At Cross Purposes

A Cathedral Organist's Memoirs

Michael Smith

At Cross Purpose:

A Cathedral Organist's Memoirs

Printed and bound in Great Britain by
Marston Book Services Ltd, Oxfordshire

ISBN: 978-1-50273-527-0

To the memory of my lovely wife Marian,

who loyally supported and encouraged me

throughout more than 35 years of happy marriage.

Llandaff Cathedral and the author as a young man

'It is repulsive [to the musical profession] to obtrude the claims of their art on the Church, and to speak of religion and money, as they must, in one and the same breath. They feel also, that the Clergy either systematically disparage music, or at best view it with a cold side glance, and have ever done so since the reign of Elizabeth; and this for no better reason than that the interests of religion were far above those of the music.'

Samuel Sebastian Wesley
from A *Few Words on Cathedral Music and the Musical System of the Church, 1849*

ACKNOWLEDGEMENTS

These memoirs, written in 2008-9, might never have seen the light of day had it not been for a providential meeting with Richard Baker, who stayed at my house during the Hereford Three Choirs Festival in 2012 and began reading the manuscript. His enthusiasm for the book prompted him to go a stage further, reading the entire script and making certain recommendations involving some reduction of personal and family history. We shared this detailed operation on and off for some fifteen months, and I am greatly indebted to him for devoting so much time and care to the task. Some of the more controversial matter which he questioned I have decided to retain, and I must stress that the facts and opinions in the resulting text are entirely my responsibility.

My 26-year tenure at Llandaff Cathedral depended on recruiting and maintaining a dedicated choir, able to perform with limited rehearsal time a very extensive repertoire of music. It is no exaggeration to say that my career absolutely depended on my colleagues listed in Appendix 3, who for varying periods of time, some for many years, made a valuable contribution to the music. I hope that these memoirs will be seen as a tribute to their hard work and special skills, which I now take the opportunity to acknowledge.

FOREWORD

by Canon Jeremy Davies, former Precentor of Salisbury Cathedral

Reading Michael Smith's account of his time as organist of Llandaff Cathedral makes one aware just how toxic can be the atmosphere and relationships that prevail in Christian communities – not least cathedral communities – however much they may claim to inhabit the high moral ground. I guess that Llandaff is sadly not much different from many another cathedral in this respect, and it is perhaps a salutary reminder to such communities that far from being saints they are communities of forgiven sinners – which I suppose is a start on the road to holiness.

Michael's travails at Llandaff are characterised by deteriorating relationships with successive deans, priest vicars and chapter clerks who seem to regard cathedral music and the organist they employ to direct it, with a degree of disdain, ignorance and discourtesy which has often marked the interaction between clergy and church musicians down the centuries. Of course there are always two sides to an argument, apart from personal chemistry, and it would be interesting to hear the ripostes of the protagonists in the Smith saga, to the accounts of misunderstanding and falling out, which Michael Smith describes and meticulously supports with documentary evidence.

In between the disagreements, which provide the very readable stuff of these memoirs, there are accounts of holidays abroad, family escapes to the bolt hole in Herefordshire, examining adventures in the Far East, southern Africa and New Zealand (about which on the whole the Chapter seems to have been perfectly agreeable) and gatherings of the musical great and good (and indeed the great and good of politics, church and academe as well). Despite all the recurring pressures of recruiting good lay clerks, and dealing with successive deans who were more interested in the cathedral as parish church than as cathedral (a tension which many English parish church cathedrals have confronted and generally resolved very well) there is a sense of the cathedral choir flourishing and growing in reputation as a source of musical excellence, committed to the *opus Dei* of daily worship, which provides the rhythm of Anglican prayer and spirituality. *(I'm determined not to re-write that last sentence, despite containing some eighty words, – a feature of clerical correspondence that Michael Smith takes delight in sending up!)* When Eric Fletcher and then Robert Joyce (Michael's immediate predecessors under whom I sang as a cathedral chorister in the 1950s) succeeded Kenneth Turner as cathedral organists at Llandaff there was a seismic shift in musical standards. The quality of the cathedral choir, its repertoire and its professional training and discipline moved up several gears. For a very short period Robert Tear the illustrious tenor, originally from Barry, was recruited into the choir after his undergraduate days at Kings Cambridge, while the then Dean, forlornly, tried to secure a job for him that would keep him in the Principality. This new musical spring coincided with the restoration of the cathedral after war damage, with the rebuilding of its spire and the erection of its crowning glory, the Epstein *Majestas*, which to my mind is the finest work of religious art in the twentieth century (with all due respect to Chichester Cathedral and the Hussey legacy). Suddenly Llandaff Cathedral emerged on the ecclesiastical landscape, more as a cathedral than a parish church (though it continued to be both), with the sort of self-confidence that it had not enjoyed since the disestablishment of the Church in Wales in 1921, or indeed since the Deanship of John Henry Vaughan in the nineteenth century when he founded the Cathedral School. It was into this legacy of the late 1950s and early 60s that Michael Smith entered in 1974, and his memoirs are a record of the battles he fought (and did not always win) to build on that legacy and to recover that earlier self-confidence.

Running like a golden thread through Michael's account are

references to Salisbury and its cathedral where he was assistant organist (1967 – 74) and references to Salisbury luminaries abound. It was no surprise that Salisbury was the chosen place for Michael and Marian to retire to after Llandaff, and as mentioned in the memoir it was at Bowerchalke, outside Salisbury that I conducted Marian's funeral after her untimely death.

Two other Salisbury connections occur to me. It is ironic that while at Salisbury Michael edited the anthems of Michael Wise, organist at the Cathedral in the eighteenth century. Michael Wise was described as 'wise in name but not in nature', and was beaten up for using 'refractory language' to a night watchman in the Cathedral Close! Llandaff too has had criminal violence as part of its recent history, but maybe the relationship between Wise and his cathedral colleagues must stand as an ironic and salutary warning to all who are involved in the life of a cathedral community, and as testimony to their sometimes fraught relationships.

The other obvious connection – not alluded to in Michael's memoirs – is that of Anthony Trollope, who stood on the Harnham Bridge and looking at the cathedral of Salisbury and its spire conceived the Barchester novels[*]. No commentator has ever captured so comprehensively or so devasatingly the toxicity, as well as the virtues, (not least the ambition), both social and religious, of a Cathedral Close. As I read Michael Smith's memoirs I feel the hand of Anthony Trollope on his shoulder, and since anxiety about finances are a recurring and understandable theme in this present volume, maybe Trollope, who wrote prodigiously and yet managed his day job with the Post Office, may provide further inspiration for an indigent musician keen to earn an honest penny by recounting the exigencies of life in a Cathedral Close today.

Jeremy Davies
November 2013

---

[*] Michael Hardwick's abridged version of the Barchester Chronicles, published in 1982, perceptively shows Llandaff Cathedral on the front cover.

AUTHOR'S INTRODUCTION

'It was during a Monday evensong that the assistant verger murdered his wife'.

This was to be my opening sentence when I first contemplated acceding to the request of many who heard my yarns that I should write a book. On reflection, this seemed an unduly sensational gambit when there was such a wealth of material at my disposal, in the way of letters and diaries, for a detailed chronicle of the shenanigans dominating my life for the last quarter of the twentieth century as Organist and Master of the Choristers at Llandaff Cathedral. But how did I get to be there in the first place?

As a young boy brought up in a London suburb during the War, I was lucky to be taught the piano by Lina Collins, whose own teacher had been a pupil of Clara Schumann. Progressing quickly through graded examinations, I won the Performers' LRAM at 15, shortly before taking O-levels at my grammar school. A school friend introduced me to an influential organ teacher in London, and a visit to Norwich Cathedral while on holiday with my parents convinced me that a career as a cathedral organist was to be my goal. I was lucky enough to be accepted at Christ Church, Oxford, where I was awarded the prestigious Organ Scholarship after gaining the FRCO diploma and founding a college music society in partnership with St Hilda's. I managed to avoid national service by studying for an extra year for a BMus degree in Composition, and returning to London for the PGCE course at the university's Institute of Education. Thus qualified, my plan was to become a grammar school teacher and a church organist, as indeed I did, first at Pontefract in Yorkshire and then at Louth in Lincolnshire.

Having by now acquired a diploma in choir training and the Archbishop's Diploma in Church Music, I was evidently considered ripe for appointment as the Assistant Choirmaster and Organist at Salisbury Cathedral, where I soon met Marian in the choral society, married her in the cathedral, and lived for seven happy years in an eighteenth-century cottage, with roses not only round the door but covering the walls, in the cathedral close. I had the opportunity to teach in three more schools, and became an examiner to the Associated Board of the Royal Schools of Music, with whom I had appeared so often as a candidate. I remember saying after the birth of Rachel, 'I wonder if we shall ever be as happy as this again'. Perhaps the answer is 'We never were', and the expounding of reasons for this gloomy prognosis is the purpose of this book.

I realised that many of my contemporaries in similar posts throughout the 42 cathedrals of England would be hoping for promotion to a 'number 1' job, now often styled more accurately Director of Music. Ambitious as ever, and with an unusual propensity for acquiring qualifications, I decided to become a Doctor of Music. Easier said than done, of course, and especially at my chosen university, Edinburgh, where I found it was possible to apply as an executant, as opposed to a composer or an historian. The admission requirements were stringent: only Bachelors of Music at Oxford, Cambridge or Dublin were considered, and one had to carry out research for at least a year on an approved subject, culminating in a substantial thesis. I chose the music of a cathedral musician and composer, Michael Wise, who had held office at Salisbury 300 years earlier, studying manuscripts in a number of important libraries in the south of England and producing three bound volumes of material on his life and works. All this work at any other university might well have gained me a PhD degree, but for a DMus at Edinburgh it only entitled me to fill in the application form! Examinations, practical and in writing, followed, and the coveted degree was duly conferred on me by Professor Kenneth Leighton at the McEwan Hall in the autumn of 1973.

For better or worse (and this is for the reader to judge) it did the trick, for I succeeded in obtaining the very next job I applied for, which happened to be at a Welsh cathedral, with its own choir school, seven choral services a week, a 'free' house, a choral society, and the opportunity to teach organ students from Cardiff University. The following account of my career from that point until my retirement at the end of the century, written largely in the years 2008-9, draws extensively on diaries, correspondence and other archive material.

Michael Smith

November 2013

1974

My arrival in Llandaff on Wednesday 17th April 1974 with my wife Marian, our baby daughter Rachel and our two ginger cats, was greeted by a quarter peal of 5040 changes, known as Yorkshire Surprise Royal, on the cathedral's ten bells. Duly impressed, I rang my parents in Ilford and held the telephone out of a window of our three-story mansion on the Cathedral Green so that they could share our pleasure. When we dined with Dean John Frederick Williams (always known as 'JF') that night, he said, 'Oh no, not in your honour – they were just practising'. As we came to know him over the coming years I found this comment was not untypical of his tendency to deflate and discourage me as a newcomer, and from England at that, but a month later I was gratified to be shown an entry in the magazine *Ringing World* which read 'To celebrate Easter and to welcome the new organist, Dr Michael Smith, from Salisbury'.

Next day saw the arrival of Moody's furniture vans from Salisbury and the digging of a trench across the road for a gas supply we had requested: to a passer-by it must have seemed quite an upheaval for the Cathedral Green. By the weekend more furniture had been delivered, a cooker installed, and a lot of rubbish cleared from the garden. The choristers being away for their Easter holiday, my first two Sunday services were sung by half a dozen men known as lay clerks: four well-established Welshmen, basses Ralph Lock and Terry Dickens, tenors Maldwyn Phillips and Maldwyn Davies (then still a student but later to become renowned in oratorio and opera on the world stage), and altos Simon James and Alan Williams. I soon discovered that Simon, still a schoolboy, was temporarily covering a vacancy, and that Dr Williams was a GP who had moved to Ilminster in Somerset but commuted a distance of a hundred miles twice a week to fulfill his singing duties. This was clearly not an ideal situation.

My predecessor, Robert 'Harry' Joyce, had after eighteen years in office decided to take a full-time post at the Welsh College of Music and Drama, now the Royal Welsh College, which at that time was still occupying Victorian quarters in Cardiff Castle. He very soon introduced me to a group of RCO members who as a committee arranged a series of organ recitals in the cathedral: during the coming year we entertained the likes of Peter Hurford, Roy Massey, Margaret Cobb, Roger Fisher and Terence Duffy, and although I always wished we had a better instrument to offer them, they all made the most of it in their various ways.

Then Marian and I were invited to attend a big dinner, the main purpose of which was to launch a new Stewardship Campaign for the parish of Llandaff, of which the Dean was also the Vicar. I was feeling very tired and run down after the stress of moving, and was suffering from a temperature of over 100F, but decided nevertheless to go along to what turned out to be an unheated sports hall at the local church comprehensive school. I had imagined that the Dean would seat me next to him at High Table and take the opportunity to introduce me to the large gathering. This would certainly have happened in Salisbury, where I had worked for seven years, but not a bit of it here: my wife and I were put in our place, as it were, and not mentioned. In fact when I introduced myself to my neighbouring diners, they seemed unaware that the Cathedral had its own Organist and Master of the Choristers: they seemed to be interested only in the cathedral's parish role, and were familiar only with the parish services and their completely separate choir with its own organist, a bank clerk named Morley Lewis who turned out to be a good friend in the next few years.

It has to be said that the house known as 1 St Mary's, which was built in the latter part of the nineteenth century as a canonry, and had at one time been occupied by a bishop, was in many ways one of the best features of the job, though as we shall see later, its upkeep was to be a cause of some anxiety from time to time. Built solidly in stone, with three stories, a conservatory, a cellar and a quite decent area of garden round three sides, it came to be a fine family home. Its architect, one John Prichard, had been responsible for the Victorian restoration of the Cathedral itself, and its function as a dwelling for cathedral staff was evident in the pointed arches of its six neo-gothic windows on the north side, overlooking the cathedral and the Caerphilly mountains beyond. In 1974, although the interior had been redecorated to our own colour scheme, we found no source of heating there apart from three electric night storage heaters, two on the ground floor and one on the first-floor landing, and wall heaters in the kitchen and bathroom.

A threadbare carpet extended along the hallway and up the first flight of stairs but no further; everywhere else there were bare floorboards, and if my recollection is correct, no curtains. In due course we made up for these deficiencies, but at first we had to rely on an assortment of old rugs and a couple of Wilton Carpet rejects bought at auction, and it was to be fifteen years before we had carpeted every room at our own expense.

Before moving to Llandaff I had made various requests for improvements to the house. The Chapter Clerk, having agreed to the provision of a gas supply, would not pay for a cooker, or any gas fires, or for the kind of kitchen units we requested, and although he offered to pay up to £150 for our removal expenses, he stipulated that this sum be repaid out of my salary in monthly instalments. I would have expected a landlord to provide heating for each living room and bedroom, but apparently it was considered sufficient that all but the smallest bedroom had an 'open fireplace'. In fact on the second floor they had been blocked up, but in any case was it expected that we should carry coal up two flights of stairs throughout the winter?

The prospect of living virtually rent-free in a large house had been one of many incentives for applying for the post. The cathedral had its own choir school, with generous scholarships for up to twenty choristers who were all boarders. As in most of the great English cathedrals, Choral Evensong was sung every day except on Wednesdays, and on Sunday mornings there would be Matins or the Eucharist, sung on alternate weeks. As Cathedral Organist I was *ex officio* Conductor of the Cathedral Choral Society, and in addition to all this I was invited by Professor Alun Hoddinott to be organ tutor to the University, teaching more than twenty hours a week. The prestigious Llandaff Festival promised to present other opportunities, and I had already been employed part-time as an examiner for five years with the Associated Board of the Royal Schools of Music, so I now felt that I had secured an ideal combination of activities commensurate with my qualifications and experience. I had been selected from twenty-eight applicants who included David Gedge from Brecon Cathedral and Paul Morgan, Assistant Organist at Exeter Cathedral (both of whom remained in post until their retirement many years later), and Harry Bramma, who became Organist of Southwark Cathedral and subsequently Director of the Royal School of Church Music.

Like most cathedrals, Llandaff was 'managed', at least in theory, by a Dean and Chapter, but in Wales it is the custom for all the canons to be vicars in parishes throughout the diocese, leaving only the Dean as a permanent resident. The Chapter meets only four times a year and therefore has very little influence on the day-to-day running of the establishment. The Dean has two assistant junior clergy known in Llandaff as Priest Vicars, (though at that time erroneously as minor canons, a title relevant only to 'New Foundation' cathedrals) who had parochial duties as well as taking turns to sing those parts of cathedral services to be sung by a priest. In 1974 these two junior clergy were a young priest who was engaged to the bishop's daughter, and Clive Jones, whose voice typified the rather precious Anglican style of the time, and who conducted his own choir, the Cardiff Palestrina Singers. His choir had fortunately been engaged to sing the services on my second Sunday in office, while I was still recovering my health. Then there was my own Assistant, Anthony Burns-Cox, not long graduated as Organ Scholar of St Edmund Hall, Oxford's smallest college: he seemed bright and willing, and on the first Sunday in May accompanied the two services sung by the full choir of men and boys to begin the summer term. In these early days I also met Mr V Anthony Lewis, who invited me to teach half a dozen piano students at the Welsh College of Music, and Canon John Lewis, a very parsonical archdeacon who would have graced a novel by Anthony Trollope. As he was in overall charge of education in church schools of the diocese, I immediately solicited his help in finding a new lay clerk who might also be employed as a schoolteacher, but alas this help was not forthcoming on this or any other occasion.

Another John Lewis, who worked at the City Museum, proved to be rather more obliging: he was the vice-chairman of the Choral Society (the Chairman being the Dean *ex officio*). It had been decided that Robert Joyce should remain as the society's conductor until the end of the season, and at John's suggestion I had driven over to Llandaff in February to hear their performance of works by Haydn, Kodály and Poulenc. I managed to persuade the committee to quadruple the rather measly annual fee paid to the conductor, and in late May I was introduced, during one of my frequent visits to the Butcher's Arms, to Arnold Lewis, the Head of Music at BBC Wales, Broadcasting House, a few minutes' walk from the Cathedral Green. We discussed my plan to perform Brahms's *German Requiem* the following March, and I was very glad when he offered me the BBC Welsh Orchestra and a radio broadcast. Although this plan was discussed further with the Senior Music Producer, unfortunately it was not confirmed in writing, and I was disappointed when broaching the subject again in October to find the proposed date was no longer available. At the time I felt let down, but at least I had learned to ensure that all future verbal agreements were duly signed and sealed, and in subsequent years I was to enjoy a very fruitful relationship with the BBC. My first organ recital, advertised as an event in the Llandaff Festival in May, was in fact broadcast on national radio in two separate programmes.

The Llandaff Festival began with Robert Joyce's last appearance with the Choral Society, performing Bach's *Mass in B minor.* At that time it was the custom for male soloists and conductor to wear morning dress for evening concerts in church, but here I noticed an unseemly mixture of morning and evening wear, and made a mental note to ensure uniformity when my turn came. The Festival was directed by Christopher Cory, a notable businessman and amateur impresario: his musical tastes did not extend earlier than Bach or later than Rachmaninov, but every year the Welsh Arts Council would commission a work from a native composer, and one of this year's concerts included the 9th Symphony of Daniel Jones, a prolific composer little known outside Wales, alongside Brahms's second Piano Concerto with the Hungarian pianist Geza Anda as soloist and the Royal Liverpool Philharmonic under Sir Charles Groves.

We made it a rule to keep Wednesdays free, and during the summer often drove to the South Glamorgan coast for cliff walks at Southerndown and to enjoy the fine sandy beach at Dunraven Bay, the more rocky terrain of Llantwit Major and Ogmore-by-Sea, and the sand dunes of Merthyr Mawr. Occasionally we would make such a trip, or to see the rhododendrons at Cefn Onn Park, on a Saturday afternoon after my organ teaching, but then we always had to get back for the choir practice at 5.15 preceding Evensong, and I often felt sorry for the family, then and in later years, for having to curtail their outing. Meanwhile Marian was sewing curtains, working hard in the garden and generally making St Mary's into a home, as well as getting to know people. At the age of three Rachel quickly settled into the nearby nursery school, and we were kept busy entertaining various friends and relatives who came to stay.

Towards the end of term the Dean and Chapter celebrated the feast of St Peter and Paul by holding one of their rare meetings in the Chapter House, and I took the opportunity to send in a report for their consideration. Dr Williams had written, very reasonably, to explain that his stalwart efforts to support the choir by covering one alto place and often two, by driving over from Somerset every Tuesday and every weekend, entailed considerable financial loss. The remuneration for lay clerks, at £300 per annum for singing five services a week (Monday and Friday services being sung by boys only), was quite insultingly low, and my first plea to the Chapter was to make the job more attractive by increasing the pay by 50%, offering accommodation, and helping to provide other work, perhaps in a local church school. I offered to reinstate the former practice of appointing three extra men, known as singing-men, to augment the choir two days a week and to deputize as required. I put in a similar plea for proper remuneration for my assistant organists (Anthony and Morley), and mentioned the Song Room piano, which was constantly out of tune. Lastly, I mentioned the organ, which was a poor instrument in need of renovation. The Dean said he was glad I had 'pulled no punches', and indeed set up a special meeting a few weeks ahead to discuss my proposals, but I felt aggrieved when I saw his article in the July edition of the parish magazine *The Llandaff Monthly,* where after mentioning the choir, he wrote:

> To help them they have a grand piano, but Dr Michael Smith, our organist tells me it is not so grand now. It needs to be restored at a cost of £200. Alternatively, perhaps someone has a grand piano they no longer need. During the last war, Dr Goebbels the Nazi propagandist used to say the bigger the lie, the more likely it is to be believed. This is why we ask boldly for such a large gift. It might be forthcoming! That it is needed is no lie!

Did he honestly believe that any intelligent person would respond to such a request? If he did, he was mistaken, and I had to make do with this sub-standard instrument for a further four terms before taking matters into my own hands.

Much of July was spent marking GCE Special Studies, and my week's examining tour for the Associated Board allowed me to explore mid-Wales from Ammanford to Llandrindod Wells and to stay with my old school friend Hugh Davies and his wife Ann at their house in Langland Bay. Marian and I were already beginning to consider buying a cottage as an investment, and from time to time looked at rather derelict properties, including the occasional shepherd's cottage surrounded by fields. The long term eventually came to an end in late July, and we set off for St Davids for a week's holiday which included my giving an organ recital at the lovely cathedral there.

The following week, with a six-week break ahead of us, we set off to drive in our Peugeot 404 estate car to the Dover-Calais ferry and thence to Switzerland, with a tent lent to us by Terry Dickens, the bass lay clerk. Camping overnight at Guise and Langres, we reached the Lake of Geneva next day and stayed at my Uncle James's house in Versoix for several days. An international lawyer working in Geneva, he staged a party in our honour and took us to see the grand street carnival that marks the Fête de Genève, followed by the grandest display of fireworks that I have seen, before or since, the spectacle being enhanced by the reflections across the lake. On leaving Versoix we spent the next six days touring the country, pitching camp at a different place each evening: Villeneuve, Grindelwald and Lake Lucerne, returning through France. The following week my 300-mile cycle tour with Hugh Davies, from Swansea through mid-Wales and Cardigan Bay to Portmeirion, and returning via Plynlimon to Caerleon, was an anti-climax, owing to the disappointingly wet, cold weather, but there was no turning back and the weather improved after a few days. I personally was fascinated by Portmeirion, built in the style of an Italian village but perhaps better known for the attractive tableware that bears its name. Another week staying with Marian's mother on the edge of the New Forest allowed us to accept numerous invitations to meet friends and relatives in the Salisbury area.

After a seven-week holiday I would have welcomed a few days to rehearse with the choristers, but instead was expected to produce three weekend services out of the hat, with a depleted choir and only two hours' practice spread between the services. During my first term the choir's performance had varied in quality as I discovered their strengths and weaknesses, and although nothing ever broke down, there were some shaky moments from time to time. I soon decided that more rehearsal time was needed. The boys already came over from the school to the song room six mornings every week, in addition to a practice before every service, but I was dismayed to find that the men had been accustomed to arriving only a few minutes before their weekday services. Not only were they unrehearsed, but if anyone were absent I would not know until, seated at the organ console, I saw the remainder processing into the choir stalls. With only five men in total, this meant there was always a risk that some of the music might be unperformable. Clearly something had to be done, and so I insisted the boys should arrive 40 minutes before every weekday service, and the men not less than 30 minutes before the full choir services on Tuesdays, Thursdays and Saturdays. There was always a 45-minute full choir practice after evensong on Thursdays, followed by half an hour with the men, to prepare for the weekend and any music that was new to the choir.

When the autumn term began, I followed up my recommendation to the Chapter by approaching the relevant people at University College and the College of Music with a view to establishing choral scholarships for their students, hoping to appoint one for each voice part, but I depended on the Dean for some sense of authority and initiative to bring such a scheme about. I called at the Deanery to discuss these changes, and also ways of ensuring that each chorister should remain in the choir until the end of the term in which he reached the age of thirteen and a half (or until his voice broke, if earlier). Some weeks later I wrote to my parents:

When I went to see him, he forestalled me with a lot of bitter invective about changing Anthony's duty day. The fact is that all this was discussed *last term*. He even said that I wasn't entitled to a second day off each week, and I had to remind him that not only had this principle been agreed last term, but that he had actually had it incorporated into my contract! He then complained about my having six weeks off in the summer and not being available for weddings, funerals and 'occasional services'. I made it quite clear that I was not prepared to deal with weddings and funerals – he had to agree that this was not intended to be part of my job – and when I asked what other services had taken place, he was unable to name a single one.

I wrote to him afterwards to say that I considered his criticisms unjust and discouraging, and later he agreed to 'draw a veil over the matter'. What particularly annoyed me was that he alleged that I was 'paring down the job'. I pointed out that, unlike my predecessor, I'm always on time, I take eleven out of thirteen practices a week, and have increased the practice time by two hours a week, so that in fact I'm doing even more now than it was *possible* to do when I first came. Moreover, I use only one assistant instead of two, and always play voluntaries before and after services (not done before). I'm afraid the Dean has gone right down in my estimation, mainly because he cannot be trusted to tell the truth.

My parents' worried reaction to this account led me to attempt to explain what I considered the vital clues to the Dean's behaviour, namely forgetfulness allied to insecurity. He was generally held in disfavour for his inefficiency, emanating from his lack of 'background' and experience in cathedral matters, and his sheer unsuitability for the post. He had previously been vicar of a few small parish churches in south Wales, and was much less qualified and experienced for his job than I was for mine. He must have realised this, trying to assert himself by means of nastiness and sarcasm. I soon came to realise that if I remained firm to my vision and ambition for the cathedral, he would expect me to stand up to him and respect me for it. The only constructive decisions made at that October meeting were that he would convene two meetings, one with the school's headmaster to stop choristers leaving prematurely, and the other with University and College heads to set up a scheme for choral scholarships. In the event, he did neither of these things. When I pointed out to him that other cathedrals often offered accommodation in the precincts to attract new lay clerks, he said he had looked at the advertisements in that week's *Church Times* and found this not to be the case. He evidently expected me to believe him, but I bought a copy myself and discovered he had simply been lying again. I found out that the organist's salary, now at £1300 per annum, had not been raised for at least five years. The Dean claimed that it had been raised from the £1200 paid to my predecessor, but enquiries showed that this also was untrue. Figures provided by the Cathedral Organists' Association showed that organists recently appointed elsewhere were paid not less than £1500, and that 62% of organists occupying tied houses were paid between £1400 and £1700. To support my claim, I mentioned that in order to move to Llandaff I had had to surrender a life insurance policy. My request for better pay for the sub-organist and lay clerks was granted, but my own salary was not raised. Nor was my request for repairs to the Song Room piano approved, even though its condition meant that it was never in tune. These were early examples of the negative response I came to expect from the Chapter.

Despite these setbacks, I did establish a team of five deputies who came to be designated as Singing Men, and in November alone they put in thirty-five attendances between them. Tim German was a good student bass who later became an opera singer, Peter Foster was a very amiable vet with a particularly fruity alto voice, Marc Rochester (one of my students) later became for a short time Organist of Londonderry Cathedral, and Michael Davidson PhD turned out to be a very loyal tenor who, apart from a few years off duty after his daughter was born, remained with me until the day I retired twenty-five years later. Another man with a good countertenor voice but little sightreading skill occasionally came over from Bridgend.

Meanwhile I had taken over the conductorship of the Cathedral Choral Society. It had been founded in 1937, the year of my birth, and indeed one of the sopranos and one of the basses had joined as founder-members. Membership exceeded a hundred, and the weekly rehearsals were held in the adjoining Prebendal House, in a room barely large enough to accommodate them, so that the sound they made was exceedingly loud. When, having learned the music sufficiently well, they ventured into the Cathedral, their mouse-like tones were scarcely recognisable as the same choir – but somehow they managed to pass muster when confronted with an orchestra on 'the day'. On the 21st December we performed the first three parts of Bach's *Christmas Oratorio*, separated by seasonal congregational hymns – I reasoned that Bach himself interspersed such works with the hymns of his time – and this was the first of many occasions when we engaged the BBC Welsh Orchestra led by Barry Haskey, though in accordance with BBC policy the players were booked individually, the whole ensemble being styled 'Llandaff Cathedral Choral Society and Orchestra'. The fact that the solo soprano's husband, whom I knew quite well, was serving a prison sentence, was tactfully not mentioned: a choirmaster himself, he had, allegedly, been caught smuggling pornographic books from Sweden after a choir trip, and getting his choirboys to do the same.

At regular intervals during the year, there being no other suitable venue in Cardiff at that time for public orchestral concerts, the BBC orchestra visited the cathedral for their 'celebrity' concerts, featuring soloists such as Stuart Burrowes (tenor), Barry Tuckwell (horn), Ida Haendel (violin) and Peter Frankl (piano). In November I had to participate in an event organised by the Salvation Army to celebrate their Welsh Centenary. This involved rehearsal and concert lasting altogether five hours and involving a large chorus, a young people's choir and a local S.A. band. The noise in a relatively small building was quite overpowering, and the events included several speeches as well as seventeen musical items, with a Handel organ concerto for me with brass band! I developed a headache and began to feel sick, so that it was only by a supreme effort of will that I was able to end with Widor's grand but vulgar *Marche Pontificale*, the title of which may have seemed a little ironic in the circumstances.

My dealings with the Chapter were normally made through the Chapter Clerk, a solicitor called John Swindale Nixon. He seemed kindly enough, but proved quite incapable of drafting my Service Agreement in a way that reflected my actual duties and responsibilities. The first document was unsatisfactory: for example it said that I had to play the organ and prepare the choir for all cathedral services, any absence requiring the prior consent of the Dean, whereas I wanted my assistant to take charge one day a week, as is normal elsewhere. I was also required by contract to train and conduct the Cathedral

Choral Society, though 'If for any reason whatsoever the payment provided for... shall not be paid the Chapter shall not be liable for paying the same' – a very odd escape clause, I thought. My suggested amendments were agreed with the Dean, (and this is important to remember) but Nixon's second draft omitted several points, and there were other inadequacies pointed out by officials of the Cathedral Organists' Association and the Royal School of Church Music, to whom I had submitted it for approval. The matter was left unresolved for the next *seven months*, and meanwhile after waiting sixteen weeks for a reply I decided to put the matter into the hands of my solicitor in Salisbury, Mr William Bache. He had acted for me in the past, and was the husband of Rachel's godmother, Heather. His careful attention to detail and sheer skill as a lawyer bore fruit in later years when he acted for some very high-profile clients and achieved national fame when representing Angela Cannings in a headline-catching case concerning cot deaths; (as her solicitor he was actually portrayed by an actor in a television drama based on the case). He studied the contract and submitted his own draft to Mr Nixon for consideration in the first week of December. I had to wait until the New Year before hearing any more. Correspondence between Nixon and myself relating to other matters, particularly the recruitment of lay clerks and the introduction of choral scholarships, was similarly fraught with misunderstandings, partly because there seemed to be no proper communication between the Dean and his Clerk, and partly because when matters were discussed, agreements reached between myself and the Dean were usually either forgotten or disregarded. After the relatively business-like conduct of people in Salisbury, I found this inefficiency very frustrating.

Looking back at my diary, I am interested to recall how many times we invited people to stay at St Mary's during that autumn term: first my parents for a week, closely followed by my uncle and aunt, then by Marian's cousin Philip; then in November Bill and Heather Bache for four nights, and more briefly in December Philip's sister Ursula and her husband Ian, ending with my parents again over Christmas. I mention these names at this point because they will appear later in this discourse, and all of them have featured prominently in our lives, along with Roy and Ruth Massey and Ian and Anne Hine in Herefordshire. The cathedral routine was interrupted by just one week's examining in Plymouth, but I was to find that financial stringency obliged me to spend considerably more time away, as we shall see. Bill and I had sought to amend my contract in such a way that I would be allowed up to twelve weekdays' leave in each term for extramural work, especially for the Associated Board, and since there were no duties on

Wednesdays and my assistant was on duty on another day each week, the extra twelve days meant that I could accept up to three weeks' examining each term. In fact I never took this much time, but it did allow plenty of scope to augment my meagre earnings.

1975

It was not until the 19th February that the Chapter Clerk, having cancelled at a few hours' notice a proposed meeting, responded to my solicitor's communication of eleven weeks earlier. Nixon made further amendments to this third draft which were again questioned by the COA's solicitor. The weeks went by, until more than a year after my employment had begun, two meetings, totalling five hours, were held at the Deanery. The final form of the document was agreed between the Dean, Precentor and Archdeacon (representing the Chapter) and me, and sent to the Clerk for final drafting and signature. Unbelievably, it was not until three months had passed that Nixon complied with this request, and by then I was away for my summer holiday. On my return, I found that there were still five significant errors. Bill Bache stoically continued his efforts to negotiate, but by the end of the year Nixon had still not brought the matter to a mutually agreed conclusion; so this saga continues into my next chapter.

However, 1975 began with the good news that Tim Bateman, who had graduated in philosophy, economics and music at Lancaster University and whom I had interviewed as an alto in November, was free to join the team on trial for a term, along with Philip Drew, a music graduate and choral scholar at Durham University, who was gladly accepted on a permanent basis. I retained Dr Williams to sing alto on Thursdays and weekends for the time being to maintain continuity and to keep my options open, with Peter the cheery vet to deputise on Tuesdays. This seemed a welcome and foolproof system, along with Dr Davidson who had proved a reliable deputy tenor, having clocked up thirty attendances the previous term. Unfortunately my contribution to this successful outcome was not matched by that of my employers, and at the end of January I found myself explaining the situation to the Chapter Clerk:

I cannot understand why no accommodation was offered to Tim Bateman, although the Dean had agreed to appoint him for a probationary term. When he arrived on the 13th January as arranged, he had received no written confirmation either from you or from the Dean that he had been appointed. This omission put me in an awkward position: as I see it, I have no authority to make appointments nor to offer accommodation, yet those of you who have this authority do not exercise it. My responsibility is to form a good choir, but I need the backing of the Dean and Chapter if I am to do this successfully. In fact I had to go to the Bishop to find Mr Bateman somewhere to stay; and I think I should add that Mr Drew, who moved into his flat a few days later, found that the electricity had been disconnected: he spent his first weekend in a cold flat, with no cooker, lit by altar candles bought from SPCK. I am sure you will realise that news like this quickly spreads, and does little for the reputation of Llandaff Cathedral.

I ended the letter by emphasising that, although I was trying hard to set the choir on its feet again, I felt that I was not getting much cooperation in the way of official backing. In his reply, Mr Nixon considered my last comment to be mistaken, admitting that the choir was already growing in quality and numbers while suggesting that I should be patient and not press my claims too hard. At least this showed a glimmer of appreciation for once, but in referring to Philip Drew's plight the usual mean streak reappeared:

I did not know when he was arriving, but he seems to have been rather helpless or inexperienced and the Chapter should not be blamed for that.

I would not let him get away with this, and my last letter to him before he resigned from office expanded on my comment in the previous one:

I had in mind my lone attempt to establish choral scholarships at University College, thinking that the attempt might have been successful had the original approach come direct from yourself or the Dean. Similarly, there would have been no accommodation problem if the three flats that were vacant in the summer had been reserved, as I requested at the time.

When in the previous autumn we were invited by the BBC to broadcast Evensong in March, I told the Dean the choir was unlikely to be good enough, but now with a full complement of men, though not yet of boys, I decided to go for it; but when the Dean told me that the service must end with a hymn sung in Welsh, I objected. For one thing, none of the boys knew the language, and for another, I felt that our broadcast should be typical of our normal weekday service which was always entirely in English. The Dean snarled, 'I wish you wouldn't argue', and proceeded to telephone the BBC to propose the use of the tune *Blaenwern,* an old warhorse better suited to non-conformist chapels than to cathedral worship. When I met Arnold Lewis, head of BBC Music, in the pub, he agreed it would be inappropriate and offered to speak to the head of Religious Broadcasting in Wales, the Rev. Tregelles Williams, about it. As a result, the latter rang the Dean to suggest a more suitable alternative. So dishonest was the Dean – or was he plain stupid? – that he then told me that it was Arnold who thought that *Blaenwern* would be suitable, and that T-W had put him right: what a distortion of the facts in favour of the clergy! In the end, the Dean changed the hymn yet again, but was forced to coach the choir in his native tongue, of which I knew nothing. I can manage Latin, French and German, even Hebrew, I said, but not Welsh. When he sent in the Revd Clive Jones to assist, there were some discrepancies owing to the differences between north and south Wales as to pronunciation of certain words.

I began to feel things were looking up when after Easter I received my first letter from the new Chapter Clerk, Norman Lloyd-Edwards. The Dean had been invited to let the choir sing at St Paul's Cathedral in London for the annual festival of the Corporation of the Sons of the Clergy. We were to represent Wales, and Scotland and Ireland were to be represented by the choirs of Edinburgh and Armagh Cathedrals, along with the choir of St Paul's itself. Needless to say, the Dean failed to acknowledge the invitation, but Norman (as I came to know the new Clerk) expressed to me the Chapter's 'great delight' at the prospect, adding

> We feel this is a tribute to the standards attained by our Choir and we know that at the Festival you will justify their faith in the ability of the choir and yourself. The Chapter hopes that you have a very pleasant day, and we look forward with keen anticipation to learning how it went.

I think we all found the Good Friday Liturgy rather daunting, the music being largely unaccompanied and requiring extra concentration, but my first Easter services went well, and a few days later we escaped to England for ten days, giving us the opportunity to see Marian's family in Hampshire and, for me, four days' examining in Sussex. Having completed twelve months in Llandaff, I calculated that our combined earnings (including Marian's piano-teaching) had increased by 17% over the previous year, but that that amount had hardly kept pace with the inflation rate over this period. Around this time Marian successfully auditioned for a place in the newly-formed BBC Welsh Chorus, trained by a radio producer named Alun John, a pleasant, mild-mannered man. She continued to sing with the Palestrina Choir, and to develop the vegetable patch as well as planting new seeds in our garden.

I had few dealings with the Cathedral School's headmaster, George Hulland, a red-faced military kind of man close to retirement who tended to use warlike expressions about ordinary matters, such as 'We shall soon torpedo and scupper that idea!' He gave a hostile reception to Neil Page, who came over from Hurstpierpoint to plan his school choir's visit in August. When I told the chairman of our governors, Christopher Cory wearing another hat, about his attitude, he telephoned Hulland at once and fully endorsed the use of the school for their accommodation. Cory was one of my few supporters: in my very first term he had written, as Festival Director, to thank me for my 'magnificent' organ recital, adding:

> I would also like to say how delighted I was with the spirit of the choir on Sunday; it was good to see them looking like new pins as well as singing like a real choir, which has not always been the case in the last year or so. I felt very proud as Chairman of their school and I am sure the future is going to be most exciting. Please be assured that from the school's point of view I will always do everything I can to encourage and forward the work of the choir.

I found this very heart-warming, but how I longed for a few similar words of encouragement from the Dean and Chapter. Cory always offered me a realistic and generous fee for my work with the Festival, unlike the Chapter who had not increased the organist's salary for six years.

We also had a visit from Martin How, a very well-liked travelling choirmaster employed by the Royal School of Church music for courses and training days. He knew Dean Williams of old, because he did actually appreciate church music and had acted as chaplain to RSCM courses. I never heard Martin say an unkind word about anyone, but he lost no time in telling me that he wouldn't like to work for our Dean. I should mention at this point that the Dean's appearance matched his sinister and sarcastic character. Always dressed in a black cassock with red beading, he had smooth black hair, several missing teeth and an aquiline nose. The dental inadequacies may well have been caused by his propensity for polo mints, of which he kept a plentiful supply in his cassock pocket; and it was remarked that when he read the lesson from the aquiline brass lectern, he reminded one of a vulture mating with an eagle.

The RSCM did not flourish greatly in the neighbouring diocese of Monmouth. I was invited to conduct their diocesan choirs' festival in that least well-known of cathedrals situated in Newport and dedicated to an equally obscure Saint Woolos. Being used to seeing hundreds of singers surging into a cathedral on such occasions – nine hundred in Lincoln in the '60s – I was amazed to see only eighty-six people in front of me, some of these arriving late.

A much more memorable and enjoyable occasion in May was the wedding on Whit Monday in Broad Chalke of Richard Seal, my previous boss, and Sarah Hamilton. The former – and formidable – headmaster of Salisbury Cathedral School, who had resigned that post and become Vicar of Broad Chalke and Bowerchalke, conducted the marriage service, assisted by my good friend Canon Cyril Taylor, then the cathedral's precentor, and the cathedral choir. The reception was in the garden of the bride's house, with its own lake and extensive views of the countryside, the buffet being held in a marquee. Perhaps this experience also influenced my life after Llandaff, when we retired to the Chalke Valley. I examined in Devon and Cornwall for five days, and other events of a celebratory and social nature in June were the Llandaff Festival, the gaudy at Christ Church and the COA Conference at Jesus College, Cambridge.

Although the Festival featured several world-famous artists such as Victoria de los Angeles and Claudio Arrau, who complained when he found me watching him practising in the cathedral, but who justified fully, in performance, his legendary reputation, the chief interest for me was to conduct Mozart's *Vesperae Solennes de Confessore* and Honegger's rarely-performed cantata *King David,* which is unusual in having a part for a narrator and a small orchestra with no string section. As in March we had a big party afterwards in our house for over thirty people including the soloists, one of whom, the tenor Kenneth Bowen, had worked with me seventeen years earlier in east London concerts.

The Festival was, of course, an annual event, but only once in every six years or so is one invited to a college gaudy. In those days Christ Church still had the honour of entertaining distinguished guests on the day known as Encaenia, following the conferment upon them of honorary doctorates. On this occasion, the 20th anniversary of my matriculation and the 450th anniversary of Cardinal Wolsey's foundation of the college, guests at High Table were headed by the Chancellor Harold Macmillan and his successor as Prime Minister Lord Home, and included the 'cellist Paul Tortelier and the mezzo-soprano Janet Baker. Immediately following a Cathedral Organists' Association conference in Cambridge, I was hurtling around the country again for nine days' examining in Lincolnshire, Cambridgeshire, Hertfordshire and Somerset, with a return to Llandaff in the middle of it all for the Sunday services, which I was not allowed to miss, only to confront another crisis.

In the parts of services which for various reasons the duty organist was unable to conduct, it had long been the custom for one of the lay clerks to keep an unobtrusive beat going from his place in the choir stalls, and to bring the choir in at the start of each petition in the Responses. I found that the normally reliable bass Ralph Lock had apparently taken umbrage and refused to do it. On my return from Bath he came in for an hour to discuss the problem, and I made a few notes on what he said. I recall there was some standoffishness by the older men when two keen young graduates had arrived on the scene, one of them briefly taking over the beat, and given similar responsibilities, and I think some kind of inverted snobbery was involved. The other two most senior men originated respectively from Clydach Vale, one of the old mining valleys, and an area of Cardiff called Splott; and I suppose it was understandable that they regarded the newcomers as upstarts. Ralph found it necessary to discuss this trivial matter with the Dean, who called me in and accused me of having recorded the interview. Jumping to conclusions as usual, he had taken Ralph's statement to mean a tape-recording. What a storm in a teacup! All was amicably resolved in a day or two.

My summer report to the Chapter informed them that the appointment of the two alto lay clerks and the continued support of Dr Davidson as a deputy tenor had meant that we had the same team of six men singing together for six months, leading to increased confidence amongst the choristers and greater reliability all round. As yet nothing had come of my plans for choral scholarships, partly because of the reluctance of University College to be associated in any way with the College of Music. Four of the voice trials for choristers since my appointment had yielded only two suitable candidates, but to keep up the numbers I had accepted all five who appeared in February, including two sub-standard boys. I put forward the suggestion that we might open the choir to day-boys from the city as well as boarders from farther afield, and persisted with my plea that they must stay in the choir until the end of the term in which they became thirteen and a half. I ended the report by reminding their reverences that the organist's salary had remained static for six years, while that of my colleagues in the neighbouring cathedrals of Hereford, Gloucester and Worcester had been increased to between 23% and 54% more than mine. The new Chapter Clerk pleaded shortage of funds for his failure to attend to various repairs and security measures that were required both at St Mary's (our house) and in the song room, and brushed off my idea that the funds agreed by the Chapter to be spent in due course on choral scholars and singing-men should be put aside in readiness and not spent on something else. It was always difficult to get anything done, mainly because nobody seemed to have the responsibility for doing anything. It was not so much that the cathedral was badly run, as that it was not really run at all.

The summer term ended in time for Marian and me to go to Winchester for the Southern Cathedrals Festival, which opened with the British premiere of John Tavener's striking work *Ultimos Ritos.* The large forces distributed under the tower included the Cathedral Choir and the Wayneflete Singers, six soloists, the Southampton Youth Orchestra, percussion, a pair of alto flutes, a horn at each of the four pillars and four sets of timpani, with trumpets up on the choir screen and a group of priests reading texts in five languages. The work is based on the *Crucifixus* from Bach's B minor Mass, and in one section the Latin words are sung backwards. The work begins with all the instrumentalists making a very loud noise for a considerable time. While this was happening, the conductor Martin Neary appeared to be strenuously intoning some kind of mystic text: the words could not be heard above the din, but he told me afterwards that he was only counting the beats.

In August Marian and I set out with Rachel again for Switzerland, crossing the Channel from Weymouth to Cherbourg and driving through France, camping at five sites on our way. We heard the monks of Solesmes singing plainsong, and toured the Loire Valley, visiting the châteaux of Chinon, Amboise, Chenonceaux, Valençay, Chaumont, Blois and finally the grandiose pile of Chambord. At a place called Blanot, somewhere between Nevers and Macon, we found some illuminated natural caves in a very isolated and mountainous district.

The autumn term began uneventfully enough, but at the end of September Dr Allan Wicks, organist of Canterbury Cathedral, brought his wife Elizabeth to stay for a weekend, giving a recital and leading a discussion at a meeting of local organists and choirmasters. He was a most interesting and lively man, combining intellect and humour most appealingly. Alas, the same could not be said of Professor Hoddinott, who in addition to his University position (and therefore my other boss) was the director of the Cardiff Festival of 20th Century Music. On behalf of the Choral Society I wrote to him the following carefully-worded letter:

Dear Professor,

We are now making plans for next spring, and the most likely date for our concert is Saturday 13th March: I am told that although this falls within the period of the Cardiff Festival, you have not arranged a concert on that day. As we shall be singing two 20th century works, Duruflé's *Requiem* and Vaughan Williams's *Dona nobis pacem*, I wondered if you would be interested in the possibility of incorporating our concert into your festival, at no extra cost to yourselves?

We hope to have an orchestra made up of BBC players, though probably we shall in both cases use the composer's reduced version, and the concert will take place in the Cathedral. The third work in the programme will be either Bach's Cantata no.57 *Selig ist der Mann* or the Poulenc Organ Concerto.

I should be most grateful if you would consider this proposal, and if you could let me know your decision within the next ten days. If you are unable to fit us into the Festival as such, would you accept an advertisement in your programme, and if so, how much would you charge for it? We are making a positive effort to avoid date-clashes and to improve our publicity.

With kind regards,

Yours sincerely,

Michael Smith, Conductor

His reply, sent by return of post, was perhaps the most unkind letter I have ever received:

Dear Dr Smith,

Your information regarding concerts in the next Cardiff Festival is incorrect, we shall be having a concert on Saturday March 13th. I must say that I do feel very strongly about you putting on a concert right in the middle of the Festival which after all has been running for ten years and you have been here for two years. We have not had this problem with Llandaff Choral Society before and I have to say now that I am not prepared to assist you with advertising or in any other way.

Yours sincerely,

pp. Alun Hoddinott

Dictated by Professor Hoddinott

and signed in his absence

Further nastiness was to follow, my general disillusionment with the clergy being reinforced by one of the Dean's most bad-tempered outbursts to date, caused by my decision to hold an RSCM meeting at my house instead of his, when Martin How was in attendance. The RSCM had officially appointed me as chairman of the diocesan committee, and Martin was particularly keen that I should show myself to be the boss in this area. The meeting itself, on a Friday morning, went very well, because we had a room full of supporters who were glad to be there, and the old man was obliged to wear his Dr Jekyll hat and say how glad he was that I was taking the lead. I told Martin about the Dean's attitude, and he passed the news on to the director, Dr Lionel Dakers; moreover, he wrote me two appreciative letters about my efforts and gave Marian and Rachel and me a very good lunch at an attractive restaurant in Penarth.

There were, however, good things about October, including inviting the Baches to stay, having the new headmaster George Hill and his wife Sue to dinner with them, entertaining Richard Seal and some of Marian's relatives, attending a party in Penarth and even dining with the King's Singers, but the end of the month brought the final straw as far as the clergy were concerned, when the Bishop himself was charged with gross indecency and ordered to appear in court on the 19th November. It transpired that he had been caught 'cottaging' with another man in the toilets at Llandaff Fields. Before the court hearing when he was fined £25, he resigned from office and his name was removed from the statutory prayers in the Sunday Eucharist – just when he might have needed them, one might say. A really nice and well-loved man, who had formerly been the Dean, he had always been supportive of my work, and keen to give me advice when I needed it. My friend Graham Houghton, who happened to be staying with us at the time, helped to paint over some unpleasant graffiti daubed on the white wall of the house opposite ours.

There was a keen spirit among church musicians in the area, and around this time the South Glamorgan Association of Organist and Choirmasters was set up at the instigation of a Pontypridd man appropriately called Tallis. Sadly he died the day before the RSCM meeting, and it fell to me as president of the new association to say a few words about him at its first AGM. After receiving many ideas for suitable events in the coming year, I addressed the meeting with a survey of hymns, leading on from Dr Wicks's controversial assertion that 90% of them were 'gibberish'. I think I am more inclined to agree with him now than I was then.

November brought an interesting assignment. The BBC decided to put out a televised and partially-staged version of Schütz's *Christmas Story*, and asked me to play a chamber organ, forming the *continuo* with the 'cellist George Ives. This proved more difficult than I had anticipated, and involved us both in a long journey to Eastbourne to rehearse the recitatives with the distinguished tenor Philip Langridge. It was the only place and day that the conductor Roger Norrington could manage, and it was immediately apparent that he was meticulous about the precise length of every note. Such detail is not in the score itself, and I doubted whether sixteenth-century musicians would have gone to these lengths, but Sir Roger (as he later became) had a steely glare, not missing a single quaver, and everything had to be just right. I still remember a piece of general advice which Philip Langridge imparted to me on the train: 'Whatever fee you are offered, double it'. All right for someone as famous as he was, I thought, but I never tried it myself. The actual filming took place in Cardiff with a cast including top-ranking singers of the time including Eiddwen Harrhy, Christopher Keyte, Paul Elliott, and three men with intriguing tripartite names, Rogers Covey-Crump, David Wilson-Johnson and John York Skinner.

The day after the Eastbourne rehearsal saw me back in Llandaff coping with two major services. The Diocesan Choirs Festival, attended by some 440 singers from 22 choirs, involved my conducting an afternoon rehearsal and an evening service, separated by tea in the nearby Memorial Hall. That same evening Marian and I entertained to dinner our two junior clergy with lay clerk Philip Drew and his wife Marilyn. As if all these events weren't enough to cope with, another major event had been scheduled for the morning of the same day: the Cathedral Choir had been engaged to sing at a Requiem for the cathedral's architect, the renowned George Pace, who had recently died. He had been responsible for the complete restoration of the building following the very extensive damage wrought by a landmine during the Second World War. His distinctive style, especially the use of limed oak and black-painted steel for furnishings, his use of bare bulbs and coat-hanger-like fittings for the lighting, quickly caught on, and can be seen to this day in the hundreds of churches that were put under his care in succeeding years. He made first his mark in Llandaff with the John Piper windows over the high altar and above all for his revolutionary parabolic arch in concrete spanning the front of the quire and dividing it, in the manner of a traditional screen, from the nave. Atop this arch is a concrete cylinder, decorated by little figures rescued from the old choir stalls, which contains a new Positive organ, played from the main console – not an ideal position, but an interesting idea at the time – and hung on its west side is Sir Jacob Epstein's commanding sculpture in aluminium of the figure of Christ in Majesty, known as the *Majestas.* It was fitting that this important architect should be honoured in Llandaff Cathedral, and since his work has always been regarded as somewhat controversial, especially when it was new, I chose an anthem by Edmund Rubbra on a text from the Book of Ezra which tells of the people's reaction to the building of an equally controversial new temple in Jerusalem:

And when the builders laid the foundation of the temple of the Lord, they set the priests in their apparel with trumpets, and the Levites and the sons of Asaph with cymbals, to praise the Lord, after the ordinance of David king of Israel. And they sang together by course in praising and giving thanks unto the Lord; because he is good, for his mercy endureth for ever toward Israel. And all the people shouted with a great shout, when they praised the Lord, because the foundation of the house was laid.

But many of the priests and Levites and chiefs of the fathers, who were ancient men, that had seen the first house, when the foundation of *this* house was laid before their eyes, wept with a loud voice; and many shouted aloud for joy: so that the people could not discern the noise of the shout of joy from the noise of the weeping of the people: for the people shouted with a loud shout, and the noise was heard afar off.

This fine anthem fittingly ends with all voices singing at high pitch and very loudly. When we later recorded it, my Rachel could hear it from her bedroom a hundred yards away, and I had envisaged its being a talking point among the hundreds of people from all over Britain who might attend the service. Sadly, I had not reckoned with the inability of the cathedral authorities to organise anything properly, and there were fewer than twenty people in the congregation, which was outnumbered by the choir and the posse of stewards who had been drafted in for the occasion.

The next three days were taken up with the filming of *The Christmas Story*, and the next day I was off to St Paul's Cathedral in London for the Cathedral Organists' Conference. A few days later I accepted three boys from yet another voice trial for choristers, and was heartened at the Advent Procession to see a bigger congregation than in the previous year. The essence of this annual event is a gradual movement from the West Door to the High Altar, and from darkness to light. In most cathedrals, for obvious reasons, the service begins in the evening, but during all my time in Llandaff it had to begin at 3.30 p.m., in place of Choral Evensong, so as not to interfere with the regular Parish Evensong at 6.30. The opening versicles and responses never change: *I look from afar, and see the power of God coming, and a cloud covering the whole earth...* and thereafter comes a succession of carols and anthems alternating with readings from the lectern. Most of the choir music is unaccompanied, mainly because only in the latter part of the service does the procession reach the choir stalls, and until then we were surrounded by congregation. The last item is a very stately recessional hymn, traditionally another reference to clouds: *Lo, he comes with clouds descending*, and I still remember a lack of reverence shown by one of the older lay clerks who, trying to be funny, altered some of the words, so that *With what rapture gaze we on those glorious scars* became *With what rupture...* just as in another standard Advent hymn *Rejoice, rejoice, Emmanuel shall come to thee, O Israel* was belted out as *'Arry Joyce, 'Arry Joyce...* evoking the name of my predecessor. I must confess I found this all rather distasteful.

With the Choral Society I had decided to avoid Handel's *Messiah* if I possibly could. I succumbed to pressure for the December concert, but managed to maintain this policy for almost all the rest of my career. I considered that every time it was performed, some other worthwhile work was excluded from the repertoire, and I was further encouraged by the objects of the Society as stated in its constitution, which were chiefly 'the Glory of God in the study and performance of music, with special emphasis on lesser known works...' An audience of eight hundred packed the cathedral, no doubt bringing in some useful revenue – the usual excuse for performing *Messiah* – and thirty-five people came to our party afterwards. A little later I found myself accompanying the work on the organ in a large Welsh chapel in the centre of Cardiff, known as the Hayes Tabernacle. It was sung by the resident Welsh choir conducted by Arwel Hughes, and in rehearsal his instructions were in their native language, except on the few occasions when he noticed my playing. When he shouted 'More organ, more organ, Dr Smith', I had to call down to him: 'There isn't any more, Mr Hughes'. In later years I was to play for his better-known son, Owain.

Thus we reached my second Christmas in office, with a rare party at the Deanery for the lay clerks and organists, at which the Dean and Archdeacon Alun Davies exchanged morbid stories mainly about tramps, funerals and exhumations. The traditional Midnight Mass was sung by the parish choir, which meant that we had to take their place at the 9 o'clock Parish Eucharist as well as singing Choral Matins and Evensong on Christmas Day itself, which was a Thursday. Although we set off for the New Forest next morning to spend time with Marian's family and friends, we had to return to Cardiff very late the following night in order to cover the two Sunday services, sung respectively by the lay clerks and a local parish choir, before driving another 160 miles to Ilford to stay with my parents for a week's holiday away from it all.

1976

Looking back at these early years at Llandaff, I cannot help remarking on the extraordinary contrast there seems to have been between my own enthusiasm and drive, and the apathy and inefficiency of those to whom I looked for leadership. Dealing with the Chapter, whether through its Clerk or the Dean, was like hitting the proverbial brick wall, and copies of the correspondence between us makes sorry reading indeed. For five terms' work in the song room I had had to put up with a piano in such bad condition that both the regular tuner and my personal tuner refused to deal with it. In the New Year I made arrangements for my own Steinway to be moved into the premises, and the school accepted the old instrument as a practice piano. It must be unusual for a cathedral organist to be compelled to provide his own piano, and in this case I had to allow its use for parish choir practices as well as my own. I also had to provide a music cabinet and my own electric heater in the organ loft. When the year began I had already been negotiating with a man called David Row who came up from Exeter offering to make a commercial recording of the choir and possibly the organ. Weeks went by while I waited for some sort of endorsement of his plans, and when eventually the Dean and Chapter Clerk agreed to meet him, he was fobbed off with a very curt encounter in the cold Chapter House. He was not even offered a seat, and I felt ashamed of the way he was treated after his long journey from Devon.

It would be tedious to recount the many other irksome examples of stone-walling I encountered in my quest for improvement, especially my campaign for accommodation for prospective lay clerks. The superb student tenor Maldwyn Davies had finished his degree course and wanted to return to the choir as a proper lay clerk, but only if a flat could be found for him. Alas, nothing was offered and he moved to

St George's Chapel, Windsor Castle, where his talents were properly rewarded. One of the altos appointed a year before, who made some kind of living as an archery instructor at an activity centre in Llangorse, had fallen into disfavour when it was learnt that he was living with a divorcee in a caravan in Rover Way, and left at only a week's notice; he should have been offered a flat on the Cathedral Green as I had requested. In each of the four years before I came on the scene the number of choristers recruited had steadily declined from seven to one, so that in my first seven terms we had to stage seven voice trials. I determined to advertise more widely, including the national press, despite the predictable caution of the Chapter Clerk, and was pleased to see numbers, if not the quality, of applicants, beginning to improve. My salary was steadily losing value in relation to the accepted figure elsewhere, but I was grudgingly awarded an increase 'after very careful thought' of £100. Even my purchase of a new music stand was regarded with disfavour: I was told that one should have been requested as a gift. I told the Chapter Clerk about the Dean's disgraceful magazine article making a similar request for a piano nine months earlier and said I did not want a repeat performance. In July a letter from the Dean requested a list of my days of absence during the summer term. By then I had learned how forgetful he was, and ignored his request: sure enough, I heard nothing more about it. This was his only response to my annual report, covering three and a half pages of foolscap.

As I have mentioned, the business and policies of the Cathedral were nominally the responsibility of the Dean and his thirteen canons, but they met only four times a year. One of these meetings was always held on the Patronal Festival of St Peter and Paul. This body of men, dressed in their black cassocks with the distinctive red beading, would assemble at 10 a.m. for a corporate Communion service rather pretentiously styled a Capitular Eucharist, at which the boys were commanded to sing a setting of the Mass. This was followed by coffee in the Prebendal House, and only then did the canons move to the mediaeval Chapter House for their deliberations. By then it would have been about 11.15, and little more than an hour later they would emerge from their solemn conclave for preprandial drinks on the terrace and a rather spartan lunch back in the Prebendal House. They always invited a few members of the cathedral staff, including one lay clerk, two choristers, and a verger. How much notice the Chapter would have taken of my long report is a matter for conjecture, because I rarely received any feedback from it, and even specific requests were usually ignored. To give an all-round picture I outlined the problems concerning recruitment, pay and contracts, described the work of the sub-organist and librarian, commented on the poor state of the organ, and recounted the work of the Choral Society, the South Glamorgan Association of Organists and Choirmasters and the RSCM within the diocese. I also took the opportunity to mention three potential cathedral events which had been disallowed by the Dean's unilateral decisions. One of these was the abortive attempt to make a record which could have been sold in the cathedral shop. Another was a project by Harlech Television to film the choristers for a Christmas programme. Following the Dean's objection to using the Cathedral, the whole project was moved to Castell Coch, a small Germanic folly on a hillside north of Cardiff, where the boys had the pleasure of singing alongside Petula Clark and Sir Geraint Evans, in their different ways two of the country's best-known singers. The Dean had also been against the BBC's plan to film in the cathedral a performance of a work which the eminent Welsh composer William Mathias had originally composed for Llandaff, a cantata about the life of St Teilo, the founder of the see, who along with Saints Dyfrig and St Euddogwy is one of the cathedral's patron saints. The performers were again moved lock, stock and barrel into another venue, but ironically this turned out to be Cardiff's Roman Catholic Metropolitan Cathedral. The work involved the BBC Welsh Chorus and Orchestra, conducted by Owain Arwel Hughes, with the eminent singers Helen Watts and Kenneth Bowen and me at the organ in the west gallery, but I could not help thinking how much more apposite, and photogenic, it would have been in Llandaff Cathedral itself, not to mention the nationwide publicity this would have engendered. As a new venture, both this performance and the earlier Schütz oratorio were broadcast on radio and television simultaneously.

My report to the Chapter also outlined other developments. Marian, herself a professional musician, had nobly volunteered to coach the probationer choristers, three at a time, at our house while I was dealing with the early afternoon practice. I was planning to take the choir out once a term to sing in one or other of the churches in the diocese. I had appointed a local choirmaster and steel magnate, Dr Anthony Edwards, whom I had known at Oxford, to be the new RSCM diocesan secretary, and together we were building up a new committee of active organists and clergy to represent different parts of the diocese and organise local activities, culminating with a Choirs Festival to be conducted by the RSCM's Director, Lionel Dakers.

Having said all this, I ventured to make a quite daring request. I had been invited by the Associated Board to carry out an examining tour in the Far East from late July 1979 until late November, and requested that after ten terms at Llandaff I might be granted leave of absence for ten weeks of the autumn term. I suspect their reverences realised that the music was already sufficiently well-established to survive under my two assistants; moreover, that someone else would be paying me the money which was evidently not forthcoming from Cathedral coffers. My request on this occasion was, to my great joy, granted.

Easter Day fell very late, on the 18th April, so that no sooner did the choir go on holiday than the University summer term began, leaving only two days' holiday which, on the spur of the moment, we shared with my old friends Graham and Judy Houghton and their two children at a rented house in West Wales, spending several hours on the superb beach at Whitesand Bay. We were still looking for a suitable property to buy, and had already come close to choosing one cottage in Llandew, near Brecon, and another at Llangammarch Wells, but during the Christmas holiday we had stayed briefly with Marian's college friends Ian and Anne Hine at their house in Ledgemoor, near the well-known black and white village of Weobley in Herefordshire. It was a crisp, sunny weekend, and we immediately fell in love with the county and its many half-timbered Tudor cottages. In early May we went back and inspected several properties, settling almost at once for a tiny cottage, part of a recent conversion of barns round a farmyard, in the pretty village of Dilwyn. Looking at the old beams forming squares with wattle and daub infill, we noticed that the width of the house was no more than the length of the car, but it was in excellent condition, looking out onto the village green on one side and a lovely communal garden on the other, with a shop and pub nearby. With the help of a very generous contribution from my father we bought it at the beginning of August and, except for a few days in Hampshire, lived there for the whole of August and into September. The summer was one of the finest on record, with constant sunshine until the late bank holiday, when a little rain fell as we attended the Leominster Show for the first time. Ian and Anne were our first dinner-party guests, followed closely by Roy Massey from Hereford Cathedral with his wife Ruth. After an idyllic holiday I was more than usually reluctant to return to work.

The long-serving Head Verger, Ron Roberts, lived in a house forming the other part of St Mary's. The building was oddly divided, so that our bedroom was above his sitting-room and his bedroom above ours. His wife Elsie was a woman of few words, but I always found Ron to be kind and quietly sympathetic, even if not always to be relied on. The couple offered to put my name forward for membership of the Parochial Church Council, and I was quick to agree, for although this body was responsible for parish matters as opposed to cathedral matters, it held the purse strings for the entire enterprise, and since the members met far more frequently than the Chapter and were more closely concerned with the day-to-day running, their influence was considerable. Moreover, their Treasurer and the Chapter Clerk were one and the same person, so at last I felt I would be able to challenge him in the context of a proper meeting. Unable to attend the July meeting, I wrote to the secretary to emphasise the importance of reserving flats for lay clerks, having acquired a list showing that the cathedral owned three houses and no fewer than nine flats around the Cathedral Green and two more just round the corner; and these in addition to 1 & 2 St Mary's and other properties occupied free of rent by the second verger and the two priest vicars. I tried to forestall the objection that rents received helped to pay the lay clerks' salaries by asking why the total rent received from fourteen properties hardly exceeded £4000, less than a third of my own salary. The letter was duly discussed, but Mr Nixon told the Council that it had never been the practice to make available accommodation to lay clerks and that no accommodation had become available. I was very incensed at this statement, which I knew to be totally untrue. Neither he nor the Dean seemed to realise that I could, and did, check on such allegations. My enquiries elsewhere had elicited the information that over the past fifteen years at least five lay clerks had lived in church properties, initially at a low rent but more recently rent-free. Bishop Eryl Thomas, who had for some years been the Dean, had retired to Gilwern, near Abergavenny, and I knew he would be a more reliable source of information, so before the next meeting I wrote to him. He sent me further useful details, and thus armed I attended the September meeting and challenged Nixon's statement, adding that even during my two years one lay clerk had been living in a flat in the Old House next to mine. The former Chapter Clerk knew he had been exposed, and was unable to reply. It was typical that my intervention was not recorded in the minutes issued at the November meeting, but I was ready with a prepared addendum and made sure that it was duly incorporated. The most forceful member, John Phillips, who often crossed swords with the Dean, proposed that my argument be referred to a committee consisting of the Dean, Chapter Clerk and churchwardens, along with the hapless Mr Nixon; but I was not altogether surprised when the next meeting, two months later, was told that no such committee had met.

Early in the year, despite already having so many irons in the fire, I decided to advertise myself round the country as a recitalist, and published a promotional leaflet which I sent to all the cathedrals of England and Wales. Within a short time I received more than twenty responses, and on a single day was offered engagements at Wells, St Asaph and Guildford Cathedrals. At least eight organists offered to fit me into a future recital series, while Leicester, Birmingham and St Edmundsbury Cathedrals, and King's College, Cambridge, offered me definite invitations. I particularly relished the opportunity to play on the magnificent Harrison organ at King's after a Saturday evensong in May, and the invitation from Philip Ledger, director of that famous choir, to dine at High Table afterwards. Events tended to happen in clusters, and within five days I found myself giving recitals in my own cathedral and in Bath Abbey, separated by a two-day conference at York Minster. I was also invited by the BBC to broadcast the whole of Messiaen's fifty-minute work *La Nativité du Seigneur* on an organ of my choice. I half jokingly suggested Notre Dame in Paris, and although the idea was not rejected, I felt it would be a little too near the *Maître* for comfort, and instead suggested Coventry Cathedral, where a recent example of Harrison's work had all the right registrations prescribed by the composer.

In February we sang at the enthronement of the hundredth Bishop of Llandaff, John Poole-Hughes, who had spent many years in Africa, an apparently holy man still imbued with missionary spirit. The cathedral choir meanwhile was gradually improving, and in the week between Palm Sunday and Easter Day I was responsible for no fewer than fourteen services, of which twelve involved the choir. I had been away examining for most of the previous ten days, but had carefully planned practices two weeks in advance, so that every single item was rehearsed, and every service went well. The long Liturgy of Good Friday was particularly good, and Matins on Easter Day absolutely splendid, so that even the Dean was moved to mention these two services when addressing the congregation at the last evensong of the term. He had at last become considerably more affable, as he became more resigned to my ways, I suppose.

The reputation of the Choral Society had also improved during this season. The Festival Council had expressed some misgivings about our performance the previous year of Honegger's *King David*. It is a rather strange work, rarely performed, and its short choruses make for some lack of cohesion, but I was told the crucial part for a narrator had been underplayed by our local actor friend, and was largely inaudible. (I reminded the Artistic Director that my original request for a famous broadcaster such as Alvar Liddell or Richard Baker had been turned down.) The summer's performance of Bach's

St John Passion with the Bristol Sinfonia and a strong team of soloists was very well received. A well-balanced article by Tony Sicluna in the *South Wales Echo* said 'Months of intense preparation paid sizeable dividends, with singing that possessed devotion and deep feeling'. Glossing over the important contributions of distinguished singers such as David Johnston, Roger Stalman and Stephen Roberts, he concluded, 'But the heroes of this piece were the choral forces, impressive in *O mighty Love*, swift to settle down in the restless, ominous opening, and with reserves to rise to the final Chorale'. Our performance came at the beginning of a Festival week which included a violin recital by the young Nigel Kennedy, still a teenager, a concert by the Gabrieli Quartet, recitals by Felicity Lott and Wynford Evans and also the organist of Cologne Cathedral, Daniel Chorzempa, with orchestral concerts by the Northern Sinfonia and the New Philharmonia, the latter conducted by Lorin Maazel – so I felt we were now indeed in distinguished company. Marian had laid on her usual sumptuous fare for the party following the *St John Passion*, and the following day I had to drive to north Wales to give a recital to a very small audience in St Asaph Cathedral. On the way I listened to myself on the radio, playing the harpsichord in a broadcast recorded earlier, and I returned to Llandaff in time to enjoy Chorzempa's brief stay with us. The Festival ended with a rather stilted party at the Bishop's house, at which Marian got into conversation with an unknown lady guest. The subject turned to Marian's work, and when asked 'What do you teach?' Marian replied, 'Oh, only the piano'. At this, the lady suddenly spilt some wine on her dress and had to leave the room. 'Who was that?' asked Marian of a fellow guest, and she realised what had caused the lady's hand to shake when she heard the reply: 'Moura Lympany'. Unfortunately Marian had not attended the final concert at which this world-famous musician had played Schumann's piano concerto.

By this time the cathedral school was getting used to the new headmaster, George Hill, who had been a housemaster at Hurstpierpoint. A shortish man, with stocky build and a merry twinkle in his eye, he had a very clear idea about how to run a choir school in a way that would cater equally well for learning, sports and music. By changing the time of the choristers' daily practice in March, from 8.50 a.m. (originally 9.00) to 1.30 p.m., he ensured that they would not miss out on lessons, but at the same time opened up potential clashes with rugby matches, especially away fixtures. To be fair, he did his best to accommodate these conflicting calls, but I sometimes had to struggle to get all my boys together at the right times, pointing out that their scholarships (worth two-thirds of the fees) were awarded for singing in the choir, and not for playing rugby. In the latter part of the summer term another problem occurred, when boys were constantly arriving late for practices because someone at the school was failing to send them across to the song room in time. George became quite huffy when I protested, especially when I alleged that some of the delay had been caused by his wife. He sent me a curt note accusing me of 'wild exaggeration', but I had kept a note of the precise arrival times, showing that in a single week some boys had missed a whole hour of valuable practice time. I took the Dean with me to confront him in his study, and the problem did not occur again.

As a member of the Incorporated Society of Musicians I was invited by the President and Secretary, Ida Carroll and Susan Alcock, to attend a meeting intended to inject some life into the moribund Cardiff Centre, which had not held a meeting for seven years. To their obvious delight I offered to help rectify the situation, writing to my parents:

> My name seems to mean more in London than it does in Cardiff, where there is always this feeling of two camps, Welsh and English, not to mention the cliques within the two camps. After two and a half years here, we are ever more disillusioned by the general apathy and inefficiency of the natives, and the lack of enthusiasm for Cathedral life – so different from Salisbury – and we are already looking forward to getting back to England as soon as something good comes up, once I've completed three years here. I'm even tempted to look at Peterborough when Dr Vann retires, and even Bristol has acquired an allure it didn't always have.

A new experience came my way in the autumn, when I was called for jury service. This always involves a lot of waiting around, since far more people are summoned to attend than are actually needed. I made the mistake of dressing smartly, and on entering the court for one case was summarily rejected by one of the barristers, but the next day I found myself listening to a case in which the plaintiff was accused of receiving a stolen car from his brother-in-law, who, it emerged, had been previously convicted on seventy-five charges of stealing, including a ton of scrap metal, which, as the judge wryly remarked, was 'not the sort of quantity that you could carry away on a bicycle'. He also asked the plaintiff 'Does your brother-in-law often give you cars?' which I also found rather droll. I tried to persuade the jury that the accused, knowing of his brother-in-law's criminal tendencies, might have purposely refrained from asking him about the car's provenance, but my fellow jurors thought this an unacceptably far-fetched notion, and we reached a unanimous guilty verdict. I felt quite sad for the man in the dock, who would be spending Christmas in jail, away from his family, and I trudged home rather gloomily, walking two miles across Llandaff Fields.

My visit to Coventry Cathedral to record Messiaen's *La Nativité* was a memorable and enjoyable event, especially as the splendid organ lent itself so readily to the style, and I was very relaxed about everything, cutting an hour and a half off the planned four-hour session. It allowed us to stay with a long-lost relative, a cousin of my mother's who had lived for some time in Australia and had only recently been rediscovered. We also managed to get away to our newly-acquired cottage at Dilwyn for a couple of nights in October and again in November, leaving home after Evensong on Friday and returning on Sunday morning for the 10 o'clock practice. I reported to my parents on the Advent Carol Service in the following terms:

> The Carol Service, which is processional, interspersed with readings, was almost as well attended as last year's, despite the fact that the Dean forgot to advertise it properly, and the singing went as well as could be expected. It was spoilt to some extent by minor canon Richard Evans's infant son yelling his head off and not being either removed or stifled by his evidently insensitive (though stately and attractive) mother. Moreover, the Head Verger made a mistake in finding one of the lessons. Imagine my horror on hearing one of the Choral Scholars reading *my* lesson! I wondered what I would find on the lectern when it was my turn, and found the same lesson staring at me! There was no time to search through the Bible for Habbakuk, so I stuck to my guns and read it again...*The wilderness and the solitary place shall be glad for them...* and managed to make it sound quite different, so that even Marian didn't realise that we had both read the same thing. Perhaps the squealing infant helped to distract people's attention, and I enjoyed turning to direct a steely glare across the nave towards this kid, adding extra venom to the words *Behold, your God shall come with a recompense.*

There were only ever two other occasions in the year when I was called upon to read a lesson, and on both of these there was a passage which particularly took my attention and tempted me to inflect my enunciation to emphasise a point. If we were in residence on Palm Sunday, which was not the case if the school holidays fell before a late Easter, Evensong was by tradition replaced by a service of anthems and readings, in which I was required to read the passage from St Matthew's Gospel about the trial of Jesus by the High Priest Caiaphas, which in modern translation reads thus:

> The High Priest then said, 'By the living God I charge you to tell us: Are you the Messiah, the Son of God?' Jesus replied, 'The words are yours. But I tell you this: from now on, you will see the Son of Man seated at the right hand of God and coming on the clouds of heaven'.

In later years I decided to interpret this as the denial by Jesus of his alleged divinity, by subtly emphasising the words *yours* and *Man*. Read it aloud, and you will see the intended effect. No one ever mentioned it, so perhaps it went unnoticed or was quickly forgotten. On Christmas Eve at the Service of Nine Lessons and Carols, I was tempted to apply similar treatment to the apparent contradiction in St Matthew's account of the Nativity by taking off my glasses and looking more closely at the text with an air of astonishment at the word *Emmanuel* – but assuming that a conflict of languages was involved, I desisted:

> She will bear a son, and you shall give him the name *Jesus*... All this happened in order to fulfill what the Lord declared through the prophet: 'The virgin will conceive and bear a son, and he shall be called *Emmanuel'*

—although the New English Bible confuses the point further by translating *Jesus* as 'Saviour' and *Emmanuel* as 'God is with us'.

An unexpected contact with Judaism occurred when the local Rabbi telephoned to ask if I could recommend an organist for the Synagogue in Cardiff, as their organist was unhappy with his pay and was asking for a rise. Always on the lookout for further opportunities to increase my own earnings, and bearing in mind that Jews worship on Saturdays, I applied for the post myself, offering one of my best organ students to act as my deputy if ever there were a conflict of duties. The job did not really appeal to me, however, and eventually the incumbent organist was offered a pay rise and returned to the job.

The terms of my own employment had still not been finalised in the form of a contract, two years after I had taken up my appointment. I knew that this failure of the Dean and Chapter put them in breach of the law, and in mid-June I spent several hours typing out what I hoped would be the final document, sending it to the new Clerk, Norman Lloyd-Edwards. I sent a copy to Bill Bache, my trusty solicitor, who in turn forwarded a copy to John Nixon. Two and a half months later, no response came from either the present Clerk or the former one, who had been the cause of all the trouble right from the start. At the start of the autumn term (my eighth term in office) Lloyd-Edwards promised to examine my own version with the Dean and seek his permission to sign it. Four days later Nixon promised Lloyd-Edwards to deal with the matter within four days – but failed to do so. Meanwhile I waited for three weeks before reminding Lloyd-Edwards of the two remaining unresolved points, including the terms for sick pay – to which there was no reply. I waited for another four weeks before writing again, with a copy to my solicitor Bill Bache. At this point Bache must have been absolutely fed up to the teeth with all this delay; and in desperation he applied what he assured me was the ultimate sanction, by threatening to report John Nixon to the Law Society if he did not complete the agreement by the 8th November. This did the trick, and after a whole year's inactivity on Nixon's part, he agreed to all proposals, whereupon I signed my part of the contract and was informed that Lloyd-Edwards had done likewise. A whole month went by before I received the completed version. This disgraceful episode had wasted altogether two years and eight months since my arrival in Llandaff, and was not properly concluded until almost three years after my appointment. The unflinching efforts of Bill Bache and myself were not in vain, for the wording of the finished document put me in a virtually unassailable position for the next twenty-three years.

1977

The year 1977 began with the best part of a fortnight free of cathedral duties, including a very welcome holiday spent first in Dilwyn and then with our relatives and friends on the Hampshire/Wiltshire border, staying with my mother-in-law. The new term brought some hopes for the future, when ten boys came for audition, twice as many as at any previous trial, and the Dean was due to retire in March. I had the agreeable duty of preparing for a royal visit in June to celebrate the Queen's Silver Jubilee, and for a Festival concert which would consist of music written for royal occasions spanning four centuries. We had been hoping that the Precentor of Hereford Cathedral, Allan Shaw, might become the new Dean, but in Wales it is the Bishop's prerogative to choose the Dean, and we were moderately pleased when we read in the press that the obligatory Welshman appointed was Archdeacon Alun Davies, who had seemed relatively pleasant and intelligent when I had been negotiating the terms of my contract a few years earlier. In January I attended Dean Williams's last PCC meeting as Vicar, when he was criticised for allowing a leak to the press before notifying the Council, and indeed he was given quite a rough time, nobody so much as thanking him for his years in office. To mark his retirement in March, I persuaded Barry Rose, who was now musical adviser to the BBC's Religious Broadcasting department, to let us broadcast the Dean's last service. As usual, we were commanded to end with a hymn in Welsh, but I got the last laugh when the floor manager cancelled the hymn during the final prayers as we were running out of time. Having boycotted his farewell party, at the earliest opportunity Marian and I celebrated the end of this era with a four-course dinner at the Red Lion in Weobley. It was also very nearly the tenth anniversary of our first date, and she was expecting our second child, so there was plenty to celebrate.

My correspondence with the Chapter Clerk continued unabated. I began by reminding him that eight months had elapsed since I had enquired about the endowment life policy the Chapter had promised to provide for me, nominally worth £2000, to mature at age 65. It was found that the dreaded John Nixon had not even put this into effect: no policy existed. On my insistence, the sum assured was raised to £2300 to compensate for the late start, and it was duly set up. At the same time Lloyd-Edwards had lost one of my letters and confused the names of two lay clerk applicants whose expenses he had forgotten to pay. For two years or more I had notified him and his predecessor about necessary repairs to the house and outbuildings, where damage was being caused by rain water seepage, and also about certain security measures, and eventually most of the work was carried out.

I then turned my attention to a plea for a higher salary. One of the original features of the job was the promise of organ students from University College, and at the start I had twenty-four of them, but the number had dwindled each year to only a dozen, partly because some applicants failed to make the grade but partly also because Professor Hoddinott had allocated some of them to his wife, though how much she knew about the organ I never discovered. Not only had I lost a very significant part of my earnings, but I had found out that only four cathedral organists in England were paid less than I, including two who were responsible for only three or four services a week as opposed to my seven, and that fifteen organists were receiving between 33% and 133% more, in most cases being promised a pension, though by no means all of these having to cope with so many services. I pointed out that the cost of heating my ten-roomed house by electric fires entailed drawing out of my savings, the bill for March substantially exceeding a month's net salary. Worse still, the Professor had decided to put an end to my part-time teaching post in the summer, in order to appoint a full-time tutor covering organ, harpsichord and piano. At first I had considered myself ineligible for this post, for obvious reasons, and my suspicions were proved right when Hoddinott advertised only within the music department, interviewing two of my own students and appointing one of them. I was somewhat comforted to hear of his cavalier attitude to part-time staff in general, and even more interested to read a front-page article in the *Western Mail* headed in large print 'MP calls for University "jobs for the boys" inquiry' and declaring

> The Secretary of State for Education will be asked to investigate student complaints about the way in which two professors were appointed to jobs at University College, Cardiff. The students are claiming that the posts were filled unofficially before they were even advertised.

51

This news caused some consternation, involving even the Prime Minister, and lecturers were said to be demanding a public inquiry. Had this come about, I would have infiltrated some rather similar information about my own case, and indeed, two of my former students complained to the Musicians' Union that the post of Tutor was not publicly advertised. My own application for the new post was backed by the President of the Royal College of Organists and the Professor of Music at Edinburgh University, who had awarded me a doctorate in organ studies; Robert Court, the student appointed in my place, had not even a diploma, nor any teaching experience. No wonder that several of my other students secretly continued to come to me for their lessons. Meanwhile I had decided against applying for the posts advertised at Manchester, Peterborough and Rochester, in view of our forthcoming addition to the family. For once the Chapter considered my plight, paying most of my legal costs for the contract, my outstanding electricity bill and even the cost of my printed stationery. Constrained by a government pay freeze to increase my pay by no more than £2.50 a week, they did condescend to award this much, representing an annual increase of less than 9%, far below what I had hoped for. My application to the Synagogue was still under consideration at that time, but when neither that opportunity nor the University post came my way, the Chapter did consent to paying a percentage of my fuel bills.

By the summer I was fortunate enough to make up the total number of boys to a full complement of twenty, making it no longer necessary to consider having dayboys. Moreover, I now had a reliable team of eight men, including a good tenor choral scholar from Exeter University, and the provision of new cassocks for the whole choir was a further boost to morale. Our scheme of termly outings to parishes in the diocese was well under way, we had provided grand music for the installation of the new Dean, and had participated with the Choral Society and an orchestra of fifty-six players in my concert of royal music. This latter undertaking had involved an unprecedented amount of work, for the programme included ten separate anthems, copies of which I had to acquire from nine different libraries, ranging from the British Library to a church in Nottingham and from the Welsh Arts Council to Liverpool Public Library, in order to make up sets for the hundred and forty singers, along with orchestral parts from five other sources, altogether 1427 pieces of music. Twenty choral rehearsals had been wholly or partly devoted to this concert, and several extra practices for the cathedral choir, who began the concert by singing Byrd's *a capella* anthem for Elizabeth I, *O Lord, make thy servant Elizabeth to rejoice*, and then, accompanied, Weelkes's *Give the King thy judgements*, for James I. Then, separated by Matthew Locke's *Musicke for His Majesty's Sagbutts and Cornetts* played by BBC brass, the choir was joined by the whole Choral Society and string orchestra in two verse anthems written for the grand Coronation of James II in 1685 by Blow, *God spake sometime in visions*, and Purcell, *My heart is inditing* (and, as one wag added, My lungs are in Leatherhead). The first half of the concert added trumpets for Handel's famous Coronation anthem for George II, *Zadok the Priest*. To begin Part Two I had persuaded Novellos to reprint the *Te Deum* which my ancestor Sir George Martin had composed for the Diamond Jubilee of the Queen's ancestor Queen Victoria, and the British Library had provided the orchestral parts. The full orchestra and organ came into their own with Parry's celebrated anthem *I was glad*, including the original interposed fanfares and royal greetings to Edward VII and his Queen: *Vivat Regina Alexandra; Vivat Rex Edwardus* at their Coronation in 1903. Then followed a very fine setting of the *Gloria in excelsis* composed by Stanford for George V in 1911, and Walton's noble march *Crown Imperial* from George VI's Coronation in the year of my birth. Every available resource was required for Walton's exciting *Te Deum* from Elizabeth's Coronation in 1953, when I had been one of the school-children watching the processions from Victoria Embankment; but as the *South Wales Evening Echo* reported afterwards, 'The absolute highlight of an exhilarating, hugely-enjoyable event was Gordon Jacob's grandiose arrangement of *God save the Queen*. Llandaff Cathedral has not heard such a mighty phalanx of sound in many years'.

More regal splendour was to come in an entirely unprecedented way when Her Majesty came to the cathedral a fortnight later for the great Silver Jubilee service, one of four which she attended in the constituent countries of her kingdom. No expense was spared for this glorious occasion, when 130 horsemen of the Sovereign's Escort rode up the High Street five abreast, as the crowd watched the Queen's Bodyguard of the Yeomen of the Guard, the Honourable Corps of Gentlemen at Arms, the State Trumpeters of the Household Cavalry and other colourful personages such as the Master of the Horse, the Keeper of the Privy Purse, the Lord Chamberlain, the Lord Steward, the Lord Chancellor and even Silver Stick in Waiting. The seating in the cathedral was rather cramped, and after the service Silver Stick in Waiting was heard to remark 'I nearly got my sword stuck under Her Majesty's Private (pause) Secretary'. My ideas for the music of the service had been submitted to Buckingham Palace for approval, and I was deeply gratified to learn that in preference to a rather slighter setting by a Welsh composer the Queen had chosen the *Te Deum* by my great-grandmother's cousin, which I had incorporated into my 'royal' concert. For the introit I had chosen Sir George Dyson's brief setting, sung at the Coronation, of the words *Be strong and of a good courage*, and to please the Welsh I played Her Majesty out with a piece by William Mathias, though to many ears it must have sounded rather discordant. The rest of the organ music, shared with my sub-organist, had royal connections, including a piece by Sir Walter Alcock who had played at three successive coronations in the twentieth century. As a token of appreciation for the service the Queen invited the Dean, the Head Verger and myself, with our wives, to one of her Palace Garden Parties. It may interest some readers to read the comprehensive account of the occasion, as sent to my proud parents:

On the morning of the 21st I phoned Moss Bros in London to make sure what colour waistcoat one should wear with one's morning dress for Royal Garden Parties – grey or black. 'Grey, sir, but black for an investiture' was the reply. I must bear that in mind. Naturally they thought a top hat essential, so I quickly hired one from their Cardiff branch, and just before 1 o'clock Marian and I boarded the 'high speed' train (already fifteen minutes late) to London, wearing our respective finery. It was nice not to be carrying a case, or indeed anything else. We treated ourselves to an expensive three-course lunch on board.

Arriving at Paddington only half an hour late, this was the first time I haven't had to tell the taxi driver where to go. I just handed him a car-sticker bearing those illustrious words *Buckingham Palace* and off we went, down Park Lane and Constitution Hill, half-way up The Mall, then a U-turn and straight down the centre towards the Victoria Memorial, round the island and through the main gates into the forecourt of the Palace. The roads were even more crowded than usual, as four or five thousand extra cars converged on that famous spot. I couldn't resist waving to the sightseers as we drove in!

Our tickets were taken by a Guard in a tall fur hat, after we had walked across the inner courtyard and as we entered the main foyer, where several elegant staircases meet. We took our time admiring the golden ceilings, the paintings and the expensive-looking china and statues all around, as we followed the columns of guests through a pink drawing-room out on to the rear terrace. By this time we were actually early, for it was 3.45 when we arrived, but as we caught our first view of the garden beyond we were confronted by thousands of suavely-dressed people on the lawns, formed up in long

Her Majesty Queen Elizabeth II leaving the Cathedral Green,
escorted by the Household Cavalry, after the service to commemorate
her Silver Jubilee, 1977

Press photographs taken from the author's study window © Media Wales Ltd

lines and groups, watching us (and more thousands behind us) descending the steps. The garden is, of course, so huge as to be more properly termed a park, and all these myriads of guests seemed no more crowded than a small tea-party in our garden. We soon found that grey-suited officials were unobtrusively guiding us all into these apparently fortuitous formations, so that the royal personages might move easily down the ranks.

At 4 p.m. the band, which had been playing folky tunes in a kind of Toytown bandstand, struck up the National Anthem. The flood of guests was temporarily halted behind the glass windows and doors of the terrace, and through a side door came the Queen and Prince Philip, followed by Prince Charles and Princess Anne with her husband, the Queen Mother and a group of attendants. It seems that each of them took a different path. We found ourselves in the Duke's territory, and noticed that here and there a couple had been drawn from the crowd to stand a few yards away from the main lines.

The chances of speaking to a royal personage are very slim! However, we got a close view of the Duke engaging in quite lengthy conversation with his chosen few; then on turning round we met the Archdeacon of Sarum and Mrs Wingfield-Digby and chatted to them instead! Then we moved on to get a good view of the Queen, and were delighted to see her talking at some length to Canon Prichard, rector of Neath, whom we visited only last term when on an outing to his church. He told us immediately afterwards that the Queen actually mentioned the Jubilee Service at Llandaff, and said that she had enjoyed the music! She also said that she had been watching the congregation during the Welsh hymn, and had noticed that some evidently did not know the language, others obviously did, and the remainder *pretended* to know Welsh! Not a bad comment, eh?

Having viewed the chief characters, so to speak, we made for the very long pavilion at which tea was being served, helped ourselves to cups of tea and plates of cakes, and sat down at one of the many little tables set out on the lawn. I spotted Christopher Robinson (then Organist at St George's Chapel, Windsor Castle)and his wife Shirley coming towards us, and introduced them to Marian; it was rather pleasant to meet them again in these circumstances and to compare notes about our respective 'royal' occasions this year We also saw Douglas Guest (Organist of Westminster Abbey), the actor Robert Morley (wearing a straw hat), the broadcaster Huw Weldon, and Sir Harold Wilson, not to mention Ron (our verger) and Elsie (!) and heard that the guests also included Barry Rose,

Herbert Howells and Sir Lennox Berkeley, though we didn't see any of these, or our own Dean or Dean Emeritus who were also invited.

By this time the royal party had gathered a number of guests into their own pavilion at the opposite side of the main lawn, and we took the opportunity to stroll round the gardens and along the lakeside, before taking up a position where we could see the Royal Family leave the pavilion at 6 o'clock. As they did so, the Yeomen of the Guard, who had been in evidence all afternoon, formed up in close order to make a passage from the royal enclosure to the palace. The crowds then took another half-an-hour to move away and through the palace, and we heard the names of the more illustrious guests being called by loudspeaker, as their chauffeur-driven limousines drew up in the courtyard. We were in no hurry, and sat down to watch until half past six, when we moved back into the pink drawing-room. Marian needed no encouragement to sit down on one of the 'royal' pink chairs (with golden arms, of course) and we watched the Lord Chamberlain and the 'Comptroller' (Colonel Sir Eric Penn) gently 'comptrolling ' the orderly departure.

We were content to walk out of the palace gates, along with many others, and then made our way to Victoria Station for a taxi. We found a cafe serving pizzas and the like, but I suddenly caught sight of my reflection in the window looking like something straight from Ascot, and realised the incongruity of the situation – so off we were driven to Paddington. I suppose it was even more incongruous to be seen munching a cheese sandwich and an apricot pie in the station buffet, leaving the top hat on a shelf with the used trays – but life's like that! All second class carriages being full on the train home, there was nothing for it but to occupy first class, which turned out to be a blessing in disguise: we were not charged extra, and the carriage was much better suited to our sartorial splendour.

Nine days later saw the birth, in University College Hospital Cardiff, of our only son, Adrian. On returning home from a fortnight's holiday at Dilwyn we counted fifty-two cards welcoming Adrian into the world: I was surprised that we knew fifty-two people, let alone fifty-two who would take the trouble to write, especially as I had sent the news to fewer than half that number.

In October something untoward happened, even by Llandaff standards – the assistant verger's wife was found dead in her bath. The verger, Barry Darling, had applied for the post not many months before, and had come down from Halifax with his Yorkshire wife Glenys to take up residence in Well Cottage, a small property near the east end of the cathedral. Only three days earlier she had told Marian she had just become pregnant, and had seemed very pleased about it. I thought something odd had happened when, on a Monday evening, as I was playing the organ at evensong, the head verger's wife Elsie appeared in the cathedral, sidling up to one of the clergy to whisper something. On crossing the road after the service I saw flashing blue lights on a police car and an ambulance nearby. Next morning we found out that Glenys was discovered with an electric fire in the bath, and that Barry had been kept in a police cell overnight, and by Wednesday morning he had been charged with murder. We were quite used to hearing of various unfortunate incidents involving cathedral staff, starting with the knowledge that a former priest vicar had attempted suicide in our garage when living at St Mary's, but Barry had seemed an exceptionally nice young man, and it seemed incredible that he could possibly be involved in such a dastardly deed. The next day Marian and I were interviewed by detectives who asked me to describe my movements at the time of the alleged murder. I explained how I had walked from the song room through the Processional Way into the Cathedral and made my way to the organ loft, and that there would have been a few people sitting in the nave waiting for Evensong to begin. The murder, if indeed it was, had clearly taken place by the time the service was under way. At this point I mentioned to the detective the rumour about the electric fire, and asked whether by any chance it had a very long lead. I went on to provide what I imagined would be a very significant piece of evidence, namely that the long lead attached to the portable convector heater in the song room had mysteriously been cut off at the beginning of term: indeed I had reported the fact to the Chapter Clerk on the 19th September, when the room temperature had already dropped below 15 degrees C. The incriminating lead had been found under the verger's bed. Barry had been remanded in custody for ten days, but it was not until five months later, when he came to trial at Cardiff Crown Court, that the whole story came out and we were able to make our own assessment of the outcome, as will be described in the next chapter.

But to return to the routine of cathedral life as it was in the autumn of 1977, Marian and I began a campaign for a new organ and by inference a new lease of life for a cathedral which had acquired such a bad public image in the last few years. With a new Dean and a relatively new Chapter Clerk, and knowing that Christopher Cory was keen to promote cathedral music as far as possible, we invited all three of them to a four-course dinner with a white Burgundy, preceded by gin and whisky and followed by port. I had taken the initiative by sounding out in advance four major organ builders who were household names to any organist, and was able to report the stated opinion of the managing director of Hill, Norman & Beard, the firm responsible for maintaining the organ ever since the end of the nineteenth century: 'I therefore state categorically that one should go back to the beginning and start from scratch with a new instrument'. Noel Mander, who had just rebuilt the organ at St Paul's, said much the same. The Chapter had recently met and had evidently decided to take note of my advice, so that I was asked to recommend an independent consultant who would make a report on the situation. I took advice from Arthur Wills at Ely Cathedral and my old boss Christopher Dearnley, whose status had just been reduced to 'Organist' of St Pauls, on the appointment of Barry Rose as Master of the Choir. Both my advisers recommended Cecil Clutton CBE, FSA, the secretary of the organs advisory committee of the Council for the Care of Churches. I was aware of his reputation as an expert, having read his book *The British Organ*, and since he had advised cathedrals far grander than mine I duly commended him to the Chapter. At that stage it was hoped to mount a big appeal covering not just the organ but also an endowment for choristers' scholarships and a fairly large sum for repairs to the fabric. I prepared for the finance committee a long report explaining why the present organ was so inferior, and why we needed a new organ as opposed to another rebuild. Clutton's report was issued a few weeks later, recommending a completely new instrument with mechanical action for about £100,000, though he did consider also the possibility of a substantial rebuild at half the price. For some reason which I no longer remember it was at least six months before the chosen builders were invited to tender.

Nine days after the potentially epoch-making decanal dinner Marian provided another superlative meal for local organists and RSCM members at which the guest of honour was Dr Lionel Dakers, Director of the RSCM, who then conducted our Diocesan Choirs Festival. On my recent travels I had taken a liking to Lichfield, and included its cathedral on a list of twenty that I would like to move to if the opportunity arose. On the way to the station that night Lionel told me the post of organist there would shortly become vacant, and he thought I should apply for it. It happened that half term was just beginning, and as we had already planned to visit the north of England, there was an opportunity for a brief visit to Lichfield on the way.

With more than a hundred miles to go, we found time to visit Manchester Cathedral before arriving at our destination at Heptonstall in Yorkshire, where we stayed the night with my old friends from earlier days, Ronald and Helen Eveleigh. The next day, we stopped for coffee at Southgate House in Pontefract to visit Frank and Nora Wilcock, who had been an important influence in my first job. They showed us photos of their six grandchildren and I was saddened to learn that their eldest daughter Mary, who had been my 'cello-playing girlfriend fourteen years earlier and married a violinist, had parted company with him and been left to bring up their two daughters alone. This short break was in fact built round a lunchtime recital I gave on the very fine organ at the church of St Thomas the Martyr in Newcastle upon Tyne, where the fee of £90 was the biggest I had yet received. We took the opportunity to visit Durham Cathedral and its organist Richard Lloyd and on the way home spent rather longer in Lichfield Cathedral, where I played the organ and heard a choir practice as well as chatting to the Head Verger, who said nice things about all the clergy and said that the community was like 'a big family'. After meeting no fewer than thirty of my colleagues at the cathedral organists' conference in Coventry in November, and with the encouragement of Roy Massey, I felt sufficiently inspired to send in an application for the Lichfield post. During a weekend sandwiched between examining tours to Newcastle-under-Lyne and Dulwich I conducted a performance of that good old warhorse Mendelssohn's *Elijah;* but after three and a half years at Llandaff, following more than seven years as the number two at Salisbury I considered I had all the necessary experience and qualifications to realise my ultimate ambition, one of the great English cathedrals, and waited with eager anticipation to learn whether my name had reached the shortlist. It hadn't, and it was Marian's mother who phoned to tell me that Jonathan Rees-Williams, my successor at Salisbury, had been appointed. I knew that one of the Lichfield canons had retired to Salisbury, and wondered whether his recommendation had secured Jonathan the job. Since then I have always wished that I had stayed at Salisbury for those three extra years, and secured Lichfield for myself; but of course such ideas are always conjectural.

Dean Davies had very strict and traditional ideas about running the Church in Wales, and gave vent to some of his theories and ideas in the pages of the Cathedral's magazine *The Llandaff Monthly,* his sentences rivalling Proust in their length and complexity, abounding in subordinate clauses and always grammatically correct but, as with his sermons, intrinsically *boring.* Here is an example from the issue of December 1977 where, lamenting the likely decline by over 8% in the number of priests between 1976 and 1980, he wrote a hundred and fifty words:

In different parts of the diocese the demands on a priest in serving the community as a whole and that part of it which belongs to the Church in Wales may vary and the extent to which the priest can rely on the laity sharing the church's ministry may vary too, but everywhere there is a need for more priests who have been well trained, who have learned how to make the best use of the gifts they possess, who are ready and willing to teach the Church's faith, who care for those whom they serve, and give a great deal of time getting to know them in their homes and to praying for them, and the whole of whose work is set in the framework of the Church's daily offices of Morning and Evening Prayer and the offering of the Holy Eucharist, certainly on Sundays and Holy Days and if possible every day.

Dean Alun Davies, seen here with Rachel at Adrian's christening in 1977, saw himself first and foremost as a parish priest.

He saw himself more as a vicar than a dean, and like his predecessor had no vision of what a cathedral should be, merely tolerating the music foundation on the grounds of history. He refused to agree with me that music was there to enhance the worship, and I did not dare suggest that to many people music was probably regarded as a form of worship in itself. He also refused to allow visiting musicians, however famous, to sign the VIP visitors' book as in past years, restricting it to preachers and members of the royal family. He told his first annual vestry meeting, 'I am an unrepentant believer in a parochially based ministry', and when he died in 2003 his obituary in *The Times* summed up his ministry in two sentences:

> Llandaff offered immense scope for being a cathedral in a capital city, but had never really fulfilled that role. Some of his predecessors, particularly Glyn Simon and Eryl Thomas, had attempted to balance both roles but Davies believed the cathedral could be floated on the parish as a kind of decorative extra.

1978

As far as work was concerned, the year 1978 got off to a slow start: without my university teaching, and opportunities for examining tours being unavailable until March, I was in danger of having virtually nothing to do except for taking choir practices and services. Aware that my qualifications as an organist were higher than those of anyone else in the country, I decided to concentrate on advertising myself nationwide as a recitalist. In the first two weeks I wrote 132 personal letters, enclosing my printed leaflet, to as many organists as I could think of, and soon began receiving replies and invitations. I also applied to be Organist and Master of the Choristers at St Alban's Cathedral in succession to Peter Hurford, but again failed to reach the shortlist and Stephen Darlington, like me a former organ scholar of Christ Church and fifteen years my junior, was appointed. In theory the set-up at Llandaff was superior to that at St Alban's, where full choir services were sung only at weekends, but I knew something of the place through having competed in the first four International Organ Festivals there, twice reaching the competition finals, and felt sure that it was managed more professionally and had a more friendly atmosphere. Meanwhile I was incensed when a television producer invited a 'popular' organist called William Davies to film a recital on 'my' organ, at a time when I needed the money; I was further disillusioned when I watched him playing an 'easier-to-play' version of Widor's well-known Toccata. Things were not all bad, however, for the Dean gave me permission to miss a Sunday Evensong in order to take part in an HTV panel game called *Cuckoo in the Nest*. Each programme in this series featured three groups, each consisting of three contestants supposedly of the same occupation, but in fact including at least one fake who was merely pretending. The panel consisted of a couple of glamorous young women and was chaired by the well-known broadcaster Wynford Vaughan Thomas. One of the groups on this occasion was of hot-air balloonists, whereas mine featured street buskers, and I had been invited to be one of the fakes. I had agreed with some enthusiasm, because with my East London background I reckoned I could simulate a cockney accent and act the part quite effectively. Dressed in an old raincoat, I was provided with a street piano with a real monkey on top. A fellow contestant, I recall, was Anthony Hose, who was on the staff of the Welsh National Opera. When my turn came to answer questions put by the panel, I claimed the Whitechapel Road as my normal patch, and feigned indignation when my patter was cut short, saying, 'I've come a long way to be 'ere!' It was all good fun, though I was rumbled, allegedly because my raincoat was thought to be too smart for a busker.

This photo taken at the organ console was used in promotional material for a series of recitals throughout England and Wales in the 1970s

Although the matter of my service agreement had at long last been settled, I thought it best to check on the endowment policy, which had only just been implemented, so I asked our friend Norman Lloyd-Edwards for a copy of it. He claimed not to have received the document, though as he was able to give me the policy number I concluded that he had lost it. I wrote to the insurers, who assured me that they had sent him the policy seven months earlier, and were disinclined to send him another copy until he confirmed that 'after further extensive searches' he was still unable to find it. Hearing nothing more for six weeks, I made another application to them, but a month later I was still waiting, and asked whether, like my colleagues elsewhere, I could have a proper pension set up, but apparently a new Government scheme had been introduced which absolved the

Chapter from such a responsibility, and in his reply Norman added 'Consequently there is no further adjustments [*sic*] to the life policy'. I could have done without all this tedious letter-writing, but at least it established the existence of the actual policy.

The authorities allowed our conservatory to fall into disrepair
and eventually to collapse in the autumn of 1980

The large lean-to conservatory adjoining our house, with access from the sitting-room, was damaged by a severe winter gale. Where the woodwork was already rotten, owing to the failure of the Chapter to maintain the structure properly, one corner had now disintegrated, causing half the side to lean outwards; and several sections of the roof had been torn off, leaving shattered panes of glass on the floor. It was clearly not only uninhabitable but also dangerous, especially with young children in the family. I had also heard that the exterior woodwork of the house had not been painted for twenty years, so I added a request for this to be seen to. Norman's reply stated with regret that no work could be done 'in the foreseeable future' because of repairs needed to other properties in the precincts and the revelation that the cathedral had incurred a deficit of over £3000 in the financial year. Soon after this, a big trench was dug at the side of our garden, alongside our next-door neighbour's house, so that its old stone wall could be rendered in order to alleviate dampness. Evidently there was enough money for this, but of course our neighbour was a retired canon, which must have made all the difference. Marian and I felt sorry that this attractive wall was to be covered in cement, and I appealed to the Llandaff Society about it, but in vain, and for years there was this unsightly grey wall alongside our 'period residence'. Our garage was part of a former stable block at the end of the garden, and we were being troubled by pigeons which had occupied the loft of the adjoining garage and used ours as a way in and out, to the detriment of our car. It was a long time before they were expelled and the entrance sealed, and meanwhile Norman asserted that the damage to the conservatory was due not to any storm but to wear and tear and therefore not covered by insurance money. With insufficient funds to carry out renovation, the only alternative would be to pull it down completely; for the same reasons the house would not be painted either.

The trial at Cardiff County Court of the former assistant verger took place in March, and the local press kept us informed about what had allegedly happened on that fateful Monday last October. Barry Darling had married a woman called Susan in 1967, and had worked in Halifax as a factory labourer, a window-cleaner and a school caretaker. After bearing him a daughter and a son, Susan left him for another man and in 1976 they were divorced, Barry being given custody of the children. He then turned to the Church, joining his local parish choir and church council, and consulted the suffragan Bishop of Pontefract with a view to training for the Ministry. He befriended another choir member called Glenys Harradine, but regretted his divorce and attempted, unsuccessfully, a reconciliation with Susan. Seeing an advertisement in *The Church Times* he applied for the post of Assistant Verger at Llandaff Cathedral and attended an interview shortly before Christmas 1976. It is not clear whether the advert specified a married man, but he evidently thought this would be an advantage, claiming to be unemployed and with a wife and two children to support. Offered the job almost at once, he proposed to Glenys at Christmas and married her on the 5th February. Two days later they moved to Llandaff, taking what furniture they had and a few items from Glenys's mother including the fateful electric fan-heater, and moved into Well Cottage. The burden of looking after another woman's children, disappointment with the state of the house, and being so far from her family, soon began to take their toll, and Glenys became increasingly unhappy. There were arguments from time to time because Barry was as anxious to keep his new job as Glenys was to move back to Yorkshire, but in October her spirits rose when she found that she was pregnant. Barry claimed that he had warned her several times not to take an electric fire into the bathroom, and when she died in the bath he called an ambulance but told the police that he was in the garden when he heard screams. After intensive questioning at the station, he changed his story, and on being reminded that he was a committed man of the Church he eventually admitted that he had picked the heater up from the floor and let it slide into the bath 'to teach her a lesson'.

Evidence of premeditation was provided in the shape of a book he had borrowed from a library that very day, entitled *Home Electrics*, and the fact that the plug attached to the heater was wired in such a way was that it was not properly earthed. I found it very strange that I was not called as a witness, and that no mention was made in press reports about the severing of the lead from the Song Room heater, as it seemed to me that this in itself was sufficient evidence to show four weeks' premeditation, much more damning than that of a single afternoon. Barry pleaded guilty on a charge of manslaughter, but was convicted of murder and given a life sentence. Despite the evidence I gave the police, if I had been on the jury I would have questioned what advantage Barry could have hoped to gain by killing his wife, who after all was not only helping to look after his existing children but was also carrying his unborn baby. If he had really had a month to consider such an action, would he not realise that his subsequent conviction would deprive his existing children of their father until they were grown up, and that in losing a wife he would also lose his new baby? We were on very friendly terms with Vera Lewis, who owned a craft shop just round the corner, and indeed she had become Adrian's godmother only a fortnight earlier when he was christened by the

Dean. It so happened that her assistant Dilys was the mother-in-law of the judge, the late Sir Tasker Watkins VC , who lived in Llandaff and must have had some knowledge of the cathedral, and according to her His Honour sent the jury out three times 'to make absolutely sure'. Looking back, this must surely mean that they did not reach a unanimous verdict at first, if at all. Barry Darling was released from prison in 1990 having served twelve years of his sentence, but in 1998 it was reported that his body was found in a canal near Halifax.

The authorities were oblivious to the increasingly dilapidated state of the Song Room, in which the Cathedral Choir rehearsed six days a week.

Norman had already reported that the Chapter had absolutely no idea how to raise money for a new organ, but were prepared to consider making something better out of the existing instrument. Given this brief, Cecil Clutton set out his proposals, which were duly sent to several builders. Meanwhile there was encouraging news regarding the piano, for the Dean told me that a parishioner called Mrs Cann had bequeathed to the cathedral a Blüthner grand for use in the song room: perhaps Dean Williams's cynically-worded plea several years earlier had borne fruit at last. This seemed an ideal moment to ask for the renovation of the room itself, which was very rarely cleaned and in such a poor state of repair, not to mention the smell from the adjacent toilets, that the lay clerks were complaining, and where the temperature was liable to fluctuate by as much as 20F degrees in a week. I wanted to claim that the temperature, often only 52F, was below the legal limit, but I found that the law applying to shops and offices apparently did not extend to cathedral premises. A group of men from the parish was persuaded to redecorate the room, and the Blüthner turned out to be a very fine piano and was duly installed. At last, after two and a half years, I was able to reclaim my Steinway, but I never received a word of thanks for lending it to the cathedral free of charge for all that time. Meanwhile Norman forgot about his promise to pay the larger part of my fuel bills, and having received yet another 'final reminder' from the electricity board I decided to save postage by sending him only the original bill for each quarter. Informing him accordingly, I added, 'May I respectfully point out, however, that if our supplies are cut off, we shall go away until they are restored, unless of course you can accommodate us in your house for a while?' This threat spurred him to pay up without delay, but even then he mistook the agreed proportion of 75% and the agreed method of paying it, trying to get away with paying only half the bill. I soon reminded him of the Chapter's ruling ten months earlier, and he was forced to capitulate. In May it was also revealed that one of the choirmen had not been paid anything since July, and when reminding Norman of this for the second time I begged for the provision of pegs for the choristers' cloaks, raincoats and caps and proper accommodation for their surplices, noting that the six-foot high rail in the vestry wardrobe was out of reach by all but the tallest boys. I was refused any contribution to the cost of my travel to Durham for the summer conference of the Cathedral Organists' Association, though most other cathedrals paid these expenses in full.

The Choral Society's Festival concert this year began with Wagner's Prelude to *Die Meistersinger* and ended with Schubert's *Mass in* G, but the main attraction was a hugely-enjoyable work composed by William Mathias only four years earlier, a kind of choral Spring Symphony entitled *This Worldes Joie*. I was secretly rather pleased that we had taken the opportunity to perform the piece before it reached the Three Choirs Festival in Hereford, 1979. The composer was present, and we certainly had a strong team of soloists: Janet Price, Kenneth Bowen and Brian Rayner Cook. As a member of the festival committee, I had noted that the previous year, when the advertising was notably poor, the cost of the Festival had outstripped the budget to the extent that the Welsh Arts Council had to bail us out by covering the entire cost of a concert given by the Royal Liverpool Philharmonic Orchestra. 'Would I be right in thinking', I asked, 'that if the Arts Council had not come to the rescue, the deficit would have been payable by the Committee?' As one of its twelve members, I was not happy at the prospect of laying out my share of the loss, which I calculated to be at least £3700. This made my fellow-members sit up and take notice, and in due course the Festival achieved some degree of financial security as Llandaff Festival Ltd.

In May and June three of England's most prestigious organ builders came to inspect the ailing instrument. Mark Venning flew down from Harrison & Harrison in Durham and took an interest in Clutton's plan, and Alastair Rushworth from Rushworth & Dreaper in Liverpool soon followed suit. There was an altogether different reaction from Noel Mander of London, who appeared on my doorstep, said he had seen the organ and would in no way be associated with an attempt to rebuild it. He declined my invitation to lunch, asking me to ring for a taxi. He would not even consent to enter my house, declaring the instrument to be the worst cathedral organ he had ever come across in his forty years' experience. He confirmed my original opinion that only a brand new organ would do. Around this time he refused to tackle a rebuild of the St David's Cathedral organ and put all his energies into Canterbury Cathedral instead, having just installed a completely new action in the magnificent organ at St Paul's. I typed out a long article, based on my 1977 report to the Chapter, for the *Llandaff Monthly* to give our parishioners a clear understanding of the unsatisfactory nature of the present organ from every angle. The Dean refused to publish it. Not to be outdone, I sent copies to several of the canons whom I knew, one of whom, an archdeacon, thanked me and said he had passed on further copies to interested parties. This added to my suspicions that it was the Dean who was, to use a phrase that was not then considered taboo, the nigger in the woodpile.

My 1978 report to the Chapter was a gloomy one. It balanced the choristers' increasing confidence with the amount of illness in the Lent term, when I recorded 130 absences in five weeks. I linked this with the unacceptable condition of the song room, and added that it had been impossible to maintain a regular team of lay clerks throughout the year because of their commitments both in business and at home, the two regular basses having between them missed twenty-nine services in the previous autumn term alone. On the positive side I reported that we had fulfilled our promise to sing once every term at some parish church in the diocese, that the boys had participated in the performance of *This Worldes Joie*, that three of them had volunteered for a week's course of music in the liturgy at Edington Priory in Wiltshire, and that we were represented by three boys and three men at the Festival of the Corporation of the Sons of the Clergy at St Paul's Cathedral. This was a similar event to that of 1975 but this time involving thirty-six other cathedral choirs – a grand occasion indeed, including Howells's wonderful *Te Deum* and Parry's longest anthem *Hear my words, ye people*, both accompanied by the orchestra of the Royal College of Music and conducted by Sir David Willcocks. I added that one-day schools for members of parish choirs had been organised in three towns by my RSCM committee and various events for amateur organists had been arranged by the local Association.

The year may have begun with time on my hands, but I made full use of the weeks available to me for Associated Board examining. In the three weeks leading up to Maundy Thursday my attendance at the cathedral was restricted to the Sundays, apart from a Monday concert when I conducted four works accompanied on the organ by Morley Lewis: a *Chandos* anthem by Handel, Vaughan Williams's prototype war requiem *Dona nobis pacem*, Britten's *Rejoice in the Lamb* and Kodály's *Missa Brevis.* My copious letter-writing in January yielded a dozen recitals between April and October, including King's and St John's college chapels in Cambridge, New College Oxford, the Priories at Christchurch and Malvern and, best of all, a four-day stint in July covering St David's Cathedral and the main churches at St Helier and St Peter Port in the Channel Islands. This latter circuit made a good start to the summer holidays, and after attending the Associated Board's annual luncheon at the Café Royal in London and the Southern Cathedrals Festival in Winchester I was ready to set out with our tent in the car for a drive to the Peak District.

As the autumn term started, I was pleased to be invited to address the Chapter as they sat in solemn conclave around the walls of the mediaeval Chapter House, sombre in their black cassocks and attended by their Clerk. I was actually invited to comment on the Clutton report, and then spent some forty minutes answering questions. The canons seemed to show genuine interest and concern as I did my utmost to persuade them to adopt Harrison's plan for an extensive rebuild, but had the impression that the least likely to be convinced was the Dean himself. This was the problem with the Chapter: they met so rarely that they seemed to leave decisions to the Dean, in the way that a parochial church council might defer to their vicar, and it seemed to me that they never did more than rubber-stamp the Dean's plans. For his part the Dean was not inclined to invite me to the Deanery for a discussion, let alone call at my house for a chat, his preferred method of communication being to push a letter through my letterbox and sneak quietly away. In this way he could announce his decision on any matter and expect no come-back. In this instance, however, he paid me the compliment of entering the house for a brief talk. The inevitable letter followed, setting out the position thus:

> We agreed that we are quite unable from our own resources to pay £90,000 or even half that amount for what amounts to a major reconstruction of the organ. Our income, the greater part of which comes from the parish of Llandaff, needs to be increased in order to meet our normal commitments and to carry out a fabric maintenance programme over a number of years... There is certainly no money available for a project about which a great many people have hesitations; and among these are some to whom an approach might be made if they thought the expense was justified *and* if the uneconomic climate was such that they could help.
>
> At the same time we acknowledge that the reliability of the existing organ could be improved, and approaches will be made to Organ Builders who would be prepared to carry out such work as is absolutely necessary. I should add that the Chapter does not rule out the possibility of, or commit itself to, replacing the present organ at a future date with a new organ that is suitable for the worship needs of the cathedral.

This was indeed deflating: a whole year had passed since our inaugural dinner party, and I felt we were virtually back to square one. In the event only two builders were prepared to carry out what was essentially envisaged as a repair job, namely Rushworth & Dreaper whose reputation was already beginning to decline, and Hill Norman & Beard, who recanted their original reluctance and submitted a tender.

Two completely different interests came my way in the autumn. One of them involved the Karen Court Maintenance Company, in effect a residents' association for all the property owners around us in Dilwyn, where about twenty attractive little cottages had been fashioned out of the original farm buildings, facing inwards on to a landscaped garden with a communal lawn which our children soon christened 'everybody's field'. I attended a meeting at The Crown of the five elected directors and was amazed to find how vociferous certain residents were. The main argument centred on the failure of the secretary to report truthfully in the minutes the majority opinion of the gardener! Some members walked out, and by the end of the agenda both the secretary and the accountant had resigned their offices. When the time came to elect two new directors to replace those due to retire, I found myself the first nominee and was duly elected with the largest number of votes. What an insight into village life, I thought, relishing my hastily elevated status to Company Director. By the end of the year I had been promoted to Chairman of the Directors!

The other new experience was working as a répétiteur for Welsh National Opera. I was invited to take three choristers for auditions for solo parts in *The Magic Flute* and the much larger role of Miles in Britten's *The Turn of the Screw*. Our very intelligent head chorister David Hubbard was chosen for the latter part, and I also had the task of coaching him for a vocal part in a ballet (unusually) by the contemporary American composer George Crumb called *Ancient Voices of Children,* about to be performed by the Ballet Rambert for three nights at the Sherman Theatre. David was required to sing the text in Spanish, in the orchestra pit with a professional soprano and an array of strange percussion instruments, a musical saw, electric piano, Tibetan prayer stones and other oddities. The WNO staff suddenly realised I could sight-read on the piano, and soon offered me a lot of work as a répétiteur. This job entails, in effect, coaching professional singers and helping them to learn and memorise their parts. In only four days I was expected to study the score of Britten's opera *Billy Budd,* running to 335 pages of very complex music, mostly very fast, and be able not only to accompany the singers but to feed them the vocal lines of other characters and give advice on interpretation. My first morning entailed a three-hour session with the distinguished tenor Arthur Davies in the title rôle, and after lunch I was handed a score of *The Magic Flute* for a rehearsal with John Treleaven, another star singer. This was relatively easy, but was quickly followed by a section of Tippett's complex opera *Midsummer Marriage* with a mezzo-soprano. On the way out I was handed the score of *Madam Butterfly* for the following day. Opera had never been one of my chief interests, and I knew very little about any aspect of it, but luckily my ability to sightread almost anything within reason stood me in good stead with the singers, who, realising the problems, were very appreciative, only rarely showing any dismay at finding me deputising for the regular répétiteur. On my second afternoon I found myself sitting next to the conductor in the pit at a stage rehearsal, where I was expected to offer advice to the producer as well as taking over some accompanying: it certainly made a fascinating change from Evensong, but somehow I did not acquire any kind of longing to change horses, even if the opportunity should arise. In any event, my efforts evidently met with approval, for I was engaged for the next three weeks, ending with an audition session to choose a violinist for the orchestra, when I found myself accompanying at sight a variety of showpieces including a difficult work by Szymanovsky.

It was during his second year of his tenure of office that Dean Davies began to make himself felt as someone reluctant to promote almost anything beyond the Holy Eucharist and the day-to-day parish worship. In May he had declared his outlook in these words:

> Music and Drama have their place in worship, particularly in a cathedral church which provides a fine setting for them, but they must be recognised as first of all expressions of worship. I am, however, more than a little worried by requests for the use of the cathedral for concerts which their promoters want to hold there simply because we provide a desirable auditorium, and by the disturbance of the cathedral when elaborate staging is erected and left there for long periods. I know how many of you are distressed, particularly at weekends, when you see the cathedral disarranged, and I very much share your feelings.

The Dean was quite happy to acknowledge the legitimacy of the Cathedral Choral Society, of which he was *ex officio* Chairman, and he apparently acquired the backing of the Chapter when ruling that we should henceforward have the exclusive right to concerts on Saturdays, to ensure that on all other weekends the vergers should be free after Evensong to rearrange the chairs in preparation for the Sunday services. In his further capacity as Chairman of the Llandaff Festival, he was much less inclined to be supportive, feeling that it was run by outsiders and caused regrettable 'disruption'; to this day I think of Dean Davies whenever I hear that word, which typified his attitude to musicians. At this stage plans were already in hand for the building of a great new concert hall in Cardiff, and one could imagine the Dean rubbing his hands with glee as he looked forward to its completion, giving him the ideal excuse for purging the cathedral of anything as vulgar as an orchestral platform. He told the festival committee in November that he had been looking into Chapter records and found that

> permission had been granted for a Festival to cover one week with a stage to be erected after the services on Sunday and to be taken down on Saturday night. The Festival had now

spread into two, almost three weeks, and the stage was much larger and remained in position for two weekends. This caused inconvenience to the people of the Parish and was not popular, and the Chapter had decided that... once the concert hall had been completed the whole concept of the Festival would have to be reconsidered.

Christopher Cory pointed out that many other cathedrals had festivals which appeared not to cause complications, and Roy Bohana representing the Arts Council reminded the Dean that people travelled to the Festival from an area much larger than the parish, adding that it would be a great loss to a very large number of people who looked forward to hearing outstanding concerts in a lovely setting, if these were not allowed to continue. On a number of occasions thereafter the Dean caused irritation by, for example, giving precedence for a wedding to take place at a time already scheduled for a large-scale rehearsal, and even confiscating a supply of publicity leaflets left in the cathedral for visitors, because the secretary had not specifically sought his permission. Yet he was the Festival Chairman, for goodness' sake. His plot to secure the ultimate demise of the Festival turned out to be the thin end of the wedge, as will become apparent in later chapters.

Towards the end of the year I was talked into yet another responsibility by the general secretary of the Incorporated Society of Musicians, who wanted to nominate me as the honorary local representative for the whole of South Wales. I knew that the equivalent post in North Wales was held by the composer Professor William Mathias, and heard that it was the President himself supported by an executive of very well-known figures in the world of music, who wanted me to 'get things going' in the way of members' activities in the south. I did not like to admit that I had no idea who the current president might be, but when I consulted the Yearbook and found it was Sir David Willcocks I felt I had no option but to accept, and was in due course elected to office. It did seem that I was becoming a recognised figure outside Wales, especially when I was invited to send a biographical paragraph for inclusion in two American publications, *Men of Achievement* and *Who's Who in the World.* Within Wales I was asked to advise the Dean of Monmouth on the appointment of a new Organist at his cathedral of St Woolos in Newport. There was a shortlist of four, one of whom had been interviewed with me at Louth Parish Church as long ago as 1964. After five hours of interviews, organ-playing and sample choir practices, we chose Michael Anderson, but when he asked to be allowed to return at a later date with his wife to consider the invitation more carefully, the Dean became slightly impatient and asked me for my second choice. Thus it was that Christopher Barton, then aged only 22 and fresh from Worcester College Oxford, gave up his teacher training course to become Britain's youngest cathedral organist. He is still there to this day, and I have sometimes wondered whether he regretted the move: he was certainly crestfallen when he was not even shortlisted for my job when I retired more than twenty years later.

My files contain a letter written home to my parents in Ilford later in the year, describing the fate of the retired canon that lived next door to us:

> There's something definitely odd about this place. You will see from the enclosed cutting that even old Canon Rew managed to be found dead in the river last week. Why can't people round here behave normally? Of course, we had all the usual paraphernalia of six or seven white vans and cars outside the house on Monday night, when he was reported missing. A dozen policemen were out there with noisy radios and tracker-dogs, with a raincoated detective issuing instructions. We never had all this in Ilford!

The four weeks leading up to Christmas were certainly action-packed, starting with the choral society concert containing two Bach Cantatas and Britten's *Saint Nicolas* which tells the legend of the original Santa Claus. The semi-chorus in the west gallery consisted of a girls' choir from Howell's School, and David Johnston was an ideal tenor for the title role. I noted with interest that our customary party for forty people included a judge, a barrister and a solicitor, a professor of gynaecology and a research biochemist, as well as a few of my in-laws. Marian and I were delighted to receive an appreciative letter from the baritone Peter Savidge, one of the Bach soloists, whose distinguished career in oratorio and opera is still flourishing even as I write:

> On my way home I decided that in my list of 1978 concerts this was the most enjoyable – certainly I've not come across such atmosphere as was created in the Britten for a long time. I also think that peripatetic singers ought to compile a Good Food Guide of Choral Societies – in which you would undoubtedly come out top by a long way. I've spent all week

enthusing about the spread – particularly the chocolate creation!

The following morning the Cathedral Choir sang Britten's *Festival Te Deum in E* for the first time, and that evening I drove across England to Harpenden to stay with Marian's cousin Richard Hickman and his wife Anthea. A graduate of the Royal College of Music, he had played the 'cello in the college orchestra next to Mary Wilcock, who had been my girlfriend four years before I met Marian, and who was to reappear in my life decades later. Richard had been Director of Music at Wells Cathedral School and now had a similar title in the Royal County of Berkshire: it was a busy time of year for both of them, and one or both of them were out every evening, leaving me to look after their three young children. I returned home to deal with my own responsibilities for Advent Sunday before setting off for a week in Oxfordshire. Here I was in my element, taking the opportunity to hear Evensong at Christ Church, New College and Magdalen, drinking sherry with Simon Preston at my own college and with James Dalton, my mentor when preparing for my doctorate, at Queen's, and having tea with Bernard Rose, one of my former tutors, at Magdalen, where I also attended a student concert in the ante-chapel and was invited to their party afterwards at Christ Church. I even attended the AGM of the Oxford Bach Choir, so altogether it was like old times and I enjoyed every minute of it. Moreover, my candidates at Oxford High School for Girls were quite exceptional, taking high grades and earning mainly merits and distinctions. Virginia Strawson, who achieved an astonishing 145 out of 150 for Grade 8 Violin (and proceeded to accompany on the piano another Grade 8 pupil) turned out to be the daughter of the Professor of Philosophy, and no doubt other candidates were also the offspring of dons.

From Oxford I travelled to Surrey and stayed overnight at Addington Palace, then the grandiose headquarters of the Royal School of Church Music and formerly the country residence of the Archbishops of Canterbury. After breakfast with the staff (Lionel Dakers, Martin How and Cyril Taylor, all of whom figured quite prominently in my career), I did another day's examining in Purley before returning home once again for my Sunday duties.

Life was definitely looking up, ('What a jolly time we have!' I wrote to my parents), especially as over a dozen enquiries about vacant lay clerkships had come in, and my importunities had borne fruit to the extent that two flats were now available for those appointed. Following negotiations with Welsh National Opera we finally allowed our top chorister David Hubbard to sing opposite Dame Felicity Lott on tour during the first half of 1979 with *The Turn of the Screw*. He took to the part like a duck to water, with natural stage gestures which evidently paved the way for further ventures, for some ten years later I heard that he had been elected President of Oxford University Dramatic Society.

1979

This was the year when I managed to escape from cathedral life for eighteen weeks while on my first examining tour overseas covering the months July to October. I was lucky to have maintained a group of six lay clerks for four years, but changes sooner or later were inevitable, and now Ralph Lock, who had sung bass for twenty years, decided to retire, and Philip Drew, who had joined us in 1975, took up a post as organist and choirmaster at a local parish church. There had been a good response to my advertising, and at last I was able to offer accommodation, for two flats had been set aside on the second floor of the house next to mine for this purpose; but in a typical mix-up, the Chapter Clerk, influenced by some maternal pressure, managed to allocate one of them to an unsuccessful applicant. Somehow the error was rectified and a new alto, Spencer Basford, and baritone David Gwesyn Smith, moved in.

This was also a year in which the Dean's negative approach to things musical was increasingly apparent. The cathedral housed a Steinway concert grand piano which had been bought with Arts Council money for the Llandaff Festival. In January the Chapter Clerk was instructed to take steps to ensure its removal elsewhere, but as usual the Dean had not foreseen possible consequences, and had to be reminded that it was also at the disposal of the cathedral staff when required, and would be needed for services in the event of the organ breaking down. Most deans would be only too pleased to have the custody of a Steinway at no cost. In May I decided that the thirteen canons should be made aware of this insidious behaviour, since they as the Chapter were jointly responsible for policy, at least in theory. The easiest way for me to explain his attitude was to list the various changes made in a few months, mostly small in themselves, but in total giving cause for concern not only to the music staff, but also to a much wider circle of people:

1. There is an increasing tendency to minimise the importance of services sung by the Cathedral Choir, by not including them in announcements made from the lectern, the Weekly Notes, and the *Llandaff Monthly*. For example, this month's magazine lists eight services on Ascension Day, but makes no mention of Evensong, the only service at which the lay clerks sing. The many Parish services are vigorously promoted at the expense of Cathedral services.

2. Details of the music to be sung at weekday Sung Eucharists are now omitted from the Weekly Notes.

3. The custom of making a presentation to a Dean's Scholar during his last Evensong as a chorister was not observed last Christmas, nor was mention made of the retirement of a lay clerk after *twenty years'* service.

4. The lay clerks' salaries remained at £400 from September 1974 until March 1979, while all other cathedrals were raising theirs to as much as double that figure; this may account for the fact that not one application has been received for the alto vacancy at the end of this term (i.e. from September).

5. Saturday concerts in the cathedral have been virtually banned, effectively denying the building to hundreds of people and reducing the potential revenue. Saturdays were made unavailable even to the Cathedral Choral Society for the four weeks before Christmas and the six weeks before Easter, which are the most convenient weeks both liturgically and for musical reasons (including rehearsal time and availability of orchestras).

6. All requests for permission to televise choral works in the cathedral have been refused, with resulting loss of publicity and revenue.

7. Permission for the Cathedral Choral Society to perform Bach's *St Matthew Passion* on Palm Sunday 1980, or on any Saturday in Lent, was refused.

8. The return of the chamber organ (from the west end of the north aisle) to the Lady Chapel has ensured that it will hardly ever be played, either *in situ* or elsewhere, owing to restrictions on moving it and the prohibitive cost of doing so.

9. Serious doubts have been cast on the future of the Llandaff Festival, hitherto one of the cathedral's claims to national fame.

10. My request that I should be kept informed of concerts which *are* to be held in the Cathedral has been refused; likewise my request for details required by the Performing Right Society.

11. Permission was withheld for me to explore ways of raising money for the restoration of the organ, and my offer to write a series of articles for *Llandaff Monthly* to explain the history and resultant shortcomings of the instrument was received somewhat discouragingly.

This was indeed a formidable indictment, but my letter went on to say that, while I was not in any way questioning the Chapter's right (I refrained from saying the Dean's right) to make any of these decisions, yet the sum total of these observations, individually insignificant though some of them might be, gave cause for speculation. Concluding my attempt to make the individual members of the Chapter take some responsibility for these downward trends, and if possible reverse some of them, I added:

> If it is the Chapter's intention to discourage professional music by gradual stages, it would be a great help to me and my colleagues in the Cathedral Choir and the Cathedral Choral Society to know in good time. We would all like to feel that our work had the active support of the Chapter, and the encouragement that all the Arts need if they are to flourish and, in the process, to bring the ordinary man and woman closer to their Creator. I hope the Chapter will feel able to assure us that the future is not as bleak as many of us are beginning to fear, and that this assurance may be conveyed to me in writing before I write my Annual Report in two weeks' time.

I suspect that at least some of the more understanding canons must have felt sympathy with my heartfelt plea, but the clergy are notorious for closing ranks, and not one of them ever mentioned any of the points I had set out. The only consolation I received before setting out on my travels a few weeks later was this general reply from our trusty Norman:

> Although there are answers and explanations to all the points listed in your letter, the point was taken that what you really wanted was an assurance as to the future of the Cathedral

Choir and the professional musicians. The Chapter have asked me to inform you that they are deeply conscious of the valuable contribution made to Cathedral life by the Choir, and particularly appreciate the standard of music that we now enjoy. Our main if not sole problem is that of adequate finance, and unfortunately many of our decisions have to be governed by the money situation rather than any other. I was pleased to hear however that the BBC will be recording a service this week, and we are all looking forward to hearing the broadcast.

The Dean's Pages in the current *Llandaff Monthly* admitted that in 1978 there had been an excess of expenditure over income amounting to £9,667, and I thought it was high time they did something about it, but in fact the financial shortfall was irrelevant to all but one of my complaints, and indeed could have been partially alleviated by raising revenue from concerts by outside bodies and from the large fees that could be demanded from television companies. The Dean was oblivious to any benefit that might be gained from publicity and the projection of a public image on a national scale, and had even turned down my offer to explore possibilities for fund-raising. He had already expressed the wish that the Llandaff Festival should not occupy more than six days between two Sundays, including the erection and dismantling of the stage. While I was abroad in the summer, he arranged for one of his yes-men to propose a motion at a meeting of the Parochial Church Council to implement this restriction and insist that any platform be under the *Majestas* and not at the west end, thereby neither obstructing the west door nor requiring the reversal of the chairs in the nave. When Christopher Cory (still Festival Director) endeavoured to elicit a reason for this proposal, he was told that the platform, and indeed the Festival (of which the Dean was still Chairman!) were felt to disrupt worship, and he felt obliged to remind the Dean that the daily round of services was always maintained, and that it was only baptisms at the font that had to be arranged around the Festival. Confidentially he asked festival committee members to lobby electors and canons accordingly, and on my return I was glad to hear that, as I had half expected, the PCC did not share the Dean's views (in his capacity as Vicar). The motion was withdrawn, and so for the time being at least he was defeated. He even called a meeting in November for representatives from the three bodies to consider arrangements for future Festivals.

Because Easter fell quite late this year, on the 15th April, the Cathedral School insisted on having a three-week holiday beginning on the fourth Sunday of Lent. This meant that in addition to some examining in Manchester and Wolverhampton and a recital in Sheffield Cathedral in term-time, I could fit in some interesting activities in the holiday. Beginning with three more days' examining in Wiltshire, in early April I was allocated a single day at Coopers' Company and Coburn School in Upminster, Essex; (originally in the east end of London – it was my father's old school). From there I drove to Cambridge for the annual conference of the Incorporated Society of Musicians, where I was glad to be remembered by The King's Singers, whom I had met at their inaugural concerts in Hale Park and Salisbury some years before, and to meet current and future Presidents David Willcocks and Ian Wallace, as well as hearing concerts by the Amadeus Quartet and Janet Baker. On Palm Sunday I was back in Ilford, attending a service at St Andrew's Church, where I had been a choirboy for six years just after the War and subsequently had my first organ lesson. We drove back to Llandaff on the Wednesday of Holy Week in time to offer tea to the Aulos Ensemble, a group of a dozen professional musicians assembled by the composer Philip Wilby to perform his new work *Ground, Psalm and Surrexit Christus* at the evening Eucharist. I knew full well that it would be a somewhat *avant garde* piece, but was anxious to persuade the Dean of its suitability, mainly because Philip had been a first-form pupil at The King's School, Pontefract, when I took up my first post there as Head of Music in 1960. The group included a number of exotic percussion instruments, and was evidently not to everyone's taste on a first hearing, but in the event the only communicant to walk out was the Dean's wife. As far as I recall, the Dean himself had not thought the occasion worthy of his presence, and had presumably sent his wife along to report back. In more recent years Philip became Professor of Composition at Leeds University and a composer of sufficient significance to be commissioned to write a work for a Henry Wood Promenade Concert in 2000.

It always seemed strange to me that Llandaff Cathedral was beholden to its own choir school to be without the Choir on Passion Sunday, Palm Sunday and half of Holy Week, although at less significant parts of the year we sang doggedly on regardless. In fact at the beginning of the Lent term the Dean had written to me at some length saying that he was 'shocked' to find that the choristers were not singing on the third Tuesday of January although they had returned in time for a pantomime the day before. He did not seem to realise that music had to be learnt and rehearsed, and the system made things even more difficult by keeping the boys on holiday right up to Maundy Thursday, expecting them to absorb in one evening the complex unaccompanied music for the next day's Good Friday Liturgy and

Evensong, followed by a couple of hours' rehearsal on Easter Eve to cover another unaccompanied Evensong and the late-night Vigil and Eucharist, timed to start at midnight. No wonder they were tired on Easter Day, with another Eucharist (preceded by an hour's practice) and a Festal Evensong (also preceded by a practice). Easter Day occurred later than the first week of April roughly every other year, entailing this mad rush to prepare all the music, to the same quality as at all other times, for these seven services in three days.

In May I embarked on a new venture in my capacity as an examiner, by agreeing to travel round to various secondary schools in the county to administer the practical part of GCE Music exams. In England, it was common practice for a pass in the Associated Board's Grade 5 to count towards a GCE result, but for some reason this wasn't good enough for the Welsh Joint Matriculation Board, who insisted on having an independent assessment. This meant I had to spend eleven weekdays driving to individual schools, mostly only one or two each day, so that the driving and simply waiting around took much longer than the actual tests. As usual with practical exams, one had not only to listen to prepared pieces but also to give the candidate something to read at sight. Shortly before my first visit I realised I had not been sent any tests for this purpose, and when I phoned to request some, was told that examiners were expected to use the Associated Board tests. When I protested that this was not allowed, they said, 'Oh, not the actual exam tests, but the sample books available in a music shop'. I knew, of course, that some candidates would have worked through this easily-available material during lessons, and at the same time I didn't see why I should go out and buy the books, especially as I was not told in advance what instruments would be presented. Even if I were able to muster some suitable music, or even compose tests specially, suppose I were confronted with guitar, harp, even percussion? I cannot recall how I solved the problem, but this casualness of approach seemed reprehensible. Another anomaly applied to the sight-singing test they all had to take: the rule was to 'deduct one mark for each mistake'. The melody provided would have about twenty-five notes, and was marked out of ten. Leaving aside the fact that even really experienced singers might have difficulty in reading at sight without any accompaniment, such a long tune (as I had found when coaching opera singers), a moment's thought will show that a single error near the start would probably make all the following notes 'wrong', even if the intervals between them were correct, implying a score of nought; and the same would apply if only the first half were sung correctly, or if the entire melody bore no resemblance at all to what was written. When I rang the chief examiner for advice, he mumbled something about using discretion, to which I replied 'then our instructions are obviously wrong'. The whole system seemed flawed, but the fees were useful, so I said no more.

This year's Llandaff Festival, including orchestral concerts conducted by Vernon Handley and notably Kurt Sanderling, was for me otherwise unremarkable except that I had another opportunity to conduct Elgar's masterpiece *The Dream of Gerontius*. For a performance in Salisbury Cathedral in 1974 with the Bournemouth Symphony Orchestra I had borrowed the full score belonging to my predecessor Richard Lloyd, which he had acquired from the late Sir Percy Hull of Hereford Cathedral, with his markings derived from Elgar himself. As part of my leaving present as deputy conductor of Salisbury Musical Society, I too had been presented with a full score, duly inscribed in copperplate writing and bearing the arms of Salisbury and Llandaff Cathedrals. Thus armed, and with an insight into the authentic interpretation of the work, I had members of the BBC Welsh Symphony in front of me, with David Johnson, at that time perhaps England's finest Gerontius, Sarah Browne as the Angel, Brian Rayner Cook as the Angel of the Agony, and the Cathedral Choir as the semi-chorus in the west gallery above the chorus. Press reviews were largely favourable. The Choral Society sang Dvořák's *Stabat Mater* in February and Handel's *Messiah* (the last time I ever conducted all three parts) in November.

The question also arose again concerning the making of a recording by the Cathedral Choir. Back in 1976 the Chapter had felt unable to approve Exon Audio's scheme whereby an initial layout of £1850 for a thousand records would make us a profit of £500. At that time, before the M4 motorway was extended to bypass Cardiff to the north, the Cathedral received about twelve thousand visitors a year, including regular coach parties, so perhaps the offer was not entirely unreasonable, but the canons often seemed reluctant to spend in order to gain in the longer term. Another example of this was their refusal to contribute to the cost of those prominent brown signboards on major approach-roads which advertise important sites and buildings, apparently failing to consider the increased revenue that could result from greater numbers of visitors. We had also been approached by one Michael Smythe, who not only ran his own company Vista but also recorded for Decca, but on hearing the organ the previous autumn he had thought better of it and invited me to make a record of organ music elsewhere. He later asked me to participate with several really eminent organists in a project to record the complete organ works of Messiaen, offering me *La Nativité* which I had broadcast from Coventry in 1976, but for some reason this never happened, and I heard that Michael had died young. The BBC was quite happy to record a programme of anthems and a couple of organ pieces in June, and invited me to broadcast another recital from the Brangwyn Hall in Swansea. Thus encouraged, I took the initiative to write to Harry Mudd, already very highly regarded for his Abbey Recording Company's series 'In Choirs and places where they sing'. By now the cost of a thousand records had risen to £2220, with a possible profit to the Cathedral of £1480, so I was quite surprised when, six weeks after I had put the plan to the Chapter Clerk, he wrote to give consent for a recording to be made. Despite the Dean's lack of interest in things musical, we did stage a variety of events, ranging from the evangelistic drama of the Fisherfolk to the choir of Christ Church Oxford, via a choir and orchestra from The Hague. I was still advocating Messrs Harrison & Harrison to rebuild the organ with a much improved specification, when the time came for me to pack up and go to Singapore.

There had for many years been a great demand overseas for the graded practical examinations of the Associated Board of the Royal Schools of Music, and nowhere more so than in the Far East, with 75% of the work being concentrated in Singapore, Malaysia and Hong Kong. At the time of writing, about 120 examiners visit Hong Kong each year to cover the vast numbers of candidates, but in 1979 just eight of us spent two months in Singapore before moving on to replace eight others in Hong Kong for a further two months. It was not uncommon for an examiner to make part of the tour a holiday for his wife and family, and in these countries a hotel would provide the additional accommodation at minimal cost, so my family travelled with me on a 'Jumbo' jet with Singapore Airlines via Paris and Dubai, where in those days the little airport was surrounded by sandy desert. The airline catering was superb: even before reaching Paris we had been served Danish open sandwiches, fruit salad and coffee, and thereafter champagne preceded a four-course meal with Chablis, followed by coffee with a choice of brandy or liqueurs. Two further meals were served after Dubai, and when not eating or sleeping Rachel spent most of the time reading, while Adrian kept nearby passengers (mostly Chinese) amused with his jolly laugh and cheerful antics, settling down to sleep when expected to. We stayed in a large room on the eleventh floor of the Cockpit Hotel, with a magnificent balcony view over the city, which then had comparatively few high-rise buildings, notably one occupied by the Chinese Banking Corporation and looking rather like three calculators stacked on top of each other, and another a hexagonal tower with gold-tinted windows. It was interesting to note that the independent republic of Singapore is an island only 50% larger than the Isle of Wight, and very similar in shape, separated from mainland Malaysia by waterways similar to Spithead and the Solent, but connected by a causeway – and with a population exceeding two million.

Next morning we were brought breakfast in bed and spent most of the day lounging by the pool under palm trees, where lunch was served in the form of sandwiches and a large dish of various fruits with ice cream and a long glass of iced lemon tea. This was the life – and I was actually being paid for it! When darkness fell, as it does quite suddenly between 6.45 and 7.15   near the Equator, we investigated the nearest shopping centre, the Plaza Singapura, a modern complex six stories high and our first experience of such a building. At 8.30 the next morning the exams began in the Yamaha studios on the top floor of the plaza, ending at 4.30 and allowing a two-hour lunch break at the hotel, only a few minutes' walk away. The area known as China Town was a complete contrast with the rest of the island, with its narrow streets, 'very scruffy and dirty looking' as Marian described it in a letter,

> with people cooking and selling strange concoctions out on the streets; the smells were most unusual and not altogether pleasant. There seemed to be very few Europeans there and we felt very much foreigners, especially as we were stared at. I think it was a combination of our fair skins, Adrian in his little pushchair and my bump!

Marian's 'bump' was our next baby, and after spending five fabulous weeks in Singapore, with visits to the smaller island of Sentosa and briefly across the causeway to Johore Bahru in Malaysia, we celebrated with a Malayan show with dinner at Raffles Hotel before Marian returned to England with the children to await the birth. They had often experienced very different meals in the open market stalls mainly frequented by the local people, and became quite accustomed to various Indian, Malay and Singaporean dishes such as nasi goreng, Hokkien fried prawn mee, murtabah (which we called motorbike) and satay, along with oriental fruits and pineapple juice by the pint. For Adrian's second birthday we had commissioned from a local baker a cake in the shape of a 2, which turned out much larger than expected and took up up almost a whole table: we shared it with my fellow examiners in the 'breakfast alcove' of our room. The baker's name was

Don Log Wee, but we renamed him Don Log Enormous.

To continue on this subject, the vast majority of inhabitants were Chinese, and at first I was fascinated by their monosyllabic names such as Lee Wee Song, Ho Sio Ping and Pu Choon Choon, with just the occasional Indian with a much grander name like Jegasothi Jeevaratriam, or simply Sadandan daughter of Mahendran. Announcements and notices were sometimes in Chinese, Malay, Tamil and English, but I was surprised to find that English was the preferred language most of the time, Chinese being used not much more than was Welsh in Wales. The biggest difference from home life was the climate, with a temperature at a fairly steady 88F during the day, so that going for a walk, or even to the shops, was a much more serious undertaking than it would normally be, and it would take time to recover from it, either by going indoors to get cool, or by jumping into the hotel pool. Taking time off in Sentosa was an exotic experience, looking out across the lagoon to the coral reef and the open sea beyond, with a group of Indonesian islands between us and Sumatra, where I believe tigers still roamed. Other enticements included trishaw rides, a sailing trip in a junk, a crocodile farm, a rubber plantation, watching the art of batik, a visit to the circular restaurant on the fortieth floor of the ultra-luxurious Mandarin Hotel on Orchard Road, and a stroll round the Jurong Bird Park, by which time I had bought my first single-lens reflex camera with several lenses, at only half the price it would have been in Britain. Wheeling a pushchair in town was not easy, owing to the deep storm drains (some several feet deep to cope with the monsoons) and pavements with ever-changing levels and little flights of steps, and it took some time to get used to stepping out of an air-conditioned building and feel the heat permeating one's trousers in a few seconds, as if stepping into a bath of hot air.

The shopping plazas were a notable feature of Singapore before they became a feature of English cities. Usually six or more stories high, there would often be a supermarket at basement level, and on the ground and first floors a variety of shops selling jewellery, leather goods, watches, cameras, books, recording equipment and so on. Higher floors were for furniture, carpets and offices, surgeries and the like. At our hotel I filled in a questionnaire, praising most aspects but offering a few suggestions for improvements. At home, suggestions of this kind were generally met, as we have seen, by a deafening silence and a complete absence of action. In Singapore it was quite different: the Manager responded by having a huge basket of fruit sent to our room – twenty oranges, apples and bananas and several bunches of grapes, with a finger-bowl and four napkins. This was at 10 p.m. Next day, a maid came to the door with her own presents for the children, who never ceased to attract attention from waitresses and shop assistants who, we supposed, had never seen a child with golden hair like Adrian's.

After spending so long with the family, I was naturally sorry to see them go, especially for little Adrian who would not understand where his Daddy had gone, or when I would ever return home. Marian would have to face not only the forthcoming birth but also twelve weeks looking after all the children without me, but there was some consolation in that for once I was being well paid, and would return thousands of pounds richer. I decided to try to teach myself the principles of piano jazz, in theory at any rate, and to read a few long novels such as Hardy's *Tess of the Durbervilles.* The 9th August was celebrated as Singapore's fourteenth National Day, with a grand parade and display at Queenstown Stadium, and I invited my colleagues up to my room to watch the fireworks that evening. A more sinister reminder of the country's history was pushed under my door on morning of the 28th August in the form of the *Straits Times*, with the headline proclaiming the assassination of Earl Mountbatten, who as supreme commander of the South East Asia Command had received the surrender of the Japanese on Santosa Island in 1945. Several more parties were held in my room and elsewhere to welcome Jenny Jones, our coordinator from the Board's London office, and at other times I was content to explore on my own the Chinese and Japanese Gardens and other parts of the island until, four weeks after the departure of the family, it was my turn, along with my colleagues, to move on.

I had arranged to break my journey by staying for four nights at the Hyatt Rama Hotel in Bangkok. Here I experienced most of the delights that were readily on offer to the tourist, including visits to the Grand Palace, Thai temples and pagodas, a boat trip on the Chao Phraya river to see the famous floating market, and various demonstrations of kick-boxing, cock-fighting and other things not generally available back home. The climate was just as hot as in Singapore but more humid, the streets were full of those noisy, smoky little motorbikes, and there were images of the Buddha everywhere. In some ways it was quite a relief to resume my flight over Vietnam and the South China Sea to the British colony of Hong Kong, where for more than seven weeks I examined hundreds of Chinese candidates, mostly offering the piano but just occasionally an orchestral instrument.

The Chinese are known as a hard-working and determined race, and in general their playing was technically well-taught and assiduously practised, but in the higher grades one looks for signs of interpretative ability, and here one usually found an inability to distinguish between different styles, so that baroque, classical and romantic music tended to sound as if learnt on a typewriter. Those who had the advantage of lessons with a teacher from Europe were better able to appreciate such niceties, but I suspect that the monosyllabic nature of the native tongue, with its absence of phrasing and nuance, had much to do with their style of playing. The examiners were allocated rooms on the mainland of Kowloon in the New World Hotel, so modern that it was still being built, with low-ceilinged rooms and virtually no view of the Harbour, being incorporated with offices and a large shopping centre. I was not alone in seeking a more congenial and less expensive base, and soon moved into the Park Hotel in Chatham Road. It was far less stylish, but my room enjoyed a splendid view across the so-called harbour to Hong Kong Island. That evening I looked in at the New World to check my post, only to find a cablegram from Wales informing me that I had a new daughter, called Laura Helen. I had been expecting a message announcing the birth of a baby, but was thrilled to realise that it was an actual person, with a name! My fellow examiner Graham Matthews, then Organist of Sheffield Cathedral, took me up to the penthouse bar where we celebrated by drinking Pimms.

Jenny Jones had followed us to Hong Kong, and we all attended a dinner given in her honour (or perhaps ours too) by Tom Lee, the manager of the examination studios. It was a twelve-course meal, very elegantly served at two round tables, and included Peking Duck, chicken baked in earth and lotus leaves, and a course called 'double-boiled snow fungus in coconuts'; a misprint on the menu stated 'sweet and sour poke', which caused some merriment. Some of the other examiners had the good fortune to be invited out quite often by teachers, but this privilege had not yet come my way, so I was all the more glad to be invited to the home, at Deep Water Bay on the south side of Hong Kong Island, of a family with distant connections with an equally distant cousin. At a later date they took me out for the day on their motor launch around islands off the coast of the New Territories (so called because the land was acquired by the British more recently than the main island). On another day I gave an organ recital at the Chinese University's chapel at Chung Chi College on a small tracker-action organ by a German builder – the first recital I had given anywhere further from Great Britain than the Channel Islands. After the recital I was introduced to another Michael Smith, director of a huge company named Jardine Mattheson, who promptly invited me to a Sunday lunch by his swimming pool near Ocean Park. The daytime temperature was still around 90F, and humidity up to at least 90% left little air for breathing, making it quite exhausting to walk about for more than ten minutes at a time in such punishing heat. Towards the end of September we experienced a tropical storm, during which all public services closed down for several hours and the hoardings surrounding a building site near my hotel were smashed to the ground; after this the climate became decidedly more temperate, with temperatures down to the mid-70s in October, which was much more pleasant. The Island covers an area of twenty-nine square miles, but its population was a million; Kowloon also houses a million people, but in only four square miles, and such was the density of pedestrians on the streets on Saturdays that our free days were Sundays and Mondays when movement was thought to be a little easier. Needless to say, I made the most of my opportunities for exploring, not only on Hong Kong Island but on a much smaller island called Cheung Chau, with its fascinating narrow streets, Chinese folk in oddly-shaped straw hats, and views of the other islands. There I went for a lone swim from an empty beach, keeping a sharp lookout for the shark which had recently been biting peoples' legs off, as I informed my parents later (or was I just pulling *their* legs?). Not all my excursions were alone, however, for I found a good friend in Patrick Forbes, an examiner who had joined us after a spell in Malaysia, and we took a coach trip to the New Territories, right up to the border with China, where we looked at a long view across the paddy-fields, appropriately enough.

Paddy was a distinguished-looking man, not unlike the popular artist Rolf Harris, who had just retired as Director of the Huddersfield School of Music (he had some interesting and not wholly complimentary things to say about my erstwhile employer Professor Hoddinott and what he considered 'the mass-production of poor-quality students' at Cardiff University). I also had the occasional meal with Dr Douglas Hopkins, who had been Marian's organ teacher at the Royal Academy of Music in the '60s. I reminded him that I had first met him when I was a boy, as a family friend of a schoolmate, when we had all been taken to St Paul's Cathedral to hear the *St Matthew Passion* (not the ideal acoustic for such a work). He responded by telling me that he had been a chorister there under Sir George Martin, who, as we have seen in Chapter 4, was an ancestor of mine. Douglas had been Organist of Canterbury Cathedral for a short time, and had also been one of the four senior examiners participating in my training when I first joined the Associated Board.

For a weekend break in early October Paddy and I travelled by jetfoil to Macau, a Portuguese colony attached to China, staying at a small hotel right on the beach of a little island called Coloane, which is joined by a causeway to another island which has a bridge to the mainland.

In my quest for reading novels I worked through *Silas Marner, Sons and Lovers* and *Cakes and Ale* thereby adding Eliot, Lawrence and Maugham to my literary education. I also fell for the irresistible opportunity to have a suit made to measure in fine wool, at a surprisingly low price.

On my last free Monday I set off alone to explore the magnificently mountainous island of Lantau, where with a most rudimentary map I walked over the hills to the east of Sunset Peak right across the island, hoping to find a ferry on the other side. At one point I had to ask directions of a woman who knew no English, by drawing with a stick in the sand a sketch of a boat on the waves and pointing uncertainly in the direction I thought I had to go. Only on my very last evening did I manage to meet one of my Dilwyn neighbours, who was engaged on work for the new 'mass transit' railway, enjoying supper with him and his wife at the Royal Yacht Club and chatting until midnight. By the end of my stay in Kowloon I had examined 870 candidates in thirty-seven days, and over the whole tour 1872 in seventeen weeks. Earlier I had looked into the possibility of breaking my homeward flight, at minimal extra cost, with a few days in the Seychelles, but with a Half Term holiday week awaiting me, a family longing to see me (I hoped) and a new daughter to meet – not to mention the considerable amount of time I had spent on exotic beaches in the last four months – I soon dismissed the idea and flew back to London via Bombay and Rome. Not until nearly thirty years later did I slake my thirst for a holiday in the Seychelles. It was therefore at Heathrow Airport that I first met Laura, and we drove all the way to Herefordshire to relax at the cottage for a few days and recover from jet-lag, with a family outing to Stokesay Castle and a directors' meeting thrown in for good measure.

The return to Llandaff after eighteen weeks was not the happiest moment of my life, but I soon set about answering some of the hundred letters that were awaiting my attention. In answering them, I used up all my headed notepaper, and it is a mark of my desire to get out of Wales as soon as possible that I waited until the New Year before ordering a new supply from the printer. It was quite clear that the Dean was simply not in sympathy with music, and when the future of the Festival was under discussion had stated categorically that the Cathedral was 'first and foremost a parish church, and the

Dean an incumbent whose first duty was the cure of souls'. (It was typical of him that having stated the prime purpose of anything he would never take the matter any further). My official sub-organist Anthony had become increasingly morose and critical, no doubt resenting the burden of work imposed on him by my long absence rather than relishing the opportunity to show what he could do. One of my part-time choirmen had written to me in Hong Kong to give me advance warning of how things were going, praising the choristers and Anthony's keen discipline, but not his limited conducting technique, 'little pecks of his fingers, plucking the pulse out of thin air; no one knows when the next peck is coming'. My informant spoke well of the performance of specific items, and assessed the competence of individual boys, adding that 'Anthony's organ-playing leaves a great deal to be desired, but it has the property of inducing levity in an otherwise dull world'. I suspect he was exaggerating somewhat when commenting on Anthony's improvised variations on the anthem *Zadok the Priest* as the choir processed out one evening: 'a sound to be marvelled at: it brought tears to our eyes; in fact choir and clergy were rolling with mirth, falling over each other in the Welsh Chapel as Anthony tried to resolve some of his neo-Handelian chords'.

On my return I found that Terry Dickens, my longstanding bass, had been given three months' leave owing to family problems, and that no one had applied for the vacant alto lay clerkship, which was currently being filled on different days by three men including a student. I set about planning our long-awaited recording sessions with Harry Mudd, but shortly before the chosen dates the University authorities refused to allow my other bass, David Gwesyn Smith, to participate, as he was needed for their own concert. There was nothing I could do but postpone the session until the New Year. I derived some encouragement, however, from Sir David Willcocks, who heard one of our better Evensongs when he came to direct a choral workshop for ISM members at Howell's School; from Hereford's organist Roy Massey, who phoned to say that the organist of Chichester Cathedral (John Birch) had decided to retire; and from Allan Wicks of Canterbury asking me to be a judge at an organ competition during the annual congress of the Incorporated Association of Organists the following summer. I also discovered that some months earlier I had been elected *in absentia* to the Council of that organisation. The only good news at the cathedral was the appointment of the Rev Terry Doherty, from Londonderry Cathedral, initially as an assistant curate and later as a priest vicar, who turned out to be one of the nicest and most musical of the many young priests who fulfilled that role during my time. Personally I felt that further development could not realistically be achieved because of the many limiting factors that have already been described in this book. I decided to approach the Director of the RSCM, Dr Lionel Dakers, for advice, setting out in a letter the best and worst features of my work. At 42 my chances of promotion were already declining, and I had applied for only two other cathedral posts in the six years since my appointment. He was kind enough to invite me to meet him at the Athenaeum Club in London, where we discussed my future, but of course there was little he could do apart from offering to support any application I might make (as he had, indeed, at Llandaff).

Not until December, more than two years after I had first begun negotiations for rebuilding the organ, did the Finance Committee authorise the spending of money for 'repairs' as outlined by Rushworth's in June. With only one competitor, our existing firm Hill, Norman & Beard, Rushworth had reduced their quotation dramatically in order to get the contract, provided their offer were taken up immediately after Christmas. This news was not as good as the Chapter Clerk would have me believe, for the two plans were not at alike, and in my view there needed to be a better reason than cost for changing to a new builder after so many years. Norman added that all other forms of expenditure would have to be 'vigorously curtailed', thereby putting paid to my request for higher salaries for lay clerks, and shortly afterwards I had to report that fifteen square feet of the Song Room ceiling had collapsed during a practice, narrowly missing the singers. To add insult to injury, Norman asked me to furnish a list of any concerts already booked between Christmas and May; not only should he have had access to this information, but as I pointed out, he had categorically refused, ten months earlier, to keep me informed of such events. My last letter of the year included a request for repairs to our garage:

> The rain comes in through the roof, the yard is littered with builders' rubbish (including a lavatory), and because the doors cannot be shut properly we have just had our third burglary. This time our car and the freezer were broken into, and Anthony's motor scooter was stolen (and later found, with several parts missing, down by the river).

The two months following my return from the Far East passed uneventfully, with only some uninspiring examining in the Midlands and Cwmbran to vary the usual routine. Even the Choral Society offered nothing more exciting than *Messiah* in November, and after Christmas we were content to relax at home with my parents until the New Year when we transferred to Woodfalls to be with Marian's family and friends.

1980

When I accepted the Llandaff post, described by Lionel Dakers as a 'medium grade' cathedral, I had hoped to stay for just a few years before moving on to one of the great English cathedrals. The first two months of this year were as fallow as ever, with little work to keep me occupied during the day, but I put a lot of care into my application for the vacancy at Chichester, where I thought I had a good chance. Not a 'great' cathedral in terms of size, but nicely situated on the south coast, within easy reach of London, and in family terms not far from Marian's mother and even closer to her brother and his family in Hayling Island. Moreover, I had been associated with Chichester during my seven years as assistant organist at Salisbury, on account of the Southern Cathedrals Festival which alternated between these two cities and Winchester every July. With a wealth of experience behind me and our friend Allan Wicks of Canterbury as the assessor, I sent in my application and was, for the first time since 1973, invited to attend for interview.

At this point we at last began our recording sessions for Abbey Records, but the project was put in jeopardy again by the intransigence of Anthony Burns-Cox, who doggedly refused to alter his regular parish choir practice on the second of the three evenings. He soon changed his tune when I asked Morley Lewis to play for the entire recording; he did not like that idea at all, and agreed to cover all three sessions. We could not allow the whole venture to revolve around him, but in fact I had rather hoped that he wouldn't back down, because I felt that Morley's playing was likely to be more accurate. A couple of days later the Choral Society performed a Haydn Mass and CPE Bach's *Magnificat* (with its final *Amen* chorus occupying about five minutes). For their Festival contribution I had decided to offer *African Sanctus*, a new and unusual work by David Fanshawe involving tape-recordings of native African music made during his travels in the Sudan, and I accepted his invitation to go and hear the work in Bournemouth on the day after I had attended a meeting of the Incorporated Society of Musicians Council in London. It was typical of my hectic schedule that although these events were on consecutive days of a weekend, I had to be in Llandaff on the Sunday morning for a confirmation service incorporated into the Eucharist. I was cross with the Dean for his instruction that the *Gloria*, psalm and *Creed* which would normally be sung by the choir, should actually be *said* by the congregation, leaving no choir music for a fifty-minute stretch, when I had returned specially to conduct it. I felt it was a pity not to let an unusually large congregation, many of whom would be strangers to cathedral music, hear what we had to offer on a weekly basis at the choral Eucharist.

The Bournemouth performance, at which I met the composer, fitted in quite well with my visit to Chichester with Marian and the children, together with her mother acting as baby-sitter. The interviews and organ-playing went well enough, I thought: each of us had to play to Dr Wicks the difficult accompaniment to Stanford's A-major setting of *Magnificat*, requiring many stop-changes as well as a fair degree of prestidigitation. There were five other men up for interview: one was a university lecturer and former King's College organ scholar, Ian Hare; four of us were cathedral organists, Malcolm Archer from Bristol, John Bertalot from Blackburn, Graham Elliott from Chelmsford and I; and the remaining candidate was Alan Thurlow, the assistant at Durham. Maybe the Chapter thought that as four of us had already made it to the top, it was Alan's turn now; for sure enough, it was he who got the job, and there he remained until he retired. The other three organists have all spent time working in the United States. Malcolm worked in Chicago for a while but was head-hunted by Wells Cathedral, where he served for some years before moving on to St Paul's Cathedral; John spent the rest of his career in Princeton, and Graham eventually took up a post in Washington. Ian Hare was destined to be content with a post as assistant organist at Carlisle. I have often thought that, as an alternative to Lichfield, Chichester would have been ideal for me (though whether I would have been ideal for them is another matter), but at forty-two I had lost what was perhaps the best chance I was ever to have for promotion, at a time when my children were still young enough to cope easily with the move.

Instead of returning home after the interviews, I stayed at my mother-in-law's house with the family and then began three weeks of examining in Hampshire, Chelmsford and Luton, keeping weekends free for my cathedral work. After enjoying some really excellent services at Easter I took the whole family to Scotland, where we stayed for several days at a very grand hotel known as the Peebles Hydro. There were good facilities for the children while Marian and I attended the meetings and recitals that made up the annual Congress of the Incorporated Society of Musicians, of which I had quite recently been appointed a regional chairman, as mentioned earlier. Our host as President was Ian Wallace, a singer just as well known then for his jovial television appearances in a quiz show called *My Music*. His equally famous colleagues John Amis, Frank Muir and Dennis Norden joined him for a recording of the show, and recitals were given by the harpist Osian Ellis with the celebrated tenor Peter Pears (by then well past his prime and seriously flat), and the pianist Denis Matthews. At the Congress dinner we ate haggis, and the puddings, bedecked with sparklers, were 'piped in' on the bagpipes. We fitted in a brief visit to friends in Edinburgh, and again did not come straight home, for I was scheduled to share a concert with a local soprano at Brackley Baptist Church in Elland, in west Yorkshire. It so happened that John Foster, brother of my erstwhile lay clerk Peter, was a prosperous wholesale fruiterer living in the nearby suburb of Almondbury. He and Malcolm Cruise, music critic of the *Huddersfield Examiner,* had fixed the recital, inviting all of us to stay at John's house for the weekend. The house was so large as to be more in the 'stately home' category – it might well have been open to the public – with no fewer that twenty-eight rooms, some of which John jokingly claimed never to have seen. We all enjoyed meeting his family, and some two hundred people attended the recital. After my long drive from Scotland and nearly five hours' practice I became increasingly tired and unwell but I managed to end the performance with the famous *Toccata* from Widor's fifth organ 'symphony', by omitting the two preceding movements I had planned to play. I had already worked my way through big works by Bach, Mozart, Mendelssohn, Elgar and Howells, so with the soprano's nine songs I think the audience got their money's worth.

Thankfully we were able to unwind for a whole week at Dilwyn, but no sooner had I taken the family back to Llandaff than I was off to Scotland again, this time for the cathedral organists' conference in Edinburgh. Dennis Townhill, Organist of St Mary's Cathedral and one of my predecessors at Louth Parish Church, had asked me to give a recital at the end of the conference – something almost unheard of at these conferences, but he thought it an appropriate gesture in recognition of my Edinburgh doctorate as an organist. This time I played the whole of Widor's fifth symphony, but I fancy most of my colleagues were by then on their way home! I dined with Roy Massey at Dennis's house and caught the night train, to be met at Cardiff station by Marian next morning, in time for breakfast. Meanwhile Dr Allan Wicks had been encouraging me to apply for the post of organist of Westminster Abbey. I had sent for details on the 15th March, exactly twenty-five years after telling the Dean of Christ Church and Sir Thomas Armstrong, when interviewed there for a scholarship, that my ultimate aim was 'to play the organ at the next Coronation'. In truth I did not feel the job was for me, for various reasons, but with the promised support of the organist of Canterbury Cathedral, no less, I sent off my application just in time. When I duly informed my Dean, there was a surprising reaction – he invited me into the Deanery for sherry (a very rare event) and a long chat. He expressed an opinion that if I were to reach the shortlist, this would at any rate stand me in good stead for somewhere like Winchester: I wondered if at last he was beginning to appreciate my worth, or if he simply anticipated some reflected glory from my potential promotion. I was not in the least surprised to learn, a fortnight later, that my name was not on the Abbey shortlist, any more than I was when Roy Massey told me ten days later that his was. He had always been ahead of me since we had received our Archbishop's Diplomas in Church Music together in 1963, had made a deep impression on the music of Birmingham Cathedral; turned down an invitation to Norwich; and had already been at Hereford for six years. The others on the shortlist were the highly-respected Christopher Robinson from St George's Chapel, Windsor (my predecessor as organ scholar of Christ Church) and Martin Neary from Winchester. In the final analysis they were outshone by Simon Preston, a particularly famous organ scholar of King's College, Cambridge, who had not only become the Abbey's sub-organist immediately afterwards and subsequently acting organist at St Alban's Cathedral for a year, but had for the next eleven years adorned the prestigious post of Organist and Tutor in Music at Christ Church, Oxford.

At a much lower level, my own sub-organist Anthony Burns-Cox was, as I have indicated, becoming increasingly disillusioned with his lot. I had to remonstrate with him when, left to choose the music for a special service in Lent to be sung by the choristers of five cathedrals following a football competition, as was his right as Director of Music at the school, he selected Purcell's 'Evening Hymn' to be sung in unison. Not only would this have caused problems in rehearsal by being sung from more than one edition, but I felt that a shorter anthem in two parts would have been more suitable; more important, he had overlooked the fact that the second half of this lengthy piece consists entirely of alleluias – an acclamation always studiously avoided during the whole of Lent. Shortly afterwards there was the confrontation about his role in the recording, which I have mentioned earlier, and then he began complaining about other matters:

> I am concerned that I am expected to do so much of your work! Last term I did 45 days and this term 18 days. I am usually neither paid not even thanked for rather unrewarding work. If I was left with a super, keen choir then it would be a different matter. I can only really compare it with Peter Hurford's choir, in the days when I used to help occasionally. I ask, why are your boys so lethargic? There is a serious lack of keenness and pride in their work; consequently there is little pleasure in working with them. Next term I propose not to exceed the 12 days which your contract allows you to be absent upon professional duties.

Rather than pass judgment on Anthony at this very late stage, I think the reader can more readily draw conclusions as to his own sincerely-felt grievances and our conflicting attitudes, as well as my own philosophy about our work, if I copy the letter I drafted in reply:

> First let us get clear what the system is regarding your duties with the Cathedral Choir. As Sub-Organist you are both my assistant and my deputy, and I do not much like your implication that you are 'doing my work'. You have your share of responsibility for the Cathedral Choir, just as I have mine, and you should be willing to co-operate with me; instead of passing off the choristers as 'my' boys, our partnership would flourish much better if you regarded them as 'our' boys. The work which I allocate to you is *your* work as the Sub-Organist.
>
> You seem to have misunderstood the terms of my contract. I am indeed allowed 12 days a term for other professional work, though in actual fact I have not taken advantage of this allocation since the summer term of 1976, and on average I am away only 9 days a term. Last summer was made an exception, but even so, the spring and summer terms together accounted for only 21 days' absence. These are in addition to

my weekly free day when you are on duty regularly, and this is perhaps what you did not know. If you are doing 18 days this term, you are lucky, because I am entitled to ask you to do 23.

I would not have thought it necessary to have to explain this, but I am anxious that you should not feel unfairly treated. My trip to the Far East was a special arrangement, for which you received extra payment, taken out of my own salary. Since you like to make comparisons with other cathedrals, it may interest you to know that in my first year as Assistant at Salisbury, I calculated that I attended 177 services and 254 practices, amounting in all to 46% of the work; my annual salary then was £200. I think you will agree that your duties in comparison with these have not been unduly onerous.

I would be grateful if you would please stop grumbling about the boys. Very few choirmasters these days are satisfied with the kind of boys who apply for choristerships, and we all have to accept the available material and do our best with it. Our present choristers are some of the nicest boys I have worked with, and I must say that on the whole I find them enjoying their work – in fact even today they were asking for extra practice time this week. If you detect a lack of enthusiasm, I am sorry to say that this must be because of your own attitude towards the boys, who unfortunately do not enjoy your practices – a fact that they make abundantly clear on frequent occasions. I do not want to undermine your confidence, or I would have mentioned this before, but in view of your repeated complaints, I think it fair to let you know how they feel. It has been said recently that, not content with banging on the piano, you have taken to hitting the boys on the head: I hope this is not true, and that you will confirm that it is not, because this could lead you into serious trouble.

I know that both the boys and particularly the men would respect you much more if your own playing were more accurate and reliable, if your method of conducting were easier to follow and more helpful in complex music, and if you adopted a kindly and sympathetic attitude to their efforts – especially on those occasions when your own performance has left something to be desired. This opinion is supported by the lay clerks themselves, who often make their views clear to me, and by the junior clergy.

I hope this letter may act as an encouragement to you, because your work is an important link in the chain that holds the cathedral music together. If you are going to continue to be disillusioned, then I think the only honest course you can take is to resign your post as Sub-Organist, forthwith.

Knowing how it feels to receive such criticism in writing, I decided not to send the letter but to summon him round to my house, where I was able to elaborate in more detail on what I considered to be his shortcomings. I did, however, take the opportunity to show the letter to the chapter clerk on Maundy Thursday and recommend his dismissal. Three years earlier I had felt unable to give Anthony a good reference when he applied to be organist of Portsmouth Cathedral, and it may well be that he suspected this, for one day in the summer term he secretively went away for an interview, and when I was sitting in my garden on Ascension Day he unexpectedly appeared and announced that he had accepted an appointment at Romsey Abbey. Naturally I was just as delighted for my sake as for his, and we went round to the Butcher's Arms to celebrate in the usual way. No other work was attached to the post, nor a tied house, but Romsey Abbey is a very grand parish church with a fine organ, and it had strong connections with the Mountbatten family at Broadlands, their stately home. I mused on Anthony's impatience with his own playing, remembering how on one occasion he had in despair suddenly stopped playing a piece by Bach and had thrown the music over his shoulder. Believing that in the Abbey the Mountbatten family pew was situated in the chancel, just in front of the organ console, I imagined the copy landing on the lap of the Countess. I have no way of knowing whether this ever happened, but I think that his tenure of the post was hardly longer than his sojurn at Llandaff, if I remember correctly a conversation I had some years later with his former vicar David Shearlock, by then Dean of Truro.

Anthony's impending departure seemed to have a good effect on the Dean, who invited me round to sherry for perhaps only the second time and for over an hour discussed future plans. He evidently felt that the dual responsibility of Parish organist and assistant to the Cathedral Organist made conflicting demands, and was minded to separate the two posts. There was also the tenure of the school post, where Anthony's duties had dwindled considerably. The Headmaster, George Hill, made it clear that his responsibility was to appoint the best candidate as Director of Music at the school, and that the person chosen would not necessarily even be an organist, let alone one good enough, and willing, to take on such a burden in addition to a full-time teaching post. Looking back, I think George must have received Anthony's resignation rather earlier than I did, because my diary shows that only two days after my meeting with the Dean I was reading the letters George had received from the more promising applicants. After a period of considerable anxiety, I was informed that the man chosen was a very well-qualified and experienced organist called Michael Hoeg, who had graduated with distinction from the Royal Academy of Music, as well as being a Fellow of the Royal College of Organists with the added Choirmaster's Diploma. For several years he had been organist and master of the choristers at Londonderry Cathedral, and while living in Northern Ireland was a peripatetic teacher and an adviser in class music teaching; yet amid all this activity he had also managed to acquire a first class degree in music at University College, Dublin. After his interview for the school post I had auditioned him, and Richard Francis from Ludlow Parish Church, on the Rodgers electronic organ that was in use during the 'repair' work being done on the pipe organ by Rushworths, giving Michael the first page of the vocal score of Parry's anthem *Blest Pair of Sirens* to play at sight. This opening is a reduction of the orchestral score, not easy to manage on the organ, but he had acquitted himself well and I was delighted to offer him the job as my assistant, which he duly accepted. Llandaff thus became the only cathedral in Britain where even the assistant organist was a former cathedral organist. This event must count as one of the most fortunate in my career, as he remained a loyal, reliable colleague until I retired twenty years later, and continued until his own retirement in 2010. It is convenient to add at this stage that the Chapter's acceptance of Rushworth's cut-price job on the organ did not please their adviser Cecil Clutton. He had thoroughly approved of my long letter to the Chapter Clerk on the subject, and replied:

> After their previous performance I'm not much surprised at anything they may do, and as I then told them in pretty clear terms what I thought of their behaviour I think it unlikely that they will consult me again! Any expenditure that will perpetuate the present layout of the organ must be sheer madness, and to that extent I would be totally opposed to the Rushworth & Dreaper proposal. I still think that anything less than my scheme will be a waste of money in the not-very-long term.

At the request of David Fanshawe the Choral Society forsook their formal dress for our performance of his *African Sanctus* in favour of safari-style summer colours, and the composer, similarly attired, introduced the work to the audience in his characteristic flamboyant manner, describing his adventures with a tape-recorder in the Sudan. There was no orchestra as such, the instrumental contribution being for two electric guitars, a variety of percussion instruments involving three players from the BBC Welsh including Clifton Prior on centre stage as a rock drummer, grand piano, and an electronic organ played by Morley Lewis. As recommended in the score, Cliff and I wore headphones in order to synchronize the recorded native African music with the choral writing. I had engaged the soprano Meryl Drower as the vocal soloist, knowing that she had already performed the work elsewhere, and for the same reason Keith Swallow came down from Yorkshire to play the elaborate piano part. I did not meet him again until twenty-five years later, when quite by chance he was pointed out to me in a Huddersfield supermarket: he not only remembered our performance, but declared it to be the best of the twenty he had experienced. The audience was so large that we had to dispense with the centre aisle to get everyone in, thereby making *African Sanctus* more popular than our *Messiah* seven months earlier. Fanshawe wrote the work after wandering through parts of Africa recording ceremonial music for weddings, funerals, warrior celebrations and the like, the result being an amalgam of African and European music comprising sections from the Ordinary of the Mass and the composer's tape-recordings. A rather sentimental and incongruous setting of the Lord's Prayer as a soprano solo was not, as one critic wrote, as appealing as the sound of frogs, rain and thunder, the Love Song, Courtship Dances or the Wedding Dance. Kenneth Loveland, the doyen of music critics and a regular contributor to *The Times,* wrote in the South Wales Argus 'It was certainly the best (of the performances) I have heard, sung with great spirit by the Llandaff Cathedral Choral Society, and played with evident commitment by the instrumental ensemble gathered for the occasion.   That I found it less exciting than before is, I am sure, a suggestion that it can begin to wear thin, and not a criticism of the performance'.

I doubt whether Anthony troubled to attend the concert, for the next day I found a letter dated the same evening in which he again poured scorn on my efforts with the Cathedral Choir, mentioning specific services and my supposed lack of discipline; it is ironic that fifteen years later, long after he had left Romsey Abbey, I was criticised for 'keeping a tight ship'. His parting shot came in the last paragraph:

The last six years have been uninspiring to say the least,
and when I think of the enthusiastic choir which I handed over

to you when you came it is nothing short of a crime that morale is presently so low. No doubt you will, as usual, look to others to apportion the blame, but one is suspicious of people who always blame others! Over the last nine years I have greatly exceeded the duties laid down by my contract, so now, in all conscience, I do officially withdraw my support for you and leave you to fight your own battles. I wish you joy!

No doubt he wrote with relish, having wanted to express his feelings for some time, and it was not the first time that one of my musical triumphs had been quickly dampened in such a negative way; perhaps he had deliberately chosen the moment. Naturally Michael Hoeg had to serve out his notice at Londonderry, so I was rather concerned at this sudden throwing in of the proverbial towel, for although I could cope well enough, with Morley's assistance, for the next few weeks, I had already agreed to spend much of July on my usual examining commitments, ranging from Somerset and Hampshire to Barnet and Liverpool. I read most of the letter to the lay clerks that evening, and in response to its sinister footnote 'Copy to the Dean' went straight to the Deanery to state my views. Once again the Dean was his most affable self, enthusiastically praising *African Sanctus* and plying me with whisky (perhaps the only time he ever did). It was a very good session, and I did not get away until 11.30 p.m. When I explained my predicament regarding examining duties, he at once phoned Terry Doherty, our new Irish curate, asking him to take over my choir practices while I was away in Somerset. Terry was only too pleased to help out, did the job well and, along with Morley, saved the situation during the remaining five weeks of term. First I had a three-day assignment in Somerset, and one evening I used the backs of two mark forms to draft a reply to Anthony's letter. It was very long, pulling no punches, and I am tempted to reproduce it here, but as he had already left his job I felt that no good would be served by giving vent to my feelings, and inasmuch as I never sent it to him, nor will I publish it now, except for my last few sentences about his decision to lay down tools:

You have merely succeeded in inconveniencing the Dean, and other people who may have to finish off your job for you, but not me. I shall carry out *my* work exactly as planned, and you will be branded as a deserter. When my seven years as an Assistant came to an end, there were dinners, parties and presentations, and even songs were composed by way of a musical testimonial, duly presented to me as an illuminated manuscript. Six years later I was greeted by my largest audience ever when I returned to play at Salisbury; the Dean gave a reception in my honour. I wonder what kind of reception *you* will get if you return to Llandaff six years hence?

My hypothetical question remained unanswered, because as far as I am aware he was never seen in Llandaff again.

On the domestic front, our family was quickly outgrowing our little cottage in Dilwyn, and at intervals we had been looking at larger ones within twenty-five miles of Hereford. We liked one on a hillside above Monmouth, and made an offer on a rather remote brick cottage at Kimbolton, near Leominster, while advertising 16 Karen Court in the *Hereford Times*. Rachel took her Grade 2 'cello examination in Caerphilly, being awarded a Distinction by Rodney Slatford the double bass player. I suffered from the longest cold of my life, lasting at least four weeks, but I kept going through seventeen days of examining and was so busy that I did not write home for seven weeks. For the first time in five years I attended a summer gaudy at Christ Church. My college scout of twenty-five years earlier was still there, but elevated to be in charge of the great hall, and at dinner I sat next to my old colleague Tony Crossland, with whom I had shared the post of assistant cathedral organist there for a year after graduation. As usual, the honorary doctors were seated at high table, including the Russian 'cellist Rostropovich, and the toast to them was responded to by the Archbishop of Canterbury. The Chancellor, Harold Macmillan, sat on the other side of the Dean, and the toast to the House was proposed by Lord Dacre of Glanton, who turned out to be the recently ennobled Hugh Trevor-Roper, Professor of History. I detected no reduction in the standard of hospitality, with five different wines, including Bollinger champagne with the strawberries and a twenty-five-year-old port with the coffee. I overheard Tarquin, son of Laurence Olivier and Vivien Leigh, saying that his wife had left him: 'she was never dull', he said, 'often appalling, but never dull'. After dinner I had a chat to Simon Preston and was introduced to the Precentor, hoping that my scarlet robe was impressing him as much as it impressed Simon, and before leaving Oxford I boldly introduced myself to the Dean, presenting him with the choir recording made earlier in the year: although my chances of succeeding Simon were very slim, I at least made an effort to be noticed.

One of my examining stints was in south Hampshire, and I took the opportunity to stay with my friends Richard and Jane Godfrey in their great Victorian house overlooking Southampton Water at Netley Abbey. My Steinway grand, which had previously been housed in the song room, was now on loan to Richard, who was not only a Doctor of Medicine but also an ARCO. By then he had bought his own Steinway, so in the evenings we were able to enjoy playing two-piano music. He had also built his own organ, on which he practised for half an hour before breakfast every day, and my signal for getting out of bed in the morning was the third movement of Hindemith's third Sonata, which, oddly enough, is based on a German folksong 'I bid you then good night'. I then found myself examining in Barnet, where for the first time my work was monitored by one of the newly-appointed moderators. Who should it be but my old tutor, Dr Sydney Watson, another link with Oxford, who seemed to enjoy the experience as much as I did. For the rest of that week I was sent again to the Bluecoat Chambers in Liverpool, where I had first worked ten years before; by Thursday I was so weary that I dropped into bed as soon as I got back to the hotel, and slept for thirteen hours, feeling more lively next day when I made a lightning tour of Rushworth & Dreaper's Organ Works between sessions. My seven-hour working day on the Saturday was followed by a six-hour journey, with two breakdowns and other delays until it was past midnight when the train eventually crawled into Cardiff station. Term finished the next day, when we had a lunch party for the cathedral music staff and finished with an Evensong attended by delegates to an Anglican/Orthodox conference, with several priests wearing that strange Eastern headwear associated at the time with Archbishop Makarios. Only an RSCM committee meeting and the annual luncheon (at the Café Royal in Regent Street) of the Associated Board intervened before our escape to Dilwyn.

After celebrating Adrian's third birthday and relaxing there for a few days, picking raspberries and strawberries at a nearby farm, we took over my brother-in-law's house in nearby Hayling Island for a week, so we were able to invite Richard Godfrey's family to join us there for fish 'n' chips and a visit to the funfair on the beach. I am not an avid attender of conferences, but I had been invited by Allan Wicks, then President of the Incorporated Association of Organists, to participate in their annual assembly at the University of Surrey at Guildford in mid-August. My contribution was two-fold: to give an illustrated lecture and to be one of the judges in a national competition, along with Richard Seal whose assistant I had been in Salisbury for six years, and Allan himself. The final was held in the chapel of Charterhouse, and was won by Michael Overbury. For my lecture, attended by about seventy delegates, I used a BBC tape-recording of my 1976 broadcast of Messiaen's great organ work *La Nativité du Seigneur* to analyse the composer's technique and powers of illustration. Each of the nine sections has a title invoking some aspect of the legend of Christ's nativity, such as the angels and the wise men, and the finale is the best-known section entitled *Dieu parmi nous*, which ends with a brilliant toccata. The whole suite is based on scales other than major and minor, invented by Messiaen with different combinations of tones and semitones, and the harmonies derived from them are very distinctive. Although the work was written before I was even born, its sonorities probably still seemed foreign to some ears, and my talk was designed partly to ease the path to a deeper appreciation. The conference members were taken by coach one day to London and then to Windsor, giving us all a good opportunity to hear top players on important organs: John Scott at St Giles's, Cripplegate, Jonathan Rennert at St Michael's, Cornhill, Christopher Dearnley (my first boss at Salisbury) at St Paul's Cathedral, Alastair Sampson at Eton College Chapel, and John Porter at St George's Chapel in Windsor Castle – a veritable feast for organ buffs!

More than forty letters were awaiting my attention when I arrived home with the family after three weeks away, but the next day we set off for Devon for a fortnight's holiday, inspired by an invitation to give a recital at Exeter Cathedral. We took the family tent and pitched it in a lovely garden in Exton, at the home of a fellow examiner, Robert Gittings, for a few days. Two hundred and fifty people filled the nave to hear me play, and they responded with enthusiasm – too much, in fact, owing to a change in the advertised programme. I had planned to play a very long piece by Liszt with a sesquipedalian title to match, the Fantasia and Fugue on the chorale *Ad nos, ad salutarem undam* from Meyerbeer's opera *Le Prophète*. With so many other activities keeping me busy, I had not had time to master its complexities, and so I included in my brief talk to the audience before the recital the names of the three shorter pieces I would play instead. As luck would have it, a party of French students arrived just after my announcement, with the result that at the end of the first of these pieces they led the applause, clearly intending to prolong it until I descended from the organ loft to take a bow. Undaunted, I launched into the second of the substituted pieces, only to realise that at least part of the audience thought this was an encore. Looking on was my faithful page-turner, my old friend Graham Houghton, who happened to be visiting relatives in the area. With one last piece to play, I soldiered on, finally climbing down to receive even more rapturous applause. I think this was my largest live audience so far, as well as the most enthusiastic.

From Exton we moved on to Paddy Forbes's smallholding known as Beard's Farm near Buckfastleigh, where he and his wife Anne had allocated us a whole field for our lone tent. Here we enjoyed both peace and freedom for ten whole days, living quite primitively and undisturbed – so much so that one rainy morning Marian, Rachel and I ran naked round the field without feeling particularly odd about the unique experience.

When we returned home on the last day of August, having spent some time before the holidays looking into a comparison of my salary with that of my colleagues elsewhere, I decided that the time had come to put in for an increase. The Dean agreed that I should make an approach via the Chapter Clerk to the finance committee, which was responsible for expenditure covering both the cathedral and parish. The £200 increase awarded in April represented a rise of 9%, but the annual inflation rate at the time had reached an astonishing 22%, with the inevitable result that my salary in real terms had decreased. Moreover, this small rise had taken me into the income-tax bracket, so that the real increase was only 5%. I pointed out that my employment in the Cathedral was my main one, since examining work occupied only a few weeks each year, and that my family had increased by two since taking up the appointment. I noted also that in 1975 my pay was already lower than at all but two of about twenty-five cathedrals where daily choral services were maintained, although I was better qualified than almost all the other organists. The percentage increases since then were only half those awarded by my examining board, and it seemed likely that Llandaff would soon be at the bottom of the league in this respect. Another factor was the dire shortage of extra services for the diocese and outside bodies, and the fact that my contract did not allow me to play the organ for weddings or funerals, which were the prerogative of the Parish organist. True, a substantial contribution was being made to my fuel bills, but this was instigated in compensation for the loss of my University teaching three years earlier. I mentioned also that I needed to buy a larger house of my own for such time, be it sooner or later, that I should cease to be a cathedral organist, and that, almost alone among my colleagues, I had no occupational pension, which meant that I was paying £30 a month into a private scheme, as well as £130 a year for a sickness and accident insurance policy, in addition to paying a flat rate of over £100 a year in National Insurance contributions. There is no doubt that finance was a considerable cause of anxiety at this time, in addition to the uncertainty about the appointment of a suitable sub-organist, without whom my job would have become virtually untenable. The outcome of my impassioned plea was a further 10% increase of salary to £2640 per annum, but only with the proviso that my telephone bill would not henceforth be paid in full. It had been remarked that in sixteen months the bill had amounted to £433, and I was told that in future their contribution would be capped at £50 per quarter. Furthermore, it was suggested that I should avoid using the telephone in the mornings and possibly resort to letter-writing instead of phoning.

Ever since the refounding of the cathedral school in 1880 it had been taken for granted that the choristers would all be boarders, and in more recent years their scholarships had become worth two-thirds of their boarding and tuition fees – quite a generous deal compared with some cathedrals. Twenty of these awards were tenable at any one time, to allow for up to sixteen choristers and four probationers, and they shared a boarding house known as The Lodge with thirty other boys. The system meant that we could attract boys from a very wide area, and indeed they came from places as far apart as North Wales, Liverpool, Derby, Louth and Surrey and Somerset. Even so, it was not easy to find a full complement of alert, intelligent boys of the right quality to cope with the stringent demands made on them, with thirteen practices and seven services a week in addition to their school work. It occurred to me that from September not a single boy was from our own diocese, all of them living outside the county of South Glamorgan. This situation was partly due to the existence of the cathedral parish choir, with its twenty-four boys from the locality, but their duties were limited to Sunday services (mainly to lead congregational singing) and the occasional wedding, and it seemed a pity virtually to debar local boys from the wonderful experience of being a full-time chorister. Previously there had been a few local parents willing to let their sons board, and I began to feel that Cardiff itself was as suitable a catchment area as the rest of Britain, and that we should open the field to include day-boys. When I wrote my annual report in July, I thought it had been agreed that the next voice trial should be open to potential day-boys as well as boarders, and accordingly I submitted an article to this effect to *Llandaff Monthly* magazine, but its editor (the Dean) told me that although the idea had been discussed by the school council, it still had to be approved by the Chapter in consultation with the Woodard Corporation which had its own Board of Governors and a big input to school policy. By now it was three months since the Chapter had received my report, but apparently everyone was awaiting guidance from a fictitious cathedral music committee which had been mooted but, surprise, surprise, was yet to be set up. When I submitted a further report to the school council in the autumn, I was careful to forestall the objection, put to me by one of the canons, to the practice of depleting parish choirs to furnish our own, by pointing out that every single chorister for centuries had come from a parish! We normally needed four or five new boys each year, I wrote; 'hardly likely to make much difference to the thousands of parish choirs in Britain' (for in those days many choirs still included boys). I mentioned that I had first put forward the idea five years earlier, and that the Chapter Clerk had in 1979 expressed a wish 'to investigate the possibility of having day school boys in the choir, as it is costing the cathedral £15,000 a year to cover the boarders' fees'. At this stage we had only twelve choristers, plus five probationers, and their ages were such that we needed to find seven more boys in January to last out until Easter 1982. I predicted the cessation of boys-only evensongs on Mondays and Fridays if quantity and quality did not improve.

As far as the men were concerned, we still had five lay clerks and one so-called singing-man acting as a deputy pending a new appointment, plus two choral scholars, Dylan Roberts and Alun Jones, and I was able to appoint a third, David Cynan Jones, an alto from Brecon Cathedral whose father was the conductor of the famous Treorchy Male Voice Choir. In the absence of a sub-organist until Christmas, I was able to call on our musical curate Terry Doherty, my 'honorary assistant sub-organist' Morley Lewis, and no fewer than three other people with B.Mus degrees, as well as the accompanist to the Ardwyn Singers Janice Ball, who later gained her ARCO following a few lessons with me. Meanwhile the only satisfactory response I had to my suggestions regarding day-boy choristers came, predictably, from Christopher Cory in his capacity as *Custos* (chairman of the school council), who set out the decision against my plan, reached jointly by the Council and the Chapter for these reasons:

> For boys not boarders there is no doubt that a very considerable extra strain would be placed on parents if they were never to miss a choir practice or to be absent from a service. This, after all, is the rule of the choir except in the case of illness or some other exceptional circumstance. We could envisage accepting a day-boy in very special circumstances where his home was, for example, on the Cathedral Green – perhaps the child of a member of the Cathedral staff – but in other circumstances I do not think it would be at all satisfactory; and over and above this I think the boys would lose the special cohesion and sense of belonging to an exclusive community of the Cathedral Choir. I do realise there are choirs where some or all of the choristers are day-boys though it is difficult to know how things work, and I have heard that at Guildford the

problem of getting boys in every day had proved to be very considerable indeed. All in all, therefore, the School Council have taken this decision.

He was aware of the problem regarding numbers of boys, but expressed a hope that the forthcoming voice trial would produce the goods. As we shall see, some fifteen years were to elapse before the subject was raised again, and somehow we did manage to maintain the *status quo* without reducing the repertoire. What happened then, and after I retired, is another matter altogether.

On the eve of Advent Sunday I dreamt that a death had occurred in the family. On arriving at the song room in the morning I was told that my very good friend Ivor Meredith, who, though holding no official capacity, had given generously of his time and skill by deputising for one or other of our bass lay clerks, and augmenting the choir at other times, had died suddenly in the night. He was the kind of person often described as 'a lovely man', with a rich voice and very pleasant personality, and I felt we were all the poorer for his decease. Later in the day I learned that another trusty colleague and friend, the alto Peter Foster, was separating from his wife, selling up their nineteen-acre smallholding near Caerphilly, and moving to a much smaller but more expensive estate in Northamptonshire. But life goes on, and I managed to sandwich a performance of Bach's monumental *B minor Mass* between two weeks of examining in north Wales and Wiltshire, before the rigours of the Christmas season were upon us.

Our country retreats in Herefordshire: a cottage at Karen Court,
Dilwyn (1976-81) above, with the two dormer windows nearest the
centre of the picture;
and
Rozel Cottage, Byford (1981-99) below, the middle part of this old
farmhouse

1981

New Year's Day 1981 was spent in Wells, where Marian's cousin Richard Hickman had become director of music at the Cathedral School. He and his family occupied 92 St Thomas Street, a very large L-shaped house not far from the Cathedral, and had arranged a party there for no fewer than thirty-five members of the family. After lunch we all set out for a walk round neighbouring fields and the Bishop's great palace, returning for tea. The next few days were spent in Woodfalls, where another party was held at Marian's mother's house to celebrate her seventieth birthday, and in the course of the week I calculated that we had seen altogether forty-eight of Marian's relatives and twenty old friends, so strong were our links with the Salisbury area.

On rare occasions I was able to earn a large fee with the minimum of work, and one such occasion occurred on my return to Llandaff when I found an invitation from the BBC to play a few *continuo* parts for a concert to be televised in the cathedral, with Robert Tear as the 'star' tenor and the BBC Welsh Orchestra conducted by Andrew Davis. It turned out at the rehearsal that the scheduled pieces by Mozart and Haydn needed no keyboard part, leaving only one by Handel, the well known aria 'Waft her, angels, through the skies'. Meanwhile the contract had been signed, promising me £262 (a tenth of my annual salary) for two rehearsals and a recording, so I stood to earn £1 per chord! As luck would have it, however, on the day of the performance the tenor developed laryngitis and was unable to perform. The programme was changed, omitting all vocal items and reducing my participation to nil, so at first I thought I had been thwarted. Still, a contract is a contract, and after only a week I received a cheque for £150 to cover the Mozart pieces, of which I had played not a single note. A fortnight later I was even more delighted to receive another cheque for the remaining £112, for rehearsing 'Waft her, angels' for five minutes. This went some way to compensate for the unwelcome news that I had not been shortlisted for a fellowship at Magdalen College, Oxford, for which I had applied at the same time as for the post of organist at Christ Church.

On the bright side was the fact that at the same time I received two offers for our Dilwyn cottage, the first for £20,000, its most recent valuation, and the second for a thousand pounds more, which we accepted. Having paid only £8,500 for the cottage just five years earlier, we were more than pleased, losing no time in offering £25,500 for a lovely cottage, twice as large and five miles closer to Hereford in a small hamlet called Byford, and formerly part of the Garnons estate, the home of Sir John and Lady Cotterell and their family. I became aware that I had not written home for about five months, and the exciting news was conveyed to my parents by way of this description:

> It's the middle one of three which were a complete farmhouse till twelve years ago, and it looks across the farmyard in one direction and across the River Wye in the other. It is in a picturesque hamlet called Byford, near Bridge Sollars, and six miles west of Hereford. Its own gardens are small, but the children can play in the field next to the lane, and around the barns. A major advantage is space – the living room is 20 feet by 15 feet, bigger than ours at St Mary's, and there are three bedrooms, a big kitchen, big bathroom, electric storage heaters, telephone, mains water, regular deliveries, and most of the things *you* would approve of! Moreover, it's near Weobley (six miles) and Hereford (seven miles from the cathedral) so we shall still be seeing our friends. How do we raise the money? We reckon that the cost of the larger mortgage will be easily covered by the income from Marian's pupils, who already number sixteen at £3 a lesson. The number of people interested in the properties we've looked at recently suggests that the market is just about to move again, and we want to be in at just the right time, when prices have been almost static for a year.

Back in Llandaff, the Dean and Chapter did at last apply to the city council to demolish our conservatory, but still showed no signs of agreeing to rebuild it. Following normal practice, the council advertised in the press, and on a nearby lamp post, for 'objections' to the application, so we submitted our opinion that the cathedral authorities should demolish it only in order to restore it to its original state, preferably in brick, wood and glass. To emphasise the strength of local opinion, I drew up a petition on these lines and collected 120 signatures from local residents, including our local GP, a professor, a retired canon, the priest-vicars, local shopkeepers and all the lay clerks. We reckoned that the most valid point from the planning department's point of view was that demolition would expose an area of rendered and whitewashed wall, and the dining-room door, and spoil the appearance of the Grade II listed building. The petition evidently had some effect, for the planning committee recommended to the City Council exactly the course of action that we had put forward. Alas, one of the councillors was none other than the ubiquitous Norman Lloyd-Edwards, who in addition to being chapter clerk was also the treasurer of Llandaff Parochial Church Council. I have often wondered if he 'declared an interest' or was partly responsible for the City Council's decision, conveyed to us in May, that 'following the demolition of the conservatory the render on that section of wall exposed shall be removed, or alternatively a new conservatory erected in accordance with details to be approved by the local planning authority'. Obviously the Chapter would adopt the easier and less costly first option, but we waited to see what the house would look like when the work were completed, and meanwhile we had lost a valuable amenity and in effect one whole room, which at first had been a useful play area for the children.

In a nine-week period I bombarded the chapter clerk with five letters, receiving only one reply. I felt that my own work was producing good results, having built up the choir to a complement of eighteen choristers, six lay clerks and (a special bonus) one choral scholar for each part, alto, tenor and bass. Yet my achievements were always offset by the lack of response to my contacts with the Chapter through the clerk, and I had to spend too much time reminding him to pay deputies' fees and to get something done about the deteriorating state of our house, which it was partly his responsibility to maintain. An application from a lay clerk at Chester Cathedral included the telling comment 'I was disappointed to learn that the gentlemen sing on only two weekdays, and that the remuneration is much smaller than that which I received at Chester; however, the reputation of Llandaff is such that I have decided to apply for the position'. When conveying this comment to Norman, I added a paragraph concerning the pay of cathedral organists:

The text of a resolution passed at a meeting of Deans, Provosts and Organists at Westminster Abbey last July stated 'that this meeting recommends that where a cathedral organist is considered to be in full-time employment, his salary and conditions should be comparable with those of a residentiary canon'. This proposal was put by the Dean of Wells, seconded by the Provost of Sheffield, and carried unanimously. I am told that a residentiary canon receives about £5600 per annum. At the time of the meeting, the Dean of Wells was paying his organist about £3000; he then increased it by £1000, and is to increase it by another £1000 this year. Along with this proposal, it was emphasised that adequate pension arrangements should form part of the package.

When I wrote this, I was still awaiting replies to letters written up to nine weeks earlier, and a few days later I wrote in about broken gutters and loose slates which were letting in water, and mentioned that the city council planning officer, when inspecting the derelict conservatory, had noticed several structural defects in the house, namely long cracks in both chimney stacks and a broken lintel which was giving rise to another crack extending up to a first-floor window. Norman did eventually send me a letter, the longest paragraph being concerned with the fees to be paid to the five organists who had assisted me during the autumn term, which he tried to whittle down to a total of £120, so that I had to go to some lengths to explain why well-qualified professional players should be properly remunerated, in proportion to the fees of semi-professional singers. My reference to the deliberations of the deans and provosts was dismissed in a single sentence: 'It does not apply to us of course, as your appointment is deemed part time – originally the other time was to be taken up with the University - and we do not have a residentiary canon'. One could see his point of view, but I found that the Church in Wales did determine a suitable salary for such a canon, in the event of one being appointed, and more important, that other cathedral organists coping with responsibilities similar to mine did not have to rely on university teaching in order to make a decent living. Two months after my complaint about the state of our garage roof nothing had been done, resulting in the garage and an adjoining storeroom being flooded, with water continuously dripping from the ceiling. I reminded him of a clause of my service agreement which he had signed five years earlier stating that the Chapter 'in particular shall be responsible for external and structural repairs and external painting', and sent a copy of the letter to my solicitor in Salisbury. As late as mid-May, my ex-student

David Thomas had still not been paid for the work he did the previous autumn, and the choral scholars had not been paid for the Lent term. I declared that I would play for no extra services until these matters had been attended to, and meanwhile would withhold my contribution to my fuel bills. I also put in a plea for a pay increase for my new assistant, Michael Hoeg, who unlike his predecessor was now playing the organ at almost every service and yet was being paid less than a lay clerk; I calculated that the newest probationer-chorister was, in effect, being paid five times as much as the Assistant Organist. This last request was duly considered, but declined.

There were often times when I felt that the Dean was trying to minimise the importance of the cathedral music. However, there were small signs that he was becoming reconciled to our distinctive contribution. Previously, the cathedral choir had been expected to sing at a 'Parish' Eucharist at 9am on Christmas Day, as well as singing Matins and Evensong. In 1980 The Dean made several changes, inviting volunteers from the Choral Society to form a mixed choir at the midnight Eucharist (which attracted 568 communicants), thereby releasing the parish choir to sing the 9 o'clock service (as on Sundays), and replacing Matins by a choral Eucharist. In the February edition of *The Llandaff Monthly* he actually mentioned our carol service, and even wrote, albeit rather awkwardly, that 'The Cathedral Choir's Schubert's Mass in G at 11 o'clock was a fitting climax in the morning'. Congregations at Matins and Evensong were never counted, and indeed these services were not even recorded in the register, but by adding yet another Eucharist the Dean was able to claim an extra 155 communicants; I suspect the statistics appealed to him rather more than the music. In July the Dean wrote a three-page article on the origin and history of the 'daily offices' of Matins and Evensong which included one of his mammoth sentences, 130 words long, and ended with this sentence consisting of a mere sixty-three:

> In Llandaff, where it has so far been possible to maintain the great tradition of English Church Music, we can find something very valuable to help us realise that in the daily office we are doing so much more than saying our own prayers or joining in an act of worship which begins when we begin and ends when we have finished.

As the years went by, I was to introduce with his blessing a number of Latin Masses into the service, with several settings by Mozart and Haydn as well as two more by Schubert, in many cases including even the Latin Creed. I reckoned that these works were probably being sung at Llandaff for the first time since the Reformation, because only when the Roman Catholic Church decreed that the Mass should be sung in the vernacular was it deemed appropriate for the Anglican Church to sing in Latin, and they had not been in the repertoire since then until I introduced them. For worshippers who felt the need to participate in the singing, there were of course always the parish services, where they could sing everything except the anthem.

The parish magazine *The Llandaff Monthly* provided a useful way for me to acquaint a wide range of parishioners with what was happening in the way of cathedral music. Far more people attended the 'parish' services, but I felt they should be aware of developments, especially as we relied to a large extent on the money they put in the collection week by week. I reported that on St David's Day we would be singing for the first time in Llandaff a setting of the evening canticles by William Mathias – one of very few by any Welsh composer – and on Ash Wednesday the world-famous setting of Psalm 51 known as the *Miserere* by Gregorio Allegri, once the exclusive property of the Sistine Chapel in Rome. It was not every year that we had a treble who could cope easily with the top Cs that occur in the solo embellishments added by a later hand. I also advertised the spring concert of the Choral Society, with a group of brass players for a change, consisting of music from four centuries by Gabrieli, Bach, Bruckner and Vaughan Williams, and a series of organ recitals to be given by Félix Moreau, the cathedral organist of Nantes, Cardiff's twin city, along with Michael Hoeg and myself. In June I paid tribute to the nine men who were now regular members of the cathedral choir, explaining that although short articles tend to mention only newcomers, yet

the adult members, like car parks, fall into two categories, 'long stay' and 'short stay'. After Christmas Timothy Parish joined us as an alto lay clerk: he is a law student, and a former chorister at Salisbury Cathedral. One of our own former choristers, Nigel Edwards, has returned as a bass Choral Scholar, completing the team of nine men in a most satisfactory way. There is a most harmonious relationship, in more senses than one, between these newcomers and those who have served as long as seven years or, in two cases, much longer: I refer to Dr Michael Davidson, who has hardly missed a service since 1974, and those two stalwarts, Maldwyn Phillips and

Terry Dickens, whose very presence bespeaks the value of a continuing and developing tradition.

I went on to mention that the choristers had broken their Lenten holiday twice, first to play rugby in Bristol against several other cathedral choirs, followed by a joint Evensong; and second to take part in a televised performance of Carl Orff's *Carmina Burana* in Cardiff. After singing 250 services since Easter 1980, I wrote, and with a heavy schedule ahead of them, they might well have shown some reluctance! I also announced the appointment of two boys taken from St Asaph Cathedral and another from the choir of Oswestry Parish Church, and finally paid tribute to the choir librarians, Mr and Mrs Ralph Stephens, who in an average month handled about 1,500 pieces of music: from Maundy Thursday to Easter Day, a mere four days, some 550 copies were in use.

In May, after spending two weeks traipsing around the Valleys on my tedious GCSE assignments, I ventured alone across the Channel in my recently-acquired red Volvo estate car, crossing from Weymouth to Cherbourg and driving for nearly five hours to Nantes, where I was to give a recital on the great 18th century Clicquot organ on the west gallery of the Cathedral. When I went to practise next morning, I was rather taken aback to find a television crew awaiting me for an interview at the console, and also two students who had been detailed to help with registration (an organist's term for selecting ranks of pipes by pulling out or pushing in stop-knobs at pre-arranged points in the music). On British organs there are usually devices known as thumb pistons, push-buttons between the manuals, and larger ones operated by the feet, enabling the player to change his own stops, but on older organs on the Continent it is quite usual for assistants to manage these changes while the player confines his attention to playing the notes. Unused to this practice, I asked the students to leave me to work out a scheme and to return in the afternoon. Although I was careful to include works by Couperin and Vierne along with a big opening work by Bach, I also wanted to introduce my listeners to some substantial British works by Stanford, Howells and Francis Jackson. They were all ambitious pieces requiring many stop-changes; I wrote various instructions on the copy, but found myself shouting further instructions in French during the actual recital, which attracted an audience of 170. The following day I drove on to St Nazaire where I was scheduled to play a quite different (and rather less demanding) programme on a smaller organ at a church dedicated to St Gothard.

After a short rehearsal there, I was taken on a scenic drive as far as Boule by an organist named Marie-Thérèse, who kept up a flow of conversation. My 'A level' French, though still serviceable after twenty-six years, was rather rusty, and I had to adopt the procedure of thinking up a question to put to her whenever her rapid-fire talk dwindled, allowing her a further spate in the hope that she would not reverse the process. The evening recital, attended by sixty-six people, went well, but I was rather surprised when my well-deserved rest at my hotel was interrupted at midnight by a telephone call from this young lady. Unfortunately I was still unable to get the gist of what she was saying and was unable to respond, but I did wonder what she had in mind at that time of night.

In June I was able to point out to the recalcitrant chapter clerk that, although eight weeks had passed since our conservatory had been demolished, there was still no sign of a replacement, and that five months had passed since I had first drawn his attention to the state of the garage roof. The pigeons had returned to the adjoining loft, and the combined effect of their pecking and of the rain coming through the roof had rendered the ceiling likely to collapse. Nothing had been done to renovate the chimney stacks, which had already been declared dangerous. At this stage Norman was allegedly waiting to see what kind of conservatory would be acceptable to the planning authority, but such an enquiry was clearly of only academic interest, since he told me that the finance committee would not wish to spend more on such a building than the cost of rendering the wall! The consent of the Welsh Office was awaited for the repair of the chimneys, but the fate of the garage had to be weighed alongside the repairs needed on other properties owned or administered by the Cathedral, at an estimated cost of £30,000. Eventually I wrote to the City planning officer to complain that the landlord, having had the conservatory demolished in mid-April, had yet to fulfil, three months later, the condition attached to the granting of his application, i.e. that nothing had been done to the wall of the house, still less had the conservatory been rebuilt. At the end of term, the chapter clerk expressed the hope that all repairs would be done by the time I returned in October from the travels abroad which I was about to undertake. Some hopes! Of course nothing happened, and as late as November he was writing a sorry plea to Graham Hardy, the architect responsible for these matters, 'Just a reminder that we are anxious to have the chimney stacks, garage roof and the removal of the rendering and tidying up where the old conservatory used to be, effected as soon as possible as autumn is now ending and I would like the work done as quickly as possible before winter'.

One initiative which was to prove of value in the future was the formation of the Choristers' Parents' Association by the parents of Robin Davies, a junior chorister, in order to facilitate communications and provide an enthusiastic back-up organisation. Their first success was securing television coverage of the January voice trial for potential choristers, by arranging for the choristers to appear on an HTV (Harlech Television) news programme a few days in advance. The number of candidates was thereby almost doubled, offsetting the disappointment that many had felt at the refusal of the school to accept local boys whose parents did not wish them to board, and I liked to think that this new development had contributed to the appointment of six new boys.

Perhaps the most outstanding event of the year was the outcome of a request from one of the canons that the Llandaff Festival be more 'cathedral-orientated' and another from the PCC that some events should be staged under Epstein's *Majestas* between nave and choir, with the audience facing east. The Dean also had expressed disquiet on more than one occasion that audiences had to sit with their backs to the altar when orchestras occupied a specially-constructed platform at the west end. There was little he could do to prevent this, though he did try to reduce the width of the staging. At the daily Evensong, instead of reading a lesson from his stall in the choir as he should have done, he always insisted that a verger should lead him to the nave lectern so that he could read to those members of the congregation (usually no more than twenty on a Saturday or ten during the week) who sat there. During the Festival, when the chairs were all turned to face the west door, worshippers were encouraged to sit in the choir, but the Dean doggedly insisted on walking to the nave lectern and reading to the backs of empty chairs. I thought this was very stupid, and indeed when he was not present at Evensong at other times in the year, the junior clergy often used to read from their own appointed places in the choir. My own initiative, in response to the views expressed above, was to invite the choirs of Bath Abbey and Wells Cathedral to join us for a concert of music ranging from William Byrd to Kenneth Leighton, conducted by the three organists and accompanied by Michael Hoeg, with two organ solos played by me. The choirs were duly positioned at the front of the nave, but even this concert, with its obvious relevance to cathedral worship, failed to entice the Dean, or for that matter any of the canons, to attend. The concert was repeated later in the month at Bath Abbey before an audience of five hundred, and the Dean of Wells was very friendly when we all joined forces again in his cathedral in July. The programme in all three venues was as follows:

Hosanna to the Son of	David Weelkes
Ave, verum corpus	Byrd
O clap your hands together	Gibbons
Passacaglia and Fugue in C minor	Bach
Turn thee unto me, O Lord	Boyce
The Wilderness	S S Wesley
A Song of Wisdom, and a Hymn	Stanford
Vox dicentis: Clama	Edward Naylor
Fantasia and Toccata in D minor	Stanford
Let all the world in every corner sing	Leighton
Te Deum laudamus (Collegium Regale)	Howells

The Llandaff Festival again included a piano recital by Moura Lympany and a concert by the Royal Philharmonic Orchestra with John Lill playing Beethoven's third piano concerto. The baroque ensemble known as The English Concert *(sic),* directed by Trevor Pinnock and playing on authentic 18th century instruments, was of special interest to me, as it featured as second violinist Elizabeth Wilcock, younger sister of my girlfriend Mary of eighteen years earlier, when Liz herself was only eight and already a talented musician. I don't think she told me that Mary's marriage to violinist Harry Cawood had been dissolved only a fortnight earlier, and I was certainly unaware that Liz was soon to marry the world-famous conductor John Eliot Gardiner. Less still did I know that our paths were to meet again twenty-three years later.

For me, my second Festival triumph, if I may with due modesty call it such, was the Choral Society's performance of Verdi's *Requiem.* It may well have been the only performance of this work in the cathedral's history, and we certainly went to town, with 110 singers in the choir, four first class operatic soloists, Suzanne Murphy, Penelope Walker, Kenneth Collins and Geoffrey Moses, and an orchestra of sixty players including four trumpets and eight other brass instruments, plus four more trumpeters stationed in front of the high altar, some two hundred feet from the platform, to create a spine-tingling stereophony representing the *Tuba mirum* in the famous *Dies Irae* section. All the tickets had been sold by members of the Festival committee and Choral Society before the Festival box office opened, and the performance was greeted with rapturous applause and the stamping of feet, bringing the principals and me back to the stage for two recalls (a rare occurrence in a church!). I was delighted to read in the *South Wales Argus*, under the headline **Requiem performed with rare authority**, the opinion of seasoned music critic Kenneth Loveland, a regular contributor to *The Times,* that

From the point of view of the choir, this was the finest contribution I can recall them making to many years of the festival. The singing was admirably disciplined, and well-unified in such matters as gradually tapering *diminuendi*, it was justly proportioned, so that the complete opulence of Verdi's canvas was totally balanced, and rich in tone.

Generally, Dr Smith succeeded because, without fuss or demonstration, he was able to hurl Verdi's climaxes like thunderbolts, given a choir so well controlled. And he was always inside the character of the music, the wrath, the supplication, the fear. Particularly the wrath; it was a thrilling *Dies Irae.* The Festival Orchestra, looking exactly like the BBC Welsh Symphony, was sensitively expressive and capable of deep-shaded colour, while the extra antiphonal brass was thrilling. So, a Verdi *Requiem* conducted with a fiery sense of its apocalyptic vision and played and sung with spontaneous zest by an orchestra and chorus in inspired form.

I was keen to capitalise on these notable successes, which went virtually unacknowledged by the Dean, even in his nominal role as Festival Chairman: he made no mention of the event in the May edition of *The Llandaff Monthly*, nor did he publish the promotional article I had written. Accordingly I devoted a paragraph to the subject in my annual report to the Chapter, which was read out to them by the chapter clerk at their meeting in late June, presumably a typical ruse on the Dean's part to ensure that no canon actually received a copy to read for himself and ponder over at home:

A few weeks ago I discussed with the Dean some reservations I had about the running of the Festival, particularly with regard to the static membership of its committee, which seems to serve little purpose in its present form. Now that the Festival has become a limited company, it seems possible that new members can be introduced, who may have ideas for revitalising this important event. During the Festival itself I was much impressed by the way in which all kinds of people came together and worked together; there seemed to be a community spirit which I have not experienced so much in previous years. This is the occasion which draws together the 'cathedral' and 'parish' elements, along with members of other churches, in a way not often seen during the rest of the year, and it was most heart-warming to see the Bishop, the electrician, the girl guides, shop-keepers, BBC staff, tea-ladies, stewards, cathedral choirs, our many Methodist friends, mingling with the many musicians, amateur and professional, in a spirit of fellowship and co-operation focused on this cathedral of ours.

I can imagine the Dean becoming more and more impatient and red in the face as this description was read, being as it was at odds with his own narrow view of the cathedral – as first and foremost a parish church, whose primary purpose was the celebration of the Holy Eucharist. He rarely considered what its other functions might be, and when he did they were always worship-orientated. As for the wider image of the building and any notion of the general public's interest in it, such ideas passed him by completely. What a pity that he did not share my vision for the place which it was *his* responsibility to promote, and what a pity that his canons were reduced to mere yes-men, rubber-stamping his limited decrees. The Festival was dealt an unexpected blow (perhaps the Dean would have called it an Act of God?) when Christopher Cory, its Artistic Director since its inception eighteen years ago, died of a heart attack during the night of the 20th July at the age of fifty. He had been a major figure in Wales, serving as High Sheriff and Deputy Lieutenant for South Glamorgan and for sixteen years as Chief Commissioner for Scouts in Wales. A director of an old-established family business, he had been heavily involved in other youth work and Church in Wales activities, and was, as we have seen, the *Custos* of the cathedral school. The choristers having just left for the summer holidays, an *ad hoc* choir sang at his funeral, conducted by his Arts Council colleague Roy Bohana, and a large congregation included both Hoddinott and Mathias.

My annual report to the Chapter also stated that two of the choral scholars were due to leave at the end of term, along with the faithful lay clerk Dr Davidson, who had sung tenor for seven years. It gave me some small comfort that the Dean did bring himself to mention these men, along with four leaving choristers, at their last service; but at no time did he suggest that lay clerks should be formally welcomed into the choir (as probationer choristers were), nor that there should be a valedictory ceremony for boys and men, as happens in other cathedrals. My report was actually acknowledged by the Chapter Clerk Norman Lloyd-Edwards, who declared that everyone was heartened by its optimistic tone and pleased to hear of the good progress made in the past year; but the only mention of the Dean was that he had not been fully informed of visits by the choir to other churches, nor of the broadcasts that had been planned and, in one case, already carried out. The latter occasion was a recording for television of Carl Orff's celebrated work *Carmina Burana*, in which the choristers took part alongside the Cardiff Polyphonic Choir and the Royal Philharmonic Orchestra. As for visits to local parish churches, we had received only one invitation this year, and that almost certainly was from its vicar direct to the Dean, in the same way that the BBC would always deal direct with the Dean when planning broadcasts; indeed, two days after the meeting the Dean himself deigned to admit in a letter to me:

> I am delighted to hear about the two broadcast evensongs next year. I thought this might be coming when I was included in the distribution list for the information sent out a few weeks ago.

It is always interesting to note how contrasting events tend to happen in close proximity. For example, during the two days which separated my two major concerts, we formally took possession of our newly-purchased cottage in Byford. Also, just before joining the cathedral choir on our coach journey to Bath Abbey I was playing the organ at an afternoon service organised by the Save the Children fund, in the presence of Her Royal Highness Princess Anne, the Princess Royal. A few days later the Dean actually sent me a copy of a letter from Buckingham Palace, ostensibly from her private secretary but signed by her lady-in-waiting Shan Legge-Bourke, saying:

> The Princess was so pleased the Thanksgiving Service for the Inauguration of the Welsh Council was able to be held at the Cathedral... the children sang quite beautifully and Mr Smith played superbly.

I did from time to time receive such tokens of appreciation, and was especially pleased with a letter from the former Bishop of Llandaff, Eryl Thomas, living in retirement near Abergavenny, saying:

> I thought you might be encouraged if I dropped you a line to say that I was at Evensong last night and came away very thrilled and excited by the quality of the music and general air of renewed confidence. The twelve boys knew just what they

were doing and looked alert and dead keen, and I thought the clerks (mostly a youngish lot) were extremely well balanced and controlled. It really was a very pleasant experience. The Bruckner anthem was new to me but very satisfying.

I was also impressed by the dignified behaviour of both choristers and clerks – a very orderly walk in and out, well spaced; no restlessness or surreptitious idle chatter! I suspect that Terry Doherty has exerted his authority, or is it you and your assistant or the lot of you? Only John Jenkins (*a Priest Vicar*) was present from the local clergy ranks, but he was impeccable. It does seem such a pity that with all those retired clergy and others hanging around the cathedral city, not one of them would bother to get to Evensong sung so beautifully – a privilege which most of them never had in their parishes. I just wish I lived a little nearer.

The summer term ended, we had just two weeks of mostly sunny weather to enjoy our new cottage, which we named Rozel after the bay in Jersey where we had stayed on our honeymoon. Then I had to tear myself away from the family and fly to South Africa for my second great adventure provided by the Associated Board. Having spent several thousand pounds on the cottage and the car, I needed to recoup this money, and with all the children now eligible for air fares, I could not afford to take them with me this time. Had our financial circumstances been different, there would still have been no way of accommodating four extra people in the hotels at such an economical rate as one found in the Far East, and I knew that my itinerary would involve flying in and out of Johannesburg – hardly the most congenial city for white tourists at that time – half a dozen times. I hoped that Marian, left to look after our children aged ten, four and nearly two, would take some comfort from having a lovely country cottage to live in for the first four weeks of my absence, and I knew that both her mother and my parents would be pleased to stay with them from time to time. My parents chose a table and chairs for the kitchen, and I still use them to this day, but my mother never visited Rozel Cottage again after I returned from abroad, owing to deteriorating health, and I was sorry that we were never able to enjoy it together.

Scenically I found South Africa a marvellous country. Apartheid was still very much a reality in 1981, and I had until then not realised the differing attitudes between the whites descended from British colonists and the Afrikaaners descended from the Dutch settlers. Some of the latter proved to be remarkably bigoted about the indigenous

127

black population, regarding them in the same light as dogs but treating them less well. The divisions between races were shown quite clearly in the Town House, an 'international' hotel where I stayed in Cape Town for two weeks: the management was white, the chamber-maids brown (known as Cape coloured, being of mixed race) and the Zulu waiters black. The Associated Board would not have countenanced the holding of examinations in South Africa had they been restricted, as were so many activities, to white people. Thus I spent a day or two working in a 'black township' called Bonteheuwel, some fifteen miles out of Cape Town, at the house of a very enthusiastic piano teacher, where I was greeted by all his fifteen candidates, decked out in party wear as if to show that this was a special day in their lives. They assembled again at the end of the morning to say a smiling goodbye.

My first experience, however, was of the seaside town of Durban on the south-east coast, where I stayed for several days in the congenial company of Kenneth Abbott, whose regular job involved teaching music to members of the Royal Air Force in Uxbridge. My first day there included two hours on the beach, swimming against two currents sending waves in at right-angles to each other – rather symbolic of the racial system, I thought – and a buffet lunch given by the local Teachers' Society. The next two days were spent examining some excellent pianists at Durban Girls' College at Berea, where I was also treated to a good three-course lunch. I very soon became aware of the sumptuous nature of meals in South Africa when confronted by a buffet salad with twenty-six possible ingredients. Some exams were held in the YMCA building, and before starting there in the morning I would get up well before breakfast and enjoy a swim in the warm sea. My next assignment was even more interesting, for I was required to hire a small car and drive more than a hundred miles up the east coast to a place called Empangeni in Zululand. I had seen postcards showing local girls dressed in nothing but an elaborate arrangement of beads, and hoped I might have a chance to photograph some of them. I was advised that this would be quite in order, provided I gave them something in return, so I armed myself with a bag of sweets for the purpose and set off in my red Volkswagen Golf saloon. I stayed at a hotel where I could not understand the Zulu waiters, and spent a morning examining in a convent, but my map showed an intriguing road leading inland from there and rejoining the coast road after some twenty miles, so I decided to take this route back to Durban. It was a dirt track, and I do not know how I would have coped with a puncture, but I was lucky, and discovered some of the real Africa, with my first experience of 'bush' landscapes with the native kraals, with round thatched mud huts, plenty of cacti and the sight of women picking cotton. In a while I espied a group of half a dozen children in green school uniform (regrettably not coloured beads) sheltering from the sun under a tree. I stopped the car, and got out, eager to photograph this natural and characteristic scene; but as they saw me approach they began to undress. Perhaps I shall see their beads after all, I thought, but in fact the young girls were only taking off their cardigans in order to pose in a straight line for a proper school-type photo, so this is how they were taken, and they duly accepted the sweets I offered them. I continued on my way to the main road, stopping at small town called Stanger to examine seven more candidates at the home of a teacher.

Before tackling more work in Cape Province I was taken to Stellenbosch, an attractive university town in an Afrikaans area, with Cape Dutch style whitewashed buildings and fresh green grassy landscapes, surrounded by vineyards and rugged mountains. I stayed for a week at the Lanzerac Hotel, a converted winery which served the most sumptuous dinners I have ever seen, before or since: every night there were eight courses (including, I remember, Welsh rarebit!) though I never managed to eat more than seven of them. My work was at the Konservatorium, a fine modern building which forms part of the university, where I also tried out a sizeable organ by Marcussen and heard a concert by the Cape Town Symphony Orchestra, meeting the conductor Brian Priestman afterwards. On the Sunday I had the pleasure of meeting, by prior arrangement, a man called Xavier Reutt and his wife and Tralee, who was the sister of Betty Steynor, my neighbour in the cottage adjoining ours in Byford. They took me to lunch at their home in a nearby town, Somerset West, and to the great sandy beach known as Strand, and joined me for lunch at the Lanzerac next day, when my examining occupied only part of the afternoon. Before returning to Cape Province I had several days' work in Paarl, but my only memories of my stay there are of an unusually poor hotel with extremely dim lighting, and a massive rounded rock from which the town took its name (meaning Pearl).

In the hotel at Cape Town I enjoyed the company of an ebullient colleague, John Jordan, whom I already knew as organist of Chelmsford Cathedral. One night while dining there we were approached by a fellow diner who had overheard our conversation, and he turned out to be Maurice Handford; I recognised his name as a conductor, and we learnt that he was on a six-month contract with the Cape Town Symphony Orchestra. I went to one of their concerts, but felt that his style did little for the music; his interpretation of Elgar's *Enigma Variations* sounded very pedestrian, as if conducted by a signpost, and it was one of the very few occasions when I have felt like jumping up on to the platform and taking over. I did however get to meet the 'cellist Colin Carr and also dined with Francis Grier, who had recently been appointed organist of Christ Church Cathedral, Oxford. The Board's local representative was John Reay, a short, round man with a grey moustache and a red face, whose equally elderly wife called Elspeth had a very creased face reminding me of a tortoise, but despite their unprepossessing appearance they were good company, and took John and me out for a picnic one Sunday on a beach at the Cape of Good Hope, where on the way we passed a number of baboons. This outing followed our attendance at a Eucharist in Cape Town Cathedral, which bore a striking resemblance to St Andrew's Church in Ilford, where I had spent my early life as a choirboy and then organist to the Sunday School. Although St Andrew's is built in red brick and Cape Town Cathedral in stone, I had already known that they shared the same architect, Sir Herbert Baker, and were both probably built in the 1920s. There was something almost uncanny about looking up at those soaring arches and seeing narrow, elongated stained glass windows shaped exactly like those I had come to know as a child, and I was glad to have an opportunity to play the organ after the service.

Before setting out for Africa I had received correspondence from Japie Malan, the organist of *Die Groote Kerk*, a large Dutch Reformed Church in Cape Town, who had invited me to give a recital there on an organ that was a fine modern example of Dutch work. It seemed that some of our letters were lost in the post, so that we never managed to conclude the arrangement. It was therefore with some surprise that I saw a poster outside the church advertising my name as the next recitalist! I had taken no music, but fortunately Japie had his own collection from which I was able to choose pieces by Couperin, Bach, Franck and Jehan Alain, along with three pieces from Messiaen's *La Nativité,* Kenneth Leighton's *Paean* and a lively *Toccata* by an obscure Russian composer called Mushel.

I had been invited by the Cape Organ Guild to attend their dinner at the Mount Nelson Hotel as a Guest of Honour and to make a speech. I had accepted before learning that others present were to include not only John Jordan, Japie Malan and the cathedral organist Barry Smith, but also Gillian Weir. I had first encountered her in 1963 when, as a student at Addington Palace, a residential college at that time and headquarters of the Royal School of Church Music, she had played the organ at the ceremony in Lambeth Palace at which I received the ADCM diploma from the Archbishop of Canterbury. After beating me at the International Organ Festival competition in St Alban's in

1964 Gillian had gone on to become a recitalist of international repute. She once told me that she liked my Messiaen interpretations: I was unaware that she had heard me play Messiaen, until she explained that when doing some Christmas shopping in the record department of the Derry & Toms store in Kensington, she had heard part of *La Nativité,* and on making enquiries had found that it was my own 1976 broadcast from Coventry Cathedral. When preparing my speech in Cape Town I felt rather like a Catholic priest being told 'and by the way, the Pope will be present'. In later years her stature as one of Britain's 'top' organists was recognised when she was made a DBE. I have always admired her gracious manner, her stunning interpretations, and not least, her eloquent command of language. However, I tried to appear undaunted and as far as I know my speech was appreciated.

After hearing Haydn's *Paukenmesse* sung with orchestra at the Cathedral's Sunday Eucharist, I was driven eighty miles by car to another picturesque town named Worcester for little more than two hours' work involving a two-night stay, and the return to Cape Town was by a slow scenic train journey round the mountains which took more than four hours. Japie Malan and his wife were a very friendly couple, who took me out one weekend in their car to show me the wonderful coastline and a beautiful botanic garden, and another drive to another botanic garden at Kirstenbosch followed by tea at the most famous winery, the *Groot Constantia.* I had hoped to follow up their idea that in another year I should return with Marian for a holiday, but this was not to be, and by the time we could have afforded it I expect the Malans had left this world. Next day I again hired a small car for further exploration which included climbing over white sand dunes at Sandy Bay, finding a place oddly called Llandudno, and visiting the Kloof Nek nature reserve. My work in Cape Town was mostly at a number of rather fine schools, including one at the foot of Table Mountain. After examining there for a whole morning I took the cable car to the top, had lunch there, and went for a walk enjoying the magnificent views. Another morning's candidates consisted entirely of one teacher's organ pupils, followed by an enormous lunch at his house. Whether this was to encourage me to add on a few marks I don't know, but fortunately his students had acquitted themselves well, so we were all very pleased with each other. After my own recital at the Groote Kerk I found his expert and flattering review of it in the *Cape Town Argus* under the headline **Master of the Organ,** one particularly apposite paragraph reading:

> His varied and interesting programme was greatly assisted
> by his own brief explanations before each group. Far too often,

organists seem to be playing for the benefit of other organists only, for the devotees who attend recitals purely to wallow in the sounds of the organ. Dr Michael Smith's performance showed a very different approach, in which the essentially musical appeal was paramount. True, there were moments of power and flashes of virtuosity; but the overall features were a careful technical clarity and a beautifully judged sense of colour – which the ample resources of the Groote Kerk organ enabled him to indulge to the full.

On reflection I think that this area of South Africa is the most picturesque I have seen anywhere in the world, and it did seem a pity that the political ideology of *Apartheid* discouraged most would-be tourists from visiting. It was with some misgivings that I boarded a plane for the 822-mile flight to Johannesburg for the next leg of my tour. Unlike the Cape, the city was teeming with black Africans, to the extent that I felt quite uncomfortable walking through the streets, just occasionally being jostled, and was warned not to take a short cut through the park at dusk. My first week there involved taking an early train each morning to Roodeport on what is known as the Rand – once a prosperous centre of the gold mines – where I was taken around by an Afrikaans couple who demonstrated their low opinion of the natives in no uncertain way. They took me to a hill top looking down over Soweto, an enormous 'township' where I believe a million black Africans lived, saying 'They live down there and we live up here, and that's the way it should be'. They explained that public toilets were provided for whites only, the blacks having to make do with going behind a bush. I soon discovered that the races were similarly segregated on trains, station platforms and subways. On one occasion at Simonstown in Cape Province I was looking down on the railway station and noticed two schoolgirls, one black and one white, waiting for a train. I wondered what would happen when the train came in: whether they would make for different carriages. What actually happened was that both of them entered a carriage intended for blacks, from which I deduced that although white citizens would not tolerate rubbing shoulders with their black neighbours, the blacks harboured no such resentment against white passengers.

After a weekend in the Kruger National Park I visited a charming primary school called Wendywood, where an equally charming couple named Robert Walsh and Josephine d'Agrela took me under their wing. I mention them only because their niceness made a special impression on me, and because a whole month later, after I had made three excursions out of South Africa and back again, they were kind enough to invite me to an excellent musical put on by the pupils, under the unlikely name 'The Ghost of Doodkwaggadam'. The first of these excursions was by a small plane to Gaberone, the capital of Botswana. On arrival at its small airport I was unable to tell immigration staff where I would be staying – only that someone would be meeting me in the arrival lounge. This someone turned out to be a Dutch Professor of Physics, Prof. Cees who, with his partner, a chemist called Alveda Blomberg, took me on a long afternoon drive into bush country where I saw many interesting sights including donkey carts and the site of David Livingstone's dwelling place. I was told that ten miles further would have taken us into lion country, and that a Belgian couple had spent a night out there in a land rover, leaving their small child outside only to be eaten by lions – though I must say I find this as difficult to believe now as I did then. We dined with two more scientists from the local university and enjoyed another meal together after my morning's work in a modern art gallery and before my return flight. Gaberone was unlike any other capital I have seen, and my memory associated with the art gallery is of a very large open square surrounded by the rather shack-like buildings that one expects to see in under-developed countries. Most of Botswana is one huge desert, with towns scattered around the edge, mostly near the south east border, and Gaberone is just the largest of these settlements. One advantage of touring without my family was the hospitality I received from so many people through being a lone traveller, including meals and outings of various sorts, for example being shown round a zoo at Vereeniging, but sometimes one or two other examiners would show up, as in the Mariston Hotel in Johannesburg, where one evening at dinner three of us spotted a white man at another table. Aware that Trinity College, London, had its own board of itinerant music examiners, we murmured 'he must be either a tea planter or a Trinity examiner'. One interesting outing was to a concert given by the South African National Youth Orchestra, where virtually all the players were white – drawn from Cape Province, Natal, Orange Free State and Transvaal, but an unexpected sight in a city full of black people; this was followed by a five-course 'black tie' dinner on the twenty-ninth floor, with civic dignatories making speeches alternating English and Afrikaans, as was the custom.

The icing on the cake of this fascinating tour was undoubtedly my fortnight in Mauritius, the Indian Ocean island which at that time was virtually unknown as a tourist destination. Within days I met Yves Candasamy, the organist of what passed for a cathedral (once used, I was told, as an amunition store) and was asked to take a choir rehearsal. Years later, I discovered that one of my lay clerks, Rob

Adams, had been present at that practice when setting up a schools examination project on the island. More significantly, Helena Allan, the eccentric wife of the British High Commissioner, took a great interest in me, inviting me to stay for the weekend at Westminster House, their official residence on a hill at Floréal in the centre of the island. In fact I did stay overnight, after a dinner party for sixteen guests. She had some pretentions as a pianist and had entered for the Grade 8 exam, but had decided to withdraw. Instead she asked me to tea, in return for which I was expected to give her a lesson on playing a Bach Prelude and Fugue at her home, to which I was driven in the official green Jaguar with a Union Flag on the bonnet and bearing the registration plate BRITAIN. That same day their Excellencies took me to a party at the Chinese Embassy, where I was introduced to the French, Russian, American and Egyptian Ambassadors before returning to the Residence for dinner. Mrs Allan was adamant that during my fortnight in Mauritius I should *perform* – she had a rather menacing way of enunciating the word – and she had in mind an organ recital at the aforementioned cathedral; but a brief reconnaissance was enough to disabuse me of that idea, since the instrument turned out to be a clapped-out electronic organ, quite unsuitable for any respectable piece of music. The lady then had a better idea: a piano recital at the Residence. Her upright piano proved to be quite satisfactory, and she had a cabinet full of music, so I found myself once again selecting music to play at short notice. The recital was to be in aid of the Anglican Homes Charity, headed by no less a personage than the Right Reverend Trevor Huddleston, whose name had become something of a household word when serving in the London borough of Stepney, and who now had the unlikely title of Archbishop of the Indian Ocean in addition to being Bishop of Mauritius. At one point Mrs Allan interrupted my recital, told me that the French Ambassador had arrived late, and requested something French in his honour. Searching through her cabinet, I lighted upon some Debussy and, despite its key-signature of six flats, decided to play *La fille aux cheveux de lin*. The gesture was rewarded by a dinner invitation, this time with about sixteen other people including the Minister of Health, and I was coaxed into playing a Chopin *Nocturne* for them. The Egyptian Ambassador had had to decline on the grounds that President Sadat had just been assassinated.

An unusual feature of the schedule in Mauritius was the examining of class singing which, although provided for by the syllabus, I had never come across elsewhere, nor have I since. It seemed very old-fashioned to be confronted by forty or fifty schoolgirls lined up in their school dresses, all ready to say 'Good morning Mrs Toolsy;

good morning Dr Smith'. Some school choirs were entered for three or four Grades, in each case singing prescribed songs and a sight-singing test, which I seem to recall was done by following a tonic-solfa chart, pointed to by a teacher, such as I had not seen since my own primary school days. When it came to the aural tests, one pupil would act as spokesperson for the group, having consulted briefly with her colleagues. Altogether ten schools and colleges, including four Loreto Convents from different parts of the island, and mostly girls' schools, entered classes for these exams, amounting to twenty-three in all. I also examined about a hundred and thirty individual candidates in a fortnight, and was intrigued by some of the more exotic names, matching the opulence of their country, such as Cécile le Juge de Segrais, M Patricia V Joanne How Kong Fah, Marie-Louise S Desvaux de Marigny, Guillaume Chasteau de Balyon and Alain Georges Marcel Deschambeaux. Mauritius had been a French colony before becoming British and subsequently independent, and the French influence was still apparent not only in its place names but also in the Creole language spoken by many including my personal driver, with whom I could make myself understood by speaking French.

In due course I flew back to Johannesburg, only to be driven 120 miles to a town called Ermelo for several hours' work on my way to the small kingdom of Swaziland, where I stayed at the Swazi Inn at the capital Mbabane and did a little exploring on my own before being taken to Waterford-Kamhlaba, a multi-racial school under the auspices of the United World Colleges (like Atlantic College in South Wales). After seeing so much segregation in neighbouring South Africa, it was fascinating to see the pupils fraternising happily with each other in the grounds – even a white boy embracing a black girl. On one of my car journeys the driver stopped to pick up a young man very colourfully dressed in national costume and carrying a knobkerrie, who told us he was going for an audience with the King. We duly made a detour to the royal Palace on our way back to the exam centre! Arriving back in Johannesburg Airport for the fifth time, I took the opportunity to see the city from the fiftieth floor of the Carlton Centre, and met again Ken Abbott, John Jordan and others whom I had last seen so many weeks earlier. My last few days' examining were interspersed with a visit to a gold mine, shopping for souvenirs and curios, dining out, watching tribal dancing and attending a service at the Cathedral, until eventually I returned to the airport for the last time, bought a gold Krugerrand and boarded a Boeing 747 jet bound for Nairobi. My second flight, delayed by more than two hours, arrived at Heathrow on the morning of the 22nd October, eleven weeks after I had set out, and I travelled from there on a coach and two trains back to Hereford, where I was enthusiastically greeted by the family. Whenever I arrive on that same platform I still remember little Adrian, aged four, running round in circles with delight. My return coincided neatly with the beginning of half term week, which we thankfully spent at Rozel Cottage. The proteas that I had carried back with me did not, alas, survive the autumn chill for very long.

On the last Saturday of the month we all returned to Llandaff, where I immediately conducted Saturday Evensong and joined in a wine and cheese party at the school which raised £200 towards the forthcoming recital by my opposite number in Nantes, Félix Moreau. No time for hanging about! I had intended that Moreau's recital should be sponsored by the local association of organists and choirmasters, but for some reason they reneged on the arrangement, and the audience numbered fewer than sixty, only a third of the number I had attracted in Nantes, so we were unable to cover his travel expenses. Although the event was not even mentioned in Cathedral publications during my absence abroad, the Chapter saw fit to impose a £30 charge for it, and to make matters worse someone had mistakenly advertised the ticket price as 50p instead of £1.50 – but we had an interesting couple of days trying out our French with both Félix and the afore-mentioned Marie-Thérèse Jehan. Meanwhile the Dean had become more chatty and co-operative, so much so that the following week saw no fewer than four cathedral concerts! Hearing rumours that the cathedral choir might be run down or phased out, I quickly wrote an article for *The Llandaff Monthly* to refute such ideas, writing 'The cathedral choir exists to fulfil the main function of a cathedral, which is to perpetuate the worship of God daily, in as elaborate and sumptuous a way as circumstances will permit; it follows that any curtailment of its activities just cannot be considered'. I was encouraged when the Dean not only stopped to agree with me, when we happened to meet in the High Street, but also endorsed my article in print, saying 'How such rumours came to be circulated I do not know. It is the intention of the Chapter to maintain the cathedral's choral foundation, and it hopes that the financial and political situations which at present threaten all such foundations will not make it necessary to abandon that position'. This was indeed a welcome assurance.

It was during 1981 that we participated in a scheme whereby examiners might offer accommodation to colleagues working in the vicinity; I remember one of the first having the extraordinary name Mariegold Cowsill, and a Frenchman called Guy Cremnitz who phoned his wife each evening asking 'How do you *feel?*' I thought this was a kindly question which I might well emulate, but the next time I heard of them they were divorced. Despite the Chapter Clerk's earlier assurances, no work whatsoever had been carried out on our house and garage during my long absence, but at last a start was made. There had been further thefts from the song room, and I also discovered that I had become the lowest paid of all cathedral organists who were provided with a house in return for taking seven services a week, the *average* salary being 34% above mine – so my gloomy correspondence was reluctantly resumed, not only with the Norman, the chapter clerk, but also to the architect responsible for house repairs and the city planning officer, who expressed concern that the conditions laid down earlier in the year had not been upheld. The following letter I wrote to Norman was not untypical:

> You mentioned in your letter of 18th November that the proposed work on this house had been allocated to Graham Hardy in July. I am writing to let you know that nothing whatever has been done about the chimney-stacks or the east wall of the house, although *seven months* have passed since the conservatory was demolished.
>
> I have another complaint. Some days ago some workmen removed the ceiling from the garage: they went away and have not been seen since. Ten pigeons flew down from the loft through the cross-beams into the garage itself, where they now fly about and huddle together, unable to escape. Now they have started eating each other. The floor is covered with droppings, and I have to leave my car outside. Thus conditions are even worse than before. Will you please do something about this appalling state of affairs? Meanwhile the wet conditions seem to have caused a short circuit, so that the lights no longer come on in the garage and the adjoining room.

The remainder of the term continued with nothing more eventful than a performance of Haydn's *Creation* and a televised recording session for the Choral Society, a visit to London as a newly-elected member of the national Council of the Incorporated Association of Organists, a week's examining at Bedales School in Hampshire, an evening of carols for the choristers at a candlelight supper in a tithe barn at St Donat's Castle in Glamorgan, and a pantomime treat for them at the New Theatre, starring Tommy Trinder and Leslie Crowther in *Cinderella.* The upright Chappell piano which my mother had bought by instalments in the 1920s, and upon which I had done all my practice as a boy, was moved to St Mary's and installed in my first-floor study, to allow both Marian and me to give lessons simultaneously, upstairs and downstairs. Finally at the end of the year I took the family to stay with my parents in Ilford, stopping three times *en route* to call on friends in Great Shefford, Maidenhead and Kingston-on-Thames. No opportunity wasted!

1982

January 1982 had a character all of its own, when persistent snow prevented our leaving Rozel Cottage for Cardiff until the 16th January. During this time we had news from St Mary's, where the head verger's accommodation to some extent overlapped ours, that he needed to enter our house to deal with a problem with melting snow, and I agreed to post our door key to him so that he could take any necessary action. Somewhat later, water began dripping through one of his ceilings below our first-floor bedroom, and with my permission the Dean's son took a ladder and climbed through the window in order to open the front door: meanwhile we wondered what was happening to our second-floor rooms. We learned that milk deliveries were reduced to two a week, not to houses but for collection in the High Street. The return of the choristers and the first Choral Society rehearsal of the year had to be postponed, and Rachel's school holiday was extended by nine days, as we tried to keep warm, huddling by the fire wearing many layers of clothing and playing games such as *Scrabble, Yahtzee* and the much more cerebral *Mastermind,* but notably a very absorbing new one called *Kensington,* with a board the size of a long-playing record and small red and blue counters.

On our return to Llandaff there were more than sixty letters awaiting my attention, so the early part of the year was not entirely void, and I began to take on a few organ students, including Gillian Glasson, a timid but gifted girl from Swansea who had already passed grade 8 piano and organ and grade 7 violin at the age of fifteen. At the organ she hardly dared pull out any stops for herself, yet eventually she won an organ scholarship to Lady Margaret Hall. She was by no means the first of my students to win an Oxford scholarship: at Salisbury I had taught Philip Sibthorpe, son of the founder of the Friends of Cathedral Music, who became organ scholar at Queen's College, and Patrick Russill, son of a school caretaker, who graduated from New College and is now not only director of music at the London Oratory but head of choral conducting at the Royal Academy of Music and chief examiner to the Royal College of Organists. A more 'mature' student was a businessman, also from Swansea, called simply John Thomas, who was the head of a company turning new inventions into prototypes. When Christopher Dearnley, whose assistant I had been for a year in Salisbury, invited me to give a lunchtime recital at St Paul's Cathedral, John offered to act as my page-turner. He travelled up to London by train, but I could not afford the fare and went by coach instead. When I had finished my evening practice there, he took a short piece of music from his pocket, asking if he might play it on the mighty organ. I then enjoyed a late supper with Michael Thompson, a curate at St Mary Abbotts in Kensington, whom I had known as a theology student at Llandaff, and made my way next morning to St Paul's to play for only half an hour, suitably colourful works by Franck and Duruflé, Norman Cocker's flamboyant *Tuba Tune* featuring a powerful reed stop under the dome, and Gigout's *Grand Choeur Dialogué* in which I alternated between the main organ in the quire and the fanfare trumpets over the west door hundreds of feet from the console; their sound reached me much later, but I just had to keep going regardless, hoping that the audience below would hear the dialogue as the composer intended. The audience included Dearnley himself, the eminent Ralph Downes, who had judged my playing several times in the past, an uncle and aunt and my parents from Ilford. John Thomas kindly entertained me to lunch at the Waldorf Hotel before seeing me off, with only a small fee in my wallet, on the coach back to Cardiff. This turned out to be one of the few highlights in a generally dismal year, as we shall see.

My children do not get mentioned very much in this account, but family life with them was always good fun and never stressful, I am happy to say. Although I was so often on duty in the cathedral while they were having their tea and being put to bed, I did make the most of opportunities to accompany Rachel on various errands and expeditions, both in Cardiff and in Herefordshire, while Marian was looking after the young ones. She was one of twenty pupils from the cumbersomely-named Llandaff City Church in Wales Junior School to gain a place at the better of the two local comprehensive schools, but I took her along to sit the entrance examination at Howells, an independent school for girls within easy walking distance. We knew we could not afford the fees, but felt that she would flourish there, with their good record for top university placements. She was indeed accepted, and my irregular but generally low income allowed us to qualify for a government-assisted place which in our case covered 87% of the fees for a day pupil, leaving us only £159 to pay for the first year – good news indeed, as Marian could earn this amount with the fees paid by a single piano pupil.

February turned out to be a very fallow month, as usual, and I was again much preoccupied with another attempt to convince the Dean and Chapter that I was grossly underpaid. Conditions in Llandaff were in every way such a contrast with my three months' life in Africa and Mauritius a few months earlier, when I was properly paid for a fascinating tour, constantly looked after by friendly people who recognised my worth. In a long letter to the non-communicative Chapter Clerk (how I came to dread and despise that title!) I pointed out that my salary had not kept pace with the very high inflation rate of that time – 93% between 1976 and 1981 and a further 10% since then. I singled out for comparison the nineteen English cathedrals whose organists were provided with a house and who were responsible for choral services six days a week, as I was: their average pay was 50% higher than mine. I added that nearly all of these men, unlike me, were provided with a pension scheme, and that all but one of them received extra fees for weddings and funerals, for which I was ineligible by the terms of my contract. I put a suggestion from a recent representative meeting of deans and organists that my salary should equal that of an archdeacon, pointing out that my position involved a great deal of time, with its many attendant commitments (i.e. unpaid work which I would not be doing were I not cathedral organist), so that private teaching devolved upon Marian. I expressed the view that giving up four evenings a week to piano teaching was a heavy burden for a wife with three children to look after. To achieve a salary approaching those of my colleagues, I was in effect asking for a rise of about 37% and a further 21% to follow. It is true that since 1977 the Chapter had paid three-quarters of my household fuel bills, as well as my telephone bills and the general and water rates, but I knew that a good half of my colleagues also received similar perquisites, and since my qualifications and experience were in no way inferior to theirs, I felt I had a good case when appealing for an equitable salary. I was glad when at last I was invited to a meeting with the Dean, the Canon Treasurer (Archdeacon Lewis, whom I had first met eight years earlier), the Chapter Clerk, and for some unknown reason Dr John Baldwin, who then had a title as a 'layman licensed to administer the chalice'. An hour and a half was allowed to discuss my submissions, plus more time after I left the Deanery, and five weeks later I was informed that their recommendations had been put to the finance committee, who had decided to award me a 9.5% salary increase, which was at least a step in the right direction.

My gloom was not alleviated between these two meetings by the receipt of a closely-typed and detailed letter from the Dean concerning appointments, and in one case a young probationer who had not made the grade. He was quite right to exert his rights in this respect, but it was clear that the many comings and goings of the adult singers, in their various capacities as lay clerks, singing men and choral scholars, had not all been made clear to him. As all these appointments were technically made by the Dean and Chapter as the governing body, I usually arranged their conditions and pay with the chapter clerk, thinking that a dean would have far too much on his plate to deal with such details, but of course he wanted to know who all these people were, and felt that if a boy were found inadequate as a potential chorister, he should at least be consulted. I imagine that most deans would have adopted the simple expedient of an informal chat about such matters, but this one usually resorted to letters, and I felt obliged to reply in like manner, in a letter of eight long paragraphs, to justify my actions and point out that the lack of communication between him and his clerk was largely responsible for his being kept in the dark. I suggested that regular staff meetings might solve problems more easily, but although he grudgingly agreed with me in a postscript to his reply ('A meeting between you, the headmaster and me near the end of each term to review the progress of all boys would not be a bad thing'), he never actually implemented this in practice. We did however establish that I should inform the Dean direct about appointments, leaving him to deal with Norman as to payment, though I was not entirely convinced this process would improve the latter's efficiency. The Dean did reply quite graciously to my invitation to join us for a lay clerks' dinner at an attractive pub in the Vale of Glamorgan, but only to describe a conflicting event which prevented his acceptance. As far as I recall, he never offered hospitality to the choir men, and even when I occasionally asked for a repeat of this occasion, and the Chapter agreed to pay, none of them ever came to act as hosts or in any other capacity.

With so little to occupy me during the day apart from office work, I drifted through March somewhat disconsolately, blossoming forth only to conduct an exciting performance of Beethoven's *Missa Solemnis* and wishing that the rest of my time could be used in such a rewarding way. Workmen had arrived at St Mary's to redecorate the walls and ceilings of our bedroom and the bathroom, and to remake the ceilings of two other bedrooms, following the damage caused by melting snow and ice two months earlier, and work was at last finished on the outer wall where the conservatory had been, while Paul Morgan, Exeter Cathedral's assistant organist and an examiner (who had applied for my job in 1973) was staying with us. I could not help thinking how fortunate he had been not to be appointed at Llandaff, and indeed he remained in Exeter well into the next century. On the 11th April Easter Day coincided with the twenty-fifth anniversary of the cathedral's rededication service after being ruined during another war, so we again sang Rubbra's anthem *And when the builders* at Evensong. I also applied for the vacancy at York Minster on the retirement of Dr Francis Jackson, and Roy Massey proposed me for election to the Council of the Royal College of Organists. Only the second of these bids was successful; there were two hundred applicants for the Minster job, and although Dr Allan Wicks of Canterbury assured me he had recommended me to the Dean of York, I was not shortlisted and it was actually Allan's former assistant Philip Moore, then at Guildford Cathedral, who was appointed, retaining the post for the next twenty-six years until his retirement.

Attending a cathedral organists' conference in Wells and giving my third recital at Bath Abbey served only to remind me what many features I was missing at Llandaff, and with my own age approaching forty-five I realised that prospects for promotion were fast diminishing. I had constructed an ingenious programme for the choral society's festival concert, comprising settings of psalms by four very different composers: Liszt's virtually unknown version of Psalm 13, Kodály's *Psalmus Hungaricus*, Stravinsky's *Symphony of Psalms* – all these in Latin – and Bernstein's *Chichester Psalms* sung in Hebrew. An added attraction was that 1982 was the centenary of the births of both Kodály and Stravinsky, so I billed the concert as 'Psalms and Centenaries'. The other event to look forward to was the 800th anniversary of Wells Cathedral. A year's events had been planned, with a fat glossy brochure, and Tony Crossland had invited the choirs of Bath Abbey and our own Cathedral to take up residence there for a week and participate in the choral services and two concerts. I prepared for this summer event by introducing movements of Bruckner's *Mass in E minor* into the Sunday Eucharists, and choruses from the fine settings of the *Magnificat* by J S Bach and his son Carl Phillip Emanuel as anthems for Sunday afternoon Evensongs. None of these preparations could alleviate my gathering gloom, however, to the extent that I became increasingly disillusioned and constantly worried, sleeping only fitfully at night and sometimes taking to my bed for a whole morning or afternoon even on sunny, warm days in May – a sure sign that depression was setting in. I began considering unlikely jobs, including Derby Cathedral (offering nearly four times my salary), a Music and Worship lectureship in Liverpool, an editor's job for a music publisher, and perhaps more hopefully Director of the Llandaff

Festival. Marian was very comforting and supportive, and at night I used to cling to her so hard that I must have almost squeezed all the breath out of her. One day I decided to drive to Oxford, setting out with a small picnic which I ate in Matthew Arnold's Field at Boar's Hill. There I climbed to the top of Jarn Mound, with its view across the fields to Oxford's 'dreaming spires' where I had often gone during my student days to pray about the important goals in my life. They had all come to fruition – my FRCO diploma, my BA degree, my BMus degree, my beautiful wife, and in later years our children – and I felt that perhaps my prayers for a better future might also be answered. Looking back now, I think that perhaps, in the fullness of time, they were. At the time, I made a start by continuing to Magdalen College to interview a promising alto who had just applied – but once more the package we could offer was not good enough and he went elsewhere.

Sometime after Easter I made representations to the Dean on behalf of the choral society with a view to performing Bach's *St Matthew Passion* during Holy Week the following year, suggesting that it might be sung on Palm Sunday, the first part in the afternoon, when Evensong was by custom replaced by a service of music and readings, and the second part in the evening, allowing time for his precious parish evensong in between. The full rehearsal, I suggested, could be either elsewhere during the morning, or on the previous day in the cathedral. Anticipating some objection to this plan, I put forward an alternative by way of a performance at the West End on a Saturday. I was not altogether surprised to receive a long letter in reply, in forty lines of typing, including the following reasoning:

> A point of great importance is that a main rehearsal in the morning (but in another building) would make it necessary for church people in the Choir to miss their basic Christian duty on Palm Sunday morning. Some might have the opportunity of attending an early Mass to fulfil their Sunday obligation but Palm Sunday is a day on which it is a good thing to participate in the ceremonies proper to the day as a way of beginning to keep a good Holy Week: these, in most churches, take place somewhere in the middle of the morning – at 9 and 11 in the Cathedral – and at 11 you also have your duties with the Cathedral Choir. As far as churchpeople are concerned it would disturb me to know that membership of the Choral Society led to their omitting their primary duty, in Holy Week or at any other time.

> I am not prepared to relax my ban on Saturday concerts in

Advent and Lent, particularly in the later weeks of Lent. From the Third Sunday in Lent onwards there are special preparations to be made, and seen by me to have been made, for Sunday morning, over and above those which I like to check before I leave the Cathedral every Saturday – rows of chairs aligned properly and spaced out, books in place, kneelers in their racks and little bits of paper removed from the floor...

It is quite clear that he was trying to impose his will on our hundred and twenty members, not to mention the orchestral players, by determining how they should spend their free time As if to acknowledge that the above might seem unduly negative, he concluded with a flourish, composing his last two sentences with no fewer than 110 words:

I am sorry to be obstructive but, as I have said over and over again, Llandaff Cathedral is something which the great English Cathedrals cannot be because of their sheer size, a cathedral church whose life is centred on worship which makes use of the whole building regularly and is offered by fairly large numbers of people. This was recognised architecturally by George Pace who provided in the *Majestas* arch a unifying feature for the whole building which would also provide a liturgical setting which could also serve to draw into the whole life and worship of the Cathedral other activities that could be fitted into the worship-controlled pattern.

By long tradition the lengthy story of Christ's Passion from St Matthew's Gospel was sung at the Palm Sunday Eucharist by three priests standing beneath the *Majestas* arch. The central priest was the Narrator, the other two singing the words of Christ and other characters, with interjections by the Choir representing the disciples or a crowd of onlookers. We always used the sixteenth-century setting by the Spanish composer Victoria, and because Bach's monumental work is essentially the same thing on an infinitely grander scale, one could hardly conceive a more suitable occasion to perform it. One might have thought that, with his strong belief in liturgical correctness, the dean might have felt able to accommodate our suggestion, and it was typical of him, and duly noted by others, that he had no alternative ideas to put forward – even in his capacity as chairman of the choral society. He went one further (in his capacity as a Governor) to issue a permanent ban on the use of the Junior School, our usual Monday rehearsal venue, in Holy Week. Of course, we simply booked Howell's School hall instead, just down the road, making him look very foolish in the eyes of everyone. Adrian Heale, the secretary of the choral society, was commissioned to meet the Dean, who suggested a date four weeks ahead, and to write to the Chapter Clerk, who of course did not reply.

The Cathedral Choir's singing often seemed to lack lustre at this time, and there were considerable changes in personnel, Ralph Lock returning as a bass after a gap of three years to replace David Gwesyn Smith whose professional career was taking off, the alto Tim Parish leaving a year earlier than expected, and a number of other young men of various degrees of competence being auditioned. Several boys left for various reasons, and I warned the chapter in my summer report that of the eleven choristers left by September only two would have had more than seven terms' experience. I mentioned the year's highlights, of course, but my general sadness was reflected in my concluding paragraph:

> Set against these apparent successes, however, there is the constant disappointment, frustration and anxiety that one feels at the prospect of maintaining a family on a salary which is £4000 below this year's recommended figure for a cathedral organist in my position, on the basis of parity with a residentiary canon, or £2240 below if we take into consideration the figures applicable to the Church in Wales. I conclude my ninth report with an urgent appeal to the Chapter to reconsider their recent offer, which they may not realise is causing many sleepless nights and considerable hardship, and which I genuinely feel unable to accept.

Pope Paul II's visit to Llandaff on the 2nd June no doubt impressed the throng that turned out to greet him, but did not impinge upon my own plans for the short Whitsun holiday. He did not visit the cathedral but celebrated Mass in nearby Pontcanna Fields, where a mixed choir was conducted by the organist of Brecon Cathedral, David Gedge. It was not a task that I would have enjoyed, and I was much happier in Byford, where we launched our new inflatable dinghy on the Wye, naming her *Rosella*. Later in the week I was back at the cathedral for our second Three Choirs concert with Bath

Abbey and Wells Cathedral, with the newscaster Martin Muncaster interspersing our anthems with readings, and the choral society coped well enough with the 'Psalms and Centenaries' programme mentioned earlier. There were special services to celebrate the centenary of the Church Army and, on the day that Prince William was born, the end of the Falklands war. A memorial service for those members of the Welsh Guards who had been killed in the conflict was held on July 12th, attended by HRH the Prince of Wales, and included Francis Jackson's eminently suitable but little known anthem beginning 'Remember for good, O Father, those whom we commemorate before thee'. Two days later I made another pilgrimage to Jarn Mound when examining a few candidates in Oxfordshire, before setting off for Wells. For the next ten days the cathedral choir took up residence there to celebrate the 800th anniversary with Bath Abbey choir, singing services both singly and in various permutations, including a Bruckner Mass with fifteen wind players from Chetham's School and Wells Cathedral School, and the two *Magnificat* settings with the English Chamber Orchestra. It fell to me to conduct George Dyson's splendidly theatrical setting of the canticles at a combined Evensong on the first Saturday, and four of the anthems in the Three Choirs concert, a repeat of the Llandaff one except for the readings, which were chosen and read by another broadcaster, Richard Baker.

The summer holidays involved minimum expenditure but considerable enjoyment, starting with a few days in Wharfedale, staying at the lovely retirement cottage of our Llandaff neighbours Vera and Humphrey before moving on to a rented cottage in a village called Aislaby, near Whitby. We had much fun exploring the Yorkshire dales and coast, dropping in on old friends in Heptonstall before returning to our own retreat in Herefordshire where we happily spent the next three weeks enjoying country life: I have to say that buying a property in Herefordshire was one of the most fortunate aspects of my life. Marian and I visited the studio of the eminent sculptor Walenty Pytel (our former neighbour in Dilwyn) and attended half a dozen evening concerts in the Three Choirs Festival in Hereford Cathedral, where the organist, our old friend Roy Massey, had given us free tickets for seats in the choir stalls, next to Frederick Swann, then organist of the Riverside Church in New York, and opposite the composer William Mathias with his wife and daughter. We heard, amongst other things, a rather perfunctory performance of Walton's *Belshazzar's Feast,* the first performance of *Lux Aeterna* by Mathias, and to end the Festival, Verdi's *Requiem* again. The remainder of the holiday saw us at Rozel Cottage, the purchase of which had perhaps been the most successful investment I ever made, following on as it did from our first cottage at Dilwyn in 1976. Returning to Llandaff, I still felt very gloomy about prospects for the choir, partly because of continuing uncertainty about the availability of lay clerks, and having lost a potentially good alto to Lichfield. In early September, before term began, consecutive diary entries record 'feeling tired and gloomy again but tried to get jobs done'; 'weary again – got up late and did little all morning'; 'even more weary and despondent, back to bed until 11.30 a.m.', and a week or so later I took my troubles to our doctor, who prescribed sleeping pills. Back in June, I had decided to try putting cards into shop windows to advertise myself as a piano teacher. In Salisbury Marian and I had built up a very flourishing practice, at one time numbering over fifty pupils, and in Llandaff she still taught a dozen, but my difficulty had always been that my cathedral duties covered late afternoons and early evenings, the most convenient times for pupils to come for lessons. From 5.15 to 6.45 on three weekdays I would be dealing with Evensong followed on Mondays by the choral society rehearsals, and on Tuesdays by practices for the full choir and for the men only, lasting until 8 p.m. Saturday mornings were reserved for an early choir practice followed by organ students, and on about one Friday in four we liked to escape to the cottage for a 36-hour break, returning for Sunday duties. With most weekends on duty, I had hitherto felt that Marian and I should always keep Wednesdays free as a matter of principle. However, our quest for new pupils quite unexpectedly furnished me with a clientele of twenty new ones plus a waiting list, so we decided to make good use of both Wednesdays and Thursdays (my assistant's duty day) and somehow I found time to fit them in. I began with seven pupils on Wednesday the 8th September, taking on more each week, and in no time was earning an extra £100 a week. By the end of September I had over thirty pupils and had received £1400 in fees, so I may have wondered why it had taken me five years to venture again into this field. Within a year my income from teaching had increased by a factor of ten, and our joint practice continued for at least ten years after that. It seemed that my prayers at Jarn Mound had been answered.

The new Choir term began more hopefully than usual, with a team of eight men, and although the choristers were down to twelve, there were six probationers waiting in the wings. At Marian's suggestion we began choristers' teas, inviting three boys to tea after Evensong each Sunday and letting them play with our children if they felt so inclined. We felt that a bit of family life would appeal to them, being for so long away from their own families. Another significant innovation concerned the chanting of psalms, and having explained this in some detail to the readers of *The Llandaff Monthly*, I thought it might interest some readers, whether *cognoscenti* or not, if I were to copy my article here, even if only because the psalms are the mainstay of the daily services:

Devotees of cathedral music will have noticed that we no longer sing the 'psalms of the day' as appointed in numerical order, from time immemorial, to cover Matins and Evensong daily during each month of the year. We have now adopted the system devised by the authorities of the Church in Wales, which has the effect of reducing the amount of psalmody per service, while introducing into Evensong many of the psalms which were previously sung only at Matins (and therefore very seldom). The prospect of learning over five hundred unfamiliar verses in one term was a daunting one for the choristers, but we have taken the opportunity to devote more time to preparing them, discovering some finely-written chants not previously sung here, and have also experimented with a new style of pointing.

Most of the English cathedrals still use Coverdale's translation of the psalms, which predates the Authorised Version and which has been published in several different methods of 'pointing', i.e. the way in which the words of each verse are spread over the ten notes which form each half of a double chant. Last July we were impressed by the psalm-singing at Wells Cathedral, where the Oxford Psalter is used, and this term I have begun the task of altering our own Revised Psalter (a translation published in 1965, based on Coverdale but correcting his 'mistakes') in such a way that the words can be sung more expressively than is the case with the printed pointing, which was designed for congregational use. In so doing I have used the Oxford Psalter as a guide, adapting its principles to our own version, and I feel that this fresh approach has inspired a new interest in psalm-singing, which is all to the good.

In general, the choir began to sing more confidently again, especially when I introduced Jeremy Davies, chaplain to Cardiff's university and colleges, as a new tenor. A former Llandaff chorister, he had also been a choral scholar at Cambridge, with a very fine voice, and became a real asset to the choir.

These various developments did not stop me from looking elsewhere, however, and I was somewhat disappointed at not being short-listed for Philip Moore's job at Guildford, where the precentor had been a Llandaff priest vicar before my time. I had often wondered whether my applications were unsuccessful owing to the Dean's formal and restrictive style, but was slightly reassured when our former bishop Eryl Thomas heard from Guildford that the dean had written 'very warmly' about me. It is strange to relate that, despite all my reservations about him, my few visits to the Deanery did tend to leave me with quite a warm feeling also, so he obviously wasn't all bad. The finance committee felt unable to accede to my anguished plea for a better salary, nor was there any response to my request for a pension scheme, and a promise to paint all the exterior woodwork on the house during the summer had not been honoured, leaving some bare patches and even sections which had rotted away altogether, owing to deterioration over many years of neglect. Extracting any proper information from the Chapter Clerk relating to choir members was still like getting blood out of a stone, and nothing had been done to protect the song room from thefts of music, replacements accounting for about £400 in a few years. In December I had to ask twice for a reply to a letter written in September, adding 'Unless you can very quickly offer accommodation for our next two lay clerks to replace Tim Parish and Terry Dickens, I can see no hope of our continuing the choral music next year'. There was no such delay in informing me that, unlike other most other members of the Cathedral Organists' Association, I could not expect reimbursement of expenses incurred in attending the biannual conferences. I had also pursued the idea of allowing local boys to become dayboy choristers, but another very detailed letter from the Dean explained why such a scheme could only apply if a boy lived very near indeed, and why I could not advertise such a scheme.

In the last two months of 1982 I did only one week's examining, but the other out-of-the-ordinary event was the first recital to be given on the organ in the new St David's Hall in the centre of Cardiff, attended by my largest ever audience, said to number about 1,400. The event was shared with three other players: the organ's designer, Ralph Downes, the Welsh BBC producer Huw Tregelles Williams, and the rather glamorous Jane Parker-Smith who arrived with her agent in a Rolls-Royce. Apart from a few earlier practice sessions this was the first time I had been inside the hall, which had yet to be officially opened, and I was led by the assistant manager to a personal dressing-room laid out rather like a hotel bedroom. I was amazed at the labyrinth of passages connecting the dressing rooms with the auditorium: it was very easy to get lost on the way, so the stage manager was sent to guide me through nine doors and up two staircases when it was my turn to play. Ralph Downes, then aged 78, began the evening with César Franck's *Premier Choral;* I followed with Bach's Fantasia & Fugue in G minor and then *Dieu parmi nous,* the final part of Messiaen's *La Nativité du Seigneur.* I had originally planned to play the Variations on an Old Flemish Song by Flor Peeters, which would have shown off the individual stops and combinations in a more interesting way, but the work had some rather tricky passages and I decided to take the line of least resistance by playing the Messiaen which had been firmly in my repertoire for years; in any case, it is a spectacular piece, well-suited to a modern organ. After the interval, Huw played some Buxtehude and the inevitable Welsh contribution by Mathias, and lastly came Jane, playing a movement from Widor's *Symphonie Gothique* and the first movement of Marcel Dupré's *Symphonie-Passion.* I once read of her taking a bow at the end of a recital, when 'her backless evening dress turned out to be virtually frontless as well'. A reception was held afterwards to meet the chairman of the city council and various mayors, reporters, organists and composers; even the Dean offered his congratulations.

Our next visit to the new hall was to hear Chris Barber's jazz band, which to my dismay was quite unnecessarily amplified, the noise becoming almost unbearable when they were joined by a female vocalist in the second half. The hall was integrated into a fine new shopping mall named St David's Centre, and in early December I took the choristers and a group of volunteers from the choral society to sing there in aid of an ISM appeal for music therapy, raising £343 in four hours. A rather grander occasion that autumn was a special service to launch an appeal for the restoration of the cathedral and even the addition of new vestries (but with nothing earmarked for the organ, needless to say). In a magazine article, the Dean remarked laconically that the target sum of £400,000 over several years was only a fraction compared with the £600,000 spent in a single day on the Pope's visit to Cardiff.

There is no doubt, as I have suggested earlier, that the Dean was glad to find a good excuse to ban big orchestral concerts from the cathedral in future festivals on the grounds that they were far better suited to St David's Hall. The festival had begun in 1958 as a one-off event to mark the silver jubilee of the Friends of the Cathedral, for six days ending with the eve of the Feast of SS Peter and Paul. In an article in *The Llandaff Monthly* the Dean explained how 'permission' had been given for a similar event for the next four years, during which Christopher Cory had assumed the position of artistic director:

It gained a deserved fame far beyond Wales, but this could not but lead to its relationship with the cathedral church and the parish changing. In order to avoid clashes with other festivals, it moved away from its position in the calendar which made it an extension of the Patronal Festival, its duration became longer and the necessity of providing a large stage for orchestras of increased size led at last to concerts being presented at the West end and, because the stage was in position over one or more weekends, to the two western bays of the nave being 'lost' to the Sunday congregations. The fact that all the chairs had to be turned around also meant that if more than a few worshippers came to weekday evensongs, which were intended to be festival 'events', they had to sit or kneel with their backs to the altar and the choir!

The death of Christopher Cory undoubtedly contributed to the feeling that great changes would have to take place, and the new Director, Huw Tregelles Williams, had the task of integrating the Festival into the life and worship of the cathedral and parish of Llandaff.

Looking back, I think 1982 must have been my most depressing year, and it was undoubtedly the loving support of my wife and the cheerful spirits of the children that kept me going through my adversity, together with a little initiative on my own part.

1983

Although a number of events had already been held in St David's Hall, the official opening ceremony was not until February 1983. Prince Charles had laid the foundation stone four years earlier, and the Queen Mother, wearing a glittering pink gown and a silver and diamond tiara, came to Cardiff for the first time since 1966 to unveil a commemorative plaque in the foyer. The gala concert which followed was conducted by that amiable Welshman Owain Arwel Hughes, before an audience of 1,200 invited guests and a further 800 who had applied for tickets. The opera singer Sir Geraint Evans and the actress Angharad Rees acted as comperes, and the seventy-five players of the BBC Welsh Orchestra accompanied Welsh National Opera singers Helen Field, Elizabeth Vaughan, Dennis O'Neill and Henry Newman. Petula Clarke (who was brought up near Merthyr Tydfil) sang a medley from her old records, and there were contributions from the 120 men of the Pontarddulais Choir, the harpist Osian Ellis and even the twenty-strong Cory Band; and the fine tenor Kenneth Bowen, with whom I had worked at intervals since 1959, was allowed just one song. Youth was represented by the Young Welsh Musician of the Year Justine Phillips (flute) and by thirty young girls from the Richard Williams Singers. Above and behind this array of Welsh musical talent sat I at the organ console, poised to add further weight to the two national anthems and a few bars elsewhere. I had felt less at ease during the six-hour rehearsal on the day before, on finding that I had left at home the organ part for William Mathias's arrangement of 'God save the Queen'. Reluctant to call down to the conductor I put another piece on the music desk, pulled out a few stops, looked in the mirror and pretended to play (for at least I knew the tune!). Huw Tregelles Williams, producing the concert for a simultaneous radio and television programme, noticed the omission of the proper organ part, but fortunately the conductor did not, so I got away with it, making sure to have the part with me for the actual concert. Also, having memorised the complex route from my dressing room to the console, I had to devise another way before the concert, as the eighth of the nine doors had been locked; this aspect of the occasion was much more difficult than the event itself. After the concert I was led from my dressing room to the St Asaph Room to be presented, along with some of the stars, to Her Majesty. She made some general comments about the concert and how she had enjoyed it. I reminded her that I had played a few chords on the organ, and she asked about the instrument and who built it. I mentioned that it was doing much to promote interest in organ music in the locality and was the largest 'tracker' organ in Britain. She enquired if it were bigger than the Royal Festival Hall organ, but I explained that this one had mechanical action as opposed to electric. When she asked 'Have you a good organ at Llandaff?' I felt suitably flattered that she knew who I was and decided that a non-committal reply 'It's *quite* nice' was the most suitable in the circumstances. This being my first and last conversation with a member of the Royal Family, I was feeling rather bashful, and often wished afterwards that I had grasped the nettle and told Her Majesty what I really thought of the organ I had been complaining about for so many years; who knows, she might have become the Patron of an Appeal, as her grandson was, a quarter of a century later! This little ceremony was followed by a big party in the main foyer for all the performers, with not only wine but roast saddle of Welsh lamb with a variety of salads, and a dessert. On seeing Marian, Owain Arwel Hughes handed over his plate and glass in order to kiss her, remembering having met us years before when we were both involved in televising Mathias's work *St Teilo*. I suspect that it is his friendly personality and ability to remember people that have ensured his success, rather than any particular finesse as a conductor.

It is one of those quirks of life that barely twelve hours later I was playing the organ to two Prime Ministers. Michael Roberts, the M.P. for Cardiff North West and Under Secretary of State for Wales, had died, and his funeral at the Cathedral was attended by numerous robed mayors and two dozen of his colleagues including James Callaghan and Margaret Thatcher, along with Secretary of State Nicholas Edwards and the Speaker George Thomas (later Viscount Tonypandy – another man renowned for his ability to recognise people after a single meeting and make them feel good). Fortunately the choristers at this stage were singing very nicely, giving a good account of William Croft's setting of the Burial Sentences and a very expressive psalm, but the rest of the service was typically unimaginative, with only a single reference by name to the deceased and nothing whatever in the way of a eulogy. Like the previous night's concert, the funeral was televised live and watched by the children at home, just up the hill. Not only did Mrs Thatcher speak appreciatively about the music as she left the Cathedral, but the Dean told me (in a letter, of course) that on reaching the Green at the top of the hill 'she expressed her approval to someone who was a complete stranger to her but happened to be a churchwarden's wife!' and that 'the Bishop also telephoned to say how impressive the service was; and no small part of the credit must go to those who provided the music'. High praise indeed! He never trusted himself to pass judgment, but this was not the first time he had passed on a flattering opinion from a visiting VIP.

Later the same day, Evensong for Ash Wednesday seemed rather an anticlimax, with Rachel's young boyfriend Jonathan rather nervously tackling those famous high phrases in Allegri's *Miserere*. Not many days earlier, attending the annual dinner of the Cathedral stewards, I noted that my place had been elevated (in my tenth year) to the top table with the Dean and two bishops. I was beginning to think that if only I could get some better men in the Choir, there would be little to grumble about, though I was finding my teaching practice, now numbering thirty-four pupils a week, rather tiring.

On the family front, Laura's godmother Lesley Robinson succumbed to cancer and I took Marian to Salisbury for the funeral in the Cathedral; it was very personal and moving, quite unlike the formality of the Llandaff service, especially in the choice of Sir William Harris's moving eight-part setting of John Donne's poem 'Bring us, O Lord, at the last awakening, into the house and gate of heaven'. Little did we know that many years later I would be choosing the same anthem, to be sung by the same choir, at Marian's own funeral. Cousin Ursula took advantage of our brief visit to Wiltshire by holding a party the next day for twenty-four relatives, all cousins and their spouses. Another opportunity to meet hoards of old friends occurred in March, when we returned south for a dinner at Clarendon Park to mark the Diamond Jubilee of Salisbury Musical (choral) Society.

One of my more unusual ventures was to go to the University to take the official test of the Mensa organisation, having found informally that I had quite a high intelligence quotient (IQ). Mensa is really a club for people who can do intelligence tests, and in fact I came out with a score of 150, which put me in the top 2% of the country, which seemed great until I realised that about a million other people must be eligible for membership, the majority perhaps being less proud of themselves. On the same day as the test a couple of new canons were installed in the cathedral at a service attended by Archbishop Michael Ramsay; and two days later I was off to Leeds Town Hall, where I managed to play the half-hour work by Liszt which had not been ready some months earlier for Exeter.

Back in Llandaff, a notable dispute broke out when a university student called Michael Steer, who had for a short time been a bass in the Cathedral Parish Choir, applied for one of our choral scholarships. Alun Hoddinott had never supported the scheme, but Michael sought the Professor's permission, lest he be found out later with awful consequences. Meanwhile Morley Lewis, as Parish Choirmaster, ran to the Dean to say 'hands off', whereupon I was called in (a rare event in itself) to discuss the problem. He was in a rather difficult position, being reluctant to allow someone into one choir at the expense of the other, and of course I put forward all the obvious arguments and explained all the difficulties, not least that our stalwart bass Terry Dickens was about to move to Exeter to take up a promotion. He expressed his dilemma in another letter:

> Although it might be possible, weighing all the considerations, for us to admit a man to the Cathedral Choir against the wish of his own incumbent and choirmaster, I cannot see that I could possibly do this when the choir in which the man is singing is also one of our own. I am sure there are ways in which the two choirs who sing in the Cathedral could support one another – not only because it is sensible but also because this is a Christian foundation in which one would expect everybody to work well together. To this end I have suggested to Morley that it might be a good thing if he and I and you could meet from time to time.....perhaps before the end of each term.

Faced with the Judgement of Solomon, the Dean decided to put the matter to the Chapter at their quarterly meeting in April, but he must have done so in a very biased way, judging by the uncharacteristically aggressive tone of the notification I received from the Chapter Clerk, whose spasmodic correspondence, though usually negative, was always courteous:

> Whilst having every sympathy with you in the difficulty of finding an adequate replacement for Terry Dickens, they wish to register their total disapproval of the attempt to fill the vacancy by approaching an existing member of the Parish Choir. Neither the consent of the Dean nor of the Master of the Parish Choristers had been obtained before the young man had been approached, and this lack of liaison and consideration of the likely affect *[sic]* such an approach might have augurs ill for the future of the Choirs and the Cathedral Music. This is a great pity, as there is no doubt that Mr Michael Steer is the sort of person and singer who would have been most welcome amongst the Cathedral Choir if a different course had been followed. As it is, the Chapter felt that they could not approve his appointment, and I was instructed to write to you in these

terms *[sic]* in the hope that in future you will have greater care in your relationship with the people with whom you have to work.

In view of the obvious misrepresentation of my actions and the unfairness of the judgment, and not being prepared to take this onslaught lying down, I decided to go into battle with all guns firing. It so happened that the father of a chorister, Gerard Elias QC, had recently become an acquaintance, and he had already questioned Hoddinott's possible infringement of human rights by restricting his students' extramural freedom. I could well do without this further and more clearly expressed opposition from the very body that was ultimately responsible for the wellbeing of the cathedral's music. Because this *laissez-faire* attitude was a major drawback affecting my working life, I think it relevant to quote my reply in full:

> I have to tell you that I was in no way prepared for the disparaging tone of your letter, which seems more concerned with censuring me over a matter of protocol than with the important matter of providing men singers for the Choir. There is nothing in my terms of reference to suggest that members of the Parish Choir, or of any other choir, should not be informed about our Choral Scholarships, not is it normal practice to approach any other person before a written application has been received. In fact, Michael Steer was introduced to the choir some time ago as a member of the Anglican Chaplaincy Choir, when we urgently needed a deputy. It was in his capacity as a Music student that he was given details of the scholarships, and I discussed his case with Morley Lewis before submitting his written application to the Dean. Moreover, Michael Steer had already made his wishes known to Mr Lewis before applying.
>
> I take the greatest exception to your remark that the course I took 'augurs ill for the future of the Choirs and the Cathedral Music', for everyone knows that the present and future of the Choral Foundation are my chief interest and concern, for which I work unceasingly and (I often feel) with little active support or encouragement. This is the first time in nine years that I have been criticised for my relationships with people with whom I work, and I am sure that in general these relationships are most cordial, though I do have cause to regret Mr Lewis's attitude towards the Cathedral Choir, which is too well-known to be described. The tone of your letter is very different from that of the Dean's on the same subject a few weeks earlier, in which he

spoke of the need for mutual support in 'a Christian foundation in which one would expect everybody to work together'. The Chapter's decision is worrying for all of us here, and I strongly urge that they should reconsider the matter, setting aside the poor opinion they evidently have of my persistent attempts to find suitable singers, and thinking instead of the wellbeing of the Choir, and in particular of this committed young man who wants to make a contribution to the worship commensurate with his musical ability, and yet is for the present relegated to the congregation, whence he can only listen to our imperfect but earnest efforts to give Llandaff the music it deserves, conscious that he could so easily be helping us to carry out our exacting task more worthily. He is no longer a member of the parish choir, and therefore his case needs to be urgently re-assessed so that the cathedral music may continue to prosper.

To set the record straight, and in the hope that the injustice to Michael Steer might be rectified, I took the unprecedented step of sending copies of the correspondence to the Dean and every member of the Chapter individually, with further copies to the Bishop, the Headmaster, and to Gerard Elias in his capacity as the new Chairman of the Choristers' Parents' Association, an organisation which, having done so much work for the Choir in recent months, as I pointed out to the Chapter Clerk, might well like to know what part the Chapter was playing in furthering our choral tradition. Gerard emphasised this aspect in a carefully-worded letter to the Dean, quoting his opinion of Mr Steer as 'the sort of person and singer who would be most welcome' and adding:

> Is this Christian foundation to be subjected to the apparently political whim and wish of individuals, or is indeed 'everybody expected to work together? I urge you in fairness to Mr Steer to reconsider his application so as to permit the boys, who benefit by good example, and the Choir as a whole to further the music of Llandaff.

This was the first time that Gerard Elias acted in my favour, and by no means the last, for he and his wife Elisabeth quickly became a very positive influence for good on the Choir, effectively beginning a new era in its fortunes. As the Association's chairman, Gerard succeeded its founder, Mr Davies, who left a lasting legacy by designing and presenting two substantial silver medallions, to be worn by the two head boys in the choir (one on each side), known in Llandaff as Dean's Scholars.

The services on Easter Day went exceptionally well, and I was pleased to see Harry Gabb, one of my predecessors, in the congregation. A fellow Ilfordian, he had been Organist to the Chapel Royal for twenty years, and I had last seen him at his final appearance with his choir at a Royal Maundy Service when we both played to the Queen in Salisbury Cathedral on my last Thursday as Assistant there in 1974. At the Easter Day evensong David Elias, who had become a junior chorister in May 1981, was invested with one of the medallions, by which time his brother Robert had also joined the ranks. Robert achieved the coveted position eighteen months later, and at the same time their youngest brother James also became a chorister, being eventually Dean's Scholar from January 1988 to July 1989; so for twenty-five successive terms the Elias family held sway. I do not know whether further discussions ensued between Dean and Chapter in response to pressure from Gerard, the Headmaster George Hill and the University chaplain Jeremy Davies, and certainly my own letter received no response from them, but a month later I told the Dean that Michael Steer, who of course had left the parish choir by then, had made formal application for the lay clerkship left vacant by the impending departure of Mr Dickens, whereupon the Dean said simply that he was 'minded' to appoint him. And so it transpired, in due course.

I had not given up the idea of moving to another cathedral, and on the retirement of Clifford Harker from Bristol I retyped my *curriculum vitae* and sent in an application. Those readers who are familiar with the organists' hierarchy may be interested to know whose names were on the shortlist: notably Barry Rose, one of the most highly respected figures in church music, who had been Choirmaster at St Paul's, Ian Little from Coventry, Jonathan Rennert from St Michael's Cornhill in the City of London, Alan Spedding who had gone to Beverley Minster in 1974 and remained there until 2009, and two assistant organists, James Lancelot from Winchester and Malcolm Archer from Norwich. The winner was Malcolm Archer, on the second leg of a distinguished career leading eventually to St Paul's. I remember hearing that two notable figures in the world of church music were born on the same day in 1916, namely Bernard Rose, one of my tutors and responsible for the music of Magdalen College Chapel, and Douglas Guest, organist (after Salisbury and Worcester Cathedrals) of Westminster Abbey. I mention it at this juncture because of a similar happening in

1983, when on the 49th anniversary of Elgar's death, (23rd February) the conductor Sir Adrian Boult and the composer Herbert Howells both died – and two weeks later Sir William Walton, whose music included a small but significant number of works for cathedral use, also left this world.

It will be remembered that I had put to the Dean a year in advance the notion that the Choral Society might perform Bach's *St Matthew Passion* in Lent (even perhaps on Palm Sunday). At that time he had banned concerts on all Saturdays in Advent and Lent. I cannot recall what made him reconsider this stance, but in the event we did perform the complete work on the Saturday immediately preceding Passion Sunday, starting at 4 p.m. and allowing Evensong to take place at the usual time before launching into Part 2 at 7.30 – a total of three hours. Pre-eminent among the six soloists, with regard to fee as well as reputation, was the soprano Emma Kirkby, and the part of the Evangelist was taken by that most amiable of tenors, Neil Mackie; the orchestra on this occasion was the Oxford Pro Musica, and the choristers sang the *ripieno* line in the opening chorus from the gallery above the west door. On the same day Rachel, now aged eleven, went to Bath with her string quartet friends to play in a competitive festival, and it was Douglas Guest who awarded them first prize in a class of six instrumental ensembles, so with Marian in the chorus for the Passion we felt the family had had a thoroughly musical day.

On Easter Monday, having persuaded six of the lay clerks that a few days in Holland would be an enjoyable experience, we set off with the boys at 5 a.m. to fly from Cardiff Airport. Terry Dickens had such a wide girth that an extension to his seatbelt had to be provided. Our first day included a lunch cruise on the canals of Amsterdam and visits to a cheese farm and a tulip garden under glass, before settling in at a youth hostel in Ochenburg near the sea. The organ at the Lutherse Kerk in The Hague dates back to the time of Sweelinck in the sixteenth century, and Michael Hoeg and I spent three hours getting used to its quirks. The large wooden stops stuck out at right angles each side of the console, with an action so heavy that two assistants were needed; so when I was playing, Michael and the school's matron were on hand to pull and push the levers – it was more like an old-fashioned signal box than an organ. Moreover, we found that there were two stops which, when drawn, would put the whole organ out of action. We did not understand why this should be, but as a precaution hung a plastic shopping-bag on each as a reminder to keep clear! Another unexpected feature was the short compass of the pedal board, and I had to make some changes to the pedal part of Bach's transcription of a Vivaldi concerto to allow for this. The concert programme was quite heavy-going, consisting of a dozen of our top favourites, which are worth listing:

Zadok the Priest	Handel
Turn thee unto me, O Lord	Boyce
Concerto in D minor	Bach
Insanae et vanae curae	Haydn
Thou, O Lord God (from Let us lift up our heart)	Wesley
A Song of Wisdom (boys)	Stanford
Though I speak with the tongues of men	Bairstow
And I saw a new heaven	Bainton
I was glad when they said unto me..	Parry

Interval

Magnificat in C	BryanKelly
King of glory, King of peace (boys)	Harris
Like as the hart desireth the waterbrooks	Howells
Toccata in B minor	Jackson
Praise ye the Lord	Mathias
And when the builders laid the foundations	Rubbra

Our short tour was promoted by the Hagacantare, a mixed choir whose members my Choral Society had entertained during a visit to Wales, and who formed part of an audience of about two hundred. The next day being free, we all visited the model village at Madurodam, and I took the afternoon off to explore the art galleries and other attractions of Amsterdam. Our last visit was to Noordwijk, where the organ in the gigantic Catholic church was as usual in the west gallery. It was clearly out of the question to sing from the chancel, so we invited the small audience to sit towards the back, with the choir between them and the gallery. It was far from ideal, and even this plan created a significant time-lag so that Michael's accompaniments had to anticipate the choir throughout. I still remember how gloomy he was on the coach afterwards, thinking that the whole concert was unsynchronised, in spite of my assurances that everything sounded fine downstairs – a fact which was confirmed by the live recording that was made. This concert also marked Terry's last appearance with the choir, and I had chosen the very fine bass solo from a long anthem by Samuel Sebastian Wesley as his swansong. It had gone well at The Hague, but on this emotional occasion he briefly took a wrong turning at one point and although he recovered at the next phrase, he must have regretted the error more than I did. The success of the tour was due in no small part to Gerard and Elisabeth, paving the way for others in future years. At the end of the holiday we had an unprecedented total of twenty-two boys, but I was still very worried about the future as far as the dwindling supply of men was concerned. As usual, the Dean and his wife declined my invitation to a lay clerks' dinner at the Fox and Hounds in Llancarfan, when a clock was presented to Mr Dickens, and it was at this time that the remaining 'old stager' Maldwyn Phillips decided to retire in the summer, along with a another younger man. There was, however, a faint glimmer of light at the end of the tunnel, with the prospect of Michael Steer replacing Terry, and Jeremy Davies being available at least as a deputy tenor. Meanwhile I drafted in two former lay clerks when recording Choral Evensong for the BBC (for the first time since 1977), but even then, incredibly, the Dean failed to turn up, leaving his junior clergy in charge.

In April I gave a lunchtime recital at St David's Hall, taking the opportunity to include the Flor Peeters 'Variations on an old Flemish Song' which I had rather timidly avoided at the time of the opening recital. The audience numbered over three hundred, including Ralph Downes, and Roy Massey came over from Hereford to hear it. My RSCM committee arranged our first dinner for the diocese at the Park Hotel in Cardiff, inviting Sir Nicholas Jackson and his pretty wife as our guests of honour. Nicholas, who had inherited his father's baronetcy, was then the organist of St David's Cathedral. I thought that my speech as Chairman, introducing them and outlining their careers and achievements, may have been more interesting than his own contribution, but he was good company. Nicholas's wife is French, and was one of the Bluebell Girls in Paris at the time they met. Marian sat between Nicholas and our friendly old enemy the former Dean Williams, now known by one of the priest vicars as the Dean bloody Emeritus, with apparently only one remaining tooth (thanks to all those Polo mints) and looking more sinister than ever.

My interest in the Llandaff Festival in early June was restricted to a relatively unambitious Choral Society concert consisting of an anthem commissioned from Richard Elfyn Jones and Rossini's jolly Mass with the doubly misleading title *Petite Messe Solennelle* with

Morley Lewis at the harmonium and professional pianists Martin Jones and Richard McMahon, who also contributed Brahms's Variations on a theme of Haydn. It was at a party in the headmaster's garden that Marian and I met his chosen successor John Knapp and his wife Rosemary, who were to become close friends throughout later years and into the next century. On the Sunday William Mathias came to the Festival Eucharist to hear the first liturgical performance in Wales of his *Missa Brevis* and a short, uninteresting anthem specially commissioned from him.

The very next day I began another overseas examining tour, spending the last six weeks of term and a further six of my summer holidays working in Malaysia. After listening to 433 piano candidates in Ipoh, I moved to more congenial surroundings on the lovely island of Penang, staying throughout July at the sumptuous Eastern and Oriental Hotel, with its palm-fringed terrace right by the sea wall, looking out over the Straits of Malacca. My family came out to join me for the whole of their school holidays, including a month in Subang Jaya, not far from Kuala Lumpur.

A hundred and fifty items of post greeted me on arrival home, including notification of Rachel's Distinction in Grade 5 Cello and my election to the Council of the Royal College of Organists, both of which pleased all of us. We also learned that my first Dean, the sarcastic 'J.F.' had passed away, but no move was made to delay his funeral until the Choir returned from holiday, and I decided to boycott it altogether. Within a week I auditioned two excellent men, Neil Evans as a bass and Stephen Challenger as a tenor. As term began, Michael Steer and Stephen Challenger became fully-fledged lay clerks, together with a young man called John Peters. Only nine choristers were left, but I had no fewer than a dozen probationers to call upon, so the prospects were promising. Adrian Heale, who had been a very helpful Choral Society secretary, was succeeded by one of the Cathedral servers, Clive Westwood, who was to prove a very good friend for years to come.

Returning now to the last few months of 1983, I find it pleasing to note that for some unaccountable reason Dean Davies became so friendly that I joyfully listed his actions in turning over of a new leaf in a letter to my parents. Maybe he was pleased with the Selangor pewter plate I had given him as a gift from Malaysia? I recorded that he actually spoke to Marian and myself on the first Sunday of term, called round for a chat a few days later, and at the first choir service welcomed the choir back (from the pulpit). He agreed to the appointment of a third bass, telephoning me only ten minutes after receiving my written request, invited me into the Deanery for sherry, and readily agreed to our making a commercial recording of cathedral music and ordering 500 discs and 500 cassette tapes. After turning up at several weekday evensongs, he came to one of Marian's special lunches with the Knapps and most of the choirmen, seeming quite at ease. All these things are what would, in most other cathedrals, be taken for granted, and that they are worthy of comment here only goes to show how unusual such behaviour was in Llandaff. Friendly relations were also established with John Swindale Nixon, whose inadequacies as Chapter Clerk had wasted so much time in earlier years, but who hosted a convivial lunch party, with the Eliases and his neighbour, Professor Hibberd, Marian's gynaecologist, again to welcome the Knapps, at his modern house opposite the Cathedral's east window. Perhaps the easiest way to describe our social life that autumn is to quote extracts from another letter to my parents which I penned at Rozel Cottage during our half-term break:

> I took Marian to the New Theatre to see an extraordinary play by Peter Shaffer called *Amadeus*, based on the alleged poisoning of Mozart by his rival Salieri. We had two dinner parties two weeks apart, and between them Huw Tregelles Williams took me out to lunch, Jeremy Davies invited both of us to a Michaelmas party at his flat in the Anglican Chaplaincy, and Gerard and Elisabeth Elias had us, the Knapps and Jeremy to a dinner party which went on until nearly 2 a.m. Marian's fortieth birthday coincided with the Judges' Service, followed by sherry with members of the judiciary, *and* the Centenary Service for the Boys' Brigade, *and* our second dinner party.
>
> Three days later we were at Windsor Castle, where Sue Hill entertained us to lunch at the Headmaster's House at St George's School, with a good red wine of 1977 donated by my old acquaintance Graham Smallbone, the Director of Music at Eton. After lunch I was welcomed to my first meeting of the RCO Council by another old friend from Oxford days, Christopher Robinson, who is the current President and who lives in Merbecke's old house within the Castle: others present included Bernard Rose, George Guest, Douglas Guest, John Sanders, David Sanger and Dr William Cole (former Secretary of the Associated Board). After the meeting we changed into evening dress and attended Evensong in the Chapel, followed by sherry in the Chapter Library, where we were introduced to the famous pianist Phyllis Sellick, guest of another organist. It

was but a short walk to the Castle Hotel for the RCO's biennial dinner, attended by about 240 people with broadcaster Richard Baker as the witty and interesting guest speaker. Dinner over, we retired to the Headmaster's very spacious Georgian lounge and drank champagne until nearly midnight, returning to Llandaff in the small hours.

Three days after this we were in Worcestershire, on a choir visit to a village near Evesham called South Littleton, and four days after that Marian and I went to London by train for the Cathedral Organists' Association conference held in the Middle Temple. This was attended by over forty organists including twenty-seven at English cathedrals (two-thirds of the total). We were addressed by the Master of the Temple, then by Ernest Lough, known as 'the boy with the golden voice' when as a treble he made one of the earliest recordings of cathedral music, singing the solos in Mendelssohn's celebrated anthem *Hear my prayer.* Lastly, the Master of the Choristers at the Temple Church, John Birch, gave a very amusing account of his work there.

On Saturday we had the cathedral school's annual Commemoration Day, with the familiar succession of service, sherry party, luncheon and a prizegiving ceremony in the cathedral, with a speech by the aforementioned John Nixon, now the *Custos* (an odd title meaning Chairman of the Governors). I was sitting (doctorally garbed) with the staff, just behind the guest speaker, Sir Cenydd Traherne, who is the Lord Lieutenant and the only Welsh Knight of the Garter. In his speech he mentioned the fine singing he had heard at the recent Judges' Service, and said how fortunate the cathedral was to have such a good choir.

It was after evensong that day that we got away for a holiday at last – the longest real break I've had since Easter. At present I have thirty pupils a week, and Marian has eleven. The latest statistics show that my salary is still £2000 below the average, and £1000 below the next man on the scale – as I have pointed out to the Chapter Clerk. On Sunday we visited Ian and Anne in their new house in Broomy Hill: it is early Victorian and very grand.

Despite all these interesting events, I still felt that my life was overshadowed by the relatively poor deal I was getting from the Dean and Chapter, and in November I appealed to the Dean, explaining that when compared with other cathedral organists who, like me, were provided with a house and had to maintain six or seven services a week, my salary was only 62% of the average. I pointed out that the Deans' Conference, in consultation with the Cathedral Organists' Association, had recommended increasing organists' salaries to the level of a residentiary canon's stipend, which in Wales was then £7544, more than *double* what I was getting. I also felt that with decent remuneration I would have more time to work out more choir tours abroad, and perhaps make more frequent recordings: as it was, I calculated that to make up the shortfall as compared with my colleagues Marian and I had to give five hundred piano lessons a year, which we felt was too much to expect. There were times when choristers' parents may have wondered why there was not more extramural activity, not realising that most of my time had to be spent in other ways in order to maintain my young family. My appeal was again rejected by the finance committee, as was my request for the provision of carpeting for the two flights of stairs at St Mary's: I regarded this as a landlord's responsibility, but was told that it came under the heading of furnishings, for which the occupant was responsible. Even as the Chapter Clerk was typing a letter to this effect, I was typing another to the Dean offering to raise some money for the Cathedral's Restoration Appeal by arranging for the choristers, dressed in cloaks and mortarboards, to collect money in the new St David's Centre, although I had found that this year an edict precluded any actual singing owing to the large numbers of shoppers. Not surprisingly the Dean poured cold water on this idea, in a typed reply of five paragraphs giving his reasons for refusing permission. Once again Gerard Elias took a more positive view and led a group of choristers' parents collecting money from shoppers and raising more than £270, which was craftily divided between the Dean's Appeal and the Choir Association. I reckoned that the visual appeal, if not the voices, of the boys in their mediaeval gear might have doubled the amount collected, which could then have gone straight into the Restoration Fund.

Meanwhile the organ at St David's Hall, recently installed by the Hertfordshire builder Peter Collins, was showing teething problems and actually failed during a concert. This inspired our redoubtable Chapter Clerk, in his other guise as a City Councillor, to suggest to the hall's manager that confidence in the new instrument might be restored by using it for a recording of choral and organ music by the cathedral choir and me. This never came about, but what a pity he did not use his influence to promote the future of the cathedral organ! It was more than twenty years later that he made a move in this direction. Just before Christmas I found time to set out in detail the duties and responsibilities of lay clerks. They had been promised proper contracts at least ten years earlier, and the system needed to be put on an official basis, but once more my request was ignored and the hand-to-mouth system continued to operate. We had a team of eight men, but during the autumn term only nine full-choir services were attended by all of them.

1984

The year 1984, anticipated with some trepidation ever since the publication of George Orwell's eponymous novel, turned out to be relatively strife-free in Llandaff, and in some respects more successful than hitherto. Unfortunately this aspect did not apply to communications between me and the Chapter via its Clerk, Norman Lloyd-Edwards, who by mid-February had failed to reply to any of my letters for a staggering eight weeks. I had been invited to represent the Welsh cathedrals at the fourth biennial meeting of six deans and provosts, six organists and two choir school headmasters in the Jerusalem Chamber at Westminster Abbey, and had asked Norman to provide various pieces of information that might prove useful in the discussions there. Eventually I made an official complaint to the Dean, who must have acted quickly because Norman immediately responded to all my requests – though not always positively. He made it clear that the Chapter felt no obligation to accede to salary levels recommended by a national body, and denied ever having promised that two flats would always be available for lay clerks. He had taken no action regarding lay clerks' contracts, and indeed on that very same day one of our basses, appointed only the previous term, decided, for personal and professional reasons, to quit without warning, even though he had rehearsed the solos allocated to him for the following Sunday's Mozart Mass. With a contract he might well have given three months' notice. We had already lost one promising candidate to Lichfield and were about to lose another to Hereford, where he remained permanently. The next day I was told that the finance committee had decided that advertising for lay clerks 'should be kept to an absolute minimum in view of their expense'. Hence I was unable to present a very rosy picture to the Westminster meeting, but I had canvassed views from my colleagues in the five other Welsh cathedrals, and was able to submit a modest input on their behalf. When the Chapter Clerk eventually got round to drafting a service agreement for lay clerks, it was clear that there were considerable gaps in his knowledge, such as believing that the choir sang Evensong at 6 p.m. on Christmas Eve and Christmas Day, although during my ten years this had never been the case; there was a time when we had to sing the office at 3.30 on Christmas Day, but this practice had ceased in 1979.

In mid-March I was granted a rare audience with the Dean, when I had a list of fourteen items to discuss. In most cathedrals such a meeting is held weekly, but Dean Davies disliked discussion and, as has been noted before, preferred an exchange of letters to ensure he always had the last word: this meant we came face to face hardly more than once a year, apart from the exchange of a few sentences in passing. His fondness for committing his ideas to print has already been mentioned in connection with his regular contributions to the magazine *The Llandaff Monthly.* His propensity for sesquipedalian sentences was never shown to better effect than when discussing the proposal that from Easter 1984 it might be permissible in England for some divorcees to be remarried in church during the lifetimes of their former spouses. He was quick to point out that 'although what the Church of England may or may not decide in this or in any other matter has no authority in the Church in Wales it is most likely that a major change in the Church's marriage discipline in England will, sooner rather than later, be made by the Governing Body of the Church in Wales'. He could have said simply 'Where England goes, Wales will surely follow' but instead he expanded his thesis into a sentence 162 words long:

> In 1977 I suggested that while the promises of lifelong fidelity in marriage made by a man to a woman and a woman to a man are not simply a "declaration of intent" but the expression of a commitment which establishes a relationship which is part of the natural order (like the relationship of a parent to a child, different only in that it is freely chosen by both parties), it is sadly true that many young people enter into marriage with an inadequate understanding of the complete and absolute commitment to one another which their vows clearly express; and so, without going into the question of what constitutes a defective intention or lack of full and free consent to marriage, it might be said that some people are, under the present discipline of the Church in Wales, needlessly deprived of a "church wedding" because they or their new partners in marriage may have had a previous marriage dissolved in the courts.

Perhaps he would have been better suited to the legal profession, or as a university lecturer, but as a clergyman he emerged as a pedantic bore. A rather irritating know-all acting as third verger was given his marching orders shortly afterwards, the Dean evidently sharing my low opinion and referring to him, figuratively rather than literally, and in a rare burst of decanal scorn, as 'Big-Ears'. We were also about to lose our second verger, who was to be ordained in the Exeter diocese; and even the head verger, the quietly affable Ron Roberts, retired half way through Lent after many years' service. Our very pleasant and obliging Irish priest-vicar, Terry Doherty, was about to become the Rector of a Welsh parish, and even my youngest probationer was expelled from school for developing his uniform-slashing and piano-vandalising propensities into the wounding of other boys at knife-point, so with the added departure of several lay clerks we were seeing many changes. I found out that expenditure of the cathedral's music foundation amounted to about a seventh of the total budget, which in view of the primary function of the establishment as a place for worship of the highest artistic merit I did not think excessive. In an effort to make more funds available, the Chapter decided to sell the three-storey building next to mine, known as The Old House, to a developer. I noticed with some chagrin that when it was converted into five flats instead of the original three, the selling price of the largest flat was roughly what the Chapter had received for the whole building, making me wonder why the development had not been carried out before ownership was transferred, eventually making a huge profit for the cathedral. Following the sale, work began on the west front of the cathedral as part of the restoration plan.

On the whole we were now enjoying living in Llandaff, and were certainly well-placed for our children's schools, which were all within ten minutes' walk. However, the thought of spending the next eighteen years there was a daunting prospect, prompting me to apply for a couple of public school posts as well as that of Principal of the Welsh College of Music and Drama and of Watford School of Music, all to no avail. My regular trips to other parts of the country as an examiner made a welcome change, though I had to wait another five years before being sent overseas again.

An innovation prompted by our keen young student bass Michael Steer was the accompaniment of a Mozart Mass by a group of string players (including our daughter Rachel, then aged 12), first on the Sunday quaintly known as Quinquagesima, and again on Trinity Sunday. This was quite possibly the first time in the cathedral's history that a Eucharist had featured a Latin Mass with orchestra, but I doubt whether many were aware of this epoch-making venture. The summer term also saw the making of another record by the Abbey Recording Company, this time of music typically sung at the service of nine lessons and carols on Christmas Eve. An unusual feature of this 12-inch disc was that it was designed to be played at 45 rpm, thereby shortening the number of carols required to fill both sides. The editing of the tapes by Harry Mudd, the doyen of cathedral music recordings, was assisted by Gerard Elias and me at Harry's bungalow in Eynsham – an interesting experience for both of us, as in those days the editing was done with scissors and sticky tape, instead of the sophisticated computerised method developed at a later stage. Although customers of the cathedral shop often enquired about our previous recording of 1980, for some reason which I never understood the shopkeeper did not supply them. Some years later I was instrumental in putting Harry's name forward for the Honours List. I knew that he was held in high regard by other organists, and we all realised what a significant contribution he had made to the archives of the treasure that is cathedral music. The Director of the RSCM took the view that the opinion of a bunch of cathedral organists would not carry much weight, but undaunted by this I contacted Sir David Lumsden, who I knew had worked with Harry Mudd on one of his earliest recordings when he was Organist of New College, Oxford. I felt sure that a word from a knight would carry enough weight, and sure enough, Harry was awarded the MBE shortly afterwards.

In general my life had settled into a regular pattern of teaching, recruiting, examining, meetings, family outings to the seaside, and so on, but one weekend stood out as a remarkable combination of these activities. On the last Saturday of June I took an hour's choir practice, presided at an ordination service lasting two and a half hours, helped Marian with a garden party for all the choristers' parents and went to Howell's School summer fête with her, drove to Oxford together in time for Evensong at Christ Church, and attended a dinner in hall to mark the golden jubilee of their Old Boys' Association, where we met Sir Thomas Armstrong, who had admitted me to the college in 1955 and Marian to the Royal Academy of Music in 1962. Arriving home in the small hours of Sunday, I took charge of two practices and two services as usual, before returning to Oxfordshire with Gerard for the aforementioned work on our new record which extended to Monday, though Monday afternoon saw me back in Llandaff for Evensong followed by the annual 'fayre' on the Cathedral Green forming part of the celebrations for the Festival of St Peter and St Paul, the cathedral's patron saints.

I felt considerably encouraged on receiving one of *three* letters from the Dean the following day, for although the first two were examples of his most convoluted and carefully-expressed reasonings and explanations covering nearly seventy lines of typing, one paragraph in the third letter read:

After last Thursday's Evensong attended by the Woodard Chapter and again on Sunday (as on several other occasions recently) a number of people have spoken with admiration of the Cathedral Choir's singing of the services, and I should be glad if you would tell the men and boys how much their – and, of course, your – work is appreciated. I stress this because I do not want it to be thought that any criticism of your or their work is intended in the other letters that may reach you with this.

I was moved to reply at once in suitably fulsome terms, saying:

I agree absolutely with the various points you make. I greatly appreciate the time and trouble you have taken to explain your policy on various matters, and also your kindness in showing your appreciation of our music in the cathedral.

During the Llandaff Festival the Choral Society celebrated the fiftieth anniversary of Elgar's death by performing in Whit Week his great oratorio *The Kingdom*, with a text drawn mostly from the Acts of the Apostles and telling the story of Pentecost. The schedule did not allow for the usual combined rehearsal on the afternoon of the concert, and instead I had to conduct the BBC Welsh Symphony Orchestra separately, three days earlier and in the studio at Broadcasting House, while Marian was in the cathedral watching an enactment of Britten's church parable *Curlew River*, featuring one of the choristers. The scoring of *The Kingdom* is really quite sumptuous, and requires a full symphony orchestra. This always poses problems of balance, partly because of the amount of space available in front of the chorus, and partly because the number of players can approach the number of singers. Although one can ask the fixer to engage a limited number of string players, instead of the full complement of up to sixty, one cannot reduce numbers any further if the composer demands triple woodwind plus four horns, full brass, tympani and sometimes a harp and extra percussion. Even with only forty strings the total number of players can still easily exceed sixty, which can seem quite daunting to a chorus of a hundred amateur singers, used to rehearsing with only piano accompaniment. Reducing the strings still further but keeping the normal ratio within the section can result in tilting the balance within the orchestra itself towards the brass, with only a little reduction in the volume of sound assailing the singers' ears, especially as it is these instruments that are often placed just in front of them. Added to the lack of a combined rehearsal, it was not surprising that the critics in three newspapers mentioned the problem, while praising other aspects including the four soloists Miriam Bowen, Penelope Walker, William Kendall and Michael George, all well-known figures in the concert world. The audience loved it, recalling us three times to the platform.

It used to be said that professional players were inclined to look down on the inexperience of part-time conductors like me, sometimes making life difficult for them in rehearsal, but I am glad to say I never experienced this myself, especially with the BBC members with whom I mostly worked. I was trained to read an orchestral score of up to thirty staves, and the musicians were obviously aware of this. I reckoned that if I observed the composer's directions to the letter (and Elgar's music is liberally sprinkled with instructions showing subtle nuances of dynamics and tempo) while noticing when a particular player or group had to come in after a long stretch of rests and bringing them in with a suitable gesture, no more was expected of me in a single three-hour rehearsal which might be little longer than the concert itself. They knew my limitations compared with full-time professional conductors, and so did I. I showed them that I knew what I was doing, while avoiding any pretence. Occasionally in a rehearsal an experienced player might miss an entry – possibly to see whether I would notice. At a suitable break I would find a way to mention the omission in such a way that he would not feel humiliated in front of his colleagues, yet without appearing to be a clever-dick myself, for example by saying something such as 'bass clarinet, you will be with me tonight, won't you?'

At quite short notice I was brought in to play the organ at two other Festival concerts, the first and the last. The first was at St David's Hall, with the Northern Sinfonia under Richard Hickox in a Handel anthem and Fauré's Requiem, and the other was to accompany a famous Welsh choir from Pontarddulais. The cheque resulting from these concerts more than covered the cost of a luxurious new rose-coloured carpet to cover the whole of the hall, stairs and landing from top to bottom of our house. Another notable Festival event was a recital by the Russian-American double bass virtuoso, Gary Karr in the hall of Howell's School. His instrument, an Amati made in 1611, was said to be the oldest and most valuable in the world, and at that time he could only afford to insure it for a quarter of a million dollars.

Easter occurred late this year – on 22 April – so the choir holiday preceded it. This happened on average every two years, so the choir had to miss Palm Sunday and not return until Maundy Thursday. Somehow with very little time for preparation this year we managed to produce the goods, so to speak, for the services on Good Friday, Easter Eve and Easter Day, continuing into the summer term two days later. The Easter morning Eucharist was sung exceptionally well, I thought, to Mozart's Mass in D, and ending with Haydn's joyful *Te Deum*.

On learning that our good tenor Stephen Challenger had moved to Hereford, the Dean actually agreed to reserve the first floor of a house opposite ours for his replacement. His decision was fully justified by an application from a top professional, Brian Burrows, whom I met at a concert and supper to say farewell to the retiring principal of the Welsh College of Music and Drama, Dr Raymond Edwards. Brian had just been appointed the college's Head of Vocal Studies, and was a singer of international standing. I already knew that he had been a choral scholar at St John's College, Cambridge, and a lay vicar at Salisbury Cathedral, but was amazed to read a list of his triumphs in concert halls and opera houses throughout Europe, singing Bach Passions in Switzerland, Sweden and Belgium, recitals in Austria, Italy and Portugal, Britten's *War Requiem* in Warsaw, the same composer's *Serenade for Tenor, Horn and Strings* in Israel, Elgar's *Dream of Gerontius* with Janet Baker at the Royal Festival Hall, Beethoven's *Missa Solemnis* in France, Mozart opera in Glyndebourne, Kodály's *Psalmus Hungaricus* at the Three Choirs Festival and Stravinsky's *Oedipus Rex* at a Royal Albert Hall promenade concert. I was vastly impressed, and welcomed him with open arms. Even more good luck came in the form of the Revd Jeremy Davies, then Chaplain to the university and colleges of Cardiff, who now became our other regular tenor. So we were to have a Cambridge graduate on both sides of the choir, both provided with accommodation: this was the beginning of one of the best years in my time at Llandaff. Much good feeling was also engendered by a very successful Flower Festival which attracted thousands of visitors and raised over ten thousand pounds for the Restoration fund. This was easily the most successful event ever staged there, the cathedral being thronged with people, heaving about shoulder to shoulder trying to see all the flower arrangements, which had been set up by various clubs in the diocese.

The summer holiday began at Rozel Cottage and with some fine sunny weather at Dunraven Bay, when I was lucky to be invited to fly to Guernsey for an examining session lasting ten days. I made the most of the sunshine by going down to a beach before breakfast on several mornings, and by taking the hydrofoil to Alderney on my day off, hiring a bicycle and riding all round the island. It was very pretty, but I was conscious of a rather sinister atmosphere created by the WWII fortresses built by the Germans to deter an invasion. A rather less enjoyable experience that summer was a Promenade concert comprising the first performance in Europe of Michael Tippett's latest work, *The Mask of Time,* scored for chorus and orchestra with enormous forces. I sat with my old friend Graham Houghton, and it was the ugliest and most unpleasant work I have ever experienced; indeed I have not heard of any subsequent performance of it, though I suppose there must have been one or two.

Returning to Cardiff I participated in the annual congress of the Incorporated Association of Organists, a kind of umbrella body to which are affiliated most of the organists' associations in Britain. Its president was the international recitalist Nicholas Kynaston, who had persuaded me, somewhat against my will, to learn several movements of Messiaen's organ suite *Messe de la Pentecôte* in which some of the writing features adaptations of the birdsongs which the composer painstakingly transcribed. It was difficult to learn, and not well suited to the Llandaff organ; I thought it should have been played by Nicholas himself, since it was almost certainly in his repertory, but in the event I had to play it as part of the Congress Eucharist, which was sung to a unison setting by the delegates themselves, under the direction of Malcolm Archer (later Organist of St Paul's). When an account of the Congress appeared later in the *Organists' Review* my contribution was not mentioned, so perhaps not even the listeners appreciated it. More relaxing was my proposal of a toast to the guests at the congress dinner, when I managed to flatter the Dean and get some good laughs within a few minutes.

Several months had passed since I first noticed something odd happening to the little finger of my right hand. At first my doctor failed to recognise the condition, but Gerard had put me in touch with Mr David Jenkins, an eminent surgeon well known in the profession for his work on hands, who had diagnosed a condition known as Dupuytren's Contracture. This complaint is said to be hereditary, but it was only later that I heard that it had affected one of my mother's cousins. It involves the hardening of hand tissue and the gradual contraction of one or more fingers, on either hand or both. By September the finger was decidedly bent at its middle joint, and just two days before term, I had an appointment at the Prince of Wales Hospital near Cardiff to have it straightened. The operation, under general anaesthetic, was performed by Mr Jenkins himself. I was unconscious for about an hour and twenty minutes, and three hours later the family arrived to take me home. The following day, with my right arm in a sling, I still taught five piano pupils, and two days later took the first choristers' practice of term, assisted by Michael Hoeg at the piano. I conducted the first Saturday Evensong, attended by a congregation of sixty, at which I had to use my left hand, of course, and a few days later one of the clergy noticed that a psalm we were singing included the topical verse 'Why holdest thou thy right hand in thy bosom?' The Dean said nothing, though he did later mention my plight in *The Llandaff Monthly.* Evensong the following Saturday attracted a congregation of three hundred, but only because it included the installation of two new canons. When I returned to hospital for the removal of fourteen stitches, nothing was said about physiotherapy, and it was only six weeks later, when someone I met in the pub expressed concern, that I sought another appointment with the surgeon. He sent me at once to see the senior physiotherapist for instant treatment, whereupon a course of almost daily sessions was laid on for me. In the next few years the condition gradually returned, and I sometimes wondered whether a much earlier start to restorative treatment of this kind might have prevented this. It was interesting, but hardly consoling, to discover that both Margaret Thatcher and President Reagan suffered the same complaint.

An important event for the Church in Wales around this time was the introduction of a revised Book of Common Prayer. The book was largely based on the English version dating back to 1662, but certain changes were made in the early sixties, and more were introduced into this new edition. As far as Evening Prayer was concerned, a notable difference occurred in the Versicles and Responses, sung alternately by Priest Vicar and Choir. For centuries these have included petitions for the well-being of the monarch, the clergy and the people, in that order:

> O Lord, save the Queen/King
>> And mercifully hear us when we call upon thee
> Endue thy ministers with righteousness
>> And make thy people joyful
> O Lord, save thy people
>> And bless thine inheritance

The Monarch is the Supreme Governor of the Church of England, but not of the Church in Wales, where the editors of the Welsh prayer book decided to put themselves first and the Queen last – even after 'thy people'. This was petty enough in itself (for is Wales not part of the Kingdom?), but it caused some difficulty with the various musical settings used in cathedrals, composed mostly in the sixteenth, seventeenth and twentieth centuries, because in some cases altering the order of the text upset the natural flow of the harmonies. But more inconvenient still was the alteration of some of the actual words: the next petition, originally

> Give peace in our time, O Lord
>> Because there is none other that fighteth for us, but only thou, O God.

was shortened by the Church in Wales to

> Give peace in our time, O Lord,
>> And evermore mightily defend us.

It might be thought that this is a better balanced response, but of course it did not fit the musical settings composed for the original version. I solved this problem by writing to all the living composers and asking them to compose a new setting for this shorter response, but the Dean refused to pay a fee to any of them. Bernard Rose said he would be happy to accept a crate of whisky, but I'm afraid that was not forthcoming either. Only Richard Lloyd, organist of Durham Cathedral and obviously a traditionalist, refused, though he gave me permission to make an adaptation, as of course I had to do for all the settings by the earlier composers.

Other radical changes concerned the collects. A collect is a prayer constructed in a particular way: it first addresses God, usually specifically in the person of the Father or the Son, then ascribes to him some more or less relevant attribute, before presenting a single petition; this usually ends with the words 'through Jesus Christ our Lord' – rather as in a secular meeting one might make a request 'through the Chairman'. Some of the collects end with what is known as a doxology, on the lines of 'who with Thee and the Holy Ghost art one God, ever world without end'. In Llandaff it was the custom to add these words to every collect, whether printed or not, but this does not seem to be common practice elsewhere. The second and third collects at Evensong are always the same, but the first is chosen according to the liturgical calendar, one for each Sunday and the ensuing weekdays.

The Welsh prayer book jumbles them all up, so that in most cases they are no longer appointed to their traditional Sundays. I have never heard the reason for this, and have always assumed that the changes were made just to be different from the English rite. Evensong always includes an anthem, which is a setting of a religious text either from the Bible or from a suitable poem of later provenance. A few anthems are settings of collects, and I used to ensure that such anthems were sung in the appropriate week, so it was slightly irritating to find that these age-old associations had been broken.

Much more serious, however, was the decision to avoid using the archaic version of the second person singular pronoun and adjective customarily used to address the Deity, namely *Thou, Thine* and *Thy.* Because the second phrase of a collect is always subordinate to the first, this immediately caused problems, since one could no longer use the archaic form of the verb either, for example thou *dost* and *thou seest.* The modern version of these phrases would be *you do* and *you see.* So far, so good, but using a relative clause like *O God, who seest that we put not our trust in anything that we do* sounds awkward when changed to *God, who see that we put not....* Some English versions have tried to avoid this linguistic problem by avoiding a subordinate clause, making *O God; you see that we put not....* which is only a little less awkward, but the Welsh prayerbook opted for a third-person verb when addressing the Almighty in the second person, thus: *God, who sees that we put not our trust in anything that we do.* One is tempted to add a question mark, for that is how it sounds. The doxology is eminently vulnerable to this treatment, for having begun the collect by addressing Jesus in the second person and in the vocative case as 'Lord', one would have expected it to end 'who livest and reignest with the Father and the Holy Spirit, world without end'. In an attempt to dispense with verbs ending in *-est* and *-eth* the editors would need to substitute 'who live and reign', but in fact they settled instead for 'who lives and reigns', which takes the clause into the third person. One brave vicar dared to point this out in a letter to *The Welsh Churchman,* and when the controversy reached the centre page of *The Times* the Dean responded in his own magazine by making lame excuses, saying

> This was a matter to which the Liturgical Commission gave much time and thought, and those who adopted the "purist" stance were swayed by others whose day-to-day teaching of English in the class room and lecture theatre had made them quite certain about what acceptable usage is, even

if it does not conform to strict grammatical rules.

In my view it would have been far better to retain the archaic words for the sake of the elegant and well-respected prose of Cranmer's original, instead of drawing the attention of those who are aware of such things to the faulty grammar. As it was, the clergy achieved only an unfortunate mish-mash, which savoured both of 'dumbing down' and throwing out the baby with the bathwater.

An essential ingredient of Evensong has always been the singing of one or more psalms to precede a reading from the Old Testament. For more than a century it has been the custom to fit each couple of verses into a kind of hymn tune known as a chant, consisting of a sequence of twenty chords in an unchanging pattern of 4+6+4+6. But unlike a hymn, which is written in verse with its own regular metre, the psalms (as translated from the original Hebrew by Bishop Coverdale at the Reformation) have no regular metre, but lines of variable length. Many editions have been published over the years, using a system of dashes and dots to indicate how to fit the words to the notes – a device known as pointing. The Anglican church has in recent years adapted Coverdale's version in the interests of accuracy and modern scholarship, necessitating the revision of pointing to match. The version appended to the Welsh prayer book was designed to be easy for congregational singing, by allocating several words to the first note of each section (known historically as the reciting note), and only one syllable to each of the other notes. I was certainly not the first organist to find that this was not an ideal distribution of syllables, and in fact there are various editions of the original text which allow a trained choir to spread out the text in a more artistic way. This had not been done with the new text, and every so often, following my initiative from 1982, I would invent and type out a different pointing for the choir's use, based on a method established in *The Oxford Psalter,* gradually assembling my new versions in ring-binders. I mention this as an example of work done behind the scenes to enhance the worship in a quite subtle way.

The cathedral lay clerks, over the years, were a very pleasant bunch, and after the full practice, at first on Thursdays and later on Tuesdays, usually followed by an extra half hour for the men only, we would normally meet in one of three nearby pubs, first the Butcher's Arms and later for many years at the Black Lion, where the beer was thought to be better. One or two of the men were less congenial, notably a young man not long out of school who sang with us for some time as a tenor. With the advent of two first-rate tenors, and a new choral scholar, at the start of the autumn term, I told this chap that I could not continue to offer him regular work as a tenor, but I was able to offer him an alternative. In the politest way I wrote:

> I should be pleased if you would kindly consider another possibility, which is to sing alto instead. You seemed to deal very effectively with an alto part when someone was absent last term, and if you feel you could cope with this on a regular basis, i.e. on the same understanding as hitherto, I would be prepared to take you on as an "alto singing-man" for an experimental term.... I mentioned this idea to the Dean a few weeks ago, and would be glad to have your reaction within a few days. If you decide against the plan I have outlined, would you still be prepared to make yourself available as a "reserve" tenor, or alto, in the same way as Michael Davidson?

Michael had taken leave of absence for the foreseeable future when his daughter was born, and I had adopted the term 'singing-man' to designate men who were available to sing only some of the five services a week which the lay clerks sang in return for a small salary. These reserves and deputies were paid per service, without the obligation to attend every one. I explained how the alto part would, like the tenor, be shared between three young men, two on one side and one on the other. I was quite taken aback by the reply I received eighteen days later, which read:

> I certainly don't appreciate your notion that I can be moved around like a piece of furniture after almost three years of consistently good service to you and the Cathedral Choir. While I have been quite prepared to help out on occasion by singing alto parts when desperately needed, as you know, I have a natural tenor voice which I strain by singing other parts. I find it quite preposterous that you suggest I try singing the alto part on a regular basis, and I'm sure that any regularly singing musician would react similarly. Effectively as I deal with sight-singing other parts, I have no intention whatever of placing that strain on my voice on a regular basis. I would suggest that you find your alto from wherever your two tenors were found. Neither am I interested in your offer of "reserve" tenor. I have however told the Dean that I am quite prepared for my name and telephone number to be passed on to any successor of yours upon his/her appointment, to which time I look forward to giving my services to the Dean and Chapter once more.

He went on to demand a term's fees in lieu of notice. It seemed extraordinary to me that a young fellow could respond so rudely to a polite request, but I had a good complement of men in the choir, and could well do without him. I remembered a previous occasion when we were rehearsing a very fine Latin verse anthem by Purcell, *Jehova quam multi sunt hostes mei.* At one point I asked for a *crescendo*, whereupon this callow youth blurted out 'the composer hasn't marked a *crescendo!*' Spencer Basford, an alto, rejoined, 'Purcell didn't know any morons like you!' Had the tenor known anything about seventeenth-century composition, he would have realised that Purcell and his contemporaries did not use such indications, but left matters of interpretation to the person directing the choir. He was unaware that I had written a thesis on that period in preparation for my doctorate, and had studied Purcell's actual autograph manuscript of this very work in the British Museum Library. He was not to know that he would have to wait more than fifteen years to re-apply to my successor, by which time both the Dean and *his* successor had retired. Alas, in the following century he was re-appointed by my successor before I had time to explain the earlier situation.

Shortly afterwards I was nominated by the Royal College of Organists as their examiner for the rarely-awarded diploma known as the ADCM, the Archbishop of Canterbury's Diploma in Church Music. Only FRCOs who had also gained the Choirmaster's Diploma (CHM), and were communicant members of the Church of England, were eligible to sit the examinations. There were three papers and three examiners, the others being nominated by the Royal School of Church Music and the Archbishop himself. I had received the diploma from Archbishop Ramsey in 1963 at Lambeth Palace; it had seemed a great honour at the time, and I was even more delighted to become one of the examiners. An important part of it was the study of liturgy from the first Book of Common Prayer of 1549 to the present, including the 1928 Prayerbook (which, though partly used, had never received the assent of Parliament). This paper demanded much detailed study, and the same could be said of the papers on church music and a special topic chosen by the candidate. With the issue of the Alternative Service Book in 1980 its scope became even wider, and the diploma was later awarded in alternate years by the Roman Catholic Archbishop of Westminster, with a corresponding omission of the reference to Canterbury in its title.

The Choral Society was invited to join forces with the University Choir and Cardiff Bach Choir the following spring in a performance of Walton's dramatic oratorio *Belshazzar's Feast*, so we began learning it well in advance, while also preparing to sing Bach's *Magnificat* and

Britten's cantata *Saint Nicolas* with Brian Burrows in the title role. The chorus at that time had seventy women and forty men, including fourteen tenors, so I considered myself lucky.

When attending the RCO Council meeting in London I took a rare opportunity to make a lightning visit to my parents in Ilford. My mother, already confined to her bed on her eightieth birthday in May, was now very ill, adding exfoliate eczema to her other aches and pains, and I agreed with her brother that she should be admitted to Wanstead Hospital, where she stayed for at least a fortnight. Meanwhile my own finger operation prevented me from playing the organ until November, so that when Princess Anne attended the annual service for Seafarers, I had to be content to watch her arrival from my front window. I was still able to address the occasional meeting of my local organists' association and those of Swansea to the west and Newport to the east, and the half-term holiday was spent in our cottage, as usual, when I found time to read through some of the letters I had kept since the sixties, including a bundle from my former teenage girlfriend Mary Wilcock, whom I had not seen since 1966 and would not see again until well after my retirement. I was wondering whether to apply for the post of organist at St Edmundsbury Cathedral, where an acquaintance had resigned over a dispute with his Dean about the merits of girl choristers, but at the age of 47 I thought it unlikely that I would succeed, and in fact the man appointed, Paul Trepte, was only thirty. One of my most respected advisers had advised me against applying, anticipating vacancies at Salisbury and Christ Church Oxford, where in both cases I had been assistant organist in the past. Meanwhile my assistant Michael Hoeg had a shot at a similar job in Hereford, but as far as I am aware he never tried anywhere else, and he was still working in Llandaff well into the twenty-first century.

I managed to conduct 280 singers in the annual RSCM Diocesan Festival, in early November, resumed playing the organ for the first time for four months, and took the cathedral choir to Lampeter College in West Wales for one of its very few actual concerts. I think I shared the view of the men that their five public performances each week were quite enough for them to cope with, and except for the occasional service at a church in our own diocese, we were not prepared to sing elsewhere unless offered reasonable fees. On Remembrance Day we sang Vaughan Williams's remarkable and very appropriate setting of the psalm *Lord, thou hast been our refuge.* The last part of it features the well-known tune *St Anne,* long associated with the hymn *O God, our help in ages past*, but instead of having the choir singing it, the composer continues with other words and other music while the melody is played by a solo trumpet. It so happened that one of our new tenors, the American Bill Bokerman, was also a passable trumpeter, so at my behest he smuggled his instrument into the choir stalls before the service (or perhaps under his surplice) and put it to his lips just in time to play the solo part. I thought the effect quite dramatic, but it was not mentioned to me afterwards by any of the congregation, who (if they noticed anything) probably assumed it was played on an organ stop, which indeed is the other way of doing it. My attendance at the Cathedral Organists' conference soon afterwards in Chelmsford enabled me to visit my mother in an Essex hospital, finding her health much improved.

Rachel's first opportunity to play her 'cello in a county Youth Orchestra concert occurred at St David's Hall in late November, and on the following day, being Advent Sunday, I conducted the annual processional service, often known as the Advent Carol Service, though in fact most of the choir items are proper anthems. The service traditionally begins just inside the west door, with the cathedral in darkness except for the candles carried by the choir. This aspect was not quite so effective at Llandaff, as the service replaced the 3.30 Evensong, but as the choir moved in very slow stages down the nave, lessons were read and anthems sung as the lights were progressively switched on until we reached the high altar. This was the only occasion when the Choir entered the sanctuary, and at that point we always sang Herbert Howells's lovely anthem *A spotless rose is blowing* before the final very slow recession westwards singing that very stately hymn *Lo! He comes with clouds descending.* The service always made a big impression on the capacity congregation who attended, arriving up to an hour early to secure their seats. I had first experienced the ceremony in my time at Salisbury Cathedral, when I sat at the console and heard those distant voices a hundred yards west intoning Palestrina's magical responses to the opening plainsong '*I look from afar, and lo, I see a cloud coming...*' I used to count off the number of years I had heard it, and continued to do so in Llandaff. This was my eighteenth year all told, and I had mixed feelings as I anticipated the remaining seventeen until my retirement; as it turned out, there would be for various reasons only fourteen, as we shall see – but that was quite enough!

Only four days into Advent the six top choristers found themselves providing Christmas carols for a rather posh 'county' party at the home of one Forbes Hayes, brother of the High Sheriff, who provided a dinner for the guests to raise money for the Red Cross. The boys and I were expected to enter by the tradesmen's entrance and have a separate supper in the kitchenrand piano, and by special request I played Chopin's *Fantasy-Impromptu* and that dramatic salon piece by Chaminade called *Automne* which my father used to play when I was a boy. Later in the evening I had to play suitable background music on a small chamber organ in another room, while the guests were chatting so loudly to each other that I doubt if my pieces were heard at all.

St David's Hall was getting into its stride as the major entertainment venue in South Wales, and among its offerings we saw that funniest of all entertainers, the Danish comedian and pianist Victor Borge, and a remarkable performance by the London Symphony Orchestra of Mahler's Second Symphony conducted by a millionaire businessman called Gilbert Kaplan. He was fulfilling his long-held ambition to conduct this work, and had made a thorough study of it, taking lessons from several of the world's finest conductors. He then secured engagements with the world's finest orchestras, and was acclaimed wherever he went. This symphony takes up a whole concert, and the final movement features two female singers and a large chorus. Towards the end, the chorus suddenly stands for the climactic apotheosis, creating a thrilling effect, and never before or since have I seen an audience at a symphony concert rise from their seats for a tumultuous standing ovation lasting for six minutes.

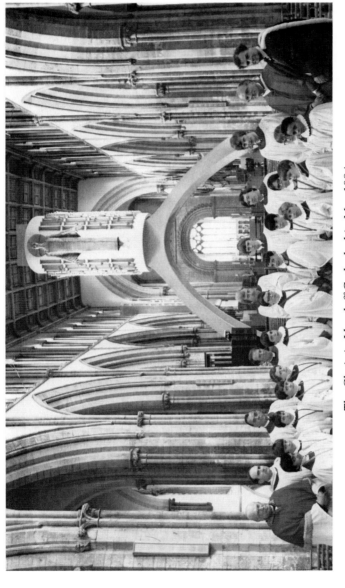

The Choir in Llandaff Cathedral in May 1984

Back row: The Very Rev Alun Davies, Michael Hoeg. Lay clerks: Ralph Lock, Rev Jeremy Davies, Spencer Basford, John Peters, Stephen Challenger; Michael Steer: Dr Michael Smith, headmaster John Knapp. Choristers: Bobby Sastry, David Cantrell, Robert Williams, Robert Hooke, David Howard-Jones, Robert Elias, David Elias and Geraint John (Dean's Scholars), Ceri Morris, Julien Sweeting, Stephen Hurn, Rhodri Crookes, Ceri Evans, Dan Edwards

Photography by the late David Mathias

185

Our annual garden party and lunch for choristers' parents, July 1985
Gerard Elias QC, standing second from right, is talking to a boy's father

The author steels himself to play the gong in Walton's 'Belshazzar's
Feast', St David's Hall, February 1985

To Michael with kind regards

The Rt. Hon. The Lord Mayor of the City of Cardiff,
(Councillor Captain Norman Lloyd-Edwards,
O.St.J., R.D.*, LL.B., D.L., R.N.R.).

*Captain Norman Lloyd-Edwards, Chapter Clerk, in ceremonial dress
as Lord Mayor of Cardiff, May 1985*

1985

In 1985 I became an examiner for the paperwork of the Associates' diploma of the Royal College of Organists (ARCO). This meant sitting in the Council Room of the College's rather grand Victorian building overlooking the Royal Albert Hall, with two other Council members, scrutinising the candidates' work. After marking several examples of the same question, we would divide the scripts into three and each mark that question, occasionally comparing notes or asking for a second opinion. That done, we would move on to the next question, and so on. Our work was somewhat hampered by the sound of the practical examinations on the organ in the room above: most of the written exercises involved writing music in the style of a particular period, for example to complete a passage (given the opening bars) of a motet by the sixteenth century composer Palestrina, add a number of bars to some two-part counterpoint by Bach, or write in the style of a Haydn string quartet; the candidates had to carry out these tasks without recourse to any musical instrument, and in the same way their examiners were required to read what they had written and assess it entirely by ear. To do this against a background of organ music from above, however faint, simply made our work more difficult, yet the situation was never changed. As a new examiner, I felt duly honoured to find Dr William Cole in the chair, for he had appointed me as an examiner to the Associated Board sixteen years earlier, and had examined me in Grade 2 piano twenty-three years before that! Moreover, the second examiner was Dr Arthur Pritchard, whose signature had been inscribed on my own ARCO diploma thirty years earlier, and it was a real pleasure to add mine next to his on the new diplomas awarded to this year's successful candidates.

Three days later I was in London again, secretly rather proud to be sharing the company of the international recitalist Nicolas Kynaston and Stephen Cleobury of King's College Cambridge at a Council meeting of the Incorporated Association of Organists. This is a kind of umbrella organisation for the many amateur organists' associations around Britain. I had been appointed liaison officer for South Wales, and it fell to me to report on the moribund state of associations in that country. The editor of *Organists' Review* evidently liked my style, for he slipped me a note asking me to contribute a 2000-word article for the magazine on Teaching the Organ. Since my approach had always been pragmatic rather than based on principles, I did not pursue this idea, thinking that the students I had helped to gain organ scholarships in three Oxford colleges and two at Cambridge would have done well anyway, and in some cases had come to me either to gain prestige or simply because there was no other suitable teacher around.

At home, two concerts were of special interest, for Rachel at the age of thirteen played her 'cello with the County Youth Orchestra in Mahler's First Symphony at the end of a three-day course, and one of my choristers, Stephen Hurn, sang the treble solo 'Walking in the Air' in an early performance of Howard Blake's work *The Snowman* at St David's Hall, with the added interest that the conductor turned out to be one Anthony Randall, a former college boyfriend of Marian's. The RSCM picked out our recording of Christmas carols as one of the top four issues of 1984, and fourteen boys attended our January voice trial. The choir was filmed for an HTV series, recording five anthems for five programmes, and we recorded a choral evensong for transmission by the BBC on St David's Day. One of the choristers, an Indian boy called Bobby Sastry, reached the finals of a national competition for cathedral singers under eleven, and to cap it all we took the boys to Nantes, Cardiff's twin city in north western France, to participate for a few days in the International Festival of Youth Choirs.

On our way to France we stayed in Windsor Castle, by invitation of George Hill who had moved from our own school to be head of St George's. On arrival at the Conservatoire in Nantes we soon found that the other sixteen choirs from all over Europe were bigger and older than our little bunch of small boys, mostly consisting of about forty buxom teenage girls, but our four anthems evidently made an impression, because we received a certificate indicating a second place, the overall winner being the Bulgarian Radio Youth Choir. It had been arranged that each choir would give a concert in the locality, and ours was in a large church in the ancient walled town of Guérande, where we sang eighteen items, interspersed with organ pieces by Couperin and others, before an audience of about two hundred. I was staying with our headmaster John Knapp and my assistant Michael Hoeg at the home of the lady Mayor of Guérande, who persuaded me to submit to being interviewed before breakfast at a local radio station, to promote the concert. On reaching the studio, which was no bigger than a petrol filling station, I found the news reader already delivering his bulletin, and I became aware that (contrary to my request) there was no time for preparation, and indeed without so much as an introduction he turned to me with his first question. I managed to muster enough French to answer about five questions satisfactorily, my only gaffe being to use the anachronistic term *les gentilhommes* when referring to the men of the choir instead of the *les messieurs*: my A-level course had perhaps concentrated too much on historic literature. Before returning home, Michael and I took the opportunity to return to Nantes to see its grand cathedral, meet the organist Félix Moreau and play the organ there.

The spring conference of the Cathedral Organists' Association was in Hereford, which gave us the opportunity to invite Canterbury Cathedral's organist, our friend Allan Wicks and his wife Elizabeth to stay at our cottage just down the road. They were a very pleasant couple, and Allan seemed enthusiastic about my prospects for promotion, including the vacancy at Durham Cathedral, one of the most desirable posts in England. He recommended me unreservedly and declared himself 'shocked and horrified' when I was not invited for interview. On phoning Durham to find out why, he was told that my name, and that of another cathedral organist, had been taken off the shortlist, in favour of someone who had not actually applied. He said that all my references were 'very good indeed', but that it was felt I already had a very full career, and that they should appoint someone who had not already achieved so much. I knew the name of my former boss Richard Seal was on the list, along with that of Roy Massey, but apparently Richard made a bad impression by giving his reason for applying that it was time for Salisbury to have a change. The Chapter evidently wanted a younger man with a fresher and more active approach and, passing over our colleagues at Rochester and Southwark Cathedrals, appointed the Sub-Organist of Winchester, James Lancelot, who had a First at Cambridge and superb references: he is still there as I write, nearly twenty-four years later. This was another example of the appointment of an assistant, rather than the promotion of someone already in charge. Durham is a very long way north, and in truth I was now finding life very pleasant in Llandaff, the house and our cottage being major assets. Moreover, my persistence for more than two years had eventually resulted in the provision of a new pension fund, the Chapter paying an annual premium calculated at 10% of my salary. This in fact turned out to be a hollow promise, because in subsequent years and right up to my retirement the premium remained static, however much my salary increased. Of course I could not have foreseen this, but in any case the limitations of the cathedral as a building, its organ and its clergy, did give me an incentive to seek something grander, even though at the age of 48 I was clearly at a disadvantage and becoming increasingly unlikely to move.

It so happened that on the very day that Richard Seal was being interviewed in Durham, his assistant Colin Walsh was being appointed organist of St Albans Cathedral. In spite of my earlier association there with the International Organ Festival, I found both the building and its organ rather austere, and knew that the full choir sang only at weekends, so I had not applied for the post. I began to turn my attention to another vacancy, at Lincoln Cathedral, where the Dean was known as an eccentric aristocrat, rejoicing in the name of the Honourable Oliver Twistleton-Wykeham-Fiennes. When that opportunity arose in October, the advisers were two of the most eminent organists I knew, Dr George Guest of St John's Cambridge, whom I had invited to be our next Festival Director and had been very complimentary about my choir, and Dr Francis Jackson of York Minster, who had known all about me since my very first job in Yorkshire. The man appointed was again an assistant organist, this time David Flood from Canterbury who, according to George was not recommended by 'any of the musicians', though my own references were again pronounced entirely satisfactory, the Dean having written very fully. This time only one cathedral organist had been put on the shortlist, the others being assistants. It looked as if I was stuck at Llandaff for another seventeen years, and I rather feared that I might lose Michael Hoeg to Windsor Castle, where the assistant at St George's Chapel had committed suicide by jumping out of a castle window: his body was found by Headmaster George Hill (formerly of Llandaff) who I felt sure would like to have Michael as his director of music - if he could persuade Christopher Robinson to accept him as his assistant. I need not have worried – Michael remained at Llandaff until 2010.

The Choral Society participated in an exciting joint venture in February, when we were invited by the University to join with their choir and orchestra and the Cardiff Bach Choir in a performance at St David's Hall of Walton's splendid work *Belshazzar's Feast*. An unusual incident happened during the final rehearsal, which was interrupted by the arrival on stage of a woman in police uniform who approached the conductor Clifford Bunford. The assembled musicians listened with bated breath and heard her tell him that his car had been stolen. She handed her hat to one of the players, and shortly afterwards her tunic as well. As we gaped with growing astonishment, she proceded to take off her blouse and then her bra, as it dawned on everyone that this was a strippagram fixed up by some of the students. To his credit, Clifford saw the joke and was persuaded to strip to the waist, whereupon there was some squirting of shaving cream as their chests touched, and the lady read out what I believe was a birthday greeting. It was certainly an unexpected diversion. I had been asked to play the organ part in the choral work, but I had other ideas. I knew that this instrument was insufficiently powerful to be heard against the full power of a symphony orchestra, so I offered instead to play the gong, which features prominently, especially in the great concluding paean of praise where the gong is struck eight times at regular intervals. I was also allocated the 'anvil' part, which illustrates the words 'Praise ye the god of iron', though instead of having an actual anvil I struck the frame of the gong with a metal stick, creating a similar effect to the real thing. I really enjoyed myself, and thought the audience must have been surprised when at the end of the performance I was called down to the front of the stage to take a bow with the conductor. Of course my bow was not as a percussionist but as chorus master of the Cathedral Choral Society – but I wonder how many of the audience knew that, as this ageing man stepped down through the ranks of young students. The other work in this hugely enjoyable event was, I recall, Rachmaninoff's second piano concerto with Martin Jones as the soloist.

The Choral Society's concert during the Llandaff Festival began with a new work, premiered in 1983 at Gloucester and now receiving its seventh performance: the *Mass of the Sea* by Paul Patterson. I think the chorus enjoyed learning it, and it was a work that can be readily appreciated on first hearing. Again I rehearsed the orchestra at Broadcasting House in Llandaff, negotiating some very tricky rhythms in 7/4 and 11/8 time, and the composer came to hear it. The other items in the concert were Sibelius's *Karelia Suite* and Poulenc's *Gloria*, another very attractive piece for chorus and orchestra.

An equally notable event was a concert shared by our Cathedral Choir and that of Bristol Cathedral, designed to celebrate no fewer than four notable centenaries – the birth of Schütz in 1585 and of Bach, Scarlatti and Handel in 1685. They were represented respectively by a German Magnificat, the motet *Lobet den Herrn*, a 10-part setting of the Stabat *Mater*, and the anthem *Zadok the Priest*. I had originally intended this to be a three choirs concert including Wells, but a visit by the Queen Mother obliged them to remain at home and the other cathedral choirs I approached were also unavailable. The Scarlatti work was the most challenging, with its four treble parts divided between Bristol and ourselves, and the divided alto, tenor and bass parts being shared quite easily by the men of both choirs. Rather naughtily I asked Malcolm Archer to conduct this long work, leaving the other three for myself, including the impressive eight-part work by Schütz. Where possible, I celebrated the composer's actual birthdays (though not Scarlatti's) by performing their music in services, as I did again later in the year for the four hundredth anniversary of the death of Thomas Tallis.

A new and not altogether welcome development affected the cathedral music during much of the Lent and Trinity terms. In January I had received a letter from the deputy chapter clerk, a friendly character called David Lambert, telling me that the Dean and Chapter and the Parochial Church Council had appointed a Music Advisory Committee 'to advise these bodies on all matters relating to music in the Cathedral'. David was to be the Secretary, and the membership consisted of the Dean, the Chapter Clerk, the Precentor, the Priest Vicar Graham Holcombe, together with David's wife Diana, who seemed to be the sole representative of the Parish (she had a diploma in Music and was head of Music at the Bishop of Llandaff High School). He explained, 'Any matter which you would like to raise relating to the Cathedral's music will be fully considered by the Committee'. On the one hand I was glad to see mention of the Precentor, because although that title had hitherto been merely honorary and usually bestowed on some elderly canon who took no interest in the music, the Bishop had now seen fit to appoint a younger man, Clive Jones, who had a music diploma, had been the senior Priest Vicar with whom I had worked amicably ten years earlier, and who ran his own chamber group known as the Palestrina Choir. On the other hand, I noted with dismay rather than surprise that I, as Organist and Master of the Choristers, was not to be a member of this new committee. Indeed, David invited me to the next meeting 'to talk informally about the Cathedral's music and the Cathedral Choir'. I also received a copy of a letter sent by the Chapter Clerk to the Cathedral School's bursar declaring that 'the Finance and Music Committees (*sic*) have decided that in future they will not be responsible for any advertisements that are placed without their prior approval, and that all such advertisements should be sent to the Precentor'. In fact I was unable to attend the meeting because on that very evening I was directing the choristers in a performance at a parents' evening at the School. One might have thought that the committee members should have known about this, especially as the Dean was one of the school governors. By then I had had several useful discussions with Clive Jones, who agreed to my request that I should be a member of the committee. In my response to the subsequent invitation I mentioned that my evenings were so full with teaching engagements 'in order to make some kind of living' that, bearing in mind my other commitments including examining tours, there seemed to be no free evening for at least two months.

The Reverend Graham Holcombe had come to me in 1974 as a student of St Michael's Theological College, asking for some organ lessons in preparation for the LTCL diploma (Licentiate of Trinity College, London). He attended one lesson, on my birthday, as it happened, but forgot to pay for it (he still hasn't) and did not arrange any further tuition. In 1984 he had been appointed as the junior Priest Vicar, and in sharp contrast to Clive Jones and the six other holders of that junior office I had worked with, he began to make himself objectionable by assuming a kind of authority over me which was entirely out of order. I quickly decided to report every manifestation of his unacceptable behaviour to the Precentor or the Dean, or both. In

January he took over from his more affable colleague Derek Belcher the preparation of the monthly service scheme, listing all the daily services including the choral music as chosen by me. This is a duty normally performed by the Precentor, but for reasons stated elsewhere had devolved upon one of the Priest Vicars as 'a person appointed by the Dean, and under his direction'. I decided that now we had an experienced musician as Precentor, he should see to the service scheme, and for once the Dean agreed with me, though I was puzzled by his written directive on the division of duties by the clause 'Fr Holcombe is responsible for making the necessary arrangements for this'. The seeds of dissent were sown, and Graham soon turned out to be a very bossy character with ideas well above his lowly station. Consternation over the function of the new committee sparked off meetings between various interested parties, and I very soon found that some decisions made by the committee were in practice quickly vetoed unilaterally by the Dean.

When singing a setting of the Mass at the Sunday Eucharist, it was our custom for the choir to sing the whole setting, comprising *Kyrie eleison, Gloria in excelsis, Credo, Sanctus & Benedictus* and *Agnus Dei.* Some of the settings were of the English text by church musicians of the twentieth century, notably Charles Stanford, Harold Darke and Herbert Howells, but I also built up a repertory of seven Viennese masses by Mozart, Haydn and Schubert, as well as an eight-part sixteenth century setting by Orlandus Lassus. Some of the Latin Creeds were too long to be sung, and were replaced by a congregational setting in English by the sixteenth-century Merbecke or the twentieth-century Martin Shaw. It was traditional to omit the *Gloria in excelsis* during Lent. Father Holcombe made himself unpopular with me and the choir on the third Sunday before Lent, quaintly known as Septuagesima, by cancelling the Gloria (which of course we had already rehearsed) and again on the two following Sundays, so that for nine Sundays in succession it had to be omitted. The Dean, when approached for a ruling, sat on the proverbial fence by declaring that on the three Sundays before Lent it should neither be omitted, nor sung, but *spoken*! I know that at least some of the choir were so incensed by this ludicrous decision that they remained silent and just let the congregation get on with it.

Looking up Fr Holcombe's credentials, just before the Septuagesima debacle, in the Diocesan Directory, I was surprised to find that he claimed to have gained an ARCM diploma way back in 1968. This is generally reckoned to be a more respectable diploma than the LTCL, for which he had requested lessons in 1974 (and I say this with no disrespect to Trinity College London, since I gained that diploma myself while still at school), so it seemed inconceivable that he should seek help for the lesser award six years after his alleged success in the other. His attitude to music in the Cathedral seemed to be at odds with his claim to some degree of professionalism, and I decided to seek the truth of the matter by writing to the Registrar of the Royal College of Music. The reply, dated 7 February, stated unequivocally:

> I am writing to confirm that we have no record of Graham William Arthur Holcombe having obtained an ARCM diploma in 1969 or at any other time. If he did obtain an ARCM he should possess a certificate and a mark sheet. I do hope this clarifies the matter.

I did not let on that I had rumbled him, and I restrained myself from informing the Bishop of the deception, but a couple of years later Holcombe received a letter from the Registrar drawing his attention to the matter. By then he had left Llandaff – and he was never rude to me again.

On Palm Sunday and Good Friday we honoured the custom of singing the very long Gospel appointed for the day. Using the simple setting by the sixteenth-century Spanish composer Victoria, the text would be narrated to quasi-plainsong by one of the priest vicars standing (unlit) under the *Majestas* and flanked by two other priests who would sing the words of Christ and other characters, while the choir would interject in four-part harmony the words of the disciples and of the crowd of onlookers at the Passion of our Lord. On Palm Sunday this year, the part of Christ was allocated to Holcombe. He may have felt in his element here, but such was his incompetence that he managed to get two of his three phrases wrong. For some reason the Good Friday Eucharist began two minutes late, putting the Dean in a bad temper from the start (not for the first time this term) and Holcombe was allocated the narrator's part in the reading of the Passion; I was not looking forward to the experience, and surely enough, not only was it full of inaccuracies but he continued to sing a further page of music provided by the composer but not included in the version being followed by the congregation. There might have been some excuse for his bumptious attitude if he had shown some competence.

When a so-called Red Letter Day fell on a weekday, we were expected to sing a Eucharist at 7.30pm instead of Evensong at 6pm. Holcombe had evidently overlooked this when it came to Lady Day on the 25th March, which fell on a Monday. The choristers had rehearsed the Evensong music that morning, and I was far from pleased when Holcombe came to the School and burst in on a piano lesson I was giving, to tell me that we must sing the Eucharist instead. This of course was a quite preposterous notion at such short notice, and I sent him off with a flea in his ear. This incident was swiftly followed by a rejoinder from the Dean, who wrote:

> I was disturbed to learn that the boys of the Cathedral Choir would not be singing the evening Eucharist of the Feast of the Annunciation of the Blessed Virgin Mary... It was too late to ask the Cathedral Parish Choir to be responsible for the service, and the result might have been that the Cathedral would have been deprived of a Sung Eucharist on a day of such importance as Lady Day if the congregation itself had not taken over and sung the service well and very happily... That any church should have a sung Evensong and not a sung Eucharist on a Sunday or Saint's Day of Red Letter rank is quite unbelievable.

Once again the Dean, by failing to talk to me about the situation, had misattributed the blame, and I had to write back to explain that the fault lay with Holcombe, who had not only made a mistake in the first place by not indicating on the draft service list that Evensong would be said, followed by the sung Eucharist, but had compounded the error by failing to send the completed sheets to the Precentor for checking, as agreed. Even worse, he had sent off the sheets to the printer during my four-day half term break, thereby preventing me from correcting various other mistakes and omissions which he had carelessly overlooked, so that these had to put right at the proof stage. Back came a paragraph from the Dean, twenty lines long, trying to justify the actions of his junior (the clergy being famous for closing ranks) and another fourteen lines on yet another contentious issue involving him. He did not respond to my request that he should take steps to ensure that Holcombe did not adopt such a dictatorial manner in future, but instead concluded his letter by predicting that the fees I had requested for an important choral service later in the year would be 'difficult to raise' and might rule us out altogether. In the event they weren't, and we weren't. In my original letter I had also reported that Holcombe had insulted Michael Hoeg and the choir during a rehearsal by sneering 'You musicians are trying to run the Cathedral', and it was this attitude towards musicians that later gave me an opportunity to expose him as a fraud, as will emerge later. I also remember him calling out to me in the street one day instead of catching up with me in a civilised way and saying 'I will not be used as a football between you and the Dean' I had to tell him that that was in fact exactly his role.

There was further unpleasantness in the summer term. The singing of the *Sanctus* is preceded by a passage known as the *Sursum corda* (Lift up your hearts...') which may be said or sung by the officiating priest (the celebrant). If sung, it must be at a pitch which will lead seamlessly into the choral setting, and to ensure this it is normal for the organist to play the opening four notes, known as the intonation. Of course Holcombe disapproved of this standard practice, saying that he could easily take his own note, thank you very much. If the setting is unaccompanied, a choir can usually follow the priest's closing words 'ever more praising thee and saying...' easily enough, provided the pitch is at a manageable level, but if there is an organ part, a very unmusical clash of keys can result, sometimes causing unfortunate confusion. When I explained this to Holcombe, he declared archly that as celebrant he could not be wrong, because he represented the Bishop. I had never heard anything so arrogant.. I sent him a list of the eighteen settings that we currently alternated, along with the note on which he should begin, courteously explaining as if to a novice:

> In an attempt to simplify matters concerning the pitch at which the *Sursum corda* should be sung for the various settings we use, I have made a list of the notes I normally give. There is no trickery or tomfoolery about this: it is simply that the music of the priest's part must establish the tonality of the *Sanctus* which follows, so that the whole passage is a satisfactory musical entity. You will appreciate that the *Sursum corda* and its attendant prefaces have a compass of a perfect fourth above the first note given on the organ. Thus the range expected is one octave from C to C. This, or course, is well within the range of the average hymn-tune, and has not previously caused problems, but I can understand that part of the range may seem a little uncomfortable for some voices. I have to admit to some surprise, however, that you were happy to choose middle C for the Collect a week ago, having found the same note unacceptable five days earlier when singing C to G. However, let us not dwell in the past, but make things right from now on.
>
> I invite you, therefore, to consider the enclosed list, and if you feel you would be happier with a different pitch in particular cases, let me know, and we will see if an alternative is possible. It is not practicable for the celebrant to take his own note, unless the organist and choir know in advance what it is; and the safest and certainly most well-tried method of ensuring accuracy is for the organist to sound the intonation.

It should not have been necessary for a cathedral organist of many years' standing to explain himself to a junior cleric, and every other priest vicar was only too pleased to comply with my requests. I had already explained the problem to the music committee, and I sent a copy of my letter to the Dean, adding 'I must tell you that I am very unhappy about a situation in which my musicianship and integrity are called into question with increasing frequency'. Naturally the Dean ignored this comment, but launched into two dozen lines of closely-typed print, laboriously setting out the thesis that 'Fr Holcombe did not raise the question on his own account only, but as the priest responsible to me for the good ordering of musical affairs in the cathedral church' and continuing:

> At every Eucharist it is the celebrant who is in command and, as he represents the Bishop, it is only the Diocesan Bishop if he happens to be present presiding who can "over-rule" him. Assistant sacred ministers, masters of ceremonies and organists and choirs take their cue from the celebrating priest... My own experience, as one who finds it difficult to take a note, has taught me that provided the priest's original pitch is within a reasonable range the congregation (and even more so a trained choir) had no difficulty in following him...

Even my long-suffering assistant more than once had cause to complain to the Dean about this troublesome man, and I took the unusual step of ending my annual report to the Chapter with a whole paragraph expressing our dissatisfaction with his incompetence and general behaviour. It was not until May that Precentor Clive Jones had an opportunity to preach, having had to take his turn with his fellow canons, and he evidently felt uncomfortable as a member of the Chapter: by August he had left the Church in Wales, seeking pastures new, first in an English parish, then for a few years as a chaplain on the Costa Blanca before returning as a parish priest to Wales, and eventually moving to the Netherlands. Holcombe survived for another year, but his tenure of office was the shortest of all the sixteen priest vicars I worked with, and we were certainly glad to see the back of him. I am glad to report that since those early days he has gained a much more affable reputation and has become very supportive of the music staff. He has played an important part in the revival of the Llandaff Festival, albeit on a reduced scale, raising much-needed funds for the cathedral. When we met again some twenty-eight years later, he had become a resident canon and welcomed me back with enthusiasm. I formed the opinion that he had achieved his ambition and had nothing to prove.

It was also something of a relief not to have to wait in vain for replies to my letters to Norman Lloyd-Edwards. The reason for this was that he was appointed Lord Mayor of Cardiff in May, so that David Lambert took over as Acting Chapter Clerk – a far more caring man, who though inevitably hamstrung by the Dean did his best to make things run smoothly. Even he was unable to persuade the Dean to link the ineffectual 'Music Committee' with the Choir Association (representing choristers' parents and the men of the choir, chaired by Gerard Elias QC).

The end of June sees the Feast of St Peter and St Paul, the cathedral's 'principal patrons', and I was disturbed to find that the choristers were expected to sing at seven services in three days. Fortunately the Headmaster agreed to ask the Dean for some respite for the poor little chaps, receiving a rather patronizing reply beginning 'My dear Headmaster' (why not just 'Dear John'?) releasing them from the Friday Evensong so that 'absolved for a day from the responsibility of providing any music, they should be more ready for the two services a day they will sing on the three following days'. On Saturday morning they began with a practice at 9 and had to sit through an ordination service lasting two and a half hours for eleven priests and six deacons. At Evensong there was a congregation of only forty despite being designated 'for the Friends of the Cathedral', after which the boys and men departed to central Cardiff to perform in some kind of musical show. Sunday saw the two usual services, but on Monday the boys had to sing not only Evensong but a morning Eucharist as well, pretentiously styled capitular (the adjective from Chapter) because it was laid on specially for the quarterly gathering of all the canons. If this had been a theatre, I believe the use of children for six public performances in three days would have been unlawful, but as usual their welfare was overlooked in favour of the clergy.

I have dwelt at some length on these problems with the clergy to show how much time and effort they wasted, but I am glad to say that the cathedral music flourished without their co-operation, and my annual Report drew attention to many aspects which should have gladdened the hearts of the Chapter (though no canon ever responded to these presentations). I was able to commend a group of fifteen particularly keen and competent boys and a team of eight men including two choral scholars, and attributed our greatest catch, the international tenor Brian Burrows, to the provision of a flat for him on the Cathedral Green. The Christmas record had sold a thousand discs in fifteen weeks, and once again two of our boys had been invited to sing at the well-established Festival of Music and the Liturgy at Edington Priory in Wiltshire for a week in August, along with choristers from well-known English cathedrals.

The RSCM committee had attracted over two hundred singers to one-day schools arranged in the diocese, and I had conducted fifteen choirs taking part in the annual Cathedral Festival service; there had also been a dinner at the Park Hotel for local members of the RSCM and of the county organists' association. Marian and I had hosted a Christmas party for the choristers and a summer garden party for their parents. I had also judged, with John Sanders of Gloucester, a national competition for young organists held in Plymouth. I did not report that I had also been applying for jobs elsewhere, notably at Christ Church (where Stephen Darlington was appointed) and Lincoln (where although I reached the last fourteen, known as their 'long list' out of 101 applicants, David Flood got the job and stayed for only eighteen months); but also at Reading University, Malvern College and Christ's Hospital, all to no avail.

Professional musicians always get very steamed up if there is any suggestion of an unauthorised recording, whether audio or visual, being made of their work. In November the Reverend Roy Davies was enthroned as Bishop of Llandaff, and on the previous day I found that a video camera was being set up by a very forceful character from the Parochial Church Council. I lost no time in taking advice from Gerard Elias QC and warning the acting Chapter Clerk that if our fees for this special were not doubled, the men might refuse to sing. I knew I had the authorities over a barrel, as they say, and managed to receive an assurance that the resulting video would be made available only to the Bishop and his 'immediate circle'; if copies were later sold, then extra fees would have to be paid to all the musicians. As the new Bishop entered the west door, there was an unexpected hiatus. According to the Order of Service the Dean was to read out a document known as the Mandate (not from the Queen, as the Welsh Church is disestablished, but presumably from its Governing Body) confirming his appointment. Meanwhile I was taking my place ready to conduct Parry's famous Coronation anthem which begins with the words *I was glad when they said unto me, Let us go into the house of the Lord.* To my surprise, there was silence. I wondered if the Mandate had been so short that I had missed it while descending the stairs from the organ loft. I looked enquiringly at one of the Priest Vicars for a signal, but he shook his head. I looked at the other one, and he nodded. Thinking that if we did not start singing the service would never get under way, we launched into that grandiose introduction and sang as if at the Coronation itself. With decanal permission I altered the words declaimed in the middle of the anthem to welcome the monarch, *Vivat Regina* (originally *Vivat Rex* for Edward VII), to *Salve sacerdos, salve Episcope Llandavensis* as an appropriate welcome for the Bishop. (He never mentioned it afterwards, so perhaps the gesture was lost on him). I found out afterwards that the Dean had left the text of the Mandate at home, and I had missed his brief announcement that it would be read later. When he reached his stall in the Choir, he had rushed out of the building by the south-east door, throwing off his vestments, and had dashed back to the Deanery to fetch it. Actually, I had suggested that we might sing Bruckner's anthem *Ecce sacerdos magnus* (Behold, a great priest) with its accompaniment for organ and three trombones, but with its papal associations the Bishop was evidently sufficiently modest to reject it in favour of an anthem designed to welcome a king.

There were two other contentious issues during the preparations for the Bishop's enthronement, both involving the Dean, as might be expected. It was customary at 'big' county or national services to expect the congregation to sing one or two hymns in Welsh. This always presented a problem, because the language was unknown to most of the choir, and I had to enlist the services of a sympathetic Welsh speaker to give us tuition in pronunciation. When I found Welsh hymns in the proposed order of service, I asked the Dean to print the words in English alongside the Welsh, so that the choir could sing in their own language and the congregation could choose either language at will. My written request took up eight lines, but his convoluted 25-line reply was typical enough to be quoted in full, as further illustration of how the man's brain worked:

> If a hymn is to be sung in Welsh, that is the language in which it is to be sung [*sic!*]; and though it may be helpful to provide an English translation of part of a service that is to be *spoken* in Welsh so that those who are unfamiliar with the language may follow it, the same cannot apply to a hymn in which it is hoped that everyone will participate to the best of his or her ability. In any case, changes cannot be made at the proof stage (even if an English version of the hymns were available, and in one case – Timothy Rees's hymn – it is not) as proofs are submitted for the correction of errors made by the printer and possibly consultation with him about lay-out: very rarely some change in material circumstances (e.g., in the case of our service sheet, the Bishop's choice of a date for the installation of a canon) makes a change in substance necessary.
>
> It surprises me that a choir which I have heard sing Latin and on occasion even German, a language which has never had a place in worship in this country, is unable to sing a Welsh hymn: many of its members live and have always lived in Wales and more of those connected with it have been in Wales long enough to gain some ability to pronounce the language. I know that the Cathedral choir is the only "endowed choir" in the English choral tradition that we have in this Province but the cathedral in which it sings stands in the Welsh tradition

of the Church's worship, one feature of which is a greater or lesser degree of bilingualism. Very many non-Welsh-speaking Welsh people and a great number of our English cousins who have never lived in Wales but who respect Welsh culture would share my surprise and might well use a harsher word. I have no doubt that the congregation, at least, will have little difficulty with the two Welsh hymns on November 16.

My reply took up only half the space, reading as follows:

> I think it would be useful to discuss the matter of Welsh hymns at the next meeting of the Music Committee. Meanwhile I am arranging for a translation of those chosen for the Enthronement to be made for the benefit of the choir, as I cannot agree with your suggestion that it is unnecessary to know what one is singing about. When we sing in Latin I always explain to the boys the meaning of the text – likewise in the case of German. Since I have 'A' levels in Latin and French and 'O' level in German, I think it unreasonable to suggest that I should have studied a fourth language. Moreover, as you know, the choristers are not taught Welsh; and the English, Scottish and American men in the choir can hardly be expected to have studied the language.

The other disputed point was the choice of a suitable setting of the *Te Deum laudamus* (used as a canticle at Matins but also as a hymn of praise elsewhere on special days). The simplest way to explain the difficulty will be to quote our correspondence: the problem arose because in some versions the last six lines, being regarded as a later accretion, are omitted. I wrote:

> I hope the words of the choir items will be printed. The Stanford *Te Deum* will have to be sung complete, as the words 'in glory everlasting' come in the middle of a section in an unrelated key!

The Dean, who had chosen Stanford's comparatively well-known setting in C major from several alternatives, replied:

> If Stanford's *Te Deum* cannot be made to end at the correct *[sic]* place, the appendix will have to be sung: but the printed version ends "…in glory everlasting". All that follows this was originally a set of suffrages to be said after the *Te Deum* had been sung. The Prayer Book of the Church in Wales indicates

this by putting verses 17 – 22 in brackets and appointing them for use as suffrages in the Burial Service, where they are more appropriate. Even the Church of England's Alternative Service Book 1980 has done something similar at Matins, while the Book of Common Prayer of the American Episcopal Church omits everything after "in glory everlasting" in Daily Morning Prayer: a place is found for the suffrages later in the service and in the Prayer Book Study dealing with the Daily Offices they are described as "the versicles added to the original hymn".

All this rigmarole was entirely superfluous, as I implied in my reply:

> I do know something of the history of the *Te Deum*, being not only a holder of the ADCM but also an examiner for it. Some weeks ago I offered to suggest suitable English settings for the 16th November, and if you had told me then that you wanted the short version, I would have recommended the setting in G by Vaughan Williams, which is the *only* setting out of the dozen we have sung in the last four years to be designed in this way. It was actually composed for an Enthronement, and I should be quite happy to use it on this occasion, since it was sung only last term and all the boys will remember it: in this way, your printed text will be what is actually sung. I shall need to know one way or the other by this weekend.

Not to be entirely outdone, the Dean found opportunity five days later to pass on some criticism by an anonymous server ('a senior member of the Guild of Servers') of the lay clerks' behaviour while assembling before services. His letter and a copy of the complaint extended to some forty lines. I passed on the complaint, but considered it not worthy of a reply.

When I first went to Llandaff, the Sunday morning choral service would be the Eucharist on the first, third and (if any) fifth Sundays of the month, with Matins on the second and fourth Sundays. Dean Davies, with his absolute obsession with the Eucharist, took it on himself to phase out Matins in easy stages. Visiting choirs singing during choir holidays were no longer required to sing Matins on any Sunday, and a few years back he had decided that it would not be sung by the cathedral choir in Lent or Advent. By 1985 he had banned it on the great Festivals such as Pentecost and on red-letter Saints' days that happened to fall on a Sunday and now he extended the ban to the three Sundays before Lent and the five Sundays after Easter, so that in the course of six years the number of times the choir sang a *Te Deum* was reduced from thirteen to two, and by 1990 Choral Matins had been wiped off the service list altogether.

In Michaelmas Term there was a grand service to commemorate the fiftieth anniversary of the King George V Trust; it was attended by many VIPs including Prince Michael of Kent. The choir sang magnificently, and the Prince was moved to donate £100 to the choir, to be spent on a 'tangible object' and not merely paid into a fund. I was allocated seventeen days' examining during November and December, enabling me to build up my own funds but without neglecting events at home, which included a performance of Mendelssohn's popular oratorio *Elijah* (which attracted an audience of 440 but still made a financial loss of £888, 30% of the cost of performing it) and a recital at St David's Hall where another large audience heard me play the whole of the *Arthur Wills Bach Book*. This was a collection of transcriptions by the Ely Cathedral organist, including that sparkling *Sinfonia* from Cantata 29 and a clever arrangement of the *Chaconne,* originally for solo violin. I had practised the pieces for hours on the very fine cathedral organ at Peterborough during one of my examining tours. At least a thousand people heard our Cathedral Choir sing ten carol arrangements at a concert in aid of the Red Cross at St David's Hall, and only days later we entertained the Lord Mayor's guests at a dinner party at his Mansion House. I also tried whenever possible to accommodate my six organ students and twenty piano pupils. Our friends the Eliases took us to Salisbury Cathedral for the installation of Jeremy Davies as Precentor, followed by a party at the Deanery.

I was sorry to lose Jeremy as a tenor, along with Brian Burrows who had fled to Sweden to escape his creditors who included Inland Revenue and the Dean and Chapter: it emerged that he owed them £1000 in rent, and had been living with one of his female students in the flat they provided. Meanwhile my friend Dudley Holroyd had run off with the mother of one of his choristers at Bath Abbey; I thought this was better than running off with the boy himself, but the boy's father kicked up a stink about it and it got into the *Western Daily Mail,* thence into the *Sun.* Dudley resigned, the vicar had a stroke and it all reminded me of the old game of Consequences.

We celebrated New Year's Eve by dining with Roy and Ruth Massey at the Rhydspence Inn, an historic black and white timber-framed building just on the Welsh border, where there was a convivial party atmosphere to round off the year.

1986

It became increasingly apparent that decisions made by the music committee and diligently minuted by David Lambert were being waved aside. Some wooden panelling had been constructed to match the choir stalls and hide a television camera used for some event in 1985. There was a good deal of space behind the choir stalls on each side, where it would have served to contain the music and improve the acoustics. I asked if the new panelling might remain in place as an experiment, but of course it was taken down. It had been decided to reinstate a sung *Gloria* at the Eucharist on the three Sundays before Lent, but on Septuagesima, a few minutes before the service, the head server requested that it be said. In view of the committee's decision I refused, but two Sundays later Graham Holcombe made a similar request on behalf of the Dean, and I had to produce photocopies of the minutes to convince the Dean of his own decision. None of this should have been necessary, and an even more irritating example occurred soon afterwards. It was customary for certain ceremonies to take place under Epstein's figure of Christ in Majesty (known as *Majestas*), between the legs of George Pace's parabolic concrete arch which was such an eye-catching feature of the building. Two floodlights had been installed as bare bulbs under the great cylinder containing the positive organ, but I had noticed that when an ordination or confirmation took place, with the Bishop seated on his throne, these lights were not switched on, putting the participants in the shade. I had put forward the view that these ceremonies should be properly lit as the centrepiece of the service. When the Dean said testily that this would make the place 'look like a theatre', I said this was exactly what was intended, and the committee agreed that in future the lights should be switched on. When a Thursday Evensong in late February was extended by twenty-five minutes' quasi-legal mumbo-jumbo for the installation of two new canons (all about their supposed 'rights and appurtenances'), I asked the head steward to remind the verger that the Dean had approved the Committee's resolution that the lights above the dais should be switched on for the occasion. This was done, but as I approached the organ loft they were switched off again, so I returned to the switch room and turned them on. As I was playing the organ before the service, the lights went off again, and the congregation must have been as baffled as I was; but I discovered afterwards that they had been switched off by the Dean himself, shouting to the verger 'Lock the switch room, lock the switch room!' I registered a complaint in a letter to Mr Lambert, declaring that this action was in direct contravention of his minuted resolution and made several of the cathedral staff look foolish: it also ensured that the long ceremony took place in relative darkness. The need to save electricity could not be cited as a reason for the Dean's action, I added, since the six floodlights in the Choir were left on for nearly two hours after the service had finished. I concluded that in the face of such ridiculous decanal conduct any further attendance at meetings would be a waste of time, so I decided to boycott the committee, and I think it must have been quietly disbanded until after the Dean retired, when rather different circumstances saw its revival some eleven years later. I also took the opportunity to complain that our song room was often left in a terrible mess by the parish choir on Monday and Friday evenings, making it necessary for my choristers to start the following mornings' practices by picking up all the sweet papers (and even pages torn out of hymnbooks), before we could begin.

Much of my time was taken up with correspondence and auditions in the attempt to recruit new men into the choir, and at one point I was told of a plan to re-order accommodation in the small house which formed about a third of St Mary's (my house being the other two thirds), which was soon to be vacated by the head verger Ron Roberts on his retirement. The concept was to create a communal sitting room and three bedrooms for lay clerks, and at one point I wondered if we might take over another room on the ground floor, but none of this came to fruition. Once more I asked for a higher salary, on finding that mine was £1100 less than the lowest paid to any other organist who had to maintain choral services six days a week, and in fact little more than half the average figure. It could of course be argued that with a wide range of salaries, someone had to be bottom of the list, but I suggested that such a position should be occupied by the youngest, least experienced and least well qualified, whereas I could claim to be one of the more senior organists, a family man of forty-eight with nearly twenty years' experience and a Doctorate in Music. I pointed out that only the organists of Canterbury, Ely, Chelmsford and Worcester had this qualification (and by the time I retired I was the very last one) and that their average salary exceeded mine by £4600. I also mentioned that the four other organists who had been, like me, organ scholars of Christ Church, were paid an average of £8850 compared with my measly £3900. As a token gesture I was awarded an interim rise of £200! pending further consideration, but months later the Clerk wrote to say that the Chapter 'were not disposed to compare my service conditions with those of other cathedral organists'. I wondered how their reverences could reconcile this statement with the case of their former assistant organist, Graham Elliott who, as organist of Chelmsford Cathedral was being paid almost twice as much as I, with only three services a week to organise.

Whether the mess made by the parish choir in the song room was part of a deliberate campaign against us, I do not know, but a dispute blew up in March involving the parish organist, Morley Lewis, who was my accompanist with the choral society and had for several years been regarded as a friend. When Michael Hoeg became my official assistant in 1980 and offered to play at every service, I no longer needed to ask Morley to help out as he had previously done, so he was needed only for occasional services when I was away, to assist Michael. Whether he felt aggrieved about this, I knew not, or perhaps he was becoming increasingly jealous of the growing prestige of the cathedral choir, but for whatever reason it came to my notice that he was doing his best to undermine our work and achievements in the eyes of his own choir. Things came to a head in a comparatively trivial incident when one of the Dean's Scholars, David Howard-Jones, entered the song room during one of Morley's practices to return some of the cathedral choir's music and was accused of 'sweeping in', smirking and failing to call him 'Sir'. This incident would hardly seem worthy of a mention, but in fact it became a storm in a teacup and Michael Hoeg bore the brunt of it. Determined to vindicate the boy (who later won a scholarship to Eton and another to Merton College, Oxford), Michael kept a detailed diary of events involving Morley and his choir for about six weeks, saying:

> There is a campaign by the Parish Choir against the cathedral choir which started before the Howard-Jones incident and which still continues. This may or may not be led by Mr Lewis, but the fact is that he has often complained of all aspects of the running of the cathedral choir, to myself and to others. His hostile attitude to us is very well-known, but it is disturbing that he has extended the campaign to the choristers, especially in an obviously doubtful issue of this sort.

Morley insisted on demanding an apology for the chorister's behaviour, but the School backed the boy and would not allow him to apologise. Michael wrote:

> As a matter of interest, I said 'Hello' to two of the parish choirboys as I went to the Song Room. They both replied politely but neither called me 'Sir'. I am not offended in the

slightest as I do not expect it from them or the cathedral boys, but it shows the double standards allowed by Mr Lewis.

Both the Headmaster and the Dean entered into the dispute, in which, thankfully, I was not involved, and the Dean offered a rather feeble solution by deciding that in future our copies should be left on a shelf outside the vestries thus obviating the need to go into Mr Lewis's practices, but implying Howard-Jones's guilt very strongly, in Michael's opinion, since no explanation was given for this judgement. The boy became ill and was unable to sing or attend lessons for several days.

Next, it was the Dean's turn again to cause trouble, and this was perhaps the most disgraceful manifestation of his own thinly-disguised antagonism to the musical profession. Once more we set aside three evenings to make an LP record on the Alpha label of the Abbey Recording Company, owned and operated by the irrepressible Harry Mudd, who had been responsible for both our earlier recordings. We began with a three-hour session on a Wednesday evening in May and continued on the following evening, after singing Evensong. The next day I received a letter from the Dean which I here reproduce in its awful entirety:

> I am very concerned about the way in which recording equipment has been disposed about the Cathedral for the last three days. My consent to the turning of the Chapter House into a "control room" and, it appears, a canteen, was neither sought nor given. There was a possibility of my having to assign it for another purpose today and, apart from this, Mr Ron Roberts spent a great deal of time at the end of last week cleaning it and polishing the floor so that when the new Head Virger arrives in ten days' time he might see the standard at which we aim in the care of the Cathedral. Today the floor is littered with pieces of squashed biscuits. Tomorrow there are two weddings in the Cathedral, the first at 11am, when the Chapter House will be needed for the completion and signing of the Registers. I must therefore ask that all equipment should be moved in good time for the Head Virger to clean and tidy the Chapter House.
>
> The microphones standing in and dominating the Nave were an obstruction when the Llandaff City Infants' School came for a service this morning. It was fortunate that the Lady Chapel was just large enough for a diocesan event which began with a Eucharist later in the morning and that Mr Charles Murray had asked for his mother's funeral this afternoon to be

in the Lady Chapel. If the funeral had (as is customary) been in the Nave the microphones would have had to be taken away. I ask that they, and the cables with them, should be removed from the Cathedral not later than early tomorrow morning.

I did not give permission for the removal of furniture from the Song Room, nor was I asked for it. Two choirs have the use of the room at different times and permission could only be given for the removal of desks if the Masters of both choirs agreed. The Master of the Cathedral Parish Choir would not be acting unreasonably if he were to make representations to me this evening when he finds that furniture needed for his choir practice is missing.

I hope that the recording has been successful.

My reading of the first two paragraphs was that in fact no one had been inconvenienced - they only might have been in different circumstances. We were due to finish recording, with the boys only, in the evening of the day he typed the letter, and the equipment was to be removed the following morning, so there was really no need for him to write anything at all. Weary of writing letters to justify myself, I took the letter straight round to Gerard Elias QC, who had made the arrangements and had offered to assist even with the editing process some days later. He was justifiably angry, and has remembered the occasion ever since, reminding me of it twenty-two years later. Fortunately I still have a copy of the broadside he fired at the Dean from his position of very considerable authority, and I reproduce it here as another significant and important document in the annals of Llandaff Cathedral:

17 May 1986

Dear Mr Dean,

The booking of the Cathedral for the recording by the Cathedral Choir was made by me on behalf of the Llandaff Cathedral Choir Association, and for that reason Dr Smith has forwarded your letter to me. I am bound to say that I read it with some perplexity and not a little anger last night.

Let me put the facts right:

1. I visited you in the Deanery earlier this year to seek your permission for the Choir to make a new record, which consent was forthcoming. You told me to book the dates through Mrs Mills.

2. I then booked the Cathedral for a recording for three evenings.

3. Mrs Mills very kindly confirmed the arrangement, but mentioned the difficulty on the Friday because of the Parish Choir practice.

4. A fortnight ago I spoke to Morley Lewis about this. For perfectly understandable reasons he informed me that he was unable to move his practice out of the Nave, but assured me that he would do everything he could to leave promptly by 8 o'clock - which in fact he did. I had nothing but encouragement and help from Morley Lewis.

5. The equipment placed in the Cathedral and Chapter House for the recording was precisely the same equipment as was placed in the Cathedral and Chapter house in May 1984 for the recording of our last record.

6. No complaint or comment of any kind was made to me about the equipment or its disposition at that time.

7. The choristers were required in the Cathedral for three hours on Wednesday and Thursday evenings. My wife provided squash and biscuits for them during a ten-minute break each evening. This was not served to them in the Chapter House. I gave a biscuit to the two producers (including the Organist from Gloucester Cathedral), Michael Smith and Michael Hoeg, and if crumbs from these were on the floor then I apologise. To describe the Chapter House floor as being "littered with pieces of squashed biscuit" does not accord with my recollection of the room on Thursday evening when I left it, or on Friday evening when I inspected it as a result of your letter. I do not understand your reference to your consent for the turning of the Chapter House into a "control room" not having been sought or given. As we both knew what was involved in making a record, was not that consent implicitly given to me at our meeting in the Deanery?

8. I did not seek your consent to use the Chapter House as "a canteen" and (of course) neither was it so used!

9. I did not seek your permission for the removal of the benches from the Song Room, but since this was precisely what occurred on the last occasion that a recording was made I assumed there would be no objection to this.. I must confess that I would not have dreamt that you would either require to be specifically asked about the matter or that you would have conceivably refused permission. (Similarly I did not ask your explicit permission to erect staging for the Pendyrus Male Choir concert and neither did you comment at the time that I should have done so).

I find your remark that Morley Lewis "would not be acting unreasonably if he were to make representations… when he finds that furniture needed for his choir practice is missing" absolutely extraordinary. Having spoken to Morley Lewis a fortnight ago and in the circumstances as he knew them, I am sure that he would not dream of being so petty - I stress that he was entirely friendly and encouraging to me.

It is depressing in the extreme to have to write in this vein. The choir, men, boys, Dr Smith and Michael Hoeg have worked very hard this week for no financial reward. The Head Verger has been most helpful and cooperative. I have returned each day from a trial in Swansea to spend four hours in concentrated effort in the cathedral to seek to achieve a good result for the benefit of us all. Elisabeth fed the party after the sessions each evening because the School's catering facility had ended. We were all quite tired and in need of encouragement - your letter, delivered I understand during Evensong yesterday, came as a deafening discouragement.

The Association aims to benefit the Cathedral Choir and the Cathedral. I think our efforts in recent years on behalf of both have achieved much. I had spoken to Morley Lewis about the possibility of his Choir making a record, which would be underwritten by the LCCA (a guarantee of about £2500) and he has expressed his positive interest in the idea. Accordingly I spoke to Mr Mudd of Abbey Records and put the proposition to him that in September/October 1986 the Parish Choir might be recorded, with all profits going to the Cathedral Appeal. Indeed, he took a short recording of their practice last evening for test purposes. He has consented and Dr Smith has agreed with me that he would be prepared to produce (that is, check the technical quality of the recording) the record without fee. I would have expected to make about £2000 from the venture, coupled with which it would have provided an opportunity for the musicians of Llandaff to work closely together.

I had intended to report my progress to Morley Lewis last night and, as is my practice, having worked out the detail, I would of course have sought your consent - as no doubt would Morley Lewis – to the venture. Having received your letter, I took the matter no further with Morley Lewis. Knowing what is involved do you wish the idea to be taken further?

The running of a Cathedral obviously has its difficulties. The running of a Choir Association has its difficulties too. I do not believe that lengthy letters across the Green assist in the running of either. I have replied to your letter at length because the contents demanded it. Surely a comment face to face, or even a phone call - critical or favourable - at the time would iron out most of our difficulties and provide the necessary stimulus to mend our ways or bring encouragement. I am sure this is the better way as I believe that we are all working in a common cause.

It was just as well that some of the problems with cathedral staff were being dealt with by my colleagues, because I had enough on my plate in dealing with my ailing parents. I had not seen them at Christmas, but the New Year presented an opportunity to visit Ilford briefly when I went to London again to mark ARCO papers. Later in the month I returned to London for the presentation of diplomas, and went on to St Albans to hear a performance of Howard Blake's new choral work *Benedictus* with a view to performing it myself, but it was clear that my parents were coming to the end of their respective tethers, so I cancelled engagements for a week and made arrangements to do something to help them. At the beginning of February I went to Cambridge to give weekend recitals in the chapels of King's College and St John's College, in both cases dining at high table with their respective organists Stephen Cleobury and George Guest. At St John's I joined the fellows in the Senior Combination Room after dinner, enjoying a 1966 vintage port and a cigar as we chatted by candlelight, and was delighted when Dr Guest described my playing in effusive terms as 'fine, dignified, noble'. I took the opportunity to ask him if he would consider becoming the Artistic Director of the Llandaff Festival. Since the untimely death of its founder, Christopher Cory, there had been two 'caretaker' directors in Roy Bohana from the Wales Arts Council and Huw Tregelles Williams from BBC Wales, but neither of them wished to continue, and I thought that George would be an ideal successor, as a figure of national fame in the field of church music who was not only Welsh but could speak the language.

Following the resounding success of the last year's three-choir performance of *Belshazzar's Feast*, the Choral Society was invited to share another concert at St David's Hall with the University Choir and Cardiff Bach Choir, totalling some four hundred voices, and this time it was Britten's *War Requiem*, first performed to celebrate the consecration of Coventry Cathedral in 1962 . The old cathedral had been destroyed by enemy action during the war, and the new one, built on a site adjacent to the ruins of the old, was intended not only as a symbol of faith but also as one of international reconciliation. The work is a setting of the Latin Mass for the Dead, scored for soprano solo with full orchestra, with a distant choir of boys' voices with organ, interspersed with settings of nine of the anti-war poems of Wilfred Owen set for tenor and baritone soloists accompanied by a separate chamber orchestra. On account of the large forces, the work had never been performed in Cardiff until now, when the size of St David's Hall made it possible. It is not unusual to have one conductor for the main forces and a second conductor for the chamber orchestra – as in the London premiere – so I gladly accepted responsibility for Martyn Hill (tenor), Stephen Roberts (baritone) and the professional players of the University Chamber Ensemble, while the cathedral choristers, positioned behind the chorus and in front of the organ were separately conducted by Michael Hoeg. It was indeed a privilege, not only for me but for my two choirs, to play such a significant part in this great work, which after twenty-four years was said to be only the second performance anywhere in Wales. The concert was followed by a champagne supper-party at which I met many musicians and university staff, and the Professor, Alan Hoddinott, wrote to thank me for my 'invaluable contribution to the success of the performance', adding 'The direction of the soloists and ensemble is probably the most vital element in the overall presentation, and this was, I must say, one of the most impressive aspects of the evening'. High praise indeed!

During the few weeks of preparation for this event, I was looking carefully into the possibility of moving my parents to Cardiff so that I could play some part in looking after them. With our packed schedules, our young family and their weakening state of health, there was no possibility of their sharing our house, but we made extensive enquiries about sheltered accommodation, residential and nursing homes, and consulted health professionals including a Dr Sastry, an Indian consultant in geriatrics (who happened by lucky chance to be the father of the chorister who had come fourth in last year's national competition). The day after *War Requiem* I put an advert in the *Ilford Recorder* to sell my old family home, and within a week was interviewing prospective buyers there. At one point my mother seemed close to death, but she was revived and was able to make her mark on various official letters. Between these two events I had to adjudicate nine church choirs in Bath Abbey as part of the West Somerset Festival, and in the evening they formed a massed choir which I conducted at a special service, in which the preacher turned out to be Fenton Morley, who had been Dean of Salisbury during my time there in the seventies and had baptised Rachel. Shortly afterwards I found myself fulfilling a rather unusual assignment at St David's Hall, giving a short organ recital at the opening of the National Congress of Obstetricians and Gynecologists, attended by the Duchess of Gloucester, followed by a concert by the Pendyrus Male Choir and several well-known musicians such as Nicholas Daniel (oboe), Caryl Thomas (harp) and Penny Walker (mezzo-soprano).

My burden of desk work, always quite heavy, was much increased by the many arrangements I had to make to secure my parents' future, until in April I drove to Essex, fetched Father from Chadwell Heath

Hospital and Mother from Barking Hospital, and after a brief goodbye to Hereford Gardens, where they had lived ever since their marriage in 1933, set off at speed for the 190 mile non-stop journey to Cardiff. I delivered them safely to an old hospital in the city centre called St David's, where they were to be looked after and assessed until they could be safely accommodated. I continued teaching my many pupils, sometimes for five hours at a stretch, and two days after depositing my parents I was back at St David's Hall, playing the organ part in a performance by the Huddersfield Choral Society with the BBC Welsh Symphony Orchestra of Elgar's *The Dream of Gerontius*, conducted by Owain Arwel Hughes. I have alluded earlier to his conducting style, with its characteristic sideways sweeps which have little meaning. There is at one point a tremendous climax, where the whole orchestra, with full organ, holds on to a C major chord for twelve bars. My view of Owain from the console, some hundred feet from the rostrum, was through a small round mirror, and having drawn all the necessary stops and carefully positioned this important chord with hands and foot, I quickly lost count of the number of bars he was beating, and was for a few seconds afraid that I would release my chord too soon, or worse, too late, leaving the organ sounding after the orchestra had stopped. By listening keenly and reacting instantaneously, I think I managed to synchronise with everyone else, but it was an anxious moment.

The large three-storey house known as the Old House, separated from St Mary's only by a narrow lane called Heol Fair, and consisting of three flats, had been sold by the Dean and Chapter for about £88,000, to a developer who promptly converted it into five flats in place of the two existing ones. I believe he sold the top-floor apartment for almost as much as he had given for the whole house, and I wondered why the Chapter had not been sufficiently astute to convert the place and make a profit, but of course a bunch of clergymen, even canons, have little idea how to manage big money. By a stroke of luck, I found that one of the ground floor flats was still on the market, and it seemed an ideal solution for my parents, so I offered £44,000 for it and signed the contract a day after Mother's eighty-second birthday, using funds from the £70,000 proceeds from the sale of their Ilford home.

For the third year running we were invited to record a Choral Evensong for the BBC, and in honour of Jeremy Davies's recent appointment to Salisbury, not to mention my own time there in the past, I hit upon the idea of choosing music with Salisbury connections. The setting of the Responses and the Lord's Prayer was that of Richard Shephard, who had begun his career there as an alto lay vicar and was now headmaster of the Minster School at York, and the canticles were by Richard Lloyd, my predecessor there as assistant organist who had moved on to Hereford and thence to Durham. The anthem, a setting of the hymn *Jesu, lover of my soul*, was by Walter Stanton who had been a Salisbury chorister, and the final responses were those of Herbert Howells, who had for a short time been assistant organist there. The remaining music was by Sidney Campbell, born in my home town and later organist of St George's Chapel, Windsor and George Guest, who had just taken over as director of the Llandaff Festival: they were represented respectively by the introit *Sing we merrily unto God* and a chant for psalm 41. I even persuaded the Dean to continue the theme by approving my choice of hymns, *All hail the power of Jesu's* name to the tune *Ladywell* and *Father, Lord of all creation* to *Abbots Leigh*; these very fine tunes were composed respectively by W.H.Ferguson and Cyril Taylor, both precentors of Salisbury Cathedral. The service was an interesting illustration, I thought, of the interaction of personalities in the world of cathedral music, as I wrote in *The Llandaff Monthly*, adding that Bernard Rose, whose responses we used, had been one of my tutors at Oxford, and Walter Stanton one of my examiners.

Three composers who all died in 1934 were similarly honoured in the Choral Society's concert in the summer Festival, when we sang Elgar's *The Music Makers* and Holst's rarely performed and unusual *Hymn of Jesus*, separated by Delius's evocative orchestral piece *A Walk to the Paradise Garden*. As a new venture I moved the annual RSCM parish choirs' Festival Service into the Llandaff Festival programme, inviting our new Director, George Guest, to conduct it. This was not an unqualified success, because George, so well known for his distinguished work with the choir of St John's College, Cambridge, seemed out of his depth when dealing with eighteen amateur choirs totalling 285 singers, who may not all have been well prepared by their own choir-trainers: he became noticeably impatient in the rehearsal, and the service was not well sung. Later that evening the cathedral choristers shared a Festival concert with a local mixed choir, the Ardwyn Singers, concentrating on music of the twentieth century. The adults sang music by Copland, Howells and Holst, and the boys sang two contrasting settings of the Mass by Fauré and Britten, and the rather unusual *Litanies à la Vierge Noire, notre Dame de Rocamadour* by Poulenc. After the Festival Service the following morning, when we sang Britten's *Festival Te Deum* in E and Shephard's exciting anthem *And when the builders,* George gave vent to his anger at the lack of co-operation from the Dean. The rest of us were obviously accustomed to his lack of interest, but to George it was plain rudeness, and indeed it was scandalous that the Dean should ignore him as he did. George did not attend Evensong that day, when a second airing of Walton's *Chichester Service* was complemented by Parry's superb setting from Milton's *At a Solemn Musick*, the grand anthem *Blest Pair of Sirens.* From time to time one comes across a work written for the opening of a building, as at Coventry Cathedral (or indeed Verdi's *Aida* for the opening of the Suez Canal) but I have often thought that this anthem by Parry ends with such an air of finality that it would grace the *closing* of something great. As it turned out, it ended the last Llandaff Festival service, for the days of the festival were numbered, and George Guest, dismayed by the Dean's negative attitude as its Chairman, together with some inefficient administration by the Welsh Arts Council staff, resigned his post as Director.

An example of the Dean's intransigence was the occasion when the festival secretary put out, on a table at the west end of the Cathedral, some printed leaflets advertising various events. When the Dean saw them, he confiscated them and hid them in one of the vestries, complaining that they had been displayed without his permission. And he was the Festival Chairman! The Festival had grown out of a more modest venture in 1958, when the then Dean, Eryl Thomas (later the Bishop, until his untimely resignation in 1975) invited the local business tycoon Christopher Cory to turn impresario and run a full-scale Festival, so it was a natural progression for successive Deans to assume the chairmanship. When I arrived in 1974, the Festival Council included such luminaries as the Lord Lieutenant, the Lord Mayor, a county alderman and senior figures from the BBC, National Museum, University and so on, but their membership had become only nominal, and in 1975 the programme listed only the members of the executive committee. There was certainly no need for a body of a dozen or more men to meet at intervals just to rubber-stamp decisions made by the Director; and I was sure that some of them were only there for the sandwiches, since they never contributed anything of note to the meetings. Sir Lincoln Hallinan's name always appeared (he was a stipendiary magistrate), but I never saw him. Other remnants from earlier times, including a retired bank clerk, a former assistant organist and an affable but ineffectual old cove called Gethyn Stoodley Thomas had little to contribute. On the other hand, the man who tuned the resident Steinway grand had too much to say for himself, and the manager of a Cardiff music shop used to make disparaging remarks about my Choral Society. Only Malcolm Boyd, a noted music scholar, had anything much to offer, and that was of little significance. It did not take Dr Guest long to spot the Committee's minimal contribution, and in a published statement he declared

> The title would approach the hilarious were the situation not so sad. Three members – and I record this with sincere gratitude – worked untiringly this year to make the festival a success. Two members, however, have not bothered to attend a single meeting of the council during the last twelve months!

Some could not bring themselves to attend a single event during the festival. Another person promised to take charge of advertising and decoration in Llandaff itself; in the event, he withdrew just before the festival, having done nothing at all and without having the common courtesy to inform the artistic director of his action. Another member of the council attended one concert, and then complained that the festival had become bilingual without authority – and this after the programme had been approved months before. Another person expressed shock that *Gwyl Llandaf* was printed in letters exactly the same size as *Llandaff Festival* – and this in the capital of Wales. It is indeed depressing when an inferiority complex reaches such depths.

The Press, he said, spoke of the festival in encouraging, indeed laudatory, terms, and in respect of programme content and performance it was an outstanding success. But at the suggestion of the Welsh Arts Council the council of management had appointed a member of its staff as our administrator, who though willing and conscientious had neither the time nor the requisite knowledge to do the work which the position demanded.

He considered that this was the main reason for the 'pathetically small' audiences at most of the concerts. He went on to say that he was leaving the job after only one year instead of three because of 'an almost unbelievable apathy from one quarter and' (in a thinly-veiled reference, no doubt, to the Dean), 'what I believe can only be described as calculated though subtle opposition to the festival as such from another'.

The young lady administrator resigned her position, as did the festival's treasurer, and news of Dr Guest's own resignation was splashed across the *Western Mail* in a bold headline an inch high and a page wide, with the by-line 'Apathy is blamed as a third resignation puts event in jeopardy'. The Dean, commenting in *The Llandaff Monthly* on the long article that followed, and quoting the sentence 'The resignation of Dr George Guest just weeks after this year's festival is the third hammer blow to hit the event', sneered 'I did not see the High Street flowing with tears at this dreadful news, but this was no doubt a sign of the apathy of which one member of the festival committee was said to have complained'. He then devoted two whole pages to the festival's history, lamenting its growth from a few days to two weeks. Citing the views of the bishop after the first festival, he said the Bishop had been less enthusiastic about an annual festival in future years as this 'would involve the regular use of the Cathedral for purposes other than those for which it primarily exists'. He had allegedly foreseen the danger of some people, 'already apt to regard the Cathedral as a museum piece', thinking of it as 'a kind of super concert hall' as well. The Dean went on to express his own view that the new St David's Hall 'would be able to offer the space needed by large orchestras and sufficient seating for an audience large enough to provide a better balance than a small cathedral could hope to do, between box office takings and Arts Council sponsorship, in meeting the cost'. He concluded ominously and not without sarcasm:

> Dr Guest's resignation, which would have been world-shattering only if the Llandaff Festival's old image was still valid, has changed the situation. The Llandaff Festival committee now has to decide what it wishes to do, but if the use of the Cathedral is included in any plans it makes for the future, it will be necessary for its proposals to be put before all the decision-making bodies of the Cathedral parish.

We shall see in my next chapter to what extent his strictures were implemented; but meanwhile Gerard Elias had been working with a fellow barrister, married to a Swedish lady, on an exciting venture for the cathedral choir immediately after the summer term. On Monday 14 July we all set out from Harwich on the 600-foot long ship *Tor Britannia* for a smooth nineteen-hour voyage to Denmark. On arrival at Esjberg, our coach driver took us right across the country to Copenhagen, and next morning we crossed the narrow strait to Halsingborg to begin our concert tour in Sweden. In nine days we gave seven concerts, mostly on the west coast, in fine churches with modern tracker-action organs in the west galleries. Audience figures ranged from 100 at Örebro in central Sweden to 360 at a Festival in Hoganas, where we were accorded a standing ovation. Our programme for each venue was chosen on the spot, with regard to the acoustics and organ specification, from a list of two dozen items ranging from unaccompanied Tudor motets to music by Britten, Howells and Leighton. Each concert included an item for boys' voices, and in two churches the organ's *trompette en chamade* stop came into its own in Kenneth Leighton's *Easter Sequence*. One Sunday morning saw us singing Mozart's Mass in D for the Eucharist at Stenkyrka, an event which was so well received that the Vicar took us all out for an excursion on a century-old sailing vessel to see the many off-shore islands to the north of Skarhamn. Our concerts ended, we continued our journey to Stockholm for a whole day's sight-seeing. Some of the men found numerous opportunities in bars, on street corners and on buses, boats and trains, to sing English and Welsh part-songs much to the delight of customers and passers-by, who in some cases contributed vocal or financial support! On our way home we spent another day looking round Copenhagen, enjoying more boat trips and the famous Tivoli Gardens. Both men and boys, and even our own children, singing Rachel's three-part arrangement of *Stand up, clap hands, say Thank you, Lord* took part in a talent competition on board the *Tor Skandinavia,* and the whole tour was notable for the tremendous spirit of *camaraderie* between all the participants and the relatives of choristers who accompanied us. The success of the tour was due in no small part to the skills of Gerard's wife Elisabeth and our headmaster John Knapp in keeping us all together. Sadly, a few weeks later one of the choristers, a twelve-year old boy called Paul Dallimore, was killed in a road accident, and when the choir returned for the autumn term we held a memorial service for him. Richard Shephard composed a moving setting of the evening canticles for boys' voices in his memory, subtly and appropriately incorporating at one point a phrase from *Tod und Verklärung* by Strauss, Richard's favourite composer.

1986 was a year when I had to consider a good many applications from potential lay clerks, and as I have mentioned earlier, there was a provisional plan to make the other part of St Mary's available to two or three new men. Quite often when I returned home from some exciting trip or relaxing holiday, there would be amongst the many letters awaiting my attention a discouraging one from the Dean. Sure enough, soon after my return there was one of these missives, to the effect that the Dean had interviewed two of my candidates and could not see

> that there would be any point in inviting them to sing in the Cathedral Choir as the interest of both of them, though perhaps not to the same degree, is in accommodation which they believe to be available. The situation is that the former head virger (*why did he not say 'Ron'?*) has now moved from 2 St Mary's, and I and others have been able to examine the property.

He continued in typical style with a 67-word sentence thus:

> When an architect's report and suggestions as to the best way in which the house might be used are available they will be studied by those with whom the responsibility of implementing what are at present only tentative proposals lies, and the likely cost of absolutely necessary structural work as well as of the refurbishing of the property will have to be given very careful consideration too.

219

A particularly irksome feature of his thinking was that any man appointed should already be involved in church life. One of these men had admitted to having 'no connections whatsoever with the Church or any other Christian body', while the other 'has experience of Church music though without any commitment to any worshipping congregation':

> All things considered, although I liked Barnes as a person I could not express much regret in saying that the lack of accommodation they seek is depriving us of two men who would make a great contribution to the worshipping life of the cathedral.

He seemed unable to understand that, whatever their lack of previous commitment might be, a job as a lay clerk would immediately involve a 'great contribution', for how many other 'worshippers' would attend five services every week, not to mention six practices, maintaining a high degree of professional musicianship in the service of the Church? Had he never heard of proselytizing? In my reply, I pointed out that he had not even mentioned the death and funeral, while I was away, of one of the choristers, and I also told him that one of the young men who had applied from Wells Cathedral for a place in the choir, and who had sung with us in Sweden, had not achieved the requisite results for a place at Cardiff University and would be going to Liverpool Cathedral and University instead.

In September I received a request from the BBC that we should broadcast a morning service on Christmas Day. This was to be transmitted only in Wales, and I lost no time in negotiating appropriate fees for a regional broadcast. My enquiries elicited yet another example of a letter criticising my actions without knowing the true facts, and as a further illustration of this tendency (earlier demonstrated, it will be recalled, by our former headmaster) I reproduce Dean Davies's letter in full:

> I understand from the BBC that you have been in touch with their Contracts Department concerning fees for the choristers for the proposed Christmas Day service which I have been asked to conduct and in which I invited you and the boys to take some part. I have made it clear to the BBC that your approach was made without my knowledge and consent and that I and the Cathedral are not in any way associated with such approaches. If you had any problems or misgivings you could have voiced them to me. I am now making other arrangements for this service which will not involve the participation of any

members of the Cathedral Choir.

Once again his letter showed a complete misunderstanding of the true situation, and again I had to waste my time explaining the truth of the matter:

> It seems that once again I have to write in order to defend myself against your accusations, though I can assure you that it gives me no pleasure to have to justify my actions so often. I have to say that I found the tone of your letter unkind and upsetting.
>
> The fact of the matter is that on the strength of the Cathedral Choir's recent reputation and what I had to say on her radio programme "All things considered" on the first of June, Lucy Hunt (who had interviewed me then) telephoned me to ask if the Choir would take part in a recorded service for transmission on Christmas Day. She explained that after using a number of amateur choirs in previous years, she now wanted a professional one. I told her that for my part, I would be pleased to co-operate, and also that her next step should be to approach the Dean.
>
> When you wrote to say that a facilities fee of £85 to the cathedral was expected to cover choir fees as well, I felt sure there had been some misunderstanding, and phoned Elaine Seer at Contracts to check. There was no question of my making any kind of demand, or re-negotiating behind your back, as you seem to imply: I simply asked what fees were proposed for the choir. In reply she quoted the current rates as agreed between the BBC and the ISM, and I was satisfied. This meant that I would be able to tell you, when discussing dates, that Llandaff would be represented, as it should be on Christmas Day, by the full resources of its cathedral music. I would not have been happy that we should make do with only the boys. The facilities fee is intended as a gift to the cathedral for the use of the building, the organ and personnel, and is quite separate from the recognised fees payable to the musicians themselves.
>
> What upsets me more than misunderstandings of this kind, is that you should think it necessary to treat me more as a naughty boy than as a responsible adult trying to organise things in an orderly way and in the best interests of the cathedral's image. As it is, the choristers, their parents, and the men will want to know why they are not to sing on the radio, and your letter is the only material I can show them by way of explanation.
>
> Since reading your letter, I have discovered that Lucy

Lunt's interest in the programme has now been transferred to Ieuan Russell Jones, who has explained to me that his budget for the service, being limited to a single region, will not cover the outlay offered by the Contracts department. He accepted that in the circumstances you had offered the services of the Parish Choir instead. I can understand this reasoning, which has always been a barrier to the use of Cathedral Choirs except throughout the national network. What I cannot understand is why I should be blamed and, by implication, censured, for creating a situation which arises merely from the ordinary facts of financial life.

As a simple way of clarifying matters to the Headmaster and the Choir, I am sending copies of our correspondence to John Knapp and Gerard Elias.

The Dean did not reply, and on Christmas Day a very plain service was broadcast by the parish choir. A much more interesting venture for the cathedral choir was to participate in the final of a competition organised by HTV for their programme *Wales on Sunday*. Viewers were invited to compose a new Christmas carol, and it was hoped that the winning composition would perhaps achieve the popularity of old favourites like *Silent Night* and *The Holly and the Ivy*. I was invited to join the panel of judges, along with the international opera singer Sir Geraint Evans, Dr George Guest and Rian Evans, a local journalist and broadcaster. We spent over six hours at the Angel Hotel, poring over the submitted manuscripts, and I soon began to feel that the terms of reference had been too vague. Did the organisers want something that could be sung under a lamp post by a few youngsters, or a four-part arrangement for a competent choir, or perhaps a congregational hymn like *While shepherds watched their flocks*? One of the unison carols reminded me of the signature tune of a current television series, but I was unable to recall the tune exactly yet felt fairly sure that Marian would know it well. The upshot of this was that Marian was taken aback to receive a phone call from Sir Geraint, asking her to sing the theme tune to him! It was felt that the similarity was only minimal, and the carol was put on the shortlist of five to be sung in the televised final by the cathedral choir under my direction. My own favourite was a lovely piece by Rhian Davies for two sopranos and piano entitled *Starshine*, but it was thought unsuitable for general popular use, and the chosen winner was a quite straightforward four-part setting with a ding-dong refrain which turned out to have been composed by a blind man. My choir duly filmed the five carols, and it fell to me to present the award to the winner. The programme was transmitted on the Sunday before Christmas, and we performed all five carols at our service of Nine Lessons and Carols on Christmas Eve. *Starshine* was sung by the choristers with organ accompaniment for some years to come. As far as I know, the five carols were not published, an oversight which I felt negated the whole point of the competition, but when a similar competition was won a few years later by Ian Gasson, one of my pupils, I believe HTV had the sense to get them into print.

In November I did something I had never done before, and have never done since, which was to agree on the spot to a very substantial purchase from a sales representative. For some time we had considered replacing the rather cheap kitchen units provided by the Chapter. An astute young lady from Kitchens Direct managed to persuade me in two hours to pay £3500 for a new kitchen on condition that I accepted the contract there and then. The new units were duly installed, and we were delighted with them. I offered to sell them to the Chapter, so that they might be offered eventually to my successor as part of the 'package', but my offer was predictably declined.

My autumn concert with the Choral Society was a performance in German of Brahms's *German Requiem*. They had sung it in English in 1975, but this time I thought it seemed silly to sing a German Requiem in English, and reckoned I knew enough about the language to deal with it, despite objections from a few of the members. When I introduced Kodály's *Missa Brevis* at a Sunday Eucharist, no fewer than seven people came up afterwards to express appreciation – an unusual occurrence indeed! It is one of the very few pieces to include a top C for the trebles, which may have contributed to their enthusiasm.

There is no doubt that the sudden resignation of such a major figure in church music as George Guest put the Llandaff Festival in jeopardy, and its Chairman the Dean in a stronger position. In 1984 I had begun a process which was to strengthen my own hand, by introducing my friend John Knapp on to the Council of Management, as it was now called, and Wynn Lloyd, an old friend of George's, also joined. By 1985 Jill Turner, Headmistress of Howell's School, who sang alto in my choral society, provided further support, and in 1986 another close friend, Clive Westwood, the Secretary of the choral society, had joined, making what I liked to call my 'gang of four'. I put forward the idea that those who thought there was no future for a Festival should resign, and that those of us who had worked hard and were still prepared to work for the Festival's success should be free to do so, and to co-opt other kindred spirits on to the management. I was in favour of a small working executive committee, knowing that Gerard Elias QC, who had amply demonstrated his own management skills by his organisation of choir tours in three countries and the promotion of two recordings, would be ready to act as its Chairman. Wynn Lloyd had resigned in sympathy with George Guest, but at a meeting in September the Council delegated to a small committee consisting of Clive and me, along with David Lambert (deputy Chapter Clerk and now the company secretary) the task of drafting an outline plan for future development. We soon co-opted the rest of the gang of four (Messrs Elias and Knapp) and persuaded Jill Turner to be our chairman. We also recruited one Michael Foster, who having joined the choral society eighteen months earlier as an experienced tenor, had soon proved to be a man of ideas and had already been elected its Treasurer. By the end of the year we had devised a series of five concerts to be spread out from mid May to early July, under the auspices of Llandaff Festival Ltd, with a small loan and with the backing of the Welsh Arts Council. The series would include a concert by three cathedral choirs, another by the choral society, and a visit by the London Festival Orchestra as part of its summer tour of cathedrals. The Dean, still hanging on to his position as company chairman, insisted that the plans be approved by both the Chapter and the parochial church council, and evidently managed to persuade both bodies to forbid the use of the West End for staging concerts, effectively ruling out all but small ensembles. The alternative was not, of course, to use the East End, where the high altar is, but to squeeze all the performers under the *Majestas* arch.

Looking back at my diary, I find certain juxtapositions interesting. In the two days between the judging of carols for the TV competition and the choral society's performance of the Brahms *Requiem*, for example, the choristers sang at a memorial service for Lady Traherne, wife of the Lord Lieutenant, before a huge congregation which included James Callaghan, the former Prime Minister. That evening Marian and I watched Claudio Abbado conducting the London Symphony Orchestra in St David's Hall, and the following night heard a marvellous performance by the Leipzig Gewandhaus Orchestra of Schubert's ninth Symphony which was greeted by five minutes' applause. The settling of my parents in Llandaff, and later visiting my increasingly ailing and despondent mother in a nearby nursing home, were matters dealt with alongside news of the failing health of mother's elder brother James, whom I helped with a move from his Kensington flat into a residential home, on hearing from a Methodist minister that he was 'destitute'. We also effected the transfer of Laura from the Llandaff infants' school to the cathedral school: John Knapp had been sufficiently impressed by her bright manner on the trip to Sweden to offer her an 'honorary choristership', worth half the fees. At the same time, Rachel had heard good reports from school friends who had moved on to the sixth form of King's College, Taunton, and wanted to follow suit: after five years in a girls' school she was looking for some male company and a change of scene, so we spent a couple of days there and she was accepted on a scholarship matching Laura's, but as a boarder. We did not look forward to the prospect of her moving away from home at sixteen, and John Knapp expressed some misgivings about the school, advocating Malvern College instead, but everything seemed to point towards Taunton, and we were pleased to accept the offer.

Among all this activity was the judicious management of the funds I had acquired from the sale of Father's house and the acquisition of his investments; from time to time buying and selling shares as well as spending thousands of pounds on refurbishing St Mary's – something which should have been the responsibility of the Cathedral authorities. Meanwhile Rachel played her 'cello in occasional concerts with the county youth orchestra, Adrian was playing his cornet with a brass class in the City Hall, and I was pleased to hear that one of my students, Nigel Hurley, had won the organ scholarship at Keble College, Oxford

All in all, 1986 proved to be perhaps the most active, varied and interesting year of my life. It closed on New Year's Eve with another quiet dinner which Marian and I shared again with Roy and Ruth Massey, this time at an old farmhouse in Wales, followed by welcoming the New Year drinking port in the lounge of their house in the cloisters of Hereford Cathedral before returning to our family in our beloved cottage in Byford.

The Cathedral Choir on board the old ship Athena in Sweden, 1986

225

*Choristers playing a game with Adrian and Laura at
our annual Christmas Eve party, 1987*

1987

The history of the transition from the long-established Llandaff Festival to the Summer Concerts almost merits a chapter to itself. The first difficulty arose over the date for the proposed opening recital by the world-famous 'cellist Paul Tortelier. It was soon realised that this event, planned for Tuesday 5th May, would involve cancelling the bellringers' regular practice and that they would have to forego their practice on the previous Tuesday as well, to allow for the Dean's insistence on a late Eucharist on St Mark's Day (already celebrated with *four* morning Eucharists). Rescheduling Tortelier's recital to Monday proved impossible, so we settled instead for Julian Lloyd-Webber, well-known but slightly less highly regarded by *cognoscenti*. In the event, for whatever reason, there was no late Eucharist on St Mark's Day, so the bell-ringers were able to practise then, and Tortelier could have accepted the date offered in the first place. To add insult to injury and cause further confusion, Lloyd-Webber telephoned the day before his recital (now moved to a Monday) pleading indisposition, and our committee met at Gerard's house for five hours, including supper, as frantic calls were made to various agents and individuals to find a substitute. Eventually we were very lucky to secure the services of a first-class 'cellist, Alexander Bailey, with the pianist Julian Jacobson.

Far more irritating was the prevarication of the Festival Council, which dithered for months about whether or not to be responsible as the promoter of the Llandaff Summer Concerts, having of course appointed its organising committee the previous September.

I came across the minutes of a meeting of the Parochial Church Council which declared that the concerts were 'wholly independent of the Cathedral and its official bodies'. I wrote to the secretary to deny this misleading statement, pointing out that

1. The organisation responsible for the series has the Bishop as its President, the Dean as its Chairman, and the Assistant Chapter Clerk as its Secretary. I refer, of course, to Llandaff Festival Ltd and its Council of Management.
2. The membership of the Executive Committee commissioned

by the Festival Council last September to plan the concerts under the chairmanship of the Headmistress of Howell's School, was deliberately designed to represent the interests of the Cathedral. It consists of the Deputy Chapter Clerk, the Cathedral Organist, the Chairman of the Cathedral Choir Association, the Headmaster of the Cathedral School, and the Secretary and Treasurer of the Cathedral Choral Society. It would be difficult to imagine a group less independent of the Cathedral and its 'official bodies'.

3. Three of the concerts involve the Cathedral Choir and Organist, and one of them features the Cathedral Choral Society, Maldwyn Davies (formerly tenor lay clerk) and the Lord Bishop himself.

Arthur Impey, the PCC's secretary, read my letter to that council and wrote in reply that while giving its approval it was in no way *financially* involved. It would have been an easy matter to insert this word into their minutes, but he had failed to do so. Moreover, the Dean failed to publish a paragraph about the venture in his *Llandaff Monthly*. It really was extraordinary, though perhaps not for Llandaff, that after the Dean had published an article expressing the view that the Festival had become too big and, by implication, inconvenient, and had stated his intention that it should be contained within a cathedral parish framework, he was now putting obstacles in the way of carefully- chosen representatives of the very bodies he had cited. Various questions were raised concerning tax and liability for loss, and I managed to engineer the co-option of both Gerard Elias and Michael Foster on to the Festival Council, whereupon David Lambert (acting Chapter Clerk) resigned from the concerts committee, and I think the Dean must have seen that he was beaten when he decided to resign the chairmanship. Shortly afterwards the Festival Council confirmed that the concerts committee had indeed been acting as a committee of Llandaff Festival Ltd in preparing the series, and when a proposal was put forward that the concerts should come under the Company's aegis, it was carried by four votes to three. The three who voted against were the parish diehards, and the motion was carried by my friends and me. Then it was the turn of the company treasurer to resign, but Michael Foster soon found a replacement upon whose appointment we agreed. David Lambert, who had distanced himself from 'my' committee but remained on the council to cover legal aspects (being a solicitor), then tried to persuade me to write my own contracts for the choirs of Bristol and Wells Cathedrals (whom I had invited to share a concert with our own cathedral choir), but was out-voted by the council and forced to do it himself. Meanwhile the Dean was obliged by articles of association to nominate a chairman in his place, and settled for his old friend Gethyn Stoodley Thomas as a safe pair of hands. As often happened, the Dean did not look ahead, and for months his exact position *vis-à-vis* the Festival remained unclear.

Matters came to a head when Michael Foster, acting as secretary to the committee, was interviewed by a reporter on the *Western Mail*. Recalling the resignation of Dr Guest after the last Festival, and outlining the new Summer Concerts series, he declared that the future looked dubious unless the council were prepared to change their attitude. 'The birth pangs of this concert season have been horrendous', he said. The *Western Mail* reporter, under an enormous headline 'Top music festival folds', wrote:

> He launched an attack on the festival council, claiming they had attempted to renege on their commitment to the concert season. Mr Foster said that at a council meeting last September he and five others had been commissioned to explore the possibility of an alternative to the festival. The invitation had been duly noted in the official minutes. Then at a meeting on March 4, just two months before the projected start date of the concert season, the council had begun backing out, Mr Foster alleged. "They attempted to distance themselves", he said. "They said they had only given us the impetus and that our committee had to be wholly independent of them. They said they would give us £1000, and if the concerts made a profit they would take the profit and expect the £1000 back. However, if it made a loss we would have to be responsible for it, although they wouldn't ask us to return the £1000". In other words, Mr Foster said, "they were expecting a group of six private individuals to withstand a loss of maybe several thousands of pounds". Finally, after a long debate, the council had agreed to back them, but the future situation still remained extremely dicey because of the council's ambiguous position.

Evidently the Dean's opinion had been sought, for he was reported as having insisted that the summer concerts committee had nothing to do with the Llandaff Festival, 'although Mr Foster would say that they had', adding that 'the Cathedral is not in any way directly involved with the concerts'. By this time, his nominee Gethyn had already thrown in the towel, and the Dean seemed uncertain what should happen next, adding that he 'had made it clear that he would wish other arrangements to be made'. Asked why he was so keen to end his association with the festival council, he allegedly replied 'I am not prepared to go into that now'. David Lambert immediately wrote to me about what he called 'Michael Foster's attack on the Festival Council and the Dean', professing astonishment that internal matters, as he saw them, had been made so public, and resigning as company secretary forthwith. The Dean, for once taking a rather more conciliatory view, reached a similar conclusion when writing to me a few days later:

> I do not think that the report accurately reflected what was said by Michael Foster or by me, and I am sorry that it is likely to damage a venture of a committee that is eager to maintain the Llandaff Festival tradition. At the same time it brings into the open a situation about which I and the Cathedral authorities have been very much concerned, and I have written to the Bishop of Llandaff as President of the Llandaff Festival to say that I am no longer prepared to act as Chairman of Llandaff Festival Ltd. Mr David Lambert has resigned as Secretary of the Company and he has informed the Registrar of Companies that neither he, nor I, now hold any office in the Company.

To present *Western Mail* readers with more positive information, a letter signed by all five members of my committee was published ten days later, with outline information and dates about the forthcoming series. At one point the Dean had tried to get the Festival's Steinway concert grand piano out of the Cathedral, and had to be reminded that it did occasionally need to be played if for some reason the organ were out of action. The Council briefly considered selling it, but fortunately wiser counsel prevailed and it is still kept in the south choir aisle to this day.

It is no small wonder that, despite all these regrettable shenanigans the Llandaff Summer Concerts took place at all. The opening 'cello recital was followed in mid May by the three cathedral choirs, the organists of Bristol and Wells, Malcolm Archer and Anthony Crossland, taking their turn to conduct a quite monumental programme of choral music interspersed with two substantial organ works:

Magnificat for three choirs	Andrea Gabrieli
Hear my prayer, O Lord (8 parts)	Henry Purcell
Crucifixus etiam pro nobis (8 parts)	Antonio Lotti
Organ Symphony no 2, first movement	Louis Vierne
In exitu Israel de Egypto (double choir)	Samuel Wesley
Ascribe unto the Lord (with organ)	Samuel Sebastian Wesley
Vox dicentis: Clama	E W Naylor

Faire is the Heaven (double choir)	William Harris
Organ Symphony no 6, Finale	Charles Widor
Te Deum (Collegium Regale)	Herbert Howells
Laudate Pueri (for three choirs)	Kenneth Leighton

The choral items here are among the most outstanding in the whole repertoire, and it was a rare privilege indeed to perform them with the combined resources of three major cathedrals.

The Choral Society had been busily rehearsing two works of a very different kind for our own three choirs concert in St David's Hall, joining forces for the third time with Clifford Bunford and his University Chorus and Cardiff Bach Choir. The works performed this time had no part for me, either as assistant conductor or as gong-player, so I sat in the audience of 1,400 listening to Constant Lambert's flamboyant work with piano and orchestra *The Rio Grande* and that popular favourite of recent times, *Carmina Burana* by Carl Orff, separated by Gershwin's Piano Concerto.

Family matters had come to the fore with the death on 13 February of my Uncle James, known to the United Nations and various publishers as Dr James Avery Joyce. I wrote his obituary for *The Times,* and the curtailing of some of my best sentences was more than compensated for by the £75 fee I unexpectedly received. I made contact with various people in Geneva with whom he had been associated over the years, and after his cremation at the City of London Cemetery a casket containing his ashes was sent to the Cimetière de St Georges for interment with those of his ex-wife, my erstwhile Aunt Barbara. I helped my cousin Colin deal with our uncle's effects, which consisted mostly of books which were accepted by appropriate libraries; Colin kept his barrister's wig, together with a small pistol – an odd item to be found in the possession of a life-long worker for Peace, but thought to be the weapon with which a burglar shot and killed his grandfather, a policeman, in 1892. I kept the police diary for that year, and also a couple of my uncle's photograph albums which included pictures showing James meeting high-ranking people such as Clement Attlee, former Prime minister, and U Thant, Director General of the United Nations - who contributed the foreword to James's book *The Story of International Cooperation* published in 1964 and dedicated to his father (my grandfather).

The 1987 edition of the Diocesan Directory still credited Father Holcombe with an ARCM, and when I again mentioned it to the editor, he replied 'Yes, Graham Holcombe is ARCM – I checked it with him, he received it in 1969'. On finding the same information in Crockford's, the recognised directory of the clergy, I again wrote to the Registrar of the Royal College of Music. Although I requested that

Holcombe should not be told of my interest, Jasper Thorogood wrote to him direct this time, saying:

> It has come to my notice that you use the letters ARCM with regard to an examination passed here in organ playing in 1969. I am afraid I can find no trace of your success in this examination and I would be very glad to hear from you so that we can get matters straight.

Ignoring my strictures, he added below his signature 'cc Dr Michael Smith – organist Llandaff Cathedral', so clearly my least favourite priest vicar knew he had been rumbled, but by then he had already left to become Vicar of Pentyrch in the Vale of Glamorgan. I felt like writing to the Bishop about my discovery, since Holcombe had no doubt claimed to have a diploma when accepting his appointment as a Priest Vicar, but when I found that the false information had been removed from the Diocesan Directory, I decided to let sleeping dogs lie. It was only many years later that the false information was removed from his entry in Crockford's, and as I write this, twenty-three years later, Fr Holcombe has been elevated to the status of residentiary canon. It would not surprise me if he eventually acquired the title of Precentor, or even became Dean.

Returning to the three concerts we organised for June, the connection with the 'authorities' which we had striven to cultivate, was strengthened by the appearance of the Bishop himself as the Narrator, standing in the pulpit to deliver passages from *The Rule of St Benedict* at the first performance in Wales of a choral work entitled *Benedictus*, composed seven years earlier by Howard Blake. The composer had become a household name for his appealing work *The Snowman,* which includes the even more celebrated song *Walking in the Air.* We all found his choral work, a setting of texts from the Psalms and the mystical poetry of Francis Thompson, very pleasant to learn and perform, and its excellent tenor solo part was sung by our former lay clerk Maldwyn Davies, who by now was at the top of his profession. A review by Kenneth Loveland in the *South Wales Argus* described its musical style succinctly and somewhat laconically:

> Mr Blake has a collection of winners up his sleeve and plays them adroitly to create atmosphere. The tolling bell over a *basso ostinato*, the occasional flirting with *Sprechgesang,* the glockenspiel decorations and harp *glissandi*, the tunes that go where we expect and common chords that occur where we do not, romantically-orientated harmonies and mystic *diminuendi*, they all work. But they have worked before... Next time we hope he will tell us more about himself.

A harp recital by Sioned Williams at Howell's School separated this event from the last of the series, when the cathedral choir contributed Mozart's so-called *Sparrow Mass* to a concert given by the London Festival Orchestra, directed by 'cellist Ross Pople and doing the rounds of British cathedrals throughout the summer. A full house heard us with celebrated soprano Heather Harper in Mozart's anthem *Laudate Dominum*, the orchestra accompanied me in the *Adagio* attributed (wrongly) to Albinoni, and a Vivaldi concerto for two trumpets and Britten's song cycle *Les Illuminations* completed a very satisfying programme.

For some reason best known to himself Clive Westwood, who did an excellent job as secretary to the Choral Society, decided to stand down for two terms, and Michael Foster, who had so quickly assumed the role of treasurer, was appointed acting secretary. As I have said, he was a man of ideas, and a hard worker, and he lost no time in preparing us all for the Society's Golden Jubilee to be celebrated in the year 1987/88. It fell to me to make a presentation to two founder members who had sung in the choir ever since I was born! The celebrations began in October with a dinner and dance at the Angel Hotel, and a very interesting concert of Christmas music by British composers kept the members on their toes throughout the term. One is sometimes hard put to it when it comes to choosing suitable works for a Christmas concert, and I was really pleased to offer the following programme of music by 20th century British composers:

Parry	Ode on the Nativity (1912, but first performance in Wales)
Finzi	*In Terra Pax* (1954)
Vaughan Williams	Fantasia on Christmas Carols (1912)
Hoddinott	Bells of Paradise (1984)
Hely-Hutchinson	Carol Symphony (1928)

Of these works only the Vaughan Williams was well-known, and although I knew the Finzi from Oxford days, I had not heard the other pieces before (or since). The first two works included a soprano soloist, Melanie Armitstead, the next two a baritone, our former lay clerk David Gwesyn Smith, and he and the choristers had parts in Hoddinott's work, which turned out to be colourful and enjoyable: the composer (who had unceremoniously cast me off from his staff, it may be remembered, ten years earlier) wrote to thank me for performing the work 'so beautifully: everything was in place and as I had imagined; I am most grateful to you for your really splendid direction which resulted in such a fine performance'. A *Western Mail* reviewer found the Parry too heavily-scored against soprano and chorus, and said of the Hely-Hutchinson: 'Popular carols were strung together in his Carol Symphony, which often threatened to outstay its welcome – and finally did so'. I suspect that if I had looked more carefully at these unheard-of works, I might have reached the same conclusion and not attempted them, but spurred on by the enthusiasm of Mr Foster, who also compiled a very informative souvenir programme book, full of information about the Society's past, its former conductors, lists of works performed and soloists engaged, I was so impressed that I made the mistake of thinking that he could do no wrong.

The committee had agreed, with the backing of the Welsh Arts Council, that we should commission a new work for the spring concert. I wanted to ask Richard Shephard, but was told that funding would be available only for a Welsh composer, or at least someone working in Wales. In the end we invited David Nevens, the English Vice-Principal of the Welsh College of Music and Drama, to compose a *Te Deum* with brass band accompaniment (making a score less expensive than one for full orchestra). It was initially proposed that this should be performed on the 12th March along with Haydn's 'Nelson' Mass and Rossini's *Stabat Mater,* though the programme was later changed and the date brought forward by a week. It gradually dawned on me that a contemporary work would present difficulties greater than usual, and that with only seven rehearsals between January and the proposed concert date we would never manage it. My next chapter will show how the problem proved impossible to solve, and how Mr Foster's ambitious ideas became even more unmanageable as time went on. Meanwhile, the first hint of trouble ahead came from the Society's auditor, who revealed 'what seems to be a serious state of affairs' in the annual accounts. I have always kept away from financial issues that do not affect me directly, believing that it is the treasurer's responsibility to keep them in check. In 1986 Michael Foster had warned the committee that despite assets of some £4000, we would need to take measures to increase our income, partly by increasing members' subscriptions. In 1987 the auditor wrote to him, warning that 'any further deterioration... will mean that the Society would be unable to pay its debts – a situation which is totally unthinkable; it is therefore essential that all future expenditure is most carefully and cautiously budgeted'. He was disturbed that full details of the accounts for the year ending in July had not been ready for the AGM in September, and he had already signified his intention to resign his position - clearly aware that Mr Foster was already planning to involve the Society in one of the most expensive choral works in the repertoire – Berlioz's Requiem, the *Grande Messe des Morts* – as part of our 1987/88 Jubilee celebrations. A tentative idea for another combined choirs concert in St David's Hall under Owain Arwel Hughes had failed to materialise, whereupon Sir David Willcocks was brought into the negotiations, but there were several more bridges yet to cross: meanwhile the last year's accounts remained unaudited until well into the following year, with further ramifications, as we shall see.

Called for the second time for jury service in June, I felt that I benefited from previous experience. I remembered not to dress too smartly, in order to avoid rejection by counsel, and during preliminary discussions in recess I made a sufficiently good impression to be elected foreman. It was an arson case involving two lads who were setting light to pieces of newspaper in a boarded-up house, causing a major fire. Only one lad appeared before us, and when we had heard all the evidence, I put it to my fellow jurors that we could not decide 'beyond reasonable doubt' that the accused was the guilty one, because the fire could just as well have been caused by his companion. I sent a note to this effect to the Judge, who responded that we had to give our verdict only according to the evidence heard. Nevertheless my intervention clearly swayed the rest of the jury, and I had the pleasure of standing up and pronouncing those life-enhancing words 'Not guilty!' Afterwards I felt that this was a good example to show that verdicts depend not so much on the obvious truth, as on the skill of a clever barrister, or in this case perhaps the lateral thinking of a clever, if misguided, juror?

A week's examining assignment in Dorset during July incorporated some fascinating diversions. I was able to stay for three nights with my niece Elizabeth at my mother-in-law's home in Woodfalls and visit friends in Salisbury. I had arranged not to work on the Wednesday, and found time to drink coffee in Jeremy Davies's garden in Salisbury Close before taking a train to London, where I met Marian for lunch at the Great Western Hotel. Changing into morning dress, I took her to Buckingham Palace for our second Royal Garden Party – this time in my capacity as a Council member of the Royal College of Organists. The guests included some famous faces such as cabinet ministers Geoffrey Howe, Norman Tebbit and Lord Murray. Then it was back to Dorset for more examining, returning to Cardiff on Saturday in time to see my choristers performing at St David's Hall in Mathias's *This Worldes Joie*, which I had introduced to Wales nine years earlier.

The year 1987 stands out in my memory for none of these things, but for the summer vacation, which was remarkable for two major events, an international conference and the longest international family holiday of our lives. The July event was the International Congress of the Incorporated Association of Organists, which this year took place in Cambridge. On arrival at Jesus College and finding my room for the week, I was surprised to find, sitting on the bed, a girl half my age, who instantly recognised me. It turned out that she had been a music student in Cardiff, a trumpeter whom I had once accompanied at a musical soirée for organists in Penarth. Sorting out the apparent double-booking, we found ourselves in adjacent rooms with a connecting kitchen, and instantly began to enjoy each other's company. I found her personality absolutely electrifying, and during the course of the week I sometimes witnessed other men taking notice of her, for she had a gift of making conversation easily, but mostly she and I had selected different events from the great many available, and tended not to meet very often. When the day was done, however, we would retire to my room, drink wine, compare our experiences and feel at home with each other before retiring to bed.

The content of the Congress was truly astonishing in its scope and interest, spread around thirty churches and college chapels with their organs of different styles: for example, at lunch time I heard each of Louis Vierne's six organ 'symphonies' in as many days. One evening I attended three sherry parties in succession, ending with supper at the home of Sir David Willcocks, who then very kindly drove me to King's College Chapel in time for a concert of Handel's music played by the Academy of Ancient Music. It would be impossible to imagine a more fascinating and diverse series of events, or a larger gathering of organists amateur and professional (it was said there were a thousand delegates) along with six professional choirs. In Cambridge there were some 160 events in seven days, and I attended about a quarter of them, hearing nineteen organists in eleven recitals, seven lectures, eleven classes, demonstrations and presentations of various kinds, and eight concerts. So many of my friends and acquaintances were there, and the heady combination of all this and my meeting with Catherine gave me such a sense of elation that I feared the rest of my life would be an anti-climax. The official Congress Banquet had to be spread round several college halls, and I looked forward to sitting with Catherine in the hall of Jesus College, only to find that as a Council member of the Royal College of Organists I was expected to dine at High Table and entertain two lady organists from America. I briefly introduced her to an FRCO called Andrew who at that time served in the diplomatic service in Brussels, and she sat with him instead, though we did meet afterwards in the bar at King's College with my old friend Michael Nicholas.

There was a coach outing to Ely Cathedral to hear Gillian Weir with the BBC Philharmonic give the world premiere of an organ concerto by Michael Berkeley; and on the last day delegates travelled to London, where some of us braved Holy Trinity, Sloane Street, to hear the first complete performance of the huge Organ Symphony no.1 by the Indian composer Kaikhosru Shapurji Sorabji, composed in 1925 but hitherto deemed (even by its composer) to be unplayable. At last, at the age of 95, Sorabji had consented to allow this performance, which was shared between two international first prize winners, Kevin Bowyer and Thomas Trotter. I have never heard such dense, turgid and unremitting counterpoint, much of it being written on four staves with hardly a rest in sight, and with many complicated cross-rhythms indistinguishable to the ear. The work is inhumanly long, and after listening to the first two movements for seventy-two minutes Catherine and I could stand it no longer. We took refuge in the Royal Court Hotel for lunch, but felt a little embarrassed when we were spotted by Tom Trotter, who was likewise seeking respite after contributing the second movement. I never heard how many people were still in the audience when Kevin's third movement eventually ground to a standstill, and I failed to understand why anybody should want to slave away for so many hours to prepare such a forbidding and unrelenting work. I said goodbye to Catherine on Victoria Station, because that is how such brief encounters are supposed to end, but we did actually walk back to Westminster Cathedral to hear yet another recital, this time shared by Nicolas Kynaston and David Hill and including grand pieces by the likes of Vierne, Widor and Reubke. Returning home the next day I still felt emotionally drained by the whole rich experience.

The other conferences I attended, for the COA in Liverpool and the newly-founded Association of British Choral Conductors in Oxford, pale into insignificance and are now forgotten, though my elevation to Chairman of the ARCO examiners, entailing setting the papers and marking them alongside John Sanders and my former tutor Dr Bernard Rose, did give me a small sense of importance which I missed elsewhere, since my unparalleled qualifications as an organist had evidently not merited an invitation to join the 160 distinguished musicians who took an active part in the IAO Congress.

August was taken up with a quite different holiday with the family, touring Europe by car. We spent a couple of days with a family in Besançon where Rachel had stayed on an orchestral course four years earlier, and a further few days at the home of an old friend of Uncle James's near Vevey before taking the lake steamer to the thirteenth century castle at Chillon. The next part of the tour found us camping on the shore of Lake Maggiore, exploring two of the islands, and then moving on to Milan Cathedral in all its glory. A 230-mile journey took us to a campsite on the Lido island which forms the Venetian lagoon, allowing the family their first sight of that wonderful city from a motor launch approaching the Doge's Palace in the magical light of the early evening. We made a brief foray into Yugoslavia, and eventually made our return journey via the spectacular Grossglockner Pass, ascending to 8,000 feet as we drove along the high Alpine road to the village of Saalbach in the Austrian Tyrol. Here we spent a whole week in a chalet overlooking the valley, leaving the car and just relaxing and walking. Our return journey followed the eastern shore of Lake Constance into the Black Forest, where I had cycled more than thirty years earlier, and took in the cathedral cities of Strasbourg, Laon and Amiens on our way back to our Herefordshire cottage.

No chapter would be complete without a few decanal anecdotes. The Dean was fanatical about Saints' days, and even on a weekday would put on seven services, including five Eucharists, the idea being that no one had an excuse not to attend, the other services being 'said' Matins and Evening Prayer. Quite often, except on Wednesdays, we would sing Evensong at 6 and the parish choir would sing the Eucharist at 7.30, having taken our place in the song room for the extra practice needed. February 2nd is a feast day known as Candlemas, which celebrates the presentation of the baby Jesus in the Temple, and the evening Eucharist would include a special ceremony of some sort. The Dean was keen that parishioners who belonged to the choral society should not miss the service by attending their regular Monday rehearsal. As the society's chairman he could not bring himself to order the cancellation of the rehearsal, so instead he banned us from our usual rehearsal room in the Church in Wales Primary School, of which he was a governor. The man often seemed unable to envisage the outcome of his more ridiculous pronouncements, and this was a case in point: we simply met a few hundred yards down the road, in the hall of Howell's School (of which he was not a governor).

My second example concerns the compiling of the monthly music scheme, which was always very nicely printed, though not very widely exhibited. The system was for the senior priest vicar to type out a list of all the statutory services (of which there were about thirty each week), leaving room for me to fill in details of the music. This had already caused trouble on one occasion with Graham Holcombe, but his place had been taken by a very nice man called John Ward, who was no Holy Joe but much more down to earth. In early April I arrived home after a week's examining in the Isle of Wight to find one of the Dean's unwelcome missives awaiting me. This time he informed me that Father Ward was surprised when the scheme, which he had delivered on the previous day, had been returned uncompleted. Sensing some sinister ulterior motive on my part, he laboriously explained that 'this sheet is published largely in order that the organist and choir may have the opportunity of publicising the music to sing at choral services'. Even more tediously he went on to request that Father Ward receive 'details for the Sundays in May, weekdays on which the choir will sing Evensong, and the Sung Eucharist on the evening of the Feast of SS. Philip and James'. He ended with a thinly-veiled threat: 'If he does not receive this information... the sheet will simply be printed without music details and consideration will be given to the question of the production of the service sheet in the future in this form'. Of course I had been following this procedure since 1974, long before the Dean was even appointed, and had no desire to stop now, so I crossed the road to see John Ward, only to discover that Marian, on seeing on the mat a brown envelope with John's name and address on it, had simply popped it through his letterbox, assuming it was some correspondence intended for him. I left him to face the Dean with this simple but unforeseen explanation. A week later, when writing to ask the Dean to promote some probationers, I added the terse sentence 'The recent misunderstanding could have been avoided by a brief phone call to Marian while I was away'. For once he felt obliged to eat humble pie, beginning 'I am sorry about what appears to be (*sic*) a misunderstanding. As far I can see, I in my generation, and you in yours, were taught to address letters and packages to the people for whom they were intended. Need I say more?'

This brings me to my third example of the Dean's shortcomings. It was unfortunate that Fr Ward had considerable difficulty singing his part in the services. The musical phrases associated with the Preces and Versicles to which the choir adds the Responses are easy enough in Tudor settings, but vary somewhat in twentieth century settings, and as everything is unaccompanied, the choir depends on the priest for finding the right notes. At John's request I actually made recordings of the music to help him, but things would have been much easier if I could have relied on the Dean to appoint a musician to the post. In fairness, most priest vicars managed well enough, but when explaining my problem to the Dean I ventured to write 'We all like him very much, and I am reluctant to offer criticism, but I am sure you would expect me to make some comment on the matter. I only wish you would permit me to audition those who apply, so that this kind of embarrassment can be avoided: I know this is the general practice elsewhere'. This request was part of a long letter dealing with various points, to which he replied at equal length, but regarding the shortcomings of Fr Ward he typed a second letter on the same day, twenty lines long, to cover this specific problem, laboriously setting out all the duties expected of the junior clergy, and ending 'Introducing a formal audition into the appointment process would be wrong as it would give the impression that the cathedral clergy should see the singing of choral services as a major part of their work'. I forebore to rise to the bait, but historically the function of a priest vicar (or, in cathedrals of the New Foundation, minor canons) was, I thought, primarily to deputise vocally for non-musical canons. Even if this were now only a minor part of their work, the fact was that they were expected to 'perform' in public six times a week without making an exhibition of incompetence while also confusing the choir.

Generally speaking, the autumn rarely yielded any particularly interesting ventures, but this year I was invited to take over from the Revd Clive Jones the direction of a small hand-picked mixed choir of up to eighteen singers, then known as the Cardiff Palestrina Choir. For logistical reasons they renamed themselves after Tallis when I took over in September. In some ways I was rather reluctant to take on regular work with a third choir, not least because we rehearsed in the song room, where I already took at least ten practices a week, but I was persuaded to do so by Mary Williams, daughter of the former Dean. They proved to be a very pleasant group, including my tenor lay clerk Michael Davidson and Diana Lambert (Head of Music at Adrian's school and wife of David), and I managed to build up an interesting repertoire which made use of the cathedral's music library while by no means being dependent upon it. We met on Thursday evenings (hitherto free of choral work) and as I sat at the grand piano week by week I never felt that my direction was sufficiently dynamic, but we were offered a sprinkling of engagements from time to time, sometimes to sing Evensong in a village church, usually followed by half a dozen extra anthems, and at other times to sing madrigals at a garden party; a Christmas carol service was a regular engagement in the modern chapel of St Michael's Theological College, and we gave the occasional concert in the cathedral's Lady Chapel, but we did not have the means of advertising ourselves widely and our audiences there were limited to local supporters. My work with the Cardiff Tallis Singers was unpaid at first, but later they agreed to contribute a small weekly subscription to my coffers.

The other major change was a family one, for Rachel took up residence at King's College, Taunton, a boys' independent school in Somerset which had decided to introduce girls into the sixth form. She soon found her feet there, and only the next month she was taking the leading part in Agatha Christie's play *Spider's Web*. Towards the end of the year, the ingenious Gerard attempted to follow our successful tour of Sweden in 1986 with an equally interesting and more ambitious tour in the United States. An agent produced detailed plans including two services and nine concerts within a fortnight, in Chicago, Illinois, Wisconsin, Milwaukee, Minnesota and Minneapolis. It seemed a wonderful way of spending most of our Easter vacation, but sadly it never came to fruition because it would have cost £850 per person, which in 1987 was more than many of us, not least myself, could afford to pay.

We moved into the cottage at Byford on Boxing Day, but celebrated New Year's Eve quite differently, returning to Llandaff and providing lunch for no fewer than nineteen members of Marian's family (including our own) squeezed round two tables in our dining room – the last such gathering until her mother's ninetieth birthday in 2001.

1988

There were many reasons why a Choral Society concert planned for March had to be cancelled. The scheduled publication of the new work had simply not happened, and we actually had to make our own photocopies of the composer's manuscript, which was, as is often the case, far from clear. It was also full of mistakes and uncertainties, of which I listed forty for correction and elucidation. This aspect, coupled with the difficulty of the music itself, was a major stumbling block for an amateur chorus accustomed to clearly-printed vocal scores. Nevens did not provide a part for the organist's use until a week before the concert date, and the young musicians of the National Youth Brass Band had nothing to rehearse until three weeks earlier. Moreover, the work included unauthorised parts for soprano and baritone soloists, entailing a potential increase in performance costs. When this was pointed out to the composer, he invited two recent graduates from his college to sing, one of them being Bryn Terfel, who was to become a household name on the international stage. The chosen concert date, 5 March, was earlier than usual for a spring concert, and a cathedral rehearsal the previous week was ruled out by the Dean on the grounds that it was the Eve of St David's Day. It was I who had thought of following this *Te Deum* with eight short Latin motets by Bruckner, mostly *a capella* in four parts, but in two cases making use of three trombones. An Arts Council representative had quite sensibly suggested suitable music by Gabrieli, Purcell and Vaughan Williams, extending the repertoire across four centuries, and it was Michael Foster who added the final straw by advocating a setting of the Mass by another contemporary composer, Jean Langlais, with accompaniment of two organs. We even had to hire an electronic chamber organ because the Dean would not allow the cathedral's small pipe organ to be moved into the right position.

There is no doubt that the cancellation of the concert at only two weeks' notice set the cat among the pigeons, so to speak, ticket money having to be refunded to some 150 people. Foster must have felt very put out by the collapse of a significant part of his plans for the Jubilee season, but in all the circumstances there was no need for him to shift the blame on to my shoulders. At the ensuing *post mortem* meeting he tabled the existing constitution, along with a draft amendment disconnecting the society from the cathedral and proposing that the chairman be elected by the society, and the conductor 'appointed in a manner specified by the committee'. I was not present at this meeting, being away examining in Taunton, but its agenda included the statement:

> Extra rehearsals should have been arranged, and the Conductor's failure to either do this or delete the difficult work from the programme had lowered confidence. It was noted that the Society is now the only choir in Wales who did not have appointment rights over its Musical Director. Steps would be taken at the AGM to 'regularise' this situation. The Chairman (the Dean) indicated that no opposition was likely from the Chapter.

At the next meeting this minute was also declared to be an inaccurate account of what was said, and the last two sentences were amended to read:

> Steps would be taken to *consider the matter.* The Chairman indicated that the Chapter *would consider the matter sympathetically.*

The reference to 'appointment rights' relates to the society's constitution, dating back to its foundation and last revised in 1978, stating that the Chairman should be *ex officio* the Dean and likewise the conductor the cathedral organist. In fact the original draft of my service agreement with the Chapter actually required me to accept the conductorship, and the constitution even required the deputy chairman (who normally presided over committee meetings) to be appointed by the Dean and Chapter. By now I had successfully chosen, prepared and conducted nearly forty cathedral concerts covering more than seventy major works, and I should have foreseen the impractical nature of Foster's ambitious project. Luckily this did not go down at all well, and both of his revolutionary proposals were voted down. Foster's minutes stated that the first proposal was defeated by eight votes, and the second by twenty, but the members later disputed these figures and insisted on attributing the defeat in both cases to 'a large majority'. At my insistence a sentence was added to the minutes of a later committee meeting at which these issues were raised, stating 'Dr Smith was displeased that a matter affecting him personally had not been brought to his attention before publication of the Agenda', and it was agreed that any future proposals to amend the constitution should first be discussed in committee.

Some efforts had been made to find a permanent treasurer to resume the work which Foster had continued after taking over as secretary, and a well-qualified young lady had volunteered, but by December 1987 she still had not received the audited accounts and declined to act. Six weeks into 1988 she wrote to the deputy chairman 'This situation is most unsatisfactory and I am therefore giving you formal notice of my resignation as treasurer. I feel that I have been very badly treated in this matter and placed in a very difficult situation'. We had planned to perform the Nevens *Te Deum* a second time at our Golden Jubilee Service in May, but had to be content with Parry's gorgeous and most appropriate eight-part anthem with organ, his setting of Milton's great poem *At a Solemn Musick* beginning with the words *Blest pair of Sirens, pledges of Heaven's joy, Sphere-born harmonious sisters, Voice and Verse.*

The committee had decided long ago that we should sing a big work in St David's Hall, combining with other choirs, and I am glad to say that this venture was a complete success. The University Choir was unavailable in late June, but our 107 singers were again joined by the Cardiff Bach Choir, and along with the 122 voices of the Morriston Tabernacle Choir and the 'chamber choir' of the Welsh College of Music and Drama numbered altogether over 300 voices. The committee had also decided to engage a 'proper' professional conductor, and I was commissioned to find one! I put forward several names, first approaching Sir David Willcocks, who expressed the opinion that I ought to conduct it myself. As he was committed elsewhere on the proposed date, I contacted Sir Charles Groves, who apparently had a reputation for being kind to amateur choirs. He agreed to take on the combined forces of the four choirs, four brass bands provided by the Welsh Guards, and the Guildford Philharmonic Orchestra, who had recently performed the massive work in their home town. For the short solo part we engaged one of Wales's best-known tenors, Robert Tear, who charged over £1600 for ten minutes (nearly as much as the conductor). Although Sir Charles was an affable chap, I found his laid-back rehearsal manner distinctly lack-lustre, and reckoned that I could have done a better job at galvanising the performers into a really exciting experience. The actual performance was one of the very few occasions when I wished I could have jumped up on to the platform and take over the baton. I could have done it, and would have relished it, but the choice of conductor was not a decision I was empowered to make.

In the Autumn Michael Foster's ambitious nature took him a step further when he persuaded Jill Turner, in her capacity as chairman of Llandaff Festival Ltd, to nominate him as a suitable member of the Welsh Arts Council's music committee, on the strength of a degree in Music from the University of Nottingham and a law degree from London.

There was just enough money available to honour our commitment to our regular BBC players in December for a cathedral performance of Bach's *Mass in B minor.* Not content with insisting that it should be at the front of the nave, the Dean also ordered us to remove all the seating and other equipment between the rehearsal and the performance, to allow for choral evensong at 6. Since a Saturday evensong was rarely attended at this time of year by more than ten people, who should in any case be sitting in the Choir, this requirement was felt to be exceptionally unreasonable; and dissatisfaction was expressed, not for the first time, at the somewhat casual way in which Barry Haskey, our orchestra fixer, dealt with certain aspects of his assignments, sometimes incurring extra expense. He tended to offer his players well above Musicians' Union rates, and the outcome of all this was that the Society was henceforth unable to afford them. Our reputation in turn was dented by the failure of many members to return their Berlioz scores, which had been hired from the BBC Library. Efforts were made to find the culprits, some of whom had left the choir meanwhile, but we had to send a cheque for nearly £300 by way of compensation for the missing copies, receiving a stern rejoinder from the BBC's library manager in London ending 'As the whole episode has been most unsatisfactory and must not recur, I have no alternative but to make it impossible for the Llandaff Choral Society to hire any material owned by this library again'. I hastened to inform him that I was in no way responsible for the missing copies, having had nothing to do with their distribution, listing, collection or recovery, nor did I conduct the performance or even take part in it. I had enjoyed very cordial relations with the BBC over many years, and did not want my reputation besmirched by the folly and incompetence of others.

The Llandaff Summer Concerts continued as planned, and although audience figures were disappointing for a recital by the young clarinettist Emma Johnson and that splendid girls' choir Cantamus which had just won the Sainsbury's Choir of the Year competition, the opening concert was something of a landmark in the cathedral's history, for it seemed likely that the Three Choirs performance of Monteverdi's *Vespers* with Bristol and Wells cathedrals was a first for Llandaff. The use of period instruments, more recently taken for granted, was not then widespread, and on this occasion we engaged the Bristol Sinfonia and three professional tenors, the *continuo* being provided by Christopher Brayne, Malcolm Archer and Michael Hoeg on two harpsichords and a chamber organ. Unlike the previous year's concert, this was not repeated in the other two cathedrals. Another collaboration with the London Festival Orchestra in their own Cathedral

245

Classics series included the cathedral choir in Schubert's *Mass in G*, but was somewhat sullied by their management's reluctance to pay the level of fees we had requested, being twice what they had paid us previously. Gerard entered into negotiations while I was away examining in Cornwall, and I took the trouble to enquire of a dozen of my colleagues in other cathedrals, finding that the majority were paid more (in one case six times as much). The orchestra's administrator failed to respond to our suggestion that the participation of our choir was likely to attract seventy or eighty people to the concert who would not otherwise support it. The orchestra's director, Ross Pople, added flames to the fire by writing to me

> 'I can't think your heart is in the event. Your letters to other cathedral organists can only be construed as mischievous. You have lost sight of your rôle as a colleague in a unifying and noble enterprise'.

Gerard, with his high profile as a QC, once again hastened to my defence, replying:

> I do find the contents of your letter entirely unreasonable. Not only are you content to describe Michael Smith's action in contacting his own Cathedral Organist colleagues as 'mischievous', patently falsely to describe my letter as 'overtly threatening', but you arrogate to yourself, with no justification that I am aware of, your concert at Llandaff as being a 'keystone' in the Llandaff Summer Concerts. What rôle are you playing in this 'unifying and noble enterprise'? Your response to our reasonable request has been extremely disappointing to the Choir, and your wild allegations most distasteful to Michael and myself. Is there any real secrecy as to the terms of engagement of a cathedral choir within the Cathedral Classics series?

The problem was partially solved when the shortfall was made up from the reserves of Llandaff Festival Ltd, but we did not engage the orchestra again. Nor were we entirely happy with the local company we had engaged to help promote and market our own series; it seemed that being operated by the sister of the prominent operatic tenor Dennis O'Neill was not a guarantee of its efficiency. The cathedral choir had a busy schedule this summer, for we put on yet another concert, in memory of our chorister who had died a year before: it was intended to raise funds to commission an anthem by Howard Blake, whose *Benedictus* we had staged around that time, but being inundated with work he was unable to produce the goods, and the commission later passed to my old friend Richard Shephard, as I have mentioned earlier.

At intervals throughout these memoirs the reader will come across my ongoing attempts to secure a better financial package from the Dean and Chapter. It was not only my meagre salary that exercised me, but also the lack of a pension to go with it. On my appointment in 1974 I had been allocated an endowment life insurance policy worth £2000, and in 1983 the Chapter Clerk had begun to explore the possibility of a proper service pension. In the autumn of 1984 there was some slow progress when a quotation was received from the Sun Alliance company, the Chapter offering at long last to pay an annual premium of £253.87 which, it was said, would produce an annual pension of £2,931 or a tax-free lump sum approaching £20,000. My own enquiries elicited the information that this figure was calculated on the assumption that my salary might increase by 8.5% per annum. I thought this most unlikely, and the sting in the tail was that the Chapter would now cease to pay into my existing endowment policy (although it was suggested that I might take over the payments myself). Sun Alliance confirmed that the annual premium *could* increase at any time, adding that it would normally keep pace with the salary, having been set as a percentage of it from the outset. I discovered in due course that the premium, worth less than 7% of my salary in the first place, was not being increased to match annual salary increments – a scandalous situation which continued right up to my retirement – although fortunately the Clerk evidently forgot to stop paying into my original policy, which therefore survived just as long.

In May I reached what I deemed to be the mid-point in my career at Llandaff, for at the age of 51 it seemed unlikely that I would ever have an opportunity to move. Again seeking the support of Gerard Elias, in his capacity as chairman of the Cathedral Choir Association, I wrote him an impassioned letter, saying that I considered it shameful and insulting to be considered worthy of only £4305 a year, less than twice the value of a probationer chorister's scholarship. Asking him to communicate my sentiments to the parents of all the choristers, I pointed out that my colleagues at Bristol and Wells, who were so willing to share concerts with my choir, were paid respectively £3545 and £6815 *more than* me, with Hereford somewhere in between. I had already aired the problem with the Cathedral Organists' Association and the Friends of Cathedral Music, but they had no power to help, nor had John Knapp, the Cathedral School's benevolent headmaster, and the Chapter Clerk had refused to let me address the finance committee in person. My final paragraph declared:

Until I receive some satisfactory answer to my plea, I

am totally withdrawing my support for any choir activities apart from the regular services, and will not give permission for any visits or tours in this country or abroad, nor for any fund-raising activities for such events. I have been grossly underpaid for fourteen years, and see no reason why I should continue to undertake any more work not covered by my service agreement. For too long I have struggled to keep the family on a mere pittance, and I now look to my friends to act on my behalf and see that justice is done.

It says a lot for Gerard that he responded by sending an important letter to the Chapter Clerk in time for consideration by the finance committee, and it gives me some pleasure to quote it in full, if only to show what a respected citizen of his eminence felt about the disgraceful way in which I had been treated for so long:

I write in support of the latest appeal that you will have received from Dr Smith for a review of his annual salary. I intervene for two reasons. Firstly, the Association is concerned to maintain and improve the standard of Cathedral music here, and we do not believe this is possible when the man at the head of the department is paid such a derisory salary. Secondly, I have not the slightest hesitation in describing the salary paid to Michael Smith – whether one assesses it upon the unrealistic basis of a 'part time' job or not – as quite scandalous. Without going into any personal detail – which may only be known outside his family to the Dean, the Headmaster, myself and some of those in regular contact with him – the financial pressures upon Michael Smith and his family result from the last few years of increasing discrepancy between his salary and that of other cathedral Organists.

I note from a letter to Michael Smith of 14 July 1986 refusing his then request that "The Committee were not disposed to compare your service conditions with those of other Cathedral Organists". Why ever not? I write this letter having made extensive enquiries. His terms of engagement vary little, if at all, from other Cathedral Organists. His commitments in terms of practices and services are as great, if not greater, than most. If Dr Smith felt constrained to resign his post because of the salary paid, I would have thought that a claim for damages for constructive dismissal might have a fair chance of success when his employer was 'not disposed to compare his service conditions with those of other Cathedral Organists'. Is it any wonder that the suspicion arises that the failure to increase his income is designed to hasten his departure? What is it expected that a new Organist would be paid?

Quite apart from any legal obligation upon the Finance Committee, I would have hoped that as a matter of fairness and justice to him – and one must have regard to his age, length of service, experience and qualifications – the Committee would appreciate that he should be paid the proper salary for the job. From my enquiries I note that Exeter has raised nearly £1,000,000 in nine months to endow its music, and I would be more than happy to play a part in trying to do the same for Llandaff now that the Appeal has run its course. I would expect that the Cathedral Organist, with his contacts developed over many years, would assist in this, but one could not dream of including him in such a project until his salary properly reflects his worth.

What a stunning letter! It should have melted hearts of steel, but I suspect that what made the members sit up and take notice was the reference by a distinguished lawyer to the prospect of legal action being taken against them. This was by no means the only time I had to use the threat of litigation to get what I deserved, since those responsible for the finances nearly always failed to respond to reasoned appeals to their judgement.

What in fact happened was that a special sub-committee decided that I should be given time sheets to fill in for four weeks, showing exactly what use I made of my time. I was not against this, because it was a good opportunity for them to see just how busy my life was. I pointed out that although some of my activities might not be directly beneficial to the Cathedral, yet they were activities that a man in my position was expected to take on in association with the job, and which were not paid for by anyone else. The four time sheets were presented on graph paper, each covering seven days from 9am to 8pm. It was immediately apparent that these hours were thought to be the extent of my working day: clearly the committee had no idea that my duties began at 8am four days a week, nor that I rarely finished work of one kind and another until at least 10 pm. Rather than fill them in as I went along, I selected four particularly busy weeks in the summer, consulted my three diaries, and did my best to remember how I had used any time not specifically covered by them. Even I found the resulting record impressive, and I trust the committee members thought likewise. I incorporated into the time sheets some colouring to show work for which I was paid by other bodies (teaching, conducting, recitals) and suggested at a subsequent meeting with the committee that the work for which the Chapter could reasonably expect to pay amounted to an average of twenty-eight hours a week, which might well be regarded as a full-time occupation.

At some stage I had mentioned that in England most cathedrals were now regarding their organist as equivalent in status to a residentiary canon, and paying him accordingly. I was reminded that there was currently no such office in the Llandaff diocese but it had been noted that when I was appointed in 1974, my salary was equal to eleven thirteenths of an incumbent's stipend, and hence that of a canon, since that office attracted no financial advantage. In the interests of fairness, it was now proposed that this ratio be reinstated, thereby raising my salary by 76% to £7590, which I found was about equal to the average salary being paid to organists in similar foundations three years earlier. It made no allowance for all the money I had lost in the intervening years, but it did represent a very substantial increase, perhaps even reflecting some confidence in my work at last, and I was gracious enough in my reply to show my appreciation of the time and attention given to considering the relevant factors. I was also interested to discover, for the first time, who these people were who had such power over my livelihood It transpired that the finance committee, chaired by the Dean, consisted of five canons (of whom two were the archdeacons) together with the Chapter Clerk (Norman) and his deputy (David) and six representatives of the parish including the two Churchwardens. The canons were all vicars, mostly concerned with running their own parishes, whereas the parish representatives were responsible to the congregations whose contribution to collections at 'parish' services largely provided the funds for running 'cathedral' worship. No wonder I had been short-changed for so many years.

However, the new offer was not without conditions. For the last eleven years the Chapter had paid three-quarters of the cost of electricity and gas at St Mary's, in response to my early request for financial assistance after losing my lucrative part-time work with University students. They now asked me to pay the whole of the fuel costs *and* a proportion of my telephone bill. From the very beginning the latter had been paid in full by the Chapter, and I had never even seen the bills: I suspect that this procedure was established for my predecessors who were mostly clergy, and went unnoticed when I took up residence. My service agreement made no mention of telephone costs, mainly because my solicitor, who doubtless noticed the omission, decided to let sleeping dogs lie. Having taken advice, I was given to understand that in the absence of any relevant clause in the written contract, established custom was considered to be part of it. Clearly, to have to pay for all these facilities myself would effectively take away a very considerable part of the salary increase. As a compromise, I offered to pay 75% of the fuel bills and £25 per quarter towards the phone bills as a gesture of good will, or alternatively to pay the whole of the fuel bills and none of the phone bills. Eventually it was agreed that my contribution to the cost of telephone calls should be 25% - but it was typical of the Chapter Clerk that the following quarter he offered to pay the 25%, leaving me to pay 75%. Another letter from me put it right. I also asked for a written guarantee that my salary in future would never fall below the agreed proportion of a canon's salary. Pointing out that I was ineligible, unlike most of my colleagues, to receive fees for weddings and funerals, I made a further request that my fees for other non-statutory services should be increased by 50%. My first option was partially accepted, with the stipulation that the Chapter would continue to pay my telephone rental charges but only a quarter of the cost of calls, or even less, representing the proportion made 'on behalf of the Cathedral'. Although I did not envisage it at the time, this latter decision was to be the subject of continuing dispute for years afterwards. I pointed out that however generous the new salary offer might be, it was still £3000 below those presently offered to my colleagues elsewhere, and that for many years my pay had dropped far below the original proportion of an incumbent's pay. I did gain some comfort from the fact that the Chapter responded positively to a request I had made earlier in the year for leave of absence the following summer for another examining tour in Malaysia, and was even more delighted when they sanctioned what I ventured to call a sabbatical term in 1990 in order to accept a similar tour in New Zealand. Provided they were not involved in extra expense, and that I could guarantee that things would run smoothly in my absence, the canons were content – but at the same time the finance committee, on becoming aware that about £200 a year had been paid to one of the lay clerks for distributing our monthly service scheme and other useful material to about seventy hotels and other establishments, immediately vetoed further payments, whereupon distribution stopped altogether. How short-sighted they were!

The cathedral choir's reputation remained high in 1988. After the Judges' service in October even the Dean wrote 'After the service on Sunday morning a great number of people told me how much they had appreciated the music, not least the fine singing of the anthem', and a week later he received a letter from the Royal Courts of Justice on similar lines. The BBC, who had for many years broadcast Choral Evensong 'live' on Wednesday afternoons, adopted a new scheme whereby a second service would be recorded, for transmission on Fridays. Now they decided to broadcast the recorded service at 10.30pm on Sunday, and Llandaff was the second cathedral to enter this scheme: it so happened that owing to some over-running of previous programmes, ours did not begin until after 11pm, running over midnight and prompting some wag to suggest that it should have been called Choral Matins! It did seem rather strange to broadcast Evensong so late, and the scheme was eventually abandoned. I had a small part to play in a series of four 'musical meditations for Holy Week' which the Dean actually allowed the BBC to *film* in the Cathedral, and was pleasantly surprised later in the year when our latest commercial recording was the subject of a letter received from someone living in Rarotonga, one of the Cook Islands in the Pacific Ocean, who declared it to be 'certainly the most beautiful recording of sacred music I have ever listened to'. For my own satisfaction I listed the full-choir settings of the evening canticles (*Magnificat* and *Nunc Dimittis*) that we had sung during the previous five years, and found there were seventy-six, along with a dozen settings of the *Te Deum* for the occasional Matins and about twenty settings of the Mass including three by Mozart and one by Schubert. There were also at least twenty more settings sung by the boys on Mondays and Fridays. We rarely repeated an anthem in the course of a year, so there must have been some two hundred in the repertoire at this time.

Following the death of one of my uncles in 1987, the other one, his younger brother Leonard, died this year. Not an international figure like James, he had nevertheless received the MBE for sterling work as a civil servant in the Air Ministry. I was also considerably saddened to hear of the death, after four years' illness, of Margaret Groves, who had been my very first girlfriend when we were teenagers: I had really loved her, and after she married one of my school mates we kept in touch, becoming god-parents to each other's daughters. We had met at St Andrew's Church in Ilford in 1953, and had been to a dozen proms together in 1954 at the Royal Albert Hall; I was so glad that I had invited her to join Marian and me in a box at that same hall in June 1987 on the occasion of the Diamond Jubilee Service of the Royal School of Church Music. It was the last time I saw her, and I was sorry that an examining tour in Cornwall prevented me from attending her funeral in Essex.

It was also in 1988 that I made my final bid to leave Llandaff for one of the great cathedrals in England, when for the second time in two years a vacancy occurred at Lincoln, David Flood having been invited back to Canterbury to succeed Dr Allan Wicks.

I felt I had a strong supporter in George Guest, and even the Dean seemed quite warmly disposed to my application. This time I was chosen for the shortlist, along with four other colleagues whom I knew well: Malcolm Archer (Bristol), Graham Elliott (Chelmsford), Colin Walsh (St Albans, having succeeded me in 1974 at Salisbury) and Peter Wright (sub-Organist at Guildford). Wives were invited to attend, and we all dined in Edward King House just south of the

Minster and met the Sub-Dean, who had achieved some notoriety over an ill-judged loan of Lincoln's *Magna Carta* to Australia. We were somewhat taken aback when he began criticising the precentor, Canon Rutter, whom I had known back in my Louth days and who was now losing his sight: it was bad form, we thought, to speak ill of one's colleague to a group of prospective employees. There were two interviews, the first with the Dean (still Oliver Twistleton-Wykeham-Fiennes) and his wife, with the Chapter Clerk and someone from the BBC; and the second with the Dean again, with his advisers Dr George Guest, Professor John Morehen, Canon Anthony Caesar, whom I also knew, and was at one time precentor of Winchester, and a 'lady from the congregation'. After lunch together in the Common Chamber and a visit to the organist's five-bedroomed house, we were interviewed by the choir school's headmaster and took it in turns to take a choir practice. Each of us had been primed to prepare the same piece, the unaccompanied motet by Walton *Drop, drop, slow tears*. I had read a book of advice about interview technique, which advised trying to be the last interviewee in order to make a fresh impression. I managed to do this, but it was not entirely to my advantage in rehearsing a motet that had already been rehearsed by four other candidates! I had meticulously prepared the little piece, even writing it all out on a large sheet of manuscript paper, and was ready to stop the choir at any point and be able to hum a chord (without recourse to a keyboard) to resume. The cathedral was extremely cold in the first week of March, and I knew from past experience that the temperature in those vast cathedrals of Eastern England could be several degrees below freezing. I think I may have been the only candidate to conduct without an overcoat on, just to show how fit and dynamic I was! The building not only felt cold, it felt *sinister*, and I remembered its reputation over the years for disputes and unfriendliness. During the night before the interviews I confided to Marian that I was not happy with the atmosphere of the place, and indeed when all the candidates met in the Eastgate Hotel for a drink before returning home, we all expressed some misgivings at the prospect of being appointed. I may never know how much influence the late Dr Guest had, though he told me later that deans quite often go against advice from musicians. Be that as it may, the mantle fell upon Colin Walsh, more than seventeen years my junior. I knew from the start that I was unlikely to be appointed at 51, and in the event I was actually quite relieved, not only because of my feelings about the job itself, but also on account of Lincoln's geographical position, surrounded by sparsely-populated and rather desolate fens and not really on the way to anywhere. On hearing that Colin had got the job, I phoned to congratulate him, only to find that although he detested his Dean at St Albans, he had his doubts about Lincoln too, and did not accept the post before making a return visit there. Meanwhile I took Marian to a concert at St David's Hall and a late supper at the *Fontana di Trevi* to celebrate my defeat! It was the day originally intended for our own cancelled concert, so everything fitted in rather nicely in the end.

As the cathedral choral society fell on hard times, I was taking more interest in my new assignment as director of the Cardiff Tallis Singers. It was good to have Marian among the altos as an already established member, and having made a cautious start in the autumn of 1987 in the village church at Bonvilston with a programme ranging chronologically from Tallis to Rutter, and the annual Christmas recital in the candlelit modern chapel of St Michael's Theological College, we managed to add three other engagements in 1988, singing Evensong with extra anthems at Lisvane and Peterston-super Ely, and a lunchtime concert at St John's in the city centre.

The month of July was mostly taken up with sixteen days' examining assignments in Rochester, Burton-on-Trent and the Mansfield area, followed by the annual luncheon in London, while August, after a couple of recitals in the RC Cathedral in Lancaster and in Cartmel Priory, was given over to a relaxing family fortnight in St Ives and a week in Woodfalls. Earlier in the year Marian and I had taken a short break in Paris to celebrate our twentieth wedding anniversary, marking the day itself with a spectacular evening river cruise on a *bateau mouche* with a five-course dinner and two wines. After visiting the *Sacré Coeur* basilica we walked along the little road pictured in the Lopexino painting I had bought in Taunton a couple of years earlier. This was fascinating in itself, but two remarkable things happened as we wandered round the adjoining *Place du Tertre* to see the artists at work. First we came across a couple who were Marian's cousins, but more importantly we detected on one easel a surprising likeness to the Lopexino. Moreover, I was able to talk to the artist himself, and could not resist the opportunity to buy another painting from him on the spot. It cost the equivalent of £200, and when we attempted to enter the Louvre with the framed picture under my arm we were rejected, having to waste time returning it to our hotel before being allowed into the museum. On another personal note, the condition known as Dupuytren's Contracture that had affected the little finger of my right hand in 1984 had gradually reasserted itself, and before the autumn term began I spent five days in a cottage hospital in Chepstow, where a second operation was followed this time by physiotherapy. For a while it seemed that the finger might remain straight, and I gave a recital in Bristol cathedral a few weeks later, but it gradually became bent again at about 45 degrees, and has remained so ever since.

The autumn term was notable for the amount of attention given to the choristers as individual soloists. I submitted an article about this for publication in *The Llandaff Monthly*, to make our parishioners aware of how much we were appreciated elsewhere:

> David Butler (Dean's Scholar) achieved just the right degree of dignity and solemnity as he placed a poppy at the Cenotaph on the stage of St David's Hall in early November at the Wales Festival of Remembrance, and sang in Hebrew an Israeli song of Peace. He was accompanied by the muted voices of Cor Meibion and the organist Huw Tregelles Williams, and a week later the occasion was shown on television. On the strength of his musicianly performance, David was invited to sing the Grace at a dinner given by the Variety Club of Great Britain at the City Hall, in the presence of the Duke of Edinburgh.
>
> On the last Saturday of November the Bach Choir came to Cardiff from London to perform Mendelssohn's oratorio *Elijah* at St David's Hall with the BBC Welsh Symphony Orchestra: the part of the youth who is sent up the mountain to look for a cloud was sung by Darren Roberts, from a perch by the organ console. The conductor, Sir David Willcocks, wrote to him afterwards praising his "excellent musicianship" and sending good wishes to the Cathedral Choir: this concert was recorded by the BBC and is expected to be broadcast this month on Radio 3. At the same time, a few yards away, another chorister, Christopher Parsons, was taking part in a concert at St John's Church in aid of Guide Dogs for the Blind. He sang with the famous Japanese soprano, Miki Sahashi, and the Ystrad Mynach Male Choir in the well-known *Pie Jesu* from the Requiem by Andrew Lloyd Webber.
>
> Just before Christmas, the voices of Christopher Parsons and Richard Jeremy were heard in a radio play, *The Vow* by Saunders Lewis, in music especially composed by William Mathias. They had recorded their duet with the BBC Welsh Chorus and Orchestra at Broadcasting House some weeks earlier, under the baton of the composer himself.

With my family in the lounge at St Mary's in October 1988
Photography © Richard Dutkowsky

St Mary's, our Victorian mansion opposite the cathedral
The white building on the right is The Old House,
where my parents owned a ground floor flat in their mid-80s

1989

During 1989 the Dean caused very little trouble in my life, and relations became quite cordial. It was time for yet another character to come forward as the *bête noire* of the year, causing a good deal more trouble than he had already. My faith in Michael Foster's abilities was sorely shaken when he was found to be acting dishonestly in his position as honorary secretary of the choral society. It all began when he invited a local chartered accountant called Lambert Lewis to sort out our accounts, which had been a bone of contention for many months, and to produce a draft budget for the current season. I had decided to perform Stainer's well-known oratorio *The Crucifixion* in March, largely to save money by incurring minimal cost (fees for an organist and two male soloists), but after rehearsals had started, along with more ambitious works for a later concert, Foster put forward many reasons for cancelling it. Our long-standing accompanist Morley Lewis, the parish choirmaster, had given notice to quit, no doubt regarding the society as a sinking ship, and the Monday rehearsal on 13 February was his last. By one of those strange coincidences it was also Fr John Ward's last day as a priest vicar, but what was even more extraordinary was that my dear old father died that very afternoon at Highfield Nursing Home, while I was teaching the piano at home. I took a short rehearsal and went home, leaving the committee to hear what Foster had to say at an 'emergency' meeting. In my absence, he persuaded them that we should abandon the planned performance. I had already noticed several misleading sentences in the secretary's report to the committee in February, and I was determined not to cancel a concert so soon after the *débâcle* of the previous spring. Remembering that Father had sung in *The Crucifixion* several times in his earlier days, and that it was his own vocal score that I was using, I decided to waive my fee, telling the chorus the following Monday that the performance would be given in his memory. This took the wind out of Foster's sails, and the concert took place as planned, with my good friend Jeremy Davies as the ideal tenor soloist. Little did I know that less than fifteen years later he would be conducting my wife's funeral. Father's own service was taken by John Ward, who had been so kind to my parents in their loneliness.

Michael Foster's less admirable qualities came to light when we received a letter from Intermusica, the concert agency representing the pianist Howard Shelley, who had played at the 1986 Festival. The letter divulged that Foster had begun negotiations in May 1988, without any consultation with the committee, eventually offering a date for the 1989 Festival and adding that I would telephone the agent to discuss Howard's programme. When the agent phoned me in December I denied all knowledge of the negotiations, but we now learned that correspondence between Foster and agent had continued until Intermusica phoned me again in February, only to be told again that we had never planned to stage a piano recital by anyone. The agent concluded a very long and detailed letter by saying 'Neither I nor my colleagues have ever come across such chaotic and contradictory behaviour, and I regard it as utterly discourteous to both agent and artist and am frankly disgusted'.

Foster produced for the next committee meeting a letter addressed to him on our new accountant's headed writing-paper, with two mini-budgets, designated general account and concert account. Examining it some days later, I spotted a discrepancy: my rehearsal fees for the year were estimated at £940, which was far more than I had ever received before. I wrote to Lambert Lewis for an explanation, stating that in no calendar year had I received more than £605 for rehearsals, and that whereas my fee per rehearsal had increased by 10%, his estimate exceeded my current remuneration by 58%. Mr Lewis's response came as a shock – he had not written the letter or its attachment. We both realised that it must be a forgery, and I put the allegation in writing to Foster, asking *him* for an explanation. On receiving my letter and knowing he had been found out, Foster tendered to the Dean (as choral society chairman) his immediate resignation. Instead of acknowledging his guilt and offering some apology, he took the opportunity to attribute his resignation principally to a deteriorating relationship with me, saying that I had given him little or no help or encouragement. These two allegations were untrue, as was his claim that he had simultaneously resigned from Llandaff Festival Ltd. On the contrary, this second resignation was prompted by the Festival Council which refused to re-elect him as secretary. It was Gerard Elias who had spoken against him, while I drew attention to his hard work, ideas and initiatives and recommended that he remain in office. Minutes of the last two AGMs also noted my own declarations of appreciation of his work. Foster's letter went on to make false allegations about his dealings with the accountant, Lambert Lewis, who hotly denied them. He ended by saying 'Resigning in this way will, I am sure, put a great strain on the society who have now lost their very valuable accompanist and almost half the membership since September 1988. Whilst many factors have contributed there seems only one common denominator'. This was, of course, a snide reference to me, but on pointing out to the

Dean at least eight untruths in the letter, I reminded him that the 'one common denominator' since 1988 was in fact Michael Foster himself, and that until then the Society had flourished quite happily under my direction for fourteen years. His letter to the deputy chairman Don Jessett referred to my 'antagonism and downright obstruction' – quite the opposite of the truth, for I was only too willing to go along with his ideas, much to my eventual disadvantage. He concluded by writing 'If it had not been for Dr Smith's action tonight at Llandaff Festival Ltd's AGM I would have been more than happy to let the choral society committee judge me'. This too was a complete distortion of the truth: before the AGM he had in fact been summoned to a private meeting by that committee's chairman, Jill Turner, supported by Gerard Elias QC, who put to him that in view of information concerning the forged letter purporting to be from Lambert Lewis, he (Foster) would not be proposed for re-election as company secretary. Gerard Elias asked if he would be prepared to continue with the organising of the current season's concerts, to which he agreed. What followed is described in a letter I wrote to the Dean in his capacity of chairman of the Choral Society:

> At the Annual General Meeting Mr Foster was asked to leave, when the matter of elections arose, while the rest of us discussed various points. On his return, he was told by Gerard of our decision, and in the ensuing discussion said that he would now resign from the Council of Management and Executive Committee. Before he left, I (*speaking for the first time on the issue*) expressed my appreciation of all the hard work that he had done, and of his ideas and initiatives, and my regret that other actions of his had made it necessary to leave us: I said I hoped there would be no personal animosity between us, and that we would still be friends. He said that he hoped the same. It is all the more regrettable that he should have written to you, in his letter of resignation from the Choral Society, in terms so detrimental to myself. I can tell you that every paragraph of it is untrue except the first and the last.

Meanwhile I had received an unequivocal and tripartite statement from the aggrieved accountant:

1. The letter dated 14 February to Mr Foster apparently from our firm is a forgery. I was aware of none of its contents and had made no recommendations. The letterhead appears to have been taken from one of our company letters, blanked off and photocopied.

259

2. I confirm that no meetings or telephone conversations had taken place with Mr Foster since August 1988 until this month, and any references to meetings in your minutes are fictitious.

3. I have now written to Mr Foster concerning the matter and enclose a copy of the letter. I understand that Mr Foster has stated that he has recently contacted me to explain the position. There has been no such contact.

A few days later Lambert Lewis did receive an apology, and I called an informal meeting of the choral society's committee, providing each member with copies of the relevant minutes and correspondence, explained the whole sorry story, and collected the papers in again. I was pleased to receive a letter from the BBC library in London concerning the lost copies of the Berlioz *Requiem* (by July sixty-three had still to be returned by the various choirs including sixteen from our own members). I had of course denied all responsibility for their loss, and I hope Michael Foster enjoyed reading a copy of the assistant library manager's letter to me which included the reassuring sentence: 'I can assure you that this incident has not in any way marred your obviously first class personal and professional relationship with the Corporation'.

Despite all these difficulties and ramifications we still managed to produce the Summer Concerts Series, which included the long-awaited performance by the Choral Society and the National Youth Brass Band of Wales of the new *Te Deum* along with a new selection of works including Bach's unique Cantata 118 with brass and just two of the Bruckner motets, John Rutter's *Gloria*, and for good measure Parry's anthem *I was glad*. The professional element was provided by Gillian Weir's organ recital and concerts by the Dufay Collective, the Tallis Scholars and the Nash Ensemble, but alas, difficulties in securing sufficient funding for future series were never overcome, and this series proved to be the last. The choral society soldiered on by presenting Bruckner's *Mass in E minor* and Fauré's *Requiem* with local soloists and my second (honorary) assistant David Geoffrey Thomas, who with my whole-hearted support had succeeded Morley Lewis as our regular accompanist. My appeal to the committee that all members should be re-auditioned was duly discussed and, not unreasonably in all the circumstances, rejected. By now there were fewer than seventy members, and a number of the better singers had defected to the recently-formed BBC National Choir of Wales, which had better facilities and much more to offer than we did at this stage.

A quite separate financial saga began in April, when Dr Gwyneth Davey, mother of one of the choristers, came into some money through a legacy and offered to make it available to the choir. My advice to her was to set up a fund to allow better remuneration for the lay clerks and choral scholars, and the initial plan was to sponsor a lay clerkship and ask the Chapter to distribute to the others in equal parts the £800 salary which they would otherwise have paid the chosen man; a similar scheme would support one choral scholar. Two months elapsed before she received a letter from David Lambert (still the deputy Chapter Clerk) proposing the establishment of a cathedral music foundation to be administered by himself, the Dean and Chapter Clerk, and Gerard Elias, but not me! It was evidently felt that the sponsorship of two individuals might pose problems, and so an alternative scheme was mooted whereby £300 would be added to the annual pay of each lay clerk and £200 in the case of choral scholars. Michael Hoeg, Assistant organist, was to receive £222, increasing his derisory salary to £800 (which the lay clerks were already getting for much less work). This was all agreed by Dr Davey, and Gerard, while recommending that I be one of the administrators, went a step further by expressing the hope that the new foundation could attract further funds, even offering to begin a campaign for the purpose, perhaps launching it at a Festival concert involving the cathedral choir, and seeking business and commercial support. Meanwhile Gerard had good cause to complain that the cathedral was now trying to charge the festival committee for the 'hire' of the building, (a term hotly refuted by the Dean in a magazine article later in the year) as well as claiming fees from the BBC for broadcasting some of our concerts – but the outcome of these quite separate initiatives will become clear in my next chapter. For myself, I made the not unreasonable request that my occupational pension be increased in line with the recent 43% increase in my salary, reminding the Chapter Clerk about the notional 8.5% p.a. salary increase mentioned when it was set up, but with his usual prevarication I was kept waiting throughout the year for a satisfactory response.

I was able to leave all these matters behind me for three months, when I undertook my second tour of Malaysia as an examiner for the Royal Schools of Music. This tour began in early June, well before the end of the children's school term; I had been working for five weeks in the northern town of Alor Setar, and enjoying several weekends in the Langkawi Islands, before the family flew out to meet me at an inland town called Taiping, and a few days later there was a holiday which gave us the opportunity to spend four nights at the Eastern & Oriental Hotel in Penang where we had stayed in 1983. The following weekend was spent in a beach hut on the lovely island of Pangkor. I must forebear to recount again our many happy experiences on this tour, which was so long that on arriving home I spent six hours opening the 243 items of correspondence that awaited me. Three days later we went to Ilford for the funeral of my remaining aunt, the wife of Leonard.

The Dean became ill, and in his absence I managed to secure permission to do a fortnight's examining in Germany, thereby missing, for the first time since 1967, the Advent Procession. I heard afterwards that he had left his hospital bed to attend the service, and enquired why I wasn't there. My arrival in Berlin was barely a fortnight after the historic fall of the Wall, and I was interested to see people chipping away at the murals for souvenirs, the empty watchtowers in no man's land between the eastern and western parts of the city, and a small exhibition at the border gates known as Checkpoint Charlie. My work was largely at army barracks, examining the children of soldiers serving in the British Army of the Rhine, and in order to be allowed in the officers' Mess I was given the honorary rank of Lieutenant Colonel! I was impressed by the standard of comfort enjoyed by the officers, with whom I shared some excellent meals and inexpensive drinks. My tour covered many other bases, involving 77 journeys in two weeks, including 51 by road and 22 by rail. My limited knowledge of German stood me in good stead when listening to platform announcements on the railways, and also when at the end of the tour I had to go to Munich to conduct examinations in a private house with pupils who knew no English. The teacher acquainted me with a little extra vocabulary before I began, with such words and phrases as *Dreiklänge* for arpeggios and *aus und zusammen* for contrary motion. At the end of each exam I would say *Das ist die Ende* until the teacher told me during a break that the phrase had much the same connotation as its exasperated English equivalent 'This is the *end!*' so I took her advice and substituted the more authentic *Das ist fertig.*

I think it was while I was in Germany that an interesting assignment was undertaken by a small group of choristers: we had accepted an invitation from an unknown but wealthy bridegroom to sing at a wedding in Athens, and off they went with Michael Hoeg to fulfil the engagement. In December the whole choir sang at the mediaeval-style folly north of Cardiff known as Castell Coch, and at Cardiff's Mansion House. Meanwhile a few contacts I had made in Germany were being followed up by Gerard's successor as chairman of the choir association, Major Davies-Jenkins, who with his wife was hoping to arrange a choir tour based on some of the army camps. Despite their enthusiasm for the idea, it had little appeal for me, and in fact never materialised.

Another unusual opportunity came our way when I was approached by John Cale, singer-songwriter and a founding member of the rock group *The Velvet Underground,* to let the choristers participate in a recording of what eventually became his best-known song, a setting of Dylan Thomas's poem *Do not go gentle into that good night.* Cale's voice had been recorded in Suffolk, and the orchestral backing by a Russian orchestra in Moscow, so the choristers had the unique experience of contributing a third track while wearing headphones.

A potential shortage of lay clerks for the coming year had become a problem, and I took the rather bold step of offering the Chapter an opportunity to rent my flat in the house next door, and then make it available for one or two new men. I thought this would be the ultimate irony: that they had sold the house which had been partly occupied for a time by lay clerks, and were now about to rent part of it back again from me for that very purpose. I was however determined to set the rent at current market value, and said that the benefit to any new lay clerk should be assessed in relation to the salaries of the others. I was not surprised to find that the two ideas were incompatible, the fair rent being considered well above the current salaries, and indeed I was told by David Lambert in October that the annual advertising budget for new singers had already been exceeded. This did surprise me, being unaware that any limit had been imposed, and I wondered how the Chapter proposed to appoint three lay clerks from January 1990 without further advertisement: I warned the Chapter that if they did nothing, the Sunday services might well have to be sung by boys only. Both the Chapter Clerk (still Norman) and his deputy (still David) were unable to tell me what the limit was, so how did they know it had been exceeded? It turned out that money spent on advertising choristerships, for which the headmaster was responsible, had been added to my expenditure in the quest for men, and in view of the rather unusual situation permission was given for further spending – although Norman's assertion that an advert would appear in the brochure of the Cardiff Festival predictably never materialised. There was a further muddle concerning my annual budget for purchasing new music for the choir, which, I was told, had also been exceeded. I suspected that this could be accounted for only by including sheet music bought to replace copies that had been lost or simply stolen during the year, the cost of which should be covered by insurance. I was told that costs incurred in this way could not be claimed on the policy, and that 'music was to be kept in cupboards with locks fitted so that only certain people would have access to it'. Norman never visited the song room and was obviously unaware that the only lockable cupboard was used to store vocal scores for the choral society, and that for the bulk of cathedral music we had to be content with cardboard boxes on some very primitive open shelving. While explaining these matters, I reminded Norman that my pension needed to be up-graded and back-dated, and that the state of the choir lavatories left much to be desired.

My bigger concern at this time was the state of St Mary's, and in the hope of persuading the Chapter to honour their responsibilities for the upkeep of the house I listed a dozen matters needing attention. Needless to say my entreaties fell on stony ground, so I took the matter further with an approach to the director of environmental services for the City of Cardiff, an amenable man who not only sang in my Choral Society but was also called Michael Smith. To my delight he invoked powers under the Housing Act 1985 and sent an inspector round, listing no fewer that fourteen faults needing attention, including rising damp, defective windows and a cracked lintel. This was the beginning of a saga which occupied much of the following year. In other respects the year moved to its end in a fairly routine way: my mother became increasingly confused, uninterested and depressed in her eighty-sixth year, feeling isolated without Father in her nursing home; I carried on with my piano pupils and the Service of Nine Lessons and Carols went exceptionally well, the congregation packing the nave and overflowing into the Lady Chapel. I was not amused when our traditional party for the choristers was interrupted at 9.30 p.m. by our neighbouring bass lay clerk complaining about the noise: he might have known that the party would soon draw to a close to allow the boys some decent sleep before singing a Schubert Mass the following morning. This was the last service for two exceptional boys who have been mentioned earlier, Christopher Parsons and Darren Roberts, whose contribution was perhaps equalled but never surpassed in later years. For a couple of days in the ensuing holiday Marian and I stayed at the Mariners' Hotel in Lyme Regis, but in the fallow period leading up to New Year it was virtually deserted and not really worth the money spent on it. All in all we felt that 1989 had been quite a satisfactory year, but there were some features of it that presaged less favourable developments to come, concerning both the proposed music foundation and the uncertain future of the choral society.

1990

The year 1990 was one of mixed fortunes. In January I noticed that my cathedral salary had doubled in two years, though a revision in the payment of expenses reduced the resulting total somewhat; at last I was able to stop calculating my pay in relation to that of my colleagues. The downside was the Chapter's mismanagement, as I saw it, of Dr Davey's generous attempt to improve the pay of the choir men. The major decline of the Choral Society and the final abandonment of the Llandaff Summer Concerts were largely offset for me by taking the opportunity to travel round the world in the course of an examining tour in New Zealand.

The leading lights of the Summer Concerts Committee, Jill Turner and Gerard Elias, made valiant attempts to get sponsorship, approaching the BBC and the *South Wales Evening Echo* (with no success) and proposing a campaign to find forty people to sponsor the season to the tune of £100 each to produce the £4000 needed. But in mid-February arrangements were made to cancel bookings already made, and a press release expressed the hope that this would not mark the permanent demise of a Festival that had run for thirty years:

> Despite the promised financial assistance of the Welsh Arts Council and the support that would doubtless have been forthcoming from local authorities and patrons, as in the past, the Committee has been unable to attract a sufficient level of sponsorship – or even guarantee against loss – to finance the proposed programmes with a reasonable expectation that it will at least break even. In recent years, artists' fees, staging and administrative costs and general running expenses have increased dramatically.

In a last ditch attempt to save the series, the indefatigable Gerard wrote to two agencies who had expressed an interest in helping to raise £20,000 for a series in 1991, but there is no record that this plan was pursued, and there has not been a similar series of professional concerts at Llandaff from that day to this.

The minutes of Choral Society committee meetings tell an equally sorry tale. My request to re-audition all the members and instigate a recruitment drive focused on singers under 45 met with disapproval, owing to a reluctance to risk losing more members, including possibly some of themselves. The accounts for 1988-89 were eventually audited by the reputable firm Peat-Marwick-McLintock, which seemed to show a loss of £5500, but I do not remember receiving a satisfactory answer when I queried a wildly inaccurate figure of £11,343 for soloists' fees; and the inclusion of a payment of over £7000 to the Guildford Philharmonic Orchestra in the accounts for both 1987-88 and 1988-89 remained a mystery to me. An 'economy' concert with organ accompaniment for Dvořák's Mass in D and a few extra instruments for John Rutter's very attractive Requiem, was staged in March, and a date in May was earmarked for Haydn's popular oratorio *The Creation* with an orchestra of forty players and the rising star Bryn Terfel as the baritone soloist. Consideration was given to selling the society's tiered staging, since we were no longer allowed to perform at the west end of the Cathedral and had to be seated at ground level, and as the season progressed several committee members stood down. By March the treasurer was reporting an overdraft approaching £800, and a request was made for a statement to members concerning the financial loss sustained by the Berlioz *Requiem* performance in 1988; members were assured that although no actual malpractice had been involved, the misrepresentation of facts by Michael Foster had been a contributory factor. It was decided in my absence that the Society could no longer afford to pay me and the accompanist (David Thomas) our proper fees, and a kindly-worded letter from the vice-chairman Don Jessett offered us honoraria respectively of £100 and £50 per term. Various ideas were put forward for fund-raising, including the promotion of 'charitable events' and the raising of members' subscriptions, or a requirement that members pay to buy or hire their vocal scores; some members generously offered interest-free loans to tide us over. Meanwhile the Summer Concerts committee, planning a fourth series, was unable to attract sufficient sponsorship, either from the Arts Council or privately, and was forced to abandon the project permanently. The Choral Society, which had always relied on such funding for its summer concert, now had to abandon it altogether, so that after Easter our Monday rehearsals became less regular, confined to sight-singing aimlessly through borrowed copies of sundry works, when not cancelled in favour of extra committee meetings and two bank holidays. My examining commitments in Wiltshire, Monmouth and Derbyshire were an excuse to hand over half the rehearsals to David, and as attendances hovered round the 35 mark they were discontinued soon after I departed with a sigh of relief for the other side of the world. Before leaving, I made what I considered a positive contribution by presenting a paper to a sub-committee comparing members' subscription rates with those of other choirs in the area, and putting forward a dozen points, agreeing to receive an honorarium for the autumn term on the understanding that my recommendations were accepted and carried into effect. My list included the aim to achieve a membership of at least eighty singers, of whom at least twenty should be tenors and basses, and with an average age not over 45, with a retiring age of 70, subject to my discretion. I also urged the committee to support the choice of music chosen, to satisfy the requirement of the society's constitution 'to promote concerts, choral works and other works of educative value, *with particular reference to little-known works.* 'This is not the choir', I wrote, 'for those who wish to sing only the most well-worn repertoire: we should still aim at a sensible mixture of styles and periods of music'. I put forward a programme for the autumn concert which would involve only a small orchestra (and, for that matter, a small chorus): Vivaldi's *Gloria* and Britten's *Saint Nicolas* (which I tended to regard as a Christmas work, the saint being the origin of Santa Claus - though I always cringe when promoters mis-spell the title). In the event, even this proved to be too expensive a venture, and was replaced by a performance, in English and with organ only, of Brahms's ever-popular *German Requiem,* together with Poulenc's *Gloria.*

Mention was made in the last chapter of the plan to set up a Cathedral Music Foundation to administer Dr Gwyneth Davey's fund for improving the remuneration of lay clerks and choral scholars. There was some considerable consternation when it was learned that the Chapter Clerk had distributed cheques to the men at Christmas in the form of a 'gift', naming Gwyneth as the donor. This, of course, was not her intention at all, and in any case she had wished her sponsorship to be anonymous: it was, it seemed, yet another example of the Chapter Clerk's bungling inefficiency. As the money had been distributed by David Lambert, without consulting Gerard (as one of the appointed administrators) or me, he was asked to convene a meeting to sort matters out. I was particularly incensed that one of the men, whom I had recently rebuked for persistent lateness, received an unexpected bonus of £300, contrary to Gwyneth's intentions. A letter from Norman Lloyd-Edwards explained that the members of the finance committee felt unable to commit themselves to a permanent increase in salaries which would have to continue after the Davey money had 'expired'; and that they could not 'simply increase the standard remuneration on a long-term basis without being certain that there would be funds to meet it'. They had therefore pre-empted any consultation with the appointed trustees by presenting the whole of the annual amount as a Christmas present. At this point Gerard Elias's experience as a lawyer prompted him to write a detailed argument for the original plan, suggesting not unreasonably that Gwyneth be a member of the administering committee and commenting

> We find the suggestion that the level of salaries cannot be increased because "the gift may cease in four years" to be both short-sighted and defeatist. It overlooks the probability that Dr Davey will continue her gift "if all goes as she hopes" whilst at the same time snubbing the purpose of her gift and making it almost inevitable that things will not go as she wishes!

Gerard's paper was duly considered by both the finance committee and the Chapter itself, resulting in a letter sent by Lloyd-Edwards to Gwyneth explaining their views, but the fact remained that they had reneged on the agreement made with David Lambert in June 1989 and a letter I had received from him in September saying 'Dr Davey has now sent the first annual payment of £1800; the fees (*sic*) can therefore now be increased in accordance with my letter of 26 June'. She quickly responded by reiterating the terms of the original agreement, adding

> I must therefore point out that unless I have your assurance that the net value of the gift plus the associated tax refund (amounting to £2400 at present tax rates) will be used to fulfil these objectives I will not be willing to continue giving to the Cathedral, and the present Deed of Covenant will be cancelled. .... It does seem that a valuable opportunity to develop and support the music of the cathedral in a substantial way will be lost if we cannot proceed broadly along the lines that I agreed to last June.

Norman Lloyd-Edwards neatly side-stepped the issue by retiring as Chapter Clerk soon afterwards, leaving his successor to pick up the pieces, but six months elapsed before the matter was mentioned again, and then only because I wrote to the new Clerk, Lindsay Ford, pointing out that he was now *ex officio* one of the administrators of the so-called Cathedral Music Foundation. After all that had been said and written, he confessed lamely that he had been able to elicit little information about the Foundation apart from David's letter of June 1989, but that meanwhile the finance committee and the Chapter had decided to deal with the fund exactly as before. He concluded by announcing the appointment of a cathedral administrator who would be responsible for handling all wages and the 'payment and receipt of monies'. Gwyneth Davey tried in vain to secure further meetings or discussions, eventually appealing to the Bishop (the Right Reverend Roy Davies) to intervene. A further seven weeks passed before he bothered even to acknowledge her letter, by which time it was 1991. Claiming to have read her submissions and discussed them with the Dean, he attributed the impasse to an earlier 'misunderstanding', concluding 'In spite of the disappointment you have felt, your generosity should not pass unacknowledged; I, for my part, would like to thank you and say how sad I am that there was not a happier outcome'. For the conclusion of this regrettable story we shall wait until my next chapter, but I am sorry to say that as I write this in 2009, exactly twenty years after the original agreement which never came to fruition, Gwyneth is dying of cancer in a London hospital.

It so happened that an appeal for funds to the Friends of Cathedral Music was granted, in the form of a £9000 endowment to be paid in six equal and annual instalments, with an undertaking that the income from the invested capital sum would be used for the maintenance of the cathedral choir and choral services and not go into a 'General Fund'. It was on that memorable day, 26th June 1989, that David Lambert assured the Friends of Cathedral Music that a separate Choral Foundation account was being created, into which would be paid not only the endowment but also the 'Davey money' *and* donations from the Friends of the Cathedral which usually amounted to some £6000 a year. David went as far as to suggest that one of the lay clerks be named the FCM Scholar, but of course this never actually happened. The Cathedral's financial statements at the end of the year did show a 'Music Endowment Fund', but although it included the first annual instalment of the FCM grant, promising five more to come, and a legacy of £500, there was nothing about the Davey money nor any contribution from the Friends of the Cathedral. A cautious footnote declared 'Income derived from the fund may be used for the maintenance of the Cathedral Choir and Choral Services'.

There were a few other interesting points about the earlier part of the year, such as the examining sessions already mentioned, attendance at RCO Council meetings, a one-day course run by the recently-formed Association of British Choral Directors, and an excellent conference of the Cathedral Organists' Association shared between the cathedrals of St Asaph and Bangor in North Wales, where the most memorable experience was the quality of the meals, exceeding all others before or since.

Another interesting invitation for choristers to sing in Europe had to be declined. We were invited to send four boys to Poland for a week to represent Great Britain in a recording and filming project promoted by UNICEF in aid of homeless children in Eastern Europe. They were to sing at a ceremony in Warsaw in the presence of Lech Walesa, then recognised at home and abroad as a charismatic leader of millions of Polish workers, chairman of the country's first independent trade union, Solidarity, and winner of the Nobel Peace Prize. At first the proposed visit, to which the Dean agreed, was to fit nicely into the February half-term holiday, but when it became apparent that it might extend to the weekend, the Dean took exception to it, especially the idea that I should take four boys to Poland when I should be working in the cathedral. He took the opportunity to remind me that I had recently contrived to be in Germany for two weekends over Advent in his absence, saying 'I am mindful of the fact that a number of people have asked why you were absent.' The choristers would have enjoyed the experience of singing at a grand final concert with boys from a dozen other countries in Warsaw's biggest concert hall; but as usual, instead of discussing the matter with me, the Dean typed a letter thirty lines long, withdrawing his permission, adding at the end the caveat:

> The proposed visit to Poland raises questions about the outside activities of choristers which seem to have been increasing: this could reach the stage at which the boys (and the choir as a whole) will not have as their first consideration their responsibility to the Church, represented by the cathedral and then the diocese of Llandaff.

Later in the term, when giving permission for various choristers to sing in three concerts elsewhere, he added:

> I think that it should be made clear that the Cathedral Choir is not an agency for trebles in ones and twos, even though we are prepared to consider sympathetically invitations for all the choristers to sing on appropriate occasions.

Another example of conflicting attitudes between the Dean and me involved the London Festival Orchestra (directed by its principal 'cellist, Ross Pople). For several years they had promoted a tour of British cathedrals, styled Cathedral Classics, in conjunction with the resident choirs, but in 1988 there had been a disagreement over fees when I discovered that other cathedral choirs were being paid more than we were. The matter had been taken up by Gerard Elias, in what turned out to be an acrimonious conversation, as a result of which we were determined not to ask them again. In May 1990 I was horrified to read in *The Llandaff Monthly* that they were scheduled to give a concert with the cathedral's amateur parish choir, evidently with the permission of the Dean (who of course was also the Vicar of the parish). I told him that the strained relations between the orchestral management and several other cathedrals had been discussed last autumn at the Cathedral Organists' Conference in Westminster Abbey, and again very recently in Bangor, where I was specifically asked to put the facts to our Dean and Chapter. As the matter was due to be referred to the Incorporated Society of Musicians, I said I would be grateful to know how the booking came to be made. In typical fashion he replied:

> It is really no concern of the Cathedral Organists' Association who is and who is not allowed to arrange a concert in Llandaff Cathedral when permission for this is sought. I learn from *The Times* that of the 25 Cathedral Classics concerts this year 15 are in cathedrals of the Church of England, including Durham, St Paul's, Canterbury and Winchester. St George's Chapel, Windsor is on the list, and the great shrine of established presbyterianism in Scotland, Glasgow Cathedral. I believe that the term "voluntary choir" has a certain meaning in some English cathedrals and would certainly not apply to the Cathedral Parish Choir here.

The month of May also saw the publication in the *Western Mail* of what were to be virtually the last two articles relating to the cathedral's music in my time. One of them actually contained a quotation from my daughter Laura. It so happened that the subject of girls' choirs in cathedrals had been discussed at a meeting of the Choir Schools' Association in York, at which their chairman, my old friend and former colleague Richard Shephard, had declared that the male domain of the cathedral choir was 'sexist'. Our own choir school had been co-educational for some years, but as far as I was aware, the question of our having girl choristers had never arisen. The article stated:

> Cathedral organist and choirmaster Dr Michael Smith felt the main barriers to introducing mixed or female choirs were the cost and musical mechanics. His 10-year-old daughter Laura, a pupil and choir member at the school, felt her father was being too cautious, and believed there was no reason why there should not be female choristers. "I think most girls would be able to sing in choirs at cathedrals and I would like to have a try. I am in a school choir and we are practising Mozart's *Requiem* at the moment", she said. Choristers Andrew Richley and Edward Jones, both aged 13, had no objections to female choristers, but were concerned that girls' voices would be too weak at preparatory school age and would be drowned out. "It might work better to have boys' choirs and girls' choirs rather than mixed; I would be in favour of that", said Edward.

The article was accompanied by a photograph of the three pupils – probably Laura's only appearance in a national daily paper. In fact a girls' choir was formed at Salisbury Cathedral and many others followed suit, but it was to be some years before girls were allowed to sing a cathedral Evensong at Llandaff.

The following day the same newspaper featured a photograph of our four tenors, along with a short article about one of them, Bill Bokerman, who was about to move to Lincoln after five years with us, and 'after 1,400 shows' as the headline quaintly referred to the number of services he must have sung. Before setting off for New Zealand I wrote a long article for the June issue of *The Llandaff Monthly*, but the Dean found an excuse not to publish it, agreeing instead to include a small part of it (about the visit of a choir from Stockholm, sponsored by our Choral Society) in the *Weekly Notes*. I tried to persuade him to publish at least most of it in July, but after I had gone he banned the entire article, which mentioned our invitations to sing in Athens and Warsaw, paid tribute to the work of the leaders of our choir association and to my two long-suffering assistants and included the following, which was, I suspect, the reason for the rejection of the article as a whole.:

It is pleasing to note that as the reputation of Cardiff as a centre for music and the Arts continues to grow, so does Llandaff's Cathedral music continue to draw people to the Cathedral, as well as making an impact much further afield. Statistics published in this magazine have shown that the number of communicants attending the Sung Eucharist at 11am on Sundays increased by 28% during the last ten years (while the already large numbers attending the Parish Eucharist increased by 4%). Last year we issued our fourth recording of the decade, and a letter from the Cook Islands in the South Pacific confirmed that our cassettes may be bought worldwide...

Further recognition of the Cathedral Choir's work has recently resulted in a munificent gift from a well-wisher to the choir, which will provide a substantial sum of money each year to improve the remuneration of the lay clerks and choral scholars... Meanwhile, last month we had a garden party to bid farewell to our tenor lay clerk, Mr Bill Bokerman, who came to us from Norwich Cathedral in September 1985 and has now accepted a post at Lincoln Cathedral, where he will sing alto (as he did here for two years) and put to good use his skills as a cathedral archivist. While in Llandaff, he not only gave good service as a very punctual and reliable singer, but also gave us the benefit of his very considerable knowledge of all aspects of the liturgy and its history: no one was more disappointed than he with the grammatical mangling of the Collects, and their apparently haphazard redistribution away from the Sundays with which they had been associated for centuries; and his interest in the history and background of the Prayer Book gave us a new insight into such matters. He also helped to publicise our work by distributing copies of the Cathedral music scheme around libraries and hotels...

During Bill's time, the men of the choir formed themselves into an independent and flexible group, sometimes augmented by ladies, known by the rather jocular title *The Kenneth Stoat Singers*, directed by David Cynan Jones (our *Decani* alto)... They will join forces with the Cathedral Choristers and the Cathedral School Choir this month in a concert organised jointly by the Cathedral School and the City of Cardiff Symphony Orchestra, conducted by Michael Hoeg, with David Geoffrey Thomas as organist, in a programme including Mozart's *Requiem.*

Not all of this pleased the Dean, as he explained in a letter. As a man who saw himself as 'first and foremost a parish priest', he did not like the idea that our special music was increasing the size of our congregations, believing that the change owed something to the fact that the Eucharist was now sung every Sunday, not alternating with Matins. He pointed out that when the 12.15 Eucharist likewise became a weekly event, its congregation increased by 100%. As Chairman of the Liturgical Commission that had sanctioned the new prayer book, he did not want to hear derogatory views from a mere lay clerk: 'Mr Bokerman's apparent dissatisfaction with the Liturgy in which he was paid to participate hardly commends him; and his distribution of monthly service notices seemed to cease when it came to the notice of the Finance Committee that he was being paid for this and the payments ceased.' He poured cold water on my statements concerning the invitations to Poland and Athens, adding grudgingly 'In the case of the millionaire's party, which most people would consider an insufficient reason for absence' (would they?), 'I was asked about it only a few days beforehand when it was rather late to say No as no doubt arrangements had already been made'. The gift from Dr Davey he similarly dismissed: 'We are still far from agreement about the administration of her gift and the Finance Committee' (how I loathed those words!) 'is still considering the setting up of a separate Music Foundation; and we must wait for the "further donation" before publicity is given to it'. When I had enquired in January about a vacant property next-door-but-one to me on the Cathedral Green,

273

which had become vacant, stressing yet again the need to provide accommodation for lay clerks, he was equally dismissive, saying 'The house is not a property in which the Cathedral Parish has any interest', a bald statement to which I responded some months later: 'I did not quite understand your reference to the "cathedral parish". I had not thought it would interest the parish, which is why I suggested its use to attract lay clerks', so he took another opportunity to put me in my place by explaining the legal technicalities involved. Incensed at the Dean's failure to publish my article, I took the rather bold step of sending a copy to all thirteen canons; only one of them acknowledged it, but he, the Archdeacon of Llandaff who had first met me and taken some interest on my appointment, wrote saying 'I have read it with great interest, as I expected to do, and I have passed copies to others who I know would have been glad to have seen it in print'.

The other matter which I tried to resolve before embarking on my tour abroad was the work needed on the house. The Chapter had been forced to carry out the requirements of the council, including measures to alleviate the rising damp on the living-rooms, but in so doing had dismantled some bookshelves next to the fireplace and thrown them out, leaving us with stacks of books lying in various parts of the house. Nothing had been done about other damp walls on first and second floor levels, nor about a number of other requests made six months earlier. In what was to be his last letter to me as Chapter Clerk, Captain Lloyd-Edwards made one more error, claiming that authority had been given for me to attend only one of the two Cathedral Organists' Association conferences each year, adding 'If you wish to attend two, no doubt you will make the appropriate application'. The reality was that although I had been attending both conferences for the past sixteen years, the Chapter had agreed to pay the costs of only one of them each year – though naturally I always claimed for the more expensive two-day course in May. This practice in itself was mean, for all my colleagues' expenses were paid in full by their respective cathedrals.

Towards the end of May I escaped from all this kind of thing. My flight from Heathrow took me to Bangkok, where I stayed briefly before continuing to Perth in Western Australia to stay with my old friend Jocelyn Forrest and his family for a few days. Perth is so far from any other city in any country that it is quite free of tourists, but it has a notably good climate and exudes freshness and spaciousness. The flight from there to Sydney crossed two and a half time zones and took nearly four hours, plus an hour's stop in Adelaide en route. I regard Sydney as the most vibrant and attractive city I have seen, even compared with Cape Town nine years earlier and, now I come to think of it, New York which I was not to see until the next century. I made the most of my two days there, just like a tourist, including a very fine concert by the Australian Chamber Orchestra at the Opera House. From Sydney I took a two and a half hour flight across 1500 miles of ocean to Auckland, New Zealand. Watching the progress of the plane on the cabin TV emphasised the great distance involved: for most people Australia is about the limit of their travels, and New Zealand seemed unimaginably far away from everywhere; how privileged I was to be given such an opportunity. Winter had just begun, in early June, and I was driven to Hamilton, where I stayed in a motel and did two weeks' examining. The climate was misty but not too cold for comfort, and notable events included a performance of Brahms's first piano concerto by Peter Frankl with the national symphony orchestra, and a Sunday spent at the World Expo 90 Agricultural Field-day. My final ten days' examining were in Hastings, and it was towards the end of that time that the family arrived in Auckland. I took a Friday evening flight to Auckland, stayed overnight, and met them in time for breakfast at my motel, then proceeded to escort them by coach to Hastings, stopping en route to stay the night in Rotorua and taking the mountain road from Taupo via Napier back to Hastings, where they were able to meet some of the friendly folk I had already encountered.

When I finished work in early August, we took the Bay Express train to Wellington, crossed the Cook Strait next day and took the Pacific Express train down the east coast of South Island to Christchurch. There we hired a campervan for the first time, and spent a fortnight touring the island via the Southern Alps as far down as Queenstown, including a flight in a tiny plane over the glaciers near Mount Cook. Our second week was spent driving up the west coast back to Picton for the ferry back to Wellington and thence via Taupo to Auckland, where we left the campervan and prepared for the long journey home. Even this was a further adventure, for I had arranged for us to spend two luxurious days on the Pacific island of Tahiti, before flying to Los Angeles for a further three-night stay. Here we devoted much of our time to the delights of Disneyland, but we also visited the Cunard liner *Queen Mary* moored as a floating hotel at Long Beach in California, and the nearby giant airliner *Spruce Goose.* During one of the children's visits to Disneyland I took time off to visit the so-called Crystal Cathedral, a huge church constructed in steel and glass like a vast conservatory, with one of the world's largest pipe organs. I had arranged to meet the resident organist, Frederick Swann, who allowed me to play just a few chords, so as not to upset men working on the windows high above. On the last Thursday evening of August I saw the family off on an Air New Zealand flight to London, following them an hour or so later on my British Airways flight and reuniting with them at Gatwick Airport the following afternoon, only to spend another four and a half hours on a coach back to Cardiff. Even at ten o'clock that evening we invited in for drinks our neighbours the alto lay clerk Spencer Basford and his wife Sheila, who reported the appointment in our absence of the new Chapter Clerk (the beginning of a new chapter?). When we eventually surfaced the following afternoon I looked through the 237 letters that awaited my attention.

The rest of the year progressed in an unremarkable way. We stayed with George Hill (our former headmaster) in his lodgings at Windsor Castle on our way to Heathrow to meet Rachel, returning from her eleven-week experience in Canada, which had reached a climax with a voyage up the coast of Alaska. I continued to direct the Cardiff Tallis Singers once a week, but decided that the current season with the Choral Society would be my last: my suggestions for concerts in 1991 had had to be pared down to a single concert in the late spring, and without the financial resources to pay for a decent orchestra in the foreseeable future, I reckoned that since I was responsible for seven choral 'performances' a week with organ accompaniment in the services, I did not need to add another one once a term with ten weeks' preparation. By resigning the following summer I would have completed seventeen years and fifty concerts with the Society, and that in my view was enough. I even applied to be *Informator Choristarum* at Magdalen College, Oxford, but at 53 it was a forlorn hope. For a fortnight we hosted a Dutch girl who came over from Utrecht to study cathedral music, and from time to time I auditioned various young hopefuls as potential lay clerks and choral scholars.

We entertained one of the canons to dinner one night with our friend Jeremy Davies, now precentor of Salisbury, and Marian provided one of her special dinners for our new Chapter Clerk and his redoubtable deputy David Lambert, with their wives, in an attempt to establish a new *rapport* with the management. I welcomed the news that a new part-time post had been established for a man called Ken Hall, with a desk in the cathedral office alongside the exceptionally inefficient secretary. He would be dealing largely with financial matters, and up to a point I found the new arrangement more congenial and less remote. At a later date I lost little time in acquainting both him and Lindsay Ford with my growing concerns about many aspects of the musical establishment, which I would later enshrine in my official report in the New Year.

It was around this time that I became increasingly aware of one of the sopranos I had admitted to the Choral Society a year earlier, who was one of a group of singers whom I met in a local pub after rehearsals. Her enthusiastic and jolly manner was a welcome breath of fresh air in otherwise rather negative circumstances, and I became fascinated with the story of her former life. Until ten years earlier she had lived with a self-made millionaire who possessed two Rolls Royces, a home in Jersey and a pet lion; moreover both of them had qualified for a pilot's licence. By December we had become very close friends.

1991

I was never entirely sure how much of the Chapter's apparent intransigence was due to sheer indifference to the management of the cathedral, how much influence the Dean had over their decisions, if indeed they were allowed to make any, and whether the Chapter Clerk ever attempted to steer them into some positive thinking. These factors were put to the test when I began the New Year by issuing a comprehensive report and appraisal of the current state of the cathedral's music, along with a number of recommendations, which I asked Lindsay Ford to put to the quarterly meeting in January. Since this book is largely intended to be a chronicle of my life as, in today's terminology, the Director of Music at Llandaff, I think it will be useful to set out in full the problems as I saw them. The magnitude of the challenge I presented will be seen all the more clearly when we come at length to the response I received from Lindsay a fortnight after their reverences had met in solemn conclave in the Chapter House.

> CHORISTERS   Serious thought must be given, as a matter of urgency, to the present shortage of choristers, and to the marked deterioration in the quality of material presented to us. The intake of choristers during the last two years has left much to be desired in comparison with former years. Although about thirty boys have attended voice trials in that period (some more than once), hardly one of the eight who were chosen has proved really satisfactory. In three cases parents withdrew the boy from the choir after a few months. Three boys who were promoted to Junior Chorister last May having already reached the age of nine and a half or ten, are failing to show the ability and promise normally expected at this stage, and of the two remaining probationers one is barely adequate, the other having made virtually no progress during the year. Further difficulty was caused when one Senior Chorister left a term early, and another's voice broke a term before he was due to leave, reducing the number of choristers to 13 last term and 12 to begin the New Year. A subsidiary problem which adversely affects their ability to read music in both treble and

bass clefs, is that half the boys are not having piano lessons. I forecast a serious situation next autumn, when two boys will have left, even if we can find the *nine* new boys we need from the applicants to be heard this month.

<u>What is the problem?   There are several possible ways of rescuing the situation:</u>

1. It has for some years been recognised that intelligent, musical boys with good voices are to be found in the Cathedral School, who are not choristers.   There is reason to believe that they could have been choristers, had day-boys been eligible for the scholarships.   Ten years ago, I recommended this procedure to the School Council via the Chapter, but the idea was rejected.   Other successful cathedral choirs rely to a large extent (Worcester) or entirely (Gloucester, Guildford) on day-boys who attend fee-paying schools.   I now call upon the Chapter to reconsider this proposal for Llandaff.   I will gladly make myself available to join in discussions and to provide any useful information.

2. After the boarding requirement, the next barrier to application for choristerships is a financial one, as the parental contribution inexorably increases. At present only one place is sponsored, but the boy holding the TSB scholarship (without which he could not have afforded to come here) is making excellent progress. My second recommendation is that further sponsorship be sought, both from firms and from individuals. Attached are some guidelines culled from three cathedrals which have benefited in this way:

BRISTOL A new organist, Christopher Brayne, has recently been appointed. He advised the Dean to seek sponsorship for the Choir. The Dean secured the sum of £250,000 from British Nuclear Fuels, to be spread over the next ten years.

GLOUCESTER During a Cathedral Appeal in 1970, a scheme was set up to provide £3000 per chorister: the capital is left intact and the interest is given to The King's School to help pay their fees. The Scholarships were secured from local firms and from individual supporters with money to spare. Sponsors in industry included ICI, Bird's Eye Walls, the Wates Foundation and Debenhams. The Dean has recently asked these sponsors to contribute more, and some have responded. The scholarships given by sponsors do not cover the full fees, but the shortfall is made up by the Chapter, and the choristers pay no fees while singing in the choir: they are all day-boys.

GUILDFORD   The boys are all day pupils at Lanesborough Prep School and the Royal Grammar School, according to their age; fees range from £3000 to over £3500. The Sponsorship Scheme for Choristers is one aspect of the cathedral's Stewardship Campaign; the sponsor's covenant supplies the Bursary for one particular chorister whose name is given to his sponsor. At the same time the boy's parents are told who is sponsoring their son. The sponsor is then enabled to watch the boy's progress in the choir and to take a personal interest in his achievements. Sponsors include firms, individuals and groups from the congregation, and the Friends of Cathedral Music. This year the scholarships will provide £900 towards school fees for each boy. This sum may be provided by a group of people, made up by themselves or by the Chapter, and the recommended method of payment is by a four-year covenant, the Cathedral recovering the tax.

> I had worked hard to acquire all this very relevant information, and the very act of typing it all out took a considerable time. I imagine that in another cathedral I would have been invited to assist the precentor and perhaps a committee under his chairmanship, to draw on these ideas and come up with some positive results. At Llandaff, the Chapter Clerk responded with just a single sentence:

> *Chapter did not feel able to make any recommendations in relation to choristers without first consulting the School Council.*

My report continued with a couple of paragraphs about me:

> MYSELF   Having just completed 50 terms as Cathedral Organist, I am also about to embark upon preparations for my 50th concert with the Cathedral Choral Society. For various reasons (which I shall be happy to explain to any interested member of the Chapter) I have decided to retire from my position as Conductor of the Society after this concert, which we hope will take place on the 1st June. This decision raises a constitutional issue for the Society, whose officers will need to consult the Chapter in due course regarding the future. I am hoping to develop my work with the Cardiff Tallis Singers, who last term promoted a successful concert in the Lady Chapel on St Cecilia's Day as well as singing Evensong here

in October.

I should like to thank the Chapter most warmly for giving me leave of absence to visit New Zealand last year, and also to say that, while being most grateful for their permission to undertake an examining tour during the summer of this year in Hong Kong (which was to have extended for a few weeks into the autumn term) I have decided to withdraw from this offer. This means that I shall be in Llandaff from the first day of term, hoping to get the year off to a good start despite my forebodings expressed earlier.

One might have thought that someone might have taken a little interest in the fact that I had conducted their Choral Society for longer than any former conductor, or that I had decided to forego a tour in the Far East and devote myself to cathedral duties (though to be fair, I was thinking more of my family and my reluctance to spend a third summer holiday in succession working my socks off). The actual response was nil. My report went on to mention the current situation regarding the men:

> GENTLEMEN OF THE CHOIR   The present complement is four lay clerks, one choral scholar, one choral exhibitioner and three singing-men, two of whom operate a rota system for the *Decani* Tenor position. We cannot continue to rely on Colin Wyver's regular attendance as in the past year, and will need to seek a regular lay clerk. The present allowance of only £500 p.a. for advertising places for both men and boys needs to be increased forthwith. I hope to provide a Full Choir for the service marking the end of the Restoration Appeal, in the presence of the Princess of Wales, and I think the men will agree to this being their final contribution to its success.

My request for a larger budget for nationwide advertising was squashed quite firmly: apparently unaware that we already had two university students in the choir, Lindsay wrote:

> *In relation to the Gentlemen of the Choir, Chapter did not feel able to agree an increase in the advertising allowance. The members felt that perhaps a closer relationship with the University should be pursued with a view to attracting singers.*

> THE ORGAN   Some thirty-five years after its last rebuild, the organ is beginning to develop faults and to fall into disrepair. From time to time the builders recommend improvements, but

it would be wrong at this stage to spend hundreds of pounds to patch up an unworthy instrument. I would not like to leave Llandaff without having seen through a major reconstruction or a completely new instrument worthy of the Cathedral. With the recent restoration of the Rossetti triptych, with the restoration of the building almost complete (save the choir lavatory and the adjoining area) and the forthcoming recasting of the bells, I recommend the Chapter to look ahead to the implementation of the plans put before them in 1978 and never realised, so that when the time is ripe the necessary funds may be forthcoming. Meanwhile I hope to write a much overdue booklet on the organ, and perhaps a series of educative articles for *Llandaff Monthly* to explain in layman's terms what an organ should be, and what this one is not.

All the canons could think of in response to this was expressed thus:

Chapter are not prepared to consider an organ appeal at present. They wanted to be assured that every attempt is being made to keep the present organ in good repair and condition, and have asked that the organ book be presented to each Chapter meeting.

As if the jottings of the tuner would mean anything to them, even if relevant to the poor quality of the organ from its very beginning! My last plea was for sympathetic consideration of the status of my two very well-qualified assistants, Michael Hoeg and David Geoffrey Thomas:

ASSISTANT ORGANISTS Throughout the last four terms, David Geoffrey Thomas has accompanied the Choir at Evensong on Thursdays, when Michael Hoeg is in charge. He has done this voluntarily, but I feel it would be unfair to expect him to continue this valuable contribution to the music without being paid, at least as much as a singing-man receives for a service. With two degrees and two diplomas in Music, Mr Thomas is a real asset to us, and I think this should now be recognised.

It is now ten years since Michael Hoeg was appointed Assistant Organist. In 1980, when George Hill was Headmaster, it was envisaged that the Assistant's duties would be severely limited by his school commitments. As a result of this, his letter of appointment indicated duties only on Sundays and the Organist's free day (Thursday), though it was known even then that the duties would necessarily include the late practice on Tuesdays. In actual fact, it proved possible almost from the beginning of his appointment for Mr Hoeg to attend all the services, and for many years he has done so of his own volition, with a correspondingly marked improvement in the standard we are able to achieve throughout the week. With his increased responsibilities at the School over the years, he has at times been overworked (as has become more obvious in recent months) but although I have offered to decrease his work in the Cathedral, he has insisted on maintaining it. The anomaly is that for all this time he has been paid for seven services a week, less than a lay clerk who sings at only five; and this is the more remarkable when one considers his high qualifications and the fact that he is quite often in charge. Present figures indicate that a lay clerk may actually be paid twice as much as the Assistant Organist, and a chorister more than three times as much! <u>Recommendation</u>: that the role and pay of Messrs Hoeg and Thomas be discussed and re-assessed.

Again, it seems that the clergy were unimpressed by my reasoned arguments, for their Clerk demolished them in a sentence:

> *Whilst Chapter appreciated the contributions made by David Geoffrey Thomas and Michael Hoeg they did not agree that Mr Thomas should receive payment and did not wish to alter Mr Hoeg's contract.*

Is it any wonder that in sheer desperation I even applied, at this late stage in my career, for a post at Blundell's School? A few weeks later there was a letter from the new administrator, Ken Hall, who like David Lambert was a pleasant, well-meaning man who managed to get embroiled in the inefficiency and antagonism of others. He had misunderstood the arrangements agreed a few years earlier regarding the payment of my telephone bill. I had to send him copies of the relevant correspondence, for he was clearly not in full possession of the facts, and indeed admitted as much, writing 'Norman was not a great one for maintaining good order files'. This was by no means the end of the matter, which was later to become one of the major problems of my time at Llandaff. The first inkling of a dispute came in June, when a letter from the Chapter Clerk informed me that at last the finance committee had agreed to spend £1000 on necessary renovation of the Blüthner grand piano in the song room, – except that they could not afford to do so! 'There is little hope', he said, 'of our finding the funds unless, of course, they come from an unexpected source'. He took the opportunity to impart further bad news:

> The Committee were very disappointed to learn that despite my writing to you in respect of the advertisement for a lay clerk, you proceeded with the advertisement offering accommodation. The Committee were of the view that that was not a correct expenditure of money, but I presume you had already committed Cathedral funds before raising the matter with me. We need to save money rather than spend it, and you are asked not to incur any further non-essential expenditure without referral to the Administrator or me.

By way of a punishment for having to consider spending money on the piano – which had been given to the cathedral some fifteen years earlier and was played for many hours every week – he added a declaration that no accommodation would be offered to any potential lay clerk in future, and introduced an issue that was to prove such a bone of contention for months to come:

> On the subject of expenditure the Committee have asked me to bring to your attention that both the PCC and the Finance Committee are disappointed with the amount that the cathedral had to pay towards your telephone. The question of staff expenses is under review at present, and no doubt I will be asked to communicate with you on this subject very shortly.

By this time, the Cathedral Choir Association had been in the hands of Major Mike Davies-Jenkins and his wife Captain Sue Davies-Jenkins for a year, and as retired army officers they had enlisted the support of a General Llewellyn and his colleague Lieutenant Colonel Keith Prentice, serving with the Royal Artillery in Dortmund, for a ten-day choir tour to be sponsored by the British Army of the Rhine. The proposal was well received, with an offer of 'very basic accommodation based on our transit wing'. The plan was to make daily excursions from Dortmund but also to go further afield, suggestions including Munich, Paderborn or Berlin. At my insistence they sought to arrange concerts principally in churches and possibly visits to schools, with the added bonus of possible recruitment of choristers. They sensibly conceded that the choir might not have a strong appeal in most garrisons. By October 1990 these ambitious plans had been whittled down to the Dortmund area, in consideration of the much greater costs of travelling to Bavaria or even Stuttgart (Cardiff's twin city) and the fact that the Royal Welsh Fusiliers in Berlin were unable to accommodate us on the proposed dates in July. Moreover, some of the choir men not unreasonably refused to take ten days off from work, asking if they might instead fly out (at further expense) for the second half of the tour. I had long had my doubts about these plans, and when the Davies-Jenkinses pressed on regardless, making a five-day booking with the Tourotel Valkenburg Hotelgroup, I decided to set out the position as I saw it:

The first consideration should be the purpose of a Cathedral Choir tour, which is two-fold. By travelling, living and giving concerts together, the boys and men get to know each other better socially, and a very good sense of morale is fostered. The Swedish trip in 1986 was exemplary in this respect, involving as it did several sea voyages on what amounted to a liner rather than a ferry, as well as various coach journeys. At every point of call, the whole choir was accommodated together. The other objective of a tour is to present concerts of music sung in an Anglican cathedral, in small or medium-sized churches with good acoustics and a fine organ, in return for a substantial fee in each case. In 1986, as you know, the fee asked was in the region of £500, and nowhere did we receive less than £200, I believe. The fees were guaranteed at the time the concert was arranged, and covered a large part of the total cost of the tour.

Now let us look at the present scenario. What was envisaged in the early stages proved impracticable when it was discovered that the men could not be available for a nine-day tour, and it was only with reluctance that I conceded the possibility of giving concerts for five days with a group of twelve small boys. It is true that some years ago, when we had a full complement of boys, we gave one concert in a fine old church in Guérande, an ancient walled town near Nantes, but the boys had to sing a lot of music to make up a whole programme, and it was largely the setting that made the event a success, and the fact that it was arranged as a feature of the International Competition they had just taken part in (hence with plenty of backing and publicity). Now it seems that the arrangements being contemplated involve the segregation of men and boys on both outward and return journeys, and completely separate accommodation for them. Even now, I know of not a single definite arrangement, nor has there been any mention of fees of any kind at all.

At this stage I must make it clear that I am not implying any criticism of your valiant efforts to promote a successful tour. On the contrary, I am extremely grateful that you have taken on the arduous and often discouraging task. But I have made it clear all the way along that I cannot commit myself to something that is not, in my own mind, clear-cut and workable, and something we can all look forward to with confidence. My contact in BAOR, Gwynn Lewis, has telephoned again, giving his opinion that the Gulf War has completely altered people's attitudes to concert-going, at a time when they live in constant fear of the return of wounded soldiers. He was unable to offer any kind of encouragement. Furthermore, I understand that two of the engagements which have been tentatively offered in Holland are not in churches, and therefore will be without an organ, which of course is an essential ingredient in Cathedral music. It must always be remembered that we are not attempting to arrange a holiday for a small group of schoolboys and some of their parents (or we would choose a more scenic part of Europe) but a Cathedral Choir Tour.

The last factor which gives me cause for concern (and by no means an unimportant factor) is the budget. I have no idea how much money the Association has in hand, nor do I know what the cost of accommodation is likely to be, though you did make an estimate of £4270 minimum for coach and air travel. You also realise that the boys and men have not agreed to pay anything, and that I have asked for £200 compensation for loss of earnings. We are also assuming that the members of the choir will not receive any fees for their work, although they are paid for all their work here. I would need to see a detailed assessment of the outgoings and receipts for the tour before agreeing to its going ahead, to ensure that no unexpected expenditure would devolve upon any of our members.

It will be clear from the above that I am far from satisfied that the necessary criteria have been met (though through no fault on your part). I am sure that everyone will understand the main reason for this, i.e. the changed circumstances on the military front, but I feel bound to ask you not to proceed further with plans for this year. No doubt in a more propitious year it will be possible to make good use of the money already raised, and the contacts already made – with the added assistance of our Dutch student friend – and it goes without saying that I am sorry your hard work has not, after such a long period of gestation, borne fruit.

In advance of a meeting of choristers' parents at half term they were notified that although an ex-student of mine working in Paderborn had helped to arrange two or three concerts in that area, no fees were offered and we would need to rely on audience donations. Moreover, in August 1990 Iraq had invaded Kuwait, and the transit camp accommodation offered in Paderborn could no longer be guaranteed as our troops were likely to need it en route to the Middle East. Likewise the Dortmund base originally offered by the Welsh Gunners was no longer an option. Estimated travel costs and the need for hotel or hostel accommodation exacerbated the situation still further, and, clearly with some regrets, the meeting decided to call off the whole venture. I set off with the family for our week at Rozel Cottage feeling considerably relieved.

The half term holidays in the spring and summer terms still allowed us only five days off work, as we had to sing the weekend services at both ends. In this instance my holiday involved a trip to London for the official opening of the Royal College of Organists' new premises at St Andrew's, Holborn, having vacated the original building next to the Royal Albert Hall in order to avoid extending the lease at a revised and no doubt prohibitive rental. I returned to Herefordshire that night, only to set out for Llandaff next day to teach pupils and conduct the Tallis Singers' rehearsal, returning again to the cottage: so much for a relaxing break!

A few days later, fittingly on St David's Day, the completion of a five-year programme of restoration work was royally celebrated by a Service of Praise and Thanksgiving to be attended by Diana, Princess of Wales. In the event, she was accompanied by her husband, Prince Charles, and their son, Prince William, making his first public appearance at the age of eight. I chose Richard Shephard's fine anthem *And when the builders* on Old Testament accounts of the rebuilding of the Temple, and proudly noted in my diary that we had performed it in front of the future King Charles III, Queen Diana and King William V. As all the world knows, at least one of these predictions was not to be fulfilled. My own contributions were a Handel Organ Concerto arrangement, the Finale of Vierne's First Symphony, a *Processional* by Mathias, and Lefébure-Wély's naughty *Sortie* to send the Royal Family on its way.

I was anxious about the quality of material presented to us at the January voice trial, when only one of the fourteen applicants for choristerships met the requirements of age, musical promise and, crucially, willingness to board. A second trial attracted a further eleven candidates, of whom six were the right age and musical potential, but most of whom were unwilling to be boarders, at least in the early stages. It was fairly obvious that many parents were just looking desperately for a way of paying reduced fees at the school, rather than presenting their sons for audition as potential cathedral choristers. My request in January that we should begin to accept dayboys had been cold-shouldered, and I now wrote to each canon individually to explain the gravity of the situation. It was known that boarding nationwide for this age group was decreasing annually, and Llandaff was no exception to the trend. A further undesirable trend was the increasing demand from public schools that choristers awarded scholarships should start in September, which meant that some boys who were contracted to retain their places until the end of the term in which they became thirteen and a half might have to leave the choir five months too early, exacerbating the situation still further. Two of the previous year's probationers had already left the choir because of the boarding requirement, while still being pupils at the school. I estimated that no fewer than eight suitable boys might be lost unless the boarding requirement were waived. I also renewed my plea for accommodation for lay clerks, quoting the minutes of a recent meeting of the working party of deans, provosts, cathedral organists and choir schools which concluded that low salaries were less relevant to recruitment problems.

The Cardiff Tallis Singers showed their support for me by offering remuneration of £450 per annum for my work as their director, while the Choral Society's committee continued to flounder. I formally announced to them my intention to retire from the conductorship in the summer, pointing out that few of the requirements I had put forward had been met. My conditions for a way forward had been submitted nine months earlier, discussion being postponed more than once. There was still no requirement for members to purchase their own vocal scores, there had not been an adequate recruiting campaign, attendance registers had not been kept, though I knew that my stipulated average attendance of 65 had not been achieved (it was in fact down to about 50), no one had a copy of the constitution, the spread of age-bands was still unknown because eighteen members had failed to divulge their ages, and there were still major errors in posters and programmes because I had not had sight of them at the proof stage. No sponsorship had been forthcoming, and my own honorarium at £700 was lower than in any of the previous ten seasons. The chief problems, I explained, were the inexorable increase in the average age of the members, along with a decrease in vocal quality, together with the difficulty in finding suitable music without orchestral accompaniment. The minutes of the committee meetings at this time make depressing reading, not least the decision to abandon plans for a spring concert and concentrate our efforts on the 1st June, my final concert, with a small orchestra called the Welsh Sinfonia and a colourful programme consisting of two works last sung in 1976, *Dona Nobis Pacem* by Vaughan Williams and Duruflé's *Requiem,* concluding with Bernstein's *Chichester Psalms* which had been enjoyed in 1984. My earnings for all the rehearsals were reduced to £200, and David my accompanist being offered only £100, declared his intention to resign with me.

There were a few ladies in the chorus who tried to persuade me to stay on, not least Joanne, the soprano who had caught my attention in the last few months of 1990. As I learnt more of her earlier life and responded to her cheerful, optimistic manner, I became quite fascinated by her. As time went on she associated herself more with the cathedral, taking responsibility for the laundering and upkeep of choir robes, attending a good many services, and becoming a frequent visitor to our home. An attractive lady of 45, shortish, with long blond hair, brown eyes and a voluptuous bosom, she alternated between rather mundane jobs, like collecting insurance premiums and delivering car parts, and periods of unemployment, which enabled us to meet rather more often than most people would have known, until for a time she became a taxi driver. Looking back, I realise that her influence on me went a long way towards alleviating the various tiresome aspects of my work at this stage in my career, though perhaps my family may have come to think more in terms of a mid-life crisis, and although at the end of my work with the choral society she did her best to make friends with Adrian and Laura (now aged 13 and 11), they tended to regard her somewhat forced jollity with some suspicion. She and Marian, however, became friends and even considered setting up business together, selling 'nearly new' clothes, but this idea never came to fruition.

My examining trips for the Associated Board continued to provide a welcome release from cathedral duties and opportunities to be away from home. In March, when staying in Aberystwyth, I went to a chamber music concert at the Arts Centre featuring violin, horn and piano in various combinations, and was pleased to meet Elizabeth Wilcock, the younger sister of my Yorkshire girlfriend Mary and by now a well-regarded professional violinist. Ten years had passed since she came to play at the Llandaff Festival with the English Concert, and in the meantime she had married the conductor John Eliot Gardiner and produced three daughters. Looking back at this distance of time, I note that my work as an examiner seems to have been adversely affected by my relationship with Joanne, perhaps because of certain aspects which I am omitting from this story. Two days at a school in Somerset elicited at least three letters of complaint to examination headquarters from teachers or parents, expressing disquiet at my manner, which in their view contrasted sharply with the Board's promise that examiners have 'a kind, pleasant, sympathetic personality to bring out the best in a candidate'; I allegedly came over as cold, clinical, impatient, inflexible, impassive and daunting, giving some candidates 'a real sense of inferiority and insufficiency'. This was before they received the actual results, which reflected several performances so poor that in one case I felt unable to give any mark at all – a situation which, though allowed by the Board in extreme cases, is fortunately very rare. Clearly my mind was on other things that week. One wrote 'some children were taking their first exam, but the examiner did nothing to put them at their ease or to encourage them, not even saying hello or asking their names in some cases. He was also very abrupt in manner and hurried them into making mistakes in the scales etc'. This was my twenty-third year as an examiner, and the first time that I had ever been made aware of a complaint, let alone several.

More than two years had passed since the death of my father, during which time my mother's health gradually deteriorated. To break my journey back from Cambridge, having taken Rachel there at the start of Trinity Term, I stayed overnight at a guest house in Malmesbury. As I was driving along the motorway in darkness, a bird hit the car's windscreen. This has never happened before or since, and I had heard that it was an omen of death. Sure enough, on my return home next morning I learnt that Mother had died at the very same time – just after 8 p.m. I consoled myself with the thought that had I driven straight home, I would still have been too late to be with her. She was 86, and ready to leave this life. Her funeral, like Father's, was in the cathedral's Lady chapel, and her ashes were scattered at Thornhill Crematorium and by family agreement with no memorial apart from an entry in the Book of Remembrance.

When calculating our income for the financial year, I was gratified to find that by letting Rozel Cottage to holiday makers for much of the year and my parents' flat continuously on a short lease, we had made over £30,000, of which less than a third was my cathedral salary. As a result, we were no longer eligible for the assisted place awarded to Laura on merit (and based on our lower earnings the previous year) which we had hoped would allow a considerable reduction of the fees for keeping Laura at Howell's School, but we managed to come to an agreement that we would pay the fees by instalments. It has to be said that my low salary was an incentive all along to find ways of making money elsewhere, and that I was fortunate to have the potential to earn rent from two properties and in due course to profit by the sale of both of them. Sometimes I look back and wish that I had been able to find a nicer nursing home for my parents when they had to leave their flat, but at the time we looked carefully into the finances and evidently felt we could not afford anything more expensive than Highfields. I am still not sure whether we were right about this, but at this late stage there is no one to pass judgment on the matter.

As we prepared for my last concert with the Choral Society, I engaged the vocal soloists as usual, deciding to include one of my bass lay clerks, a neighbour who had better remain nameless, for he had made difficulties some years earlier over his fee. This time he failed to acknowledge the offer in writing, despite several requests. At last, only two weeks before the concert, I warned him that I would engage someone else. He made the mistake of calling my bluff, and indeed I did engage another bass who turned out to have a more flexible voice and a much nicer personality. The lay clerk thereby lost a £100 fee, and of course was not offered any engagement thereafter. The concert went well, and we had thirty people round to a party afterwards. A week later I applied to be director of the Cardiff Polyphonic Choir, knowing its membership to be younger and more vibrant, but although I was interviewed, I was not offered the post.

It was at this time that Marian also completed an artistic undertaking, in the form of a stiff rectangular cushion in cross-stitch for the headmaster's stall to the east of the choirstalls in the Cathedral. She had designed it specifically for John Knapp, with a grey background and maroon edging to match the school uniform, and incorporating motifs associated with school life and John himself, such as his University's coat of arms, a French horn (which he had played) and even the opening bars of Fauré's aria *Pie Jesu Domine* which he always chose for school commemoration services. Marian worked devotedly on it for sixteen months, calculating that it consisted of an astonishing 95,787 stitches. I watched John show it to his staff in the common room, but they showed little enthusiasm, and when it was duly placed in the cathedral, the Dean could not bring himself even to mention it, even after I had suggested that a word of appreciation would not go amiss. Maybe he resented that it honoured a mere headmaster, and in fact when John Knapp retired he took it with him, had it framed and hung it in his own house where it has been admired ever since. His successor had to sit on the hard wooden seat, with no cushion.

Having given up the Choral Society, I continued to work with the Cardiff Tallis Singers most Thursdays, directing another seven performances in the year. One of these was a Solemn Mass in Margam Abbey on the 18th May, celebrated by the Bishop, when I assembled seven string players and we sang a setting by Mozart to commemorate his bicentenary year. In June there was a cathedral service to commemorate the end of the Gulf War, when the paltry sum of £120 was offered for the participation of the cathedral choir. I argued that proper fees should be paid, since a few hundred pounds would be a very trifling sum compared with the millions spent on the war we were expected to commemorate, but the Dean assured me that the offer was final, so I arranged for the boys to sing Stanford's unison anthem *A Song of Peace* as an acceptable compromise in the circumstances. At the annual ordination service on the Feast of SS Peter and Paul, lasting for two and a quarter hours, the Chapter Clerk Lindsay Ford was ordained Deacon, along with two women (being now accepted without protest). He had recently declared that in future no lay clerk would be offered accommodation, in spite of my frequent pleas. These events were separated by three examining tours, one of which took me to Essex, where I stayed with my trusty friends Graham and Judy Houghton and visited others, including Colin Groves, a fellow Old Heronian and widower of my first girlfriend Margaret, returning home in time for a party marking the retirement of Jill Turner, headmistress of Howell's School, who had been one of the most helpful colleagues I had come across during my Cardiff years. Two days later it was my turn, when the Choral Society staged a dinner for about sixty members at Radyr Golf Club to mark my retirement. Unusually, I made a speech consisting mainly of funny stories, which went down well, but I also pointed out that in seventeen years I had conducted some four hundred auditions, as well as eighty-five choral works in the course of fifty concerts.

For six nights before term ended I was staying at Cwm Craig Farmhouse in Little Dewchurch, within easy reach of Hereford where I was examining for the week, and gave an organ recital in Hereford Cathedral one evening, playing works by Bach, Mozart, Franck, Elgar, Whitlock, Mulet and Lefébure-Wély. The last day of term featured Schubert's Mass in B flat and at Evensong that fine anthem by Walter Stanton *Jesu, lover of my soul* with its glorious climax guaranteed to bring tears to the eyes of the four choristers who were leaving**. Marian and I were invited to Salisbury for another farewell – a dinner in honour of Tom Gambold who had been a tenor lay clerk there ever since (and no doubt long before) I had heard him sing a solo verse in *Lord of the Dance* in a televised event back in 1968 – the occasion when I was introduced to Marian. The summer holiday began with another week's examining in West Wales, only to return there shortly afterwards to stay with the family in a flat attached to the Old Rectory, Llandeloy, the home of the former organist of St David's Cathedral, Peter Boorman, (who had famously described his tenure there as 'seven years of famine, followed by seven years of famine') and his second wife Susan, who was younger by several decades.

It was during the autumn that some extensive work was at last undertaken on our family home, St Mary's. The man responsible for getting the work done in accordance with the order made by the environmental health department was generally off-hand about the

---

** This anthem is featured on a recording made in 1994 – see Appendix 1

whole business, and days went by with no work being done. For four weeks we were unable to use the dining room because of the work, which included the renewal of two cracked lintels over the sash windows, but my attempt to claim reimbursement for the cost of meals bought for various members of the family in local cafés was predictably unsuccessful. Because the room over our dining room and kitchen was occupied by a different household, having been added to the second verger's accommodation, our ceilings were given a fire-proof lining of plasterboard.

The Chapter Clerk had warned me in June that he would 'soon' be writing to me about my telephone bills. It was in fact five months later that he broached the subject again. The good news was that some funds had become available which would allow restoration of the song room piano, but he counteracted this information with responses to more recent requests in the following order:

> I read out your observations concerning the accommodation for Lay Clerks to the Finance Committee. The Committee was not prepared to alter its decision in this matter.
>
> I read out your request in relation to conference expenses and I regret to have to inform you that the Committee did not accede to your request.
>
> Your request for an increase in fees was rejected by the Committee.
>
> The members of the PCC take the view that the Cathedral's contribution to your telephone bill is inordinately high, and instructed the Finance Committee to report to them upon the matter. The Finance Committee recommendations were considered by the PCC on 10th November and it was resolved that the Cathedral's contribution to your telephone bill be reduced to paying the rental of the telephone and the cost of the first 100 units. The arrangement is to have immediate effect from the presentation of the next bill.

I was not in a mood to accept all these negative responses, and as far as the telephone was concerned, decided to fight tooth and nail for my rights, starting with this broadside dated 27th November:

> Regarding the telephone account, this matter was discussed at some length with your predecessor in 1988/89, when it was established that the payment in full of my telephone bills by the Chapter had in the course of fourteen and a half years become an implied term of my Service Agreement, and as such should be continued. At that time, as a gesture of goodwill, I offered

to pay £25 per quarter to allow for calls made by my family, and subsequently agreed to the Chapter's proposal that this contribution be amended to 25% of the cost of calls. ....

It would seem that the Parochial Church Council, which is not a contracting party to the Agreement, is attempting to vary it, and moreover without my consent. Would you be kind enough to let me know whether the Council was advised that such an amendment would involve breaking an implied term of my contract with the Dean and Chapter? Furthermore, when it was declared that the directive should have immediate effect, (assuming that the PCC thought it had the right to make such amendments) was the Council advised that I should be given time to consider my position and take legal advice if necessary?

Lastly, I think I should be asking why in the first place the Finance Committee should have put this recommendation to the PCC (to whom I am not responsible) and not to the Dean and Chapter (with whom the agreement was made).

Perhaps I could be forgiven for wondering if I should have taken up the law as a profession, as I seemed to be more aware of correct procedures than this man who, like Norman Lloyd-Edwards before him, earned a good living as a solicitor.

There had been significant changes in the membership of the cathedral choir. Although many of the readers of *The Llandaff Monthly* were 'parish' worshippers, I was keen to inform them from time to time about our 'cathedral' music and musicians, to show connections between ourselves and the better-known English cathedrals:

This term we have welcomed two experienced gentlemen to the Cathedral Choir. The alto lay clerkship left vacant by the departure of David Cynon Jones in July, has been taken up by Kenneth Robinson, who previously sang in the choir of Lichfield Cathedral. Our two choral scholars, Julian Paisey and Mark Davies (both from Salisbury) are joined by a new tenor, Edward Williamson, who comes to Cardiff to read Music at the University: he was a chorister at Christ Church Cathedral, Oxford, before going on to Cranleigh. The tenor lay clerkship on *Cantoris* side was taken up by Gary Beauchamp last year, when Bill Bokerman moved to Lincoln Cathedral to sing alto; it is interesting to note that Gary, like Julian and Mark, attended Bishop Wordsworth School in Salisbury Close. The tenor position on *Decani* side has for a few years been occupied on a rota system by Michael Davidson and Colin

Wyver, with Charles Lewis as an occasional deputy. For the record, the other three lay clerks are Spencer Basford (alto) and Robert Adams and Stephen Hamnett (baritone). Although we have only eleven choristers this term, there is a large contingent of probationers in training...

How nice it would have been if the Dean could have shown some recognition of the significance of our contribution to the cathedral! For some people who do not regularly attend cathedral services, the 'First Eucharist of Christmas', more commonly known as Midnight Mass, is a 'must', and many others would be sorry to miss the service of nine lessons and carols on Christmas Eve: we could always guarantee a full house for this most most popular of services. The Dean was loath to admit such popularity for an act of worship which put the musicians in the spotlight and the clergy in the wings, so to speak. The *Llandaff Weekly Notes* issued on the previous Sunday gave full details of the seven services on that day, and the times of services for the Sunday after Christmas. On the reverse side, a special panel listed no fewer than five Eucharists on Christmas Day, mentioning also that Matins would be said at 7.30am and Evensong said at the unlikely time of 12.20pm. Another panel showed four services a day on the three weekdays following Christmas Day, and below this were listed another nine services on the two days before Christmas Eve and a parish service on that evening. *Only then*, at the bottom of the page and under the heading 'Other events this week', with the words Christmas Eve and Cathedral Choir *in brackets* on a single line, appeared the notice '3.30 p.m. Service of Nine Lessons and Carols'. Unimportant to him, perhaps, but his exasperating meanness in no way diminished the size or enthusiasm of the congregation attending it.

*Diana, Princess of Wales, greeting crowds outside the author's house
with Norman Lloyd-Edwards (in uniform, left) as Lord Lieutenant of
Glamorgan, March 1991*

*Marian presenting her hand-stitched cushion to headmaster John
Knapp in the Cathedral School, 1991*

1992

The Reverend Lindsay Ford was proving no more efficient or cooperative as Chapter Clerk than his predecessor, so to make sure that the thirteen Canons were aware of the increasingly worrying plight of the Choir, I again wrote to them individually, with a copy of my report that Lindsay was to present to them at their quarterly meeting on the 8th January. Although letters of appointment had at last been sent to the men appointed in 1991, one of the four had been forgotten. Thus continued my constant battle to force the authorities to honour their obligations in full. I also reminded the Dean that his finance committee had recently recommended an increase in fees for 'special' services and the reinstatement of the payment of my expenses for at least one of the two cathedral organists' conferences. Just three of the canons had the courtesy to acknowledge having received the report in advance, although the style of one of them, the Archdeacon of Margam, was as arch as his title and as pedantic as the Dean:

> Lest the absence of such should be seen as a mark of personal unconcern or studied discourtesy, I acknowledge receipt of your letter of 1st January 1992. The Chapter is, of course, however, a corporate body, the responsibility for the communication of whose collegiate Acts is, if not by the Dean, as its Numeral Head, by the Chapter Clerk. I trust this will follow the Chapter's consideration of your present missive.

Could anything be more 'studied' or impersonal than this? No wonder I regarded these clerics as cardboard cut-outs, or, as Prince Charles once described a group of Chinese dignitaries, 'appalling old waxworks'. I have no record of any response to my report, which, for the sake of a historical record of my unstinting attempts to maintain and secure the future of the cathedral's music, I reproduce here:

> CHORISTERS   We managed to survive the autumn term with only the nine boys who remained from the previous term (as I predicted last April) plus one long-standing but weak probationer and one other who was promoted after only one term. The reason for the current shortage of choristers is two-fold:

297

1. The new insistence by Public Schools that choristers should join them in September, even if this entails their breaking their contract with the Cathedral which requires them to stay on until the end of the term in which they become thirteen and a half. This meant our losing two experienced boys to Wells Cathedral School and Lancing College. Hitherto, it has been accepted that some boys will stay on until Christmas; between 1987 and 1990 no fewer than seven choristers did this.

2. The new nationwide trend away from boarding in prep. schools. This trend has reduced boarding places by 4% per annum for the last three years, and is now apparent here. In 1990 we lost two promising probationers because of the boarding requirement, and last October we lost another one - a boy who lives a few hundred yards from the Cathedral. He came as a day-boy probationer, and would now been a chorister had the Chapter accepted my recommendation a year ago that we should have a mixture of boarders and day-boys (as at St John's College Cambridge, Worcester and Hereford Cathedrals, etc.) Our refusal to move with the times has lost us three good boys between May 1990 and October 1991, and has reduced the Cathedral Choir to its smallest membership within memory.

I predict the continuation of these two trends. The first is not in our competence to change, but we can accommodate the second by announcing immediately that day-boys will be accepted as choristers. This will greatly increase the catchment and enable us to select intelligent and musical boys from Cardiff whose parents do not wish, or cannot afford, their boys to be boarders.

It has been stated recently by the President of the Choir Schools Association and the President of the Cathedral Organists', that choir schools which continue to insist on choristers being boarders cannot any longer expect to maintain a Cathedral Choir. I am very concerned and disappointed that my advice to the Chapter a year ago should have been rejected, and that my letters to the individual canons in April were not even acknowledged. Without your support I cannot realistically be expected to guarantee the continuation of the cathedral music after July 1992: it is therefore essential that you act now, in order to preserve the tradition into the next century. A further consideration is the current expansion scheme for the music of the Metropolitan (Roman Catholic) Cathedral in

Cardiff, based on their own Choir School which takes day-boys and advertises extensively. Surely the Chapter would not wish the Roman Church to usurp our own pre-eminent position in Wales where cathedral music is concerned?

LAY CLERKS, CHORAL SCHOLARS, etc.

We were fortunate last term to have five lay clerks, a full complement of three students (alto, tenor and bass) and two singing-men. Our new alto lay clerk, Ken Robinson, whose voice was heard by all the canons when he sang the solo in the anthem *This is the record of John* on 14 December, has made a very good impression However, concern has been expressed by other men in the choir that he was not offered accommodation on the Cathedral Green. Having sung previously at Lichfield Cathedral, he is used to the communal spirit of a Close community, and misses it here. Without a car, he has difficulty in reaching Llandaff from his lodgings in Roath. It is well known that several houses and flats owned by the Church stand empty on the Cathedral Green, and equally well known that other cathedrals provide flats for their lay clerks. I fear that we are in danger of losing a fine singer unless accommodation is offered quickly, and since our alto Choral Exhibitioner has just left, this would put the musical repertoire in jeopardy.

In April I asked the Chapter Clerk to pass on to the Chapter the following Minute from a meeting of the Working Party of Deans, Provosts and Cathedral Organists:

The main drawbacks to recruitment of lay clerks were thought to be lack of accommodation and heavy commitment in terms of time; low salaries were not thought too relevant. It was felt necessary for Deans and Chapters to establish an atmosphere of confidence between themselves and lay clerks.

Two months later, without any consultation with the Chapter, I received the following reply from the Chapter Clerk:

It has been resolved that accommodation no longer be provided for lay clerks. This does not mean that the present arrangements are to be upset, but no accommodation will be provided for any future appointee.

This seems like a deliberate attempt by the Chapter to

discourage men from applying for lay clerkships, and I should like your assurance that this is not so. There has been much talk of late about the lack of communal support from the Chapter, and the potential destruction of the cultural heritage to which we musicians are proud to belong. I consider it my duty to bring these opinions (which come also from members of the public) to your attention, and to take what steps may be necessary to protect my own position and reputation.

As it happened, by great fortune the voice trial ten days later yielded a record number of nineteen candidates, and took nearly eight hours, including the discussion which followed between me, Michael Hoeg and Steven Kirk the senior priest vicar (now more grandly styled Succentor). We decided that no fewer than eight boys had made the grade, so the future began to look more secure. But four weeks after the Chapter had considered my report, I received a very long letter from Lindsay Ford, giving no glimmer of hope that anything would ever improve. Its ten paragraphs may be summarised as follows:

1. It was agreed that my fee for non-statutory services be increased from £25 to £30 (but of course this was payable by whoever promoted the service, and by then I had asked the Dean for £35 or £40).

2. A grudging acknowledgment that the custom of paying £100 (and no more) towards my attendance at one Cathedral Organists' Conference a year would be maintained

3. He declared that an agreement made in a letter from his predecessor in May 1989 had been a mistake, and should have required me to pay for *all* my telephone calls. It was recognised that in practice the Cathedral had been paying 75% of the cost, but 'whether this amounts to a legal obligation to do so is doubtful'.

4. It was emphasised that the PCC had 'a very strong voice' in the finances of the Cathedral, and that they and the Finance Committee and indeed the Chapter were unanimous in declaring it unreasonable that they should pay so much.

5. If I felt aggrieved it was for me to calculate whether my calls on behalf of the Cathedral exceeded 100 units (about £5) in any quarter, in which case I should log all calls and provide evidence for my claim.

6. I was censured for sending copies of my Reports to individual members.

7. Since the Cathedral School was founded to provide board and education for the choristers, the financial basis would have to be reconsidered if day-boys were to admitted; therefore this would be kept 'under review'.

8. The cost of advertising nationally for lay clerks, offering accommodation, was regarded with disfavour; as it was felt that a city the size of Cardiff should be able to supply suitable men who already lived there.

9. Chapter were very concerned that I persisted in offering accommodation to potential lay clerks – a practice which must stop forthwith.

10. Only £500 would be allowed this year for advertising for both men and boys (not, as hitherto, just for choristers). The £700 allowance for new music and replacement of worn copies would not be increased.

I was invited two weeks later to spend an hour with Lindsay Ford to discuss these points, though it is symptomatic that although he lived in Cardiff and might have considered meeting me in Llandaff, I was expected to drive to his office in Caerphilly. I referred especially to the telephone bill and to my pension premiums, pointing out that they had not increased in line with the salary increase of a few years earlier, and that for many years there had been no provision at all. I came away with a clear impression that he intended to look into ways of bringing it into line, and before leaving the meeting, I ventured to ask whether I might actually address the Chapter in person at their next meeting. Five weeks later he told me he had put me on their agenda, though with the rather ambiguously worded proviso 'I am sure you will agree that Chapter will have to agree to hear you' and a further note of discouragement: 'I doubt if it is realistic to expect any level of discussion with members of Chapter if you intend to make representations about your terms of employment. I should imagine that 15 minutes could be made available to you'. The meeting was held on the Tuesday of Holy Week, not in the mediaeval Chapter House where the canons normally met, (perhaps they thought it too sacrosanct for a mere layman like myself) but in the Prebendal House, which though more often used for 'parish' meetings, was adorned with a rather daunting series of photographs of previous deans going back to Victorian times. I was allowed to address them for twenty minutes, during which I covered six topics, first mentioning my recent attempts to negotiate with the Chapter Clerk and then expressing appreciation for restoration work done on my house and the choir lavatories, and the planned renovation of the piano. Then I outlined the position regarding boys and men, asked again for an appeal for a new organ, possibly linked with the proposed Choral Foundation, and finally expressed my anxiety that it was predicted that after twenty-eight years' service, my pension would be only in the region of £1500 per annum.

I was very lucky to have Gerard Elias QC as a supportive friend and neighbour, willing to advise on my next move, and took pleasure in telling the administrator that he was legally responsible to pay the agreed proportion of the telephone bill. I was quite willing to discuss the matter with him, and offered to ask my solicitor to clarify the legal aspects in writing.

In May I wrote my longest-ever letter to the Dean, appealing to his sense of justice by explaining my reasons for refusing to accept conditions which in effect actually decreased my earnings. In so far as this book is a chronicle of my relationship with the clergy, and to establish in the mind of the reader the causes of my grievances, I think it right to reproduce the points I made:

1. In 1988 I was able to report that the difference between my salary and that of the organist of Hereford, £100 when we were both appointed in 1974, had risen to £6000. The increase awarded in 1989 narrowed the gap to something nearer £3000, but there was no compensation made for all those intervening years when my salary never exceeded £4300. Even now, my salary is about £4000 less than the average paid to organists in English cathedrals. I had thought that the payment of the telephone bill was intended to go some part of the way to make up for such an obvious deficiency.

2. At a meeting with Norman Lloyd-Edwards and John Phillips in the autumn of 1988, when my new salary was being negotiated, I was told that my Pension would in due course be adjusted accordingly, to be commensurate with the increase in pay. Now, three and a half years later, no steps have been taken to do this, even though Ken Hall drew my attention to the anomaly last year, and Lindsay Ford promised more recently to attend to the matter. The latest projection from Sun Alliance assumes that my pension, after 28 years' service (as I said to the Chapter last month) will be something between £1150 and £1950, depending on the growth rate between now and my 65th birthday. I wonder if you genuinely consider that this will be a just reward for my work here for so many years? In fact, I cannot look forward to my retirement with anything but foreboding, to say the least: in reality, it is very worrying indeed.

302

3.   In recent years, in addition to bearing the cost of redecorating most of the interior of this house, and carpeting it from top to bottom (a most unusual requirement for a resident cathedral organist), not to mention providing all the curtains, I have spent £3500 on installing a new kitchen and £1000 on a fine Victorian-style fireplace in the dining-room, thereby enhancing the property quite considerably. On the other hand, the Cathedral authorities have been so reluctant to maintain the exterior fabric (the woodwork having been painted only once in the first seventeen years of my tenure) that when dry rot attacked the kitchen I had to enlist the support of the local authority before any action was taken. I should add that the money spent on the house came not from my earnings, but was available when my parents sold their house in London.

4. In a time of recession, the maintenance of a family of five, with three dependent children aged between 12 and 21, is particularly difficult, and one is constantly confronted by debts to this and that body. To be asked in these circumstances to pay yet another bill four times a year presents not merely a dilemma but an impossibility.

I concluded with a suggestion that might satisfy all parties, namely that my earnings might be shown in a differently apportioned form in the accounts, by increasing my salary by a sum equal to an increased contribution to my phone calls by myself, and pointing out that in three years these bills had remained virtually static. I added a postscript to the effect that when before Christmas a new immersion heater had been fitted to our hot water tank, the fitter had failed to connect it to our economy system, so that for several weeks it was using electricity at the full rate, increasing my share of that bill by nearly £250, an amount which I felt should be reimbursed, the extra cost being no fault of mine.

The Dean acted typically by forwarding my letter to the Chapter Clerk, and atypically with a single lame sentence of his own, 'All I can do is to assure you that I will once again bring the points you raise to the attention of the Finance Committee when it next meets'. I have reason to believe, in the light of later correspondence, that he did not. The Chapter Clerk's letter was more dismissive, declaring:

> I wish to place on record that I was not the initiator of your attending Chapter. Neither did I promise to attend to the pension arrangements. My recollection of our meeting at the office is that I was at pains to convey to you that no one in

the cathedral was prepared to pay such large amounts towards your phone bill. My impression was that you had accepted that position, but clearly your recent letters show that you have not.

I challenged these assertions in a letter to the Dean, reasserting my memory that the one positive thing that did come out of my meeting with Ford was his agreement that my pension arrangements should be reviewed, adding that he promised Marian that he would deal with it, when in some anguish she telephoned him.

The Dean took some trouble to explain how his own telephone calls were apportioned. He need not have bothered, because my bill remained unpaid and I was threatened by British Telecom with the imminent disconnection of the telephone. At this stage I asked my solicitor, a Mr Rees, to intervene. Quoting the agreement reached in 1988, he advised the Chapter Clerk that in the event of disconnection there would be a breach of my terms of employment, and that the cost of reconnection, as well as my consequent loss of earnings as a result of not having a telephone, would entitle me to claim for breach of contract. Lindsay Ford replied at once (for a change), agreeing to pay the current bill on condition that I should obtain an itemised bill and make a personal log to show the calls made on behalf of the cathedral which would not appear on the bill if they cost less than 50p each. My solicitor agreed on my behalf that this system would be adopted for the next nine months, but he also made a condition – that my pension should be reviewed as promised when the 1988 agreement was made. There was further muddle when it was disclosed that Ford had no cheque book, and that with the Dean and the administrator on holiday only the Clerk of Works had access to one. Ford simply reiterated decisions made in May that my request for a better pension had been rejected. I duly reported the situation to British Telecom.

I explained to Mr Rees the solicitor that although my salary had been suddenly increased by 68% in 1988, the pension provision had not followed suit. It had been proposed that I should pay the entire amount of each telephone bill, and 75% of the cost of fuel bills at St Mary's instead of the 25% paid hitherto. The existing pension had been calculated on the assumption of a salary increase of about 8% per annum, but there had been no compensation for the many years when I was grossly underpaid. My telephone was in fact disconnected, whereupon I withdrew my offer to log calls from September onwards. Mr Rees sought 'leading Counsel's opinion' (i.e. the opinion of a QC) which confirmed his own view, and requested reimbursement of the amount I had to pay to resume the service. The QC was in fact Patrick Elias, the brother of Gerard, who as my personal friend did not wish his own name to be used. Lindsay Ford's office demanded the full substance of Counsel's opinion. I took this opportunity to mention that it had taken two and a half years to finalise my original service agreement, and that another pile of letters, a centimetre thick, could be used as evidence of the Chapter's failure to keep my house in good repair until forced to do so after two years of litigation involving the City Council.

At the start of the autumn term my telephone was again cut off, whereupon my solicitor told Ford that it was a time of year when I would expect to advertise for pupils, and that not having the telephone would undoubtedly cause me a loss of income for which I would hold the Chapter responsible, noting that in any case by the end of the summer vacation I did not have sufficient funds available. Later I did actually get a bank loan to restore the service as an interim measure, and the relevant papers were sent to Patrick Elias. I told the Dean that Rachel's prospective employer in London would be unable to contact her (this being long before mobile phones were in general use) and that nobody could contact me about cathedral business or anything else. Moreover, no prospective pupil had been able to respond to the advertisements I had displayed in shops and post offices around the city. I described the horror and dismay expressed by everyone, including choristers' parents, school staff, lay clerks, and staff members of the Arts Council, the Welsh College of Music and Drama and the Royal College of Organists. I also said that two very senior lawyers from outside Cardiff had advised that the situation was of sufficient gravity and significance to be reported to the national press. I decided that it would not be in my best interests to involve the media, but to rely instead on the legal process. Accordingly a batch of papers, along with my solicitor's instructions, was sent to Patrick Elias QC. In order to disguise its provenance from a member of the Elias family, his advice was actually attributed to James Goudie QC, who issued it from his chambers in King's Bench Walk at the Temple in London.

QC's Opinion questioned whether the Chapter Clerk had the power to bind the Dean and Chapter, and quoted case law to prove that he had. Goudie noted that the office of Clerk had changed hands since the original negotiations, and quoted the Dean's view that my claim was considered unreasonable. He concluded with a strong point:

> Legally, of course, the question is not what is reasonable but what has been effected as a matter of contract. Moreover, what is reasonable will in any event vary from individual to individual and has to be assessed in the light of all the relevant contractual terms. No doubt others employed by the Dean and Chapter in positions of similar status to Dr Smith will be paid a

larger salary; I cannot imagine that any would be employed on such a parsimonious pension.

This was good stuff indeed, and I was delighted to read his conclusions in my favour:

> In my view Dr Smith has a clear right to have the whole costs paid in respect of his telephone, save as to 25% of the cost of calls. The Dean and Chapter are not entitled unilaterally to alter that agreement which was struck on their behalf by the predecessor of the present Chapter Clerk. I advise Dr Smith if necessary to sue for sums due, together with interests and costs, if the Dean and Chapter insist on maintaining their current stance.

Thus my campaign seemed thoroughly vindicated, and I had a clear mandate to sue my employers at last. However, I again decided to let justice run its course, and waited to see what would happen next. My solicitor sent to the Chapter an account for £176 in respect of my latest bill, deducting my 25% but including a reconnection charge. Incredibly, Lindsay Ford doggedly insisted that it was my responsibility not only to contribute 75% but also to have avoided disconnection. He also disregarded the QC's opinion on the strength of a sentence written in 1988 basing my 25% contribution on a proviso that it might be adjusted if later calculations showed it to be unrealistic. He quoted another letter of 1988, (which of course had been superseded) but weakened his case by stating the wrong date. In conclusion, he wrote:

> All this indicates that he (Goudie) has not been appraised fully of the Cathedral's case and, accordingly, I do not regard the Advice as particularly persuasive.

As the year drew to a close the matter remained unsettled, so I will now move on to other problems I had to deal with, concerning choir membership. Towards the end of 1991 I had been warned in a letter from our loyal choral scholar Mark Davies, whose career determined that he should leave us before Christmas, that his equally talented colleague Ken Robinson was feeling disheartened and might well seek pastures new. 'Something City-wide or public needs to be said' he wrote, 'about the Cathedral's future.... I know you are under-valued as much as anyone in the business and I sincerely regret that'. I had used some of his other choice phrases in my report, and Mark went on to express an intention to write an article on the subject for the student newspaper. Sure enough, Ken sought a better-paid appointment at the Roman Catholic cathedral, and I spent half an hour on the telephone to its director of music in the hope that he would not be 'poached'. In the event, he decided to join the Catholic Cathedral for Mass on Sunday mornings, returning to us for Evensong and on the three weekday evensongs sung by the full choir. This occasioned disapproval from the Dean, who wrote later in the year, when another man was considering a similar offer,

> Whether or not singers with a commitment to the Roman Catholic cathedral should be allowed to sing here when they are available, is a policy decision which the Chapter will have to make. My own view is that we only want men who are committed to the Church in Wales and its worship and are therefore attracted by the privilege of singing in the Cathedral Choir without weighing the financial terms: if someone prefers to accept 'a better offer' we are better off without him.

Mark Davies had indicated that Ken's discontent was partly due to remarks made to him during Thursday practices taken by Michael Hoeg on my day off, and rather strangely, I received another warning from Russell Warren, a teacher at the cathedral school, who believed that Michael Hoeg and the singing teacher Alun Jones were making critical remarks about me and causing discontent among the boys in some way which I did not understand. These rumours were never substantiated, but Russell was well known to me, not only as Laura's favourite teacher but also as an amateur flautist for whom I used to provide piano accompaniment on a regular (and paid) basis. We shall hear more about him later. Further evidence that all was not well at the school was provided by a young lady teacher who had become one of my pupils: she came to see us one morning in tears to talk about her discontentment there.

I auditioned a number of women as potential members of my Tallis Singers, but none was sufficiently experienced in reading at sight. There were new pupils too, including ten boys whom I began teaching at the cathedral school, not only for extra money but also in order to be recognised there not just as an outsider. I also wrote a paragraph about the cathedral for a small book being compiled by a lady called Enid Bird about the organists of Welsh Cathedrals: when it was published, the picture on the front cover was a photograph of the interior of Llandaff Cathedral taken by Graham Cooper, my brother-in-law. Marian took a job at a bookshop in town, which prevented her from playing badminton on Mondays, though I continued for a while.

After my summer session as an examiner I was told about 'another batch of strong complaints'. Only one of these reached me in detail, in the form of a letter from St Mary's Convent in Worcester. This was the second occasion in twenty-three years' examining that I had had to defend myself from false allegations, and it is perhaps interesting to explain them here. The initial invitation had been to examine in Mount Battenhall and the next day in Pwlleli. The latter place I knew to be in the Lleyn Peninsula of north Wales, but I could not find the former in my atlas. When further material arrived, I was surprised to find that the first place was a street in Worcester, some 150 miles from Pwlleli. I had a good reason to break my journey from Cardiff, staying overnight at a farmhouse in Herefordshire, but was given incorrect instructions, as it turned out, for negotiating the rather complicated one-way system in Worcester, resulting in much confusion and a late arrival. In her letter to the Board, the head of the junior school exaggerated the extent of my lateness and falsely claimed that I was late on the second day also. The lady's reference to my 'cavalier attitude' and 'disparaging remarks' I was anxious to refute in view of similar criticisms made the previous year, so when writing back to Philip Mundey, the director of examinations, I asked how it was that my work had not been inspected by a moderator for more than five years, and that he had seen fit to invite me five times in the previous four years to examine overseas. In fact my work had been moderated only twice, the first time in 1980. I was even accused of pouring glasses of water during exams, but I pointed out that not only did the 'notes for the guidance of teachers' recommend the provision of water, but that it was not at my request that it was provided. The lady was probably incensed by the high percentage of failures I gave, but should not have magnified my 32% to 50% in her complaint; she also omitted to mention that I had awarded merit and distinction marks to 32% and 20% of the candidates respectively. In response to another matter, I explained that I had not complained about the inconvenience of having the candidates on a stage, with my desk on the floor below, forcing me to go up and down steps during every exam in order to administer the sight-reading and aural tests; in fact it was only on the second day that I rearranged the furniture. In response to a request from me, I was 'moderated' in December by a fellow cathedral organist, the late David Cooper, who reported that although my own friendliness did not immediately come through in examination circumstances, as I tended to be rather 'matter-of-fact', there were no real problems. My few days in north Wales are memorable in different ways, not least that I slept in my tent near Pwlleli beach, creeping out in my lounge suit with briefcase to attend examinations, and although I found time to swim in the sea at Abersoch, heavy rain put paid to camping by the time I arrived for more work in Blaenau Ffestiniog on my journey back to Cardiff.

From time to time Marian and I visited Rachel in Cambridge, sometimes staying overnight, and on occasion hearing her as an accompanist in the fellows' lounge at Girton. Nor were Adrian and Laura neglected, as I found time for them too, quite often going on a walk or cycle ride with Adrian, and taking interest in Laura's progress on the violin which included her becoming the leader of the South Glamorgan 'Transitional' Schools Orchestra. I was unexpectedly invited to examine in Malaysia again at a few months' notice, but again decided to decline in the interests of family life: they had already spent a number of weeks in that country and we decided to be free of work during the summer holidays.

Occasions for the whole of our little family to meet together were limited, fourteen weeks elapsing between holidays in Holy Week and late July, when we spent a weekend at the cottage, but although Rachel had to return to her work in London as a trainee record producer, the rest of us took our tent to the Yorkshire Dales and indulged our pleasure in walking in the countryside for a week. I had invested some money in shares with a German holiday time-share company, and in August we took the opportunity to spend a week in a very pleasant apartment in the centre of Paris, doing all the usual things that tourists do, including one day visiting Versailles in the morning and then enjoying eight hours at Euro Disneyland. It had been opened only a few months earlier, but we felt that its American-style jollity somehow did not fit with its French surroundings, compared with our 1990 experience of the original model which enjoys the benefit of the warmth and sunshine of California. One day I took Marian to the Isle of Wight to look into some of my own family history. An ancestor of my father's, it transpired, had been a yeoman farmer living at the Old Rectory, Shanklin (I had previously assumed he must have been the Rector), and although we could not decipher any family names on the weather-worn tombstones in Brading churchyard, we did meet the present owner of Shide Manor, which was apparently our family home in an earlier century. As a family we always made the most of the summer holidays (partly because free weekends were largely unavailable), but although a fuller account might well interest my offspring, they must regrettably go unrecorded for the benefit of the general reader.

My second venture into the world of advertising came to my notice through the mail. The idea was to gather advertisements, as I had already done in a small way for a theatre display board, but this time to be printed on a small folded leaflet to be delivered throughout an area of about a square mile by a professional agency. Rachel contributed a suitable cartoon for its front page, and I did collect enough material for it, including an advert for Marian's work as a piano teacher, and eventually my Neighbourhood Directory was printed and delivered; I believe the whole of this enterprise yielded a profit of just £279, eight thousand leaflets being delivered in the New Year. Desperate to widen my interests, I attended evening classes in Accountancy, but my ensuing GCSE result convinced me not to go further down that road. Instead, I decided to polish up my knowledge of German, which I had last studied in 1953 for my 'O' level exams, and joined a small group meeting weekly at the house of a congenial German lady. I also signed on for a jazz course, but soon left on finding that it was very badly run and a complete waste of time.

Rachel, having come down from Cambridge University, had almost immediately come to the notice of an elderly man called John Shuttleworth, the proprietor of a well-known recording company in south London specialising in classical music and known as Meridian. He invited her to attend a concert of Indian music at the Barbican Hall, where he quickly recognised her acute critical faculties and invited her to join his young staff in Mottingham, where his two adjoining houses were run as a kind of commune, with recording equipment on site. Thus began a career which has engaged Rachel from that day to the present time of writing.

It was in the autumn that Marian took up three new ventures which were to have considerable significance. Answering an advertisement, she was visited by one John Harrison from Cowbridge, who initiated her into the old-established door-to-door sales company known as Kleeneze (pronounced clean easy), which of course has always dealt principally with cleaning equipment for the household, but had branched out into a wide range of associated products. She decided to give it a go, purchasing fifty catalogues and preparing to walk round the streets delivering them to potential customers. It was explained as a net-working system, whereby one should persuade others to take up the same business, building a small team and making profits from the combined sales. People often think of this system as 'pyramid selling' but this is incorrect, as the agents are not required to buy anything that has not been specifically ordered by the customers, and therefore cannot lose. Another new experience for Marian at this time was to join the relatively new BBC Welsh Chorus, and her first concert with them at St David's Hall included Walton's great choral work *Belshazzar's Feast* and Elgar's Cello Concerto, with Steven Isserlis as soloist. I am glad to say that I kept a video of the Walton, in which Marian is clearly seen from time to time, and of course I little knew that Laura would one day become responsible for organising aspects of this international 'cellist's concert tours. Third, but perhaps most

310

important, Marian began a two-year City and Guilds course at a local college to study various aspects of gardening.

It had not escaped my notice that we were gradually approaching the long-awaited retirement of Dean Alan Radcliffe Davies, who without ever being really offensive or rude, had nevertheless been the bane of my life for sixteen years. I was naturally anxious that his successor should be someone more sympathetic towards the cathedral's music staff, and since in Wales the Dean is appointed directly by the Bishop, I secured an appointment with the Bishop Roy Davies, first jotting down a list of no fewer than forty-four points I wanted to raise with him, hoping that he would somehow find a man who could wave a magic wand and put everything right. He heard me out and kept a copy of my notes, but as far as I recall he declined to comment, for as we all knew, the clergy are apt to close ranks when there is any hint of criticism.

On 20 October I noted two significant events on the wider stage. The memorial service to the Welsh composer William Mathias, who had contributed numerous anthems and settings to cathedral music, was held in St Paul's Cathedral on the same day as a disastrous fire gutted a substantial part of Windsor Castle. In Cardiff, our Chapter Clerk was telling my solicitor David Rees that I was difficult to deal with, having no friends on any of his committees, and actually offering the possibility of some financial compensation if I were to resign. He must have known that the writing was on the wall, and perhaps hoped that he could oust me before the arrival of a new dean who might conceivably appreciate my point of view. At this stage, already backed by David Rees and of course Gerard Elias and his confederates, I enlisted additional help from another solicitor, Tony Jeremy, who was not only the father of two of my choristers but also a specialist in employment law. An interesting feature of all my consultations was that none of these lawyers ever charged me a fee, so confident were they about the legal validity of my case.

A week's examining in Liverpool yielded an opportunity to spend an enjoyable half hour playing the great Willis organ, the biggest organ in England's largest cathedral, and to have dinner as the guest of the managing director of the organ builders Rushworth & Dreaper. Later I attended a concert at the Royal Academy of Music to mark the retirement of the then head of the Associated Board, Ronald Smith.

1993

Having ventured into the commercial world for several years, first by letting our own property, then by selling advertisements for a display board in a local theatre, I found myself drawn to the Kleeneze business that Marian had recently taken up, first helping her with the delivery of catalogues, and soon signing up as an agent myself. By the end of January I was walking round the streets of several areas of Cardiff, ringing doorbells and inviting people to take in a catalogue, choose purchases and leave the booklet out for collection. Each week Marian would send in my orders with hers to headquarters in Bristol, whence after a few days the goods would be delivered to St Mary's for distribution by us to our customers. Selling such low-priced goods as floor polish, dish cloths, washing-up liquid, brushes and the like, I was agreeably surprised to find that we could collect £400 in a single week, of which £180 was mine at my first attempt. My second week's work yielded over £300' worth of sales, so I began to think my time was well spent; it certainly made a change from teaching the piano, which I continued to do, although the number of pupils at the school dwindled to only two, as I suspect the boys found me rather stern and impatient. The company paid us some 12% of our sales, to the thinly-veiled derision of my accountant, but at least it was extra pocket-money and there was the prospect of recruiting more agents to boost sales.

A less welcome development at the beginning of the year was a stalemate over the thorny question of my telephone bills, with the Chapter Clerk failing to accept QC's opinion. Back in 1988 I had enlisted the help of John Phillips whom I knew to be an influential member of the Parochial Church Council. He was known to be outspoken to the point of downright rudeness, and difficult to deal with: it was he who, way back in the 70s, had stood up at a council meeting, pointing an arm and a finger at Dean Williams and saying aggressively, 'If the cap fits, wear it!' He once expressed the view that I would always win any disputes with the authorities, because I was cleverer than any of them! It was he also who managed to persuade these authorities in 1988 to increase my salary by 68%, and at the time he had said that in due course my pension would increase likewise. I decided to approach him again, drawing his attention to the opinion signed by James Goudie QC, and reminding him that when it was realised in 1988 that my salary in earlier years had been thirteen fifteenths of an incumbent's stipend, it was decided that this proportion should be restored from 1989. I pointed out that no compensation had been made for the years 1980 to 1988, during which time I should have earned £15,000 more than I did. 'In the circumstances', I wrote, 'I should think any reasonable person would understand why I cannot agree to contribute more than the 25% of the cost of telephone calls, which I offered as a "gesture of good will" in 1988.' I added that I was anxious to ensure that those who made the decisions should know why I wanted to protect my position without appearing to be awkward, difficult or intransigent. Whether he cut any ice I do not know, for there was no written reply from him, and Lindsay Ford continued doggedly paying only what he considered a just amount. I might have been more sympathetic if he had taken me aside to look at the cathedral's budget, which showed that the year 1992 had yielded only about £95,000 revenue from regular donations and covenants from the congregations. The trouble was, of course, that the cathedral was financed like a parish church, which it was, even to the extent of being required to pay a considerable sum each year into diocesan funds to support other churches; moreover, the annual cost of insuring the building had risen to a staggering £23,000. How could they really expect to maintain the full panoply of a semi-professional music foundation with seven choral services a week? The problem seemed insuperable, but they had chosen me as the most highly-qualified and experienced musician on offer, and having accepted the post nineteen years earlier I was determined not to be unduly penalised for their lack of judgement and financial acumen. Meanwhile I still had not enough ready cash to pay what was required, and again approached the bank manager for a loan.

With all my new undertakings I was less interested in pursuing extra activities with the choir, but an invitation to sing at St Paul's Cathedral was not to be missed. It was once again our turn to take part in the annual Festival of the Corporation of the Sons of the Clergy, this time sharing the honours with the choirs of Wells Cathedral, York Minster and St Paul's. We were stationed in the north transept, and I had chosen a seven-part unaccompanied motet by the Tudor composer Thomas Weelkes, *O Lord, arise into thy resting place* which includes the very apt petition 'Let thy priests be clothed with righteousness'. Following the Archbishop of Canterbury's address to the congregation of three thousand we joined the other three choirs in Parry's great anthem *Hear my words, ye people*, its fine treble solo being sung by all the choristers in unison – a thrilling sound – and Vaughan Williams's grand setting of the *Old Hundredth* accompanied by organ and brass.

313

It was, as I wrote in *The Llandaff Monthly*, 'a service of unparalleled magnificence and splendour which will for ever remain in our memories'. The previous edition of that magazine was the Dean's last before retiring on 6 May, an event which was celebrated next day with champagne provided by Gerard and Elisabeth Elias.

The choir had been invited to sing at the Dean's farewell party, sharing the honours with the parish choir, but consultation with the lay clerks and others confirmed my view that to accept would be hypocritical and embarrassing in view of his unremitting lack of support for us, and we all, along with the virgers, boycotted the party altogether, just as I had boycotted the funeral of his predecessor years earlier. Not long before, we heard of the death of John Swindale Nixon, my first Chapter Clerk. Although he had proved pretty hopeless at drafting my contract, he was a nice enough chap, and a good friend to the cathedral school and its headmaster, John Knapp. Moreover, his widow wanted the cathedral choir to sing at his funeral, but the Dean put his foot down and vetoed the idea, just as he had done in the case of a former diocesan registrar, refusing to countenance the payment of any fees. Mrs Nixon, however, proved to be a good match for him, insisting on paying us, until the Dean grudgingly agreed. Even then he made a fool of himself by trying to begin a prayer after we had sung the *Agnus Dei* from Fauré's *Requiem*, forgetting that we were about to sing *In paradisum* as well (with John Rutter's lovely arrangement for piano and organ accompaniment): we just carried on regardless.

I did not give up my campaign for fair treatment as a professional, and on the advice this time of both John Phillips and Tony Jeremy, (who said the salary situation was 'disgraceful for a Christian community') wrote for the third time to each of the thirteen canons individually, attaching a copy of the QC's opinion along with tables comparing my salary and pension with those at other cathedrals, as well as my salary as a proportion of a clergy stipend, and putting forward new ideas for negotiation:

> I am disinclined to accept Mr Goudie's advice that I should sue for the monies owed to me. Instead, my proposal is that the Chapter compensate me by restoring its contributions to my pension scheme to the level agreed in 1985, i.e. 10% of my salary; (during the last eight years the contribution has fallen to 3.8%). This proposal would also bring my pension benefits up to the average level of the other great cathedrals. If the Chapter can accept this proposal, which incidentally would be a more tax-efficient way of paying benefits, I would be prepared to agree to an amendment of the contract, to reflect the Chapter's wishes with regard to my telephone accounts.

You will, I know, see some justice in such an arrangement, which would go some way towards relieving the considerable financial hardship suffered by me and my family in recent years. If my proposal commends itself, I should hope that the Clerk will be directed to open up negotiations between the Finance Committee and myself in person, avoiding further correspondence and the intervention of lawyers.

Of course I had been rebuked before for contacting the canons individually, and only one recipient was gracious enough to reply saying 'thank you for your courtesy', while the Chapter Clerk wrote to my solicitors expressing astonishment at my action, saying 'I cannot imagine that his taking direct action in this way will assist the matter'. My letter was discussed at the Chapter meeting in late June, but according to the Clerk 'they did not take kindly to having letters addressed direct to them'. However, there was a glimmer of light:

I am pleased to be able to say that I have been directed by the Members of Chapter to bring the matter to the next Finance Committee with a view to negotiating direct with you. I will be in touch with you immediately following the next Finance Committee.

The idea of my actually meeting people face to face for discussion was virtually unheard of, and it will be remembered that an attempt decades earlier to hold meetings involving me in some way soon foundered when the Dean continued to act unilaterally, defying some of the decisions made. Any optimism I may have felt was gradually dispelled as the months dragged on and no meeting was convened. As late as the end of October, more than three months after Ford's letter, my solicitor felt obliged to send him a reminder – but by then we had a new Dean.

It will be remembered that the ex-military couple who were running the Choir Association at this time had been forced by circumstances to abandon their plan to take the cathedral choir on tour in Germany. Determined not to be beaten, they instead fixed up for us a week in west Wales. Thinking still largely of the boys, and more in terms of a holiday by the sea and a recruiting drive than a money-earning concert tour, they booked a hotel on the front at Tenby and arranged for the boys to sing Evensong once in Llandeilo and twice in Tenby, plus a mid-afternoon 'informal recital' there (where charging only £1.50 a ticket had the anticipated effect of attracting only eight people). We then travelled to Cardigan for an evening concert attended by about a hundred. My family arrived in Tenby next day for a mini-holiday, but not until the Friday evening were the men able to join us for a well-attended concert in Tenby, and on Saturday we sang Evensong in St David's Cathedral before a congregation of about two hundred. I heartily wished that the Davies-Jenkinses had promoted a concert there instead, which would have been more interesting for the audience and certainly lucrative for us, as we might well have raised £1000 in ticket money. The Sunday morning Mass in Kidwelly church was sung in the west end organ loft to the music of Haydn's *Missa Sancti Nicolai*, and two hundred people attended our choral Evensong in Carmarthen that evening. The men, who had been accommodated in Saundersfoot, went home on Sunday night, leaving the choristers to sing Evensong in Brecon Cathedral on our way home. By way of contrast, Marian and I had our first taste of a full-scale business presentation at the Convention Centre in Birmingham for Kleeneze agents, including the launch of a new subsidiary catalogue expanding the range of products.

Before the autumn term began, the new Dean, John Rogers, moved into the Deanery, and late one evening, on the spur of the moment, I called in to see him, taking Laura with me. Imagine our surprise, having known his predecessor only in a black cassock, to find the new, rather corpulent man leaning back casually on his chair, wearing green dungarees and red braces! From this moment I was determined that we should be, as in other cathedrals, on Christian name terms. He readily agreed, and although we addressed each other formally in work situations, we were always John and Michael in private, and to mark this epoch-making change I have just, sixteen years later, telephoned him to arrange a reunion. Bishop Roy Davies had announced the appointment in May, telling me that John had read theology at Oriel College, Oxford, and had served for eight years in Guyana before returning to Wales to become in due course Vicar of Monmouth and latterly Rector of Ebbw Vale. With my experience of the relatively illustrious careers of English deans, this did not sound very promising as a background for a cathedral post, but Eryl Thomas, the former Bishop, reassured me that John would be diligent, caring, amenable and flexible, giving me a free hand; although he had 'lacked polish' for Monmouth, was a very good parish priest and very well liked. 'It could be a lot worse', he said, 'and it may work out better than I think!' In his very first article in *The Llandaff Monthly*, written shortly before he took office, John Rogers named a few people he had already met, including Laura and me. This was indeed a promising start, and I was further delighted to be mentioned in his first sermon. How different from his predecessor, who had scarcely acknowledged our existence!

September saw another exciting event in St Paul's Cathedral. Graham Elliott, organist of Chelmsford Cathedral, thought of an unusual way of raising funds for an appeal for a new organ there. Finding that no fewer than eight serving cathedral organists had originated in the Essex diocese of Chelmsford, his first idea was to ask each of us to give a recital in our own cathedral in aid of the appeal, but the response was such that he decided instead to arrange a concert at St Paul's to be given by all eight of us. This idea appealed to us all, and two Mander chamber organs were brought into the dome area, along with the so-called 'Willis on wheels' on ground level, to complement the grand Willis organ in the Quire, with its impressive five-manual console above the choirstalls. I was delighted to be allocated the latter, along with the Roger Fisher, organist of Chester Cathedral, while Graham himself and my colleagues at Belfast, Birmingham, Chichester, Gloucester, Portsmouth and St Albans had to be content with the much smaller organs on the ground. For the record, these posts at that time were held respectively by David Drinkell, Marcus Huxley, Alan Thurlow, John Sanders, Adrian Lucas and Barry Rose. Five of us were born within five miles of each other, and John and I in the same nursing home! I contributed Norman Cocker's *Tuba Tune* to exploit a particularly fine stop in a gallery under the dome, and joined Roger in a postlude duet by Robert Cundick. Graham had arranged some chorale variations by Bach and his cousin Walther to be played by all eight organists in turn, and the final item, following a Stanford motet sung by the Chelmsford choir, involved all of us again: an arrangement of the *Variations on an Easter theme* by John Rutter, in which it fell to me, seated alongside Roger Fisher at the console where my ancestor Sir George Martin once played, to draw the fanfare trumpet stop, bringing into action the section in the gallery over the west door, a hundred yards away. All in all it was a thrilling experience.

This autumn brought about two other significant changes in personnel. Only ten days after my first meeting with the new Dean, John Knapp came round to tell us that he had decided to resign as headmaster of the cathedral school, claiming that the combined demands of parents, staff and governors had become too much for him after ten years in the job. His tenure had seen the school grow tremendously in terms of number of pupils (up to 430 at one point) and new buildings. He had no new job in view, and we never knew whether there were other reasons for his resignation (I use that term rather than 'retirement', since he was then only 52), but he had always supported me and we had worked very harmoniously together, so I was sorry to hear his news. Just four days after his announcement, John Rogers was installed as Dean during a Saturday Evensong, and we were quick to invite him, his wife and twin son and daughter round to dinner, again to establish good relations. Meanwhile the second son of Mike and Sue Davies-Jenkins had become Dean's Scholar, they had organised a successful tour, and it was time for another parent to take over from them as chairman of the choir association. The new man, like their predecessor, was a friendly barrister, Peter Jacobs, who at the end of the year set out some ideas for the way ahead. Joanne continued as 'mistress of the robes' and also put together a portfolio of her experiences in the field of church music during the period from Advent to Pentecost, which she submitted to the Guild of Church Musicians under a new scheme to encourage members to acquire some degree of skill in church music. As a result she became the first person in Wales to be awarded the newly-initiated Archbishops' Award in Church Music, and was duly presented with it during Vespers at Westminster Cathedral by Cardinal Hume. It should be explained that the Roman Catholic church now shared this award, along with their certificate in church music and, in collaboration with the RSCM, the prestigious ADCM Diploma.

I began gradually to phase out my piano teaching, having become less enthusiastic after twenty-five years of it, and I had also allowed the Cardiff Tallis Singers to slip out of my grasp a year before, having directed twenty-seven services and concerts with them in five years. Although I had played the organ occasionally at St David's Hall as a solo recitalist, I sometimes felt a little disappointed that I was rarely asked to accompany a choir there, or to play with orchestras when a programme included an organ part: I think the market had been cornered by my former pupil Robert Court. I was therefore rather pleased to be invited to join the newly-named BBC National Orchestra of Wales in a performance of music from Bartók's ballet *The Miraculous Mandarin*. I duly hired full evening dress and borrowed a full score as well as my organ part. When I arrived at the rehearsal I was told that only the first section of the music was to be played. Looking at my part, I found that I was left with only *three notes* to play – and they were in the first minute and for pedals only. At the concert I took my place at the console high up behind the orchestra, in full view, and made a business of pulling out stops, looking in the mirror and no doubt giving an A for the players to tune to, so that the audience might think I had something to do. I managed to fit my three notes into the music correctly, and walked out with a very substantial fee (by my standards) for a broadcast public performance lasting only thirteen seconds and literally without lifting a finger.

Eventually the long-awaited opportunity came to meet members of the finance committee in the deanery itself to discuss my concerns. Knowing that the Parish would be represented by two men with little or no interest in my work (one being better known as a football manager) I invited to a dinner and later a lunch both Tony Jeremy (solicitor) and Dudley Austin (my new accountant) to brief them in more detail, planning to take them along to the meeting as my advisers. During the weeks that elapsed before the appointed date I again found myself in north Wales, examining this time in Bangor, but eventually 15 December arrived and we met for two hours at the deanery. My chosen advocates were not as effective as I had hoped, Dudley being a rather quiet and unassuming man, and Tony having unfortunately lost his voice; but at least the proceedings were chaired by a sympathetic Dean for the first time in my experience. I had noticed that during October the number of people attending the main Parish service on Sundays had declined every week, as the number at my own cathedral service had risen every week – perhaps an omen for my own fortunes? A dinner to mark John Knapp's retirement had been held the night before, and the name of his successor, another Lindsay (not such a good omen), was announced. And so, without really being aware of any effect my initiatives would take, on Christmas Eve I took charge for the twentieth time of the traditional service of nine lessons and carols, amid a number of social and family gatherings which included Marian's mother and brother, before escaping once more to our country retreat.

1994

There is little doubt that the main activity for Marian and me in 1994 was our Kleeneze work, not only delivering and collecting up to 130 catalogues a day, but also sponsoring and enthusing other people to join us, thereby boosting our profits. Before long, these increased to 16%, so that in one month we received a cheque for more than £700 from the company. Recruiting was done whenever we saw an opportunity, approaching all kinds of people we met, or had known for years, as well as advertising locally and further afield. We frequently went out to visit applicants and to explain the business, with varying degrees of success. So much did Kleeneze take over our lives that it was during the course of the year that I gave my last piano lesson.

Something odd happened in January, when Francis Hayes, chairman of the school governors, came round to our house to pass on a false allegation about me. I do not know how this came about, but I assume the school had requested a criminal background check on me, and had received a confidential letter from the department for education with an attached schedule from the police. The schedule showed that a Michael John Smith had been convicted at Wood Green Crown Court in 1984 and given two suspended sentences of nine months' imprisonment for indecency. I immediately noticed that the man's date of birth was shown as a month earlier than my own, which of course suggested a case of mistaken identity. It did not take me long to look up my diary for December 1984 and find that I was actually examining in Reading on the date shown, and I received a written apology from the government department. Another very odd thing that happened early in the year was the return to the cathedral of an ancient relic, in fact the upper part of a skull purporting to be that of one of our Welsh patron saints, St Teilo. It had been kept by the Mathew family for centuries, and at some stage incorporated into a chalice. They decided the time had come to surrender it, and a special Eucharist was held on a Wednesday evening to celebrate its return, to be placed in an aumbry made for the purpose. The Dean made it plain that there was no intention to venerate the object, but merely to accept it as an historical relic artefact. All the same, the whole choir turned out for the event, and sang the chorus *Hail, holy Teilo!* in a jaunty

6/8 metre from William Mathias's cantata based on the saint's life, as the skull was borne ceremoniously up the nave, and later the motet *Ecce sacerdos magnus* (Behold, a great priest) by the sixteenth century Spanish composer Victoria.

Two other happenings in the Spring, both apparently minor in themselves, are now seen as sowing the seeds for major confrontations in the future. One of them was a visit from the father of one of the choristers, expressing concern about his son's progress but more importantly about my dealings with the boys generally. I cannot recall the details, but suspect his complaint may have been similar to those made in letters received not so long before, concerning my attitude to candidates taking music exams. Another inkling of troubles to come took the form of a letter to the school's acting head from the mother of an eight-year old probationer, Rhys Harris. Mrs Harris was fussy and over-protective in a way that teachers loathe, but she felt that Michael Hoeg (who was in charge of all the school music as well as being my assistant) had treated her little darling unfairly.

The tricky matter of the telephone bill, the subject of no fewer than fifty items of correspondence in 1993 between British Telecom, the Chapter Clerk, myself and my legal advisers, was held in abeyance for a while, pending any influence the new Dean might bring to bear on the many protagonists involved. The Chapter already owed me £830 according to my advisers, including interest for two years, and since I had told my solicitor in July 1992 that I would agree to make a bigger contribution only if offered a better pension, I continued to pursue this option with Dudley, my accountant. At the beginning of March I sent in a proposal which reminded the finance committee that the annual premium they paid into my pension fund, having been set at 10% of my salary when the scheme was begun in 1985 (already eleven years late) had never been increased, whereas my salary had at least kept pace with inflation, and had risen by 43% in 1988 which meant a shortfall of £3665. I suggested that this sum, suitably enhanced by an actuarial computation, should be paid into the fund, and that the annual premium be increased forthwith to 10% of salary. In return, I would offer to increase my contribution towards telephone calls from 25% to 50%. Meanwhile I still demanded the £830 already owed to me, being the shortfall on the last eight telephone accounts plus 15% interest for 1992-3 and 8% for 1993-4. Mindful of the cathedral's own financial difficulties, I suggested they might request support from the representative body of the Church in Wales. I intended that these proposals should be put before the committee, but evidently they had to be considered by the sub-committee first, so there was further delay, and another *ten weeks* passed before my solicitor received a reply. This stated that it was not the sub-committee's remit to consider my pension at all, and that they would pay the lump sum demanded (which had now risen to £916) on condition that they would continue to pay only for the line rental and the first hundred units in each quarter. My friend Tony Jeremy, who it will be remembered was a solicitor specialising in contract law, advised that their condition was unlawful and that I should sue them in the small claims court for the £916, adding that any further recalcitrance on their part should be taken to the county court. My official solicitor, David Rees, was less sure about this, but he did threaten the Chapter with legal proceedings if the cheque were not received at once. Years before (in 1977) I had defeated a former Chapter Clerk by threatening to report him to the Law Society, and now once again the Clerk acknowledged the threat of legal action and paid up in full, specifically in order to avoid it. By then the debt had risen to over £1000, so a demand was sent in for the shortfall, but after further double miscalculation of figures Lindsay Ford (now firmly on the wrong foot again) had the gall to carry on paying only for the first hundred units of the summer account.

By now we were well into the autumn, whereupon a sixth lawyer entered the fray in the shape of our Choir Association's chairman Peter Jacobs, yet another barrister. He took the initiative to meet Lindsay Ford for a man-to-man talk lasting seventy-five minutes. Peter began by objecting strongly to a hefty hire charge of over £500 being levied by the cathedral on the Choir Association for the use of the building to make our recording for Priory Records. It was unreasonable, he maintained, for the Chapter to charge its own choir for anything, especially as many of the resulting CDs would be sold in the cathedral shop at a profit which would not come to us. Ford admitted that he was constantly being 'got at' by the parochial church council, who felt that we all did the absolute minimum required by our contracts (no wonder!) and that my relations with some sectors of cathedral life were at a low level. His predecessor (Lloyd-Edwards) whom he held responsible for the combining of funds, had overlooked the fact that the parish would then effectively control them. He alleged that there was a deficit of £17,000 for just the first half of the year. For his part, Peter Jacobs offered to set up another meeting, and suggested that the choir might make some gesture, such as a Christmas concert and/or a buffet supper, to raise money for the cathedral. I guess that Dean Rogers must have played a part at this stage, but it was still considered that the bills I was accustomed to present had 'exceeded all possible reasonable estimates'. 'Your client will have to accept', he wrote to David Rees, 'that the Dean and Chapter appeal to his Christian stewardship and ask that he put forward a reasonable proposal: the Chapter cannot use funds to pay your client 75% of an indefinite telephone bill'. David Rees would not accept this, and requested immediate payment of a further sum of £327 which had accrued. I told the Dean that I was preparing to report to the conference of the Cathedral Organists' Association, to be attended by thirty-four serving organists including the chief executives of the RCO, the RSCM and the Choir Schools' Association, on the agenda item 'the remuneration of the cathedral organists of Wales'. It would be nice to report, I said, that the Chapter had honoured the QC's opinion of 1992. Furthermore, the conference might well be aware that I was the only delegate whose travel expenses were not paid by his employer for both conferences each year. A fortnight later, Ford suggested that I might accept as a proper contribution to my phone bills a sum 'equal to that expended by the Dean for business calls'. I told the Dean that I did not wish to read my customary lesson in the Advent procession service, which would have meant sharing a platform with Lindsay Ford, and that I was substituting one of the new lay clerks. It may have been at this time that for the same reason I also stopped going up to the altar on Sunday mornings to take Communion – but no one ever mentioned it. The usual derisory telephone cheque received in December was never banked, and so this sorry affair dragged on into the following year. Lest it should be thought that I could well afford, from my other sources of income, to pay more than I did, I should explain that I had built up such large debts on my credit card accounts that around this time I was forced to take out a second mortgage of £6,000 on Rozel Cottage in order to pay them off and avoid their very high interest rates.

Meanwhile I applied to the architect responsible for the oversight of cathedral properties for various improvements to the house, including the provision of a shower in the bathroom, the absence of which was frequently lamented by our teenage children whose friends took such an amenity for granted. I even suggested the possibility of extending Adrian's tiny bedroom into the unoccupied adjoining flat which, like two others along the Cathedral Green, had been closed because of the cathedral's lack of the funds needed for implementing new fire regulations covering separate households. Nearly nine months later I found it necessary to send a copy of this request to the newly-designated, and unpaid, clerk of works.

I would not like to give the impression that these struggles dominated my life at this stage, for in other ways things were definitely looking up when we reached the summer term. In May we much enjoyed singing a Saturday Evensong in Worcester Cathedral, where the acoustics in the quire, with its extensive wooden panelling, were so much more grateful than our own. Members of the congregation commended our singing of Alan Gray's 8-part *a capella* setting of the canticles and Walter Stanton's anthem *Jesu, Lover of my soul*, judging us to be better than the resident choir. In June we fulfilled my previous year's ambition to stage a concert in St David's Cathedral, being offered this time an £800 fee and singing to an audience of 150 a programme of 8-part anthems by Gibbons, Weelkes and Purcell, along with some of my twentieth-century favourites by Rubbra and Shephard. Moreover, we were offered a rather unconventional recording engagement by a Lincolnshire firm called Cantoris Soundalive, who wanted to recreate the investiture of the Prince of Wales at Caernarvon in honour of its twenty-fifth anniversary. The resulting CDs, we were told, would be a limited edition on sale for one year only and exclusive to the royal palaces. It was an odd assignment for a choir of boys and men, since the original ceremony featured a large mixed chorus and an orchestra, but I agreed to the proposal, even though it meant singing three hymns in Welsh and learning a suite of folk-song settings entitled *Rhapsody for a Prince* by Mansel Thomas. I decided that these would have to be sung in English because of the time-scale involved, and accompanied more suitably on the Steinway grand that resided in the Cathedral, than on the organ – even though Michael Hoeg did not regard himself as a pianist, and I could well have asked David Thomas to play instead. I contributed a couple of moderately appropriate organ pieces, but do not remember ever listening to the resulting recording since it was made, except for the very grand version of *God save the Queen* by David Willcocks, with the brass and percussion of the Welsh National Opera orchestra placed well down the nave and making a quite magnificent backing to the relatively restrained singing of the choir. As if that weren't enough, our new Chairman Peter Jacobs negotiated an important recording with Priory Records, to be part of their series of *Great Cathedral Anthems**. This put us on an equal footing with some of the great English cathedrals, and it was good to be recognised in such a way by a company that had in effect succeeded Abbey as the premier source of English cathedral music. Our performance evidently pleased Neil Collier, the company's proprietor, because he invited us to be part of his next project, a collection of settings of the evening canticles.

The Chapter Clerk, true to form, complained to the cathedral school's bursar that expenditure on advertising under the heading 'music' had increased from £186 in 1992 to £1,129 in 1993, and although not all of this would have been for chorister recruitment, it had evidently worked, because we now had a full complement of twenty boys, always including at least fourteen full choristers, the number for which the stalls were designed. It was mentioned in passing that the cathedral's annual accounts had revealed a deficit of £10,000, which explained the apparently parsimonious responses I

---

* See appendix 1

always received to my financial requests.

The autumn term produced an unparalleled supply of new men in the choir. Several of our long-standing lay clerks had requested lighter duties, and Michael Davidson, Gary Beauchamp and Spencer Basford had all been demoted, so to speak, to the status of singing-men, along with Alastair Clarke: this meant that each would attend most of the choral services but not all, and was therefore paid a fee per service instead of a salary. Kenneth Robinson left to join a religious community in Durham, leaving only the two basses, Robert Adams and Stephen Hamnett, as lay clerks. It gave me considerable pleasure to inform readers of *The Llandaff Monthly* that

> These changes paved the way for the introduction of a new group of very experienced young men, two as lay clerks and three as choral scholars. The lay clerks are David Pounder (alto) who took a degree in Engineering and has joined the Welsh College of Music and Drama for the Advanced Diploma in Singing, specialising in early music; (David was a chorister at St Paul's Cathedral, Dundee and sang alto at St Mary's Cathedral, Edinburgh); and Deiniol Morgan, who, as an undergraduate at Manchester University, sang in the William Byrd Singers and *Voces Cantorum* as well as directing the University Chamber Choir for a year. Deiniol has won a three-year scholarship at the University of Wales, Cardiff to study for his doctorate. Our three new choral scholars have all been choristers at important English choral foundations, each becoming Head Chorister: Joseph Davis (alto) sang for eight years as a treble in St Chad's Cathedral, Birmingham; Andrew Dobbins (tenor) was at Exeter Cathedral for six years before going to King's College, Taunton; and Andrew Jenkins (baritone) was a chorister at St Michael's College, Tenbury and at Tewkesbury Abbey, and comes to us from Ellesmere College. All three are now reading Music at the University.

I might add that their subsequent progress was more varied, for Joe Davis ceased to attend after a few days, whereas Deiniol Morgan persevered rather longer and became precentor of Westminster Abbey before leaving in 2008 to be chaplain of the Welsh Guards.

In spite of our financial worries and limited cashflow, we still found ways of enjoying family holidays. Incorporating these into foreign examining tours was no longer a choice, for not only had I turned down such invitations for 1991 and 1992 but, perhaps owing to criticisms made about my style (which this year included a few more, relating partly to my written reports) no more international tours were offered. It was around this time that examiners working for the Associated Board were instructed to take more care over the choice of words when writing reports, and to 'evolve a written style where honesty is combined with diplomacy and sensitivity'. We were supplied with a list of twenty adjectives which should be used 'only rarely and with the greatest care', such as 'untidy', 'heavy', 'poor', 'careless' and 'insensitive', while certain words were to be avoided altogether: 'unacceptable', 'unpleasant', 'unmusical' and (perhaps with more justification) 'disastrous'. I would have thought that some of these words were necessary when justifying a failure, but it was a sign of the times that one should take measures to avoid upsetting candidates at all costs.

It perhaps did not bode well that Mr Gray, the new headmaster, shared with my least favourite man, the Chapter Clerk, the name Lindsay. A former choral scholar at King's College, Cambridge, with an ARCO diploma and plenty of experience in teaching, he seemed more than eligible for the job. We duly invited him and his wife Caro to dinner to establish good relations. Michael Hoeg was thought to be something of a misogynist where girl pupils were concerned, leaving the way open, perhaps, for Lindsay to make his mark by setting up a girls' choir himself. As early as 13 September an alert journalist questioned whether they would be allowed to sing in the cathedral choir, pointing out that Manchester Cathedral had just incorporated girls into its choir. Salisbury had set up a girls' choir in 1991, and as long ago as 1970 the trend had been started at St David's. 'The tradition is', wrote Lindsay Gray,

> that only boys and men may join the Llandaff Cathedral Choir, and we see no reason to change that; the girls can sing in several choirs within the school and regularly perform concerts. Obviously they cannot sing in the cathedral choir, but I would like to think that as their skills develop, they will eventually be of the standard that they can sing in the cathedral as other choirs do.

This statement incensed a reader from the west coast, who wrote to the newspaper: 'I would have thought it more appropriate for a modern educationist to campaign and instigate equal rights and opportunities for all pupils in his care, rather than perpetuate the myth of second-class citizenship to 50% of his children'. Lindsay swiftly countered the criticism by wholeheartedly applauding the Salisbury initiative, while offering the view that the combination of boys' and men's voices provided a unique sound, one that most cathedral composers throughout the ages had in mind when writing anthems and settings; and making the other often-heard point that the boys would become the lay clerks of tomorrow. It did not go un-noticed that his two daughters were members of his new choir, and I heard it said that he tended to choose one of them for a solo, in preference to another girl called Charlotte Church, who very soon left for Howell's School and promptly became a world-famous child singer.

After my various attempts to persuade the authorities to allow some choristers to be dayboys, a compromise had been made by which probationers could be dayboys only until such time as they were promoted to the status of junior chorister. Also, John Knapp had recently abolished Saturday morning school, an act which, though undoubtedly beneficial to most of his pupils, meant that special arrangements had to be made to allow for the choristers, who still had to attend a practice between 8 and 9 am. One of Lindsay Gray's first acts as headmaster was to propose that the boarding requirement for choristers be abolished, and that the boarding house should close down after the summer term in 1995. Peter Jacobs set out a list of predicted disadvantages for his fellow parents to consider, under four headings: extra strain on the boys; the loss of their early morning instrumental practice before the choir practice; the risk of a lowering of standards if the choir practice had to be abandoned; and the extra burden on parents having to transport their children to school at difficult hours - a specially serious problem for parents living at some distance from Cardiff. With the remission of two thirds of the boarding and tuition fees currently allowed, would a scholarship of two thirds of the *day* fee be sufficient? Peter summoned all the parents to a meeting at the end of the autumn half term holiday, inviting the headmaster to attend only after the matter had been discussed for an hour, to explain his proposals and answer questions. I do not know what Dean Davies would have thought of all this, having been against the idea throughout his time, but it was clearly a case of a new broom sweeping clean, as the old adage hath it. Some of the boys were due to remain in the choir until 1999, and all of their parents had deliberately chosen boarding for their sons, so it was not surprising that they were strongly opposed to a change, especially as Gray even suggested that some boys from further afield might be billetted with those living nearby. He did concede that boarding could continue until 1996, but the meeting insisted that proper provision should be made also for the boys who were due to remain for up to three years longer. Peter Jacobs set out in writing the strong feelings expressed, summing up in true barrister style by considering wider questions to be resolved and reflecting my own views:

The boys have made a tremendous commitment to the

School and Cathedral. I sometimes feel that many in both institutions do not realise how massive such a commitment is. For the best part of thirteen hours a day they are involved in school and cathedral matters. By and large they enjoy what they are doing, but I would be saddened to see their self-belief undermined. I would be sorry if they received the impression that the commitment elsewhere was less than that which they are required to show now.

Gerard Elias, as our former chairman for five years, was consulted by a number of the parents, and wrote to Dean Rogers saying:

> The choristers are fortunate enough to be trained by sympathetic and highly talented choir trainers who are able to develop a dedication and collegiate spirit in a group of boys who devote a considerable part of each day to their tasks in the cathedral. I would not wish to denigrate any other choir, but my travels take me to cathedral churches which now have 'day boy' choirs, and the difference in standards is obvious.

He went on to say that his third son, having begun as a day-boy probationer following the recent concession, soon preferred, as his two brothers had done, to involve himself totally in the choir, and would have chosen to board in any case (even though the family lived on the Cathedral Green itself). For the record, this is the letter I wrote to the headmaster for consideration by the Governors:

> I fully appreciate the wishes of the current choristers that they should continue to board until they leave at the age of thirteen and a half. Almost half the present boys are expected to remain in the choir until after 1996, and provisions should be made for them.
>
> 1. When policy changes are considered, it should always be uppermost in the Governors' minds that the school was founded to provide cathedral choristers. Therefore the school's ability to encourage the most musical and intelligent boys in the United Kingdom to take up choristerships should be a consideration of paramount importance, other factors (however important) concerning the school as a whole taking second place.
> 2. If Llandaff Cathedral were to change the course of history by taking away the opportunity for choristers to board, this could encourage similarly constituted foundations

328

to follow suit. Eventually choristerships (now available to boys throughout the UK) would be available only to boys living within a few miles of a cathedral.

3. The strength of the choir here has depended for more than a century on a mixture of local boys and those from far afield. In our particular circumstances, where a parish choir of local boys already exists, the nationwide catchment area for cathedral choristers should be maintained at all costs. I therefore strongly recommend (as I have on occasion for the last twenty years) a mixture of day boys and boarders, to take full advantage of talent both local and national, not forgetting that we have often taken boys who at first applied unsuccessfully to their nearest cathedral before looking to Llandaff for an opportunity.

4. It can too easily be overlooked that Llandaff Cathedral Choir, which now has a reputation for excellence fully equal to those of the major cathedrals of Britain, is still the only one in Wales able to achieve such high standards by recruiting not only boys, but also men, from all over the country. Any move to restrict applications through lack of boarding facilities should, if at all possible, be firmly rejected.

For the sake of interest, I noted that nine of the boys who had left in the past four years had come from Brecon, Llechryd, Raglan and Trecastle in Wales, and from Liverpool, Oxford, Berkshire, Surrey and Kent – a wide catchment area indeed! It soon became apparent that Lindsay Gray had a hidden agenda, possibly intending to sell the boarding house ('The Lodge') or convert it in the interests of the school's long-term future. The parents' overwhelming opposition won the day, and by December it was clear that boarding would continue until all the current choristers left.

Meanwhile Adrian had left the Bishop of Llandaff High School, not relishing the thought of a sixth form syllabus, and had taken up a course in information technology at Coleg Glan Hafren in Cardiff, leading to a 'BTec' national diploma, while we provisionally accepted a place for Laura in the sixth form at King's College Taunton for the following year, where her fees as a boarder would be much lower than if she had continued at Howell's School as a day pupil. Rachel and John came to stay for the occasional weekend, and began living together in a large house which John bought opposite his parents' in Eltham. Marian had passed several examinations in horticulture in her City and Guilds course, achieving their certificate, with distinction in two subjects.

Dean Rogers fully supported my decision in early December to suspend the 'difficult' bass lay clerk who has already cast a few shadows over these chronicles, actually summoning him to the Chapter House for a formal warning, and later resisting his request to be allowed to sing at the Christmas services. I remember my concise admonition to this man: 'You're too late, too loud, and too rude'. The Dean was also kind enough to invite Michael Hoeg to lunch on Christmas Day, so that for the first time in years we enjoyed our own lunch purely *en famille*.

1995

The New Year began with a novel idea, which was to rent a cottage near the sea in Dorset for a few days, where we enjoyed crisp, fine weather as we explored Lulworth Cove, Weymouth, Portland and Corfe Castle before returning home. We continued our Kleeneze activities, travelling miles to meet prospective agents as far afield as Hackney, Barking and Ilford. When I knew that I would be examining in Swindon, I advertised in the area and arranged to meet applicants in their homes after work. In February, still feeling the pinch financially, I felt obliged to sell a Krugerrand and a smaller coin which I had bought in South Africa in 1981. I took Marian with me to the deanery and spent an hour with John Rogers to plead with him about our financial problems. I told him that because the Chapter now again owed me £460 in respect of the telephone, I could not afford to pay my three-quarters portion of our electricity bill. I also pointed out that my submission for an enhanced pension fund, made almost a year ago, had been totally disregarded. Furthermore, I asked him to bear in mind that the recommendation of the Incorporated Society of Musicians (which he had recently accepted concerning fees for special services) stated that the minimum salary for a cathedral organist who enjoyed rent-free accommodation and worked for sixteen or more hours a week should be £15,000, which was 32% higher than mine. I think he must have taken pity on us, for a few weeks later he authorised Lindsay Ford to meet my claim and resume paying the line rental and 75% of the cost of all calls. It had taken me three years and four months to achieve this victory - considerably longer than it had taken me to settle my service agreement some eighteen years earlier.

Thus emboldened, I next tackled a neighbour called Keith Morris, who had assumed some degree of responsibility for the properties in and around the Cathedral Green. After all these years, St Mary's was still the only staff house without a central heating system, and Adrian and Laura had good reason to complain, especially during the weeks of cold and wet weather in January and February. My enquiries had shown that the cost of installing the system would be less than the current cost of three years' fuel for our assortment of storage heaters and separate convector and radiant heaters, thereby in the long run saving money for the Chapter as well as for us. I mentioned also that the woodwork of the garage and outhouses had not been repainted for at least twenty years, and that several damp patches in the walls needed attention. In fact, the work required by the environmental health department had still not been completed. It was the Dean himself who responded to these requests, albeit fifteen weeks later (why did everything take so long?) Even he had failed to persuade his own finance committee to improve my pension or to contribute more for my attendance at conferences, but he did authorise the repairs to the premises and went so far as to say that our request for the installation of central heating would be passed on to the Church's representative body as the owners of the property.

Members of the Sunday morning congregations seemed to favour the Viennese settings I had gradually introduced, by Mozart, Haydn and Schubert, including the latter's *Mass in* C, though I did find the eighty-five pages of his *Mass in B flat* rather repetitive. Two days after that experience we acknowledged Purcell's tercentenary at a Tuesday evensong by performing his long verse anthem *O sing unto the Lord* with a small string ensemble. Peter Jacobs's idea that we should give a concert in aid of cathedral funds came to fruition in March when, for only the second, and last, time this actually happened, with a performance in aid of the restoration of the north-west tower, of a programme of ten anthems and two settings of evening canticles for boys' voices. We were a strong team, with fourteen choristers and nine men, and it was in my view a very fine concert. Looking back, I am tempted to wonder why we did not bring our wide repertory to an equally wide audience in this way, but at the time I considered that seven public performances a week, albeit to an audience usually numbering no more than fifty (more like a hundred on Sunday mornings) were quite enough for us to manage. Sundry lords and ladies (not to mention James Callaghan, a former Prime Minister) heard us sing at a memorial service to the former Lord Lieutenant, and the Prince of Wales again graced us with his presence at an ecumenical service to commemorate the fiftieth anniversary of our victory in Europe. On that occasion we sang that very fine but little known anthem by Vaughan Williams, *Lord, thou hast been our refuge*, a setting of Psalm 90 which, as I have mentioned earlier, incorporates the tune of *O God, our help in ages past* as a trumpet solo, fittingly played on this occasion by a sergeant-major. One of my rare opportunities to accompany an oratorio on the organ was realised in March, when I was engaged by the Dyfed Choir to play Dvořák's *Stabat Mater* in the Cathedral.

April brought another complaining letter from Mrs Harris, this time addressed to me, with copies to the Dean and Headmaster (an ominous sign). This began such a significant chain of events that it is perhaps worthwhile to trace her young son's background. Born Rhys ap Dafydd in May 1986, he was brought to my house for piano lessons at the tender age of five, made good progress and passed his first two graded examinations in a year and a half. In September 1993 he joined the choir as a probationer, and I continued teaching him at the cathedral school, though his mother still drove over from Pontypridd every week to attend his lessons. The following year, his father decreed, against his wife's wishes, that his piano tuition should not cause him to miss any school lessons, and as I was not prepared to teach him at home again, his mother had no option but to seek another teacher. By half term her quest was unsuccessful, but I turned down her request that I should teach Rhys on Saturday mornings. In February 1995 Mrs Harris told me, apologising for the short notice, that Rhys would be absent for a fortnight in order to sing in America. She had assumed, wrongly, that the headmaster would have told me five months earlier about this arrangement. The Dean asked her for a full explanation, which was duly delivered above the father's signature, including some criticism of me. Unfortunately when Rhys returned I made some quip pretending that I had forgotten who he was. Obviously he passed this on to his mother, who told me in no uncertain terms how he had been recognised as an 'outstanding young talent' when only eight, at an international choral summer school in Hertfordshire, where he was selected by two prominent American musicians to be the only boy from Great Britain to sing in the first National Honor Boychoir of the American Choral Directors' Association in Colorado. Mentioning some of his achievements in America, she wrote 'Everyone in America was very impressed with our son: he represented the school well, and promoted much goodwill between Wales and the American Boychoir'. Indeed, I received a letter from the chairman and guest conductor of the course, praising Rhys's contribution in fulsome terms and commending me for 'the excellent training extended to this fine young chorister'. His mother wrongly claimed that on his return I had demoted him, an allegation easily disproved by the list of boys posted on a notice board, and had singled him out as someone I could not remember – a deed regarded as 'a cruel and unusual stunt committed for the sole purpose of breaking the spirit of an innocent eight-year-old boy who loves to sing'. After the Easter holiday I took the matter up with Mrs Harris, explaining to her in my reply, that my remark was a standing joke often made when a man or boy returned after absence of a week or so, and that everyone else accepted such banter with good humour. I went on:

This is a happy choir, and stunts, cruel or otherwise, and spirit-breaking devices play no part in the methods I have evolved in twenty-one years as a Cathedral Organist; and most parents have expressed only gratitude at the results achieved. I take a serious view of your allegation of cruelty, which was not only unjust but also, being communicated to my colleagues, defamatory. I am taking steps to protect my personal position, and think that you and your husband would be wise not to write to me again in this unacceptable manner.

I told the story to my solicitor, who advised that on no account should the boy become a chorister, since his mother would never change her behaviour and I would have to suffer similar treatment for the next five years. My rebuke seemed to have had the desired effect on the parents, but an incident happened a little later, when a few choristers were off duty and I let probationers take their place at a Sunday morning service. Looking down from the organ loft, I noticed that Rhys, instead of starting each musical phrase at the beginning, would purse his lips as if in preparation, thereby omitting two or three words every time. His parents, having heard that he had sung in the morning, expected him to do so at Evensong, and indeed Mr Harris was observed putting a hassock in the choir stalls at the place where Rhys had stood in the morning, presumably so that he could stand on it and not look smaller than the choristers. I did not ask the boy to sing that afternoon, and the next day I explained to him that he should begin each phrase promptly, without making 'rabbit faces'. I thought this an apt phrase for a boy aged nine, but on hearing what I had said Mrs Harris took the boy to a consultant paediatrician, telling me afterwards that Rhys was 'severely stressed' and had been advised to stay away from the choir for a further two weeks. I demanded to see the doctor's report, but it was not until near the end of the summer term that he wrote to me. He had recommended a three week break from choir duties, but there was no mention of any 'stress'. The mother had mentioned the development of a 'facial tick', but the doctor said that such things were common in children 'and we would expect an excellent prognosis here'. He saw nothing that would adversely affect the boy's potential in any way. For my part, I challenged Mrs Harris (who had told me that no report had been issued) and told her that if she felt his work with the choir caused Rhys severe stress, I would have to take this into account when assessing his suitability as a chorister. I also stressed the importance of parents' faith in the choirmaster, and asked for a retraction of her accusations of cruelty, should she wish to express some confidence in me. I also requested, at a meeting in the school, that her own attendance there should be limited to bringing him from home and taking him home in the evening – but this requirement was vetoed by Lindsay Gray for fear of singling her out for a special ban.

Easter was unusually late this year. Although in earlier days the choir's Lent term continued until Easter Day, for some years the school terms had dictated that the break of two or three weeks enjoyed by the choir quite often occurred before Easter. This year was unique in that the holiday was partly before Easter and partly after, requiring the choristers to return after a fortnight, be on duty for five days, and then take five days off again before beginning the summer term. This must have been rather unsettling, and for some reason there had been far more absences than usual in the early part of the year; so much so that I began keeping a register of attendances. I found that of the eighty-nine services sung by 20 May the three youngest choristers had missed a total of seventy and that Andrew Lewis was absent twenty-seven times; there were two others with a poor attendance record, and I calculated that four boys had accumulated a staggering total of 150 absences. As this state of affairs had never happened before, I looked for reasons. A number of boys had been complaining about a poor selection of food provided at the school, so I obtained a few details from them and asked the catering manager for a typical menu, which was duly provided, but it covered only weekdays, with no indication of how choristers were fed on Sundays; there was no cooked breakfast on Wednesdays, and there seemed to be a preponderance of sandwiches in the evenings. I am no nutritionist, but it did seem that there was some cost-cutting involved here, possibly to the detriment of the energy of these hard-worked boys. This, and the introduction of terms like 'middle management' rather than 'heads of department' made me think that the school was being run more like a profit-making business than a school.

It was now the turn of Peter Lewis, who had complained last year, to deliver a report on Andrew Lewis, privately commissioned from a psychologist and former child protection officer, to the effect that there was in his view cause for concern which should be investigated further, specifically in relation to my 'negative and damaging interaction' towards some of the choristers. It later turned out that this man had been called in as a result of disagreement between Peter Lewis and Andrew's mother, who, it emerged, was a medic known professionally as Sheila Lawrence, having separated from her husband in 1989 and set up home with Andrew at a different address. It was apparently Andrew's idea that he should be a boarder at the school, but the parents arranged for him to stay with one of them on Wednesdays and at other times. I did observe that some kind of parental break-up was an element in most of the problems we had to deal with. The psychiatrist expressed concern that the effect of the alleged 'disassociation' in the long term would have a major psychological effect on Andrew. These allegations, he concluded, should either be investigated internally, or formally under Section 47 of the Children Act of 1989: The Duty to Investigate by the Police / local authority. Clearly, as often in these cases, it was felt that Andrew was being unfairly 'picked on'. For my own protection I began to write notes on his misdemeanours, which, though trivial in themselves, amounted to a formidable array. His misbehaviour in practices was easily summarised as fidgeting, turning his head sideways, talking and writing in his copies of the music being sung. It was a firm rule that no boy should write anything in his copy unless I instructed all of them to do so, yet Andrew made a show of deliberately flouting this rule, on one occasion producing not one but five pencils. In short, he was a nuisance, and I agreed to see Dr Lewis (who was a senior lecturer in the College of Medicine) again in June. Expecting trouble, I invited for moral support the succentor, an intelligent and rather eccentric man called Jonathan Redvers-Harris who had a law degree; and Clive Westwood, who combined the useful attributes of friend, school teacher and cathedral server with first-hand knowledge of the life of a chorister, his son being one at the Chapel of St John's College, Cambridge. We had a useful discussion, but Clive told me afterwards that as they left the house Dr Lewis muttered 'We've got to put a stop to Dr Smith', and by July the parents met the Dean and alleged that I had subjected Andrew to psychological abuse. How different, I thought, from the attitude towards me of the majority of parents. Unknown to me, though headed 'To whom it may concern', another report had been issued in May by the consultant psychiatrist, expressing a hope that the school would do something to promote the welfare of children rather than ignore the evidence. He felt that the pattern of interaction which had been described by Andrew in a further interview was both psychically (*sic*) damaging in the short term and was having an effect in the long term, citing 'psychosomatic illness for Andrew and a number of his peers in the choir'. This report was not shown to me until December, but in September, when Andrew's voice was breaking, it was suggested that he might join the ranks of the men as an alto and therefore no longer attend the practices for trebles where he was making a nuisance of himself. Dean Rogers, it seemed, had successfully defused the situation and the plan was accepted by all concerned, even the proviso that in the event of further misbehaviour on Andrew's part I had the parents' approval to discipline him. In the event, for some reason now forgotten, this scheme did not come to fruition, and in October the parents saw fit to rake up the whole business again by writing to the chairman of the school governors, of whom we shall read more later.

I had been given an inkling of Peter Lewis's position some months earlier, by Roger Lallemant, a father of five including two boys in the choir. Mr Lallemant was an itinerant welder by trade, but I found him very perceptive of character and human relationships. Without actually naming names, he made it clear that Dr Lewis offered his 'close friendship' with Michael Hoeg as cause for confidence that his son would become a Dean's Scholar. 'I have made my own observations', he wrote, 'but others, more regular observers of the choir, have commented upon his almost shameless display of politics'. It seemed that the Lewis boy himself was apt to undermine Oliver Lallemant, exploiting his rather diminutive stature in subtle ways. When the time came for promotions, Oliver, as by far the more worthy contender, gained the silver medallion. I was a conscientious choirmaster, and could do without criticism from choristers' parents: Marian and I sometimes discussed our future, and decided that I should plan to retire at sixty, in two years' time.

During the month of June I had the good fortune to spend four days examining in Salisbury, enabling me to look up some of the many friends I had made there, followed by a garden party at Christ Church, Oxford. Unfortunately, while I was away from home a burglar broke into the dining room at St Mary's, breaking a window, forcing the inside shutters and making off with several items, the most regrettable loss being a late nineteenth century clock which had been given to my ancestor Sir George Martin in 1897, the year that he was knighted after conducting Queen Victoria's Diamond Jubilee service on the steps of St Paul's Cathedral. The clock was inscribed with the names of men who I always supposed to be the cathedral lay clerks, and was the only heirloom I had, apart from a pair of cufflinks. I made vain attempts to find the clock in a few local antiques markets, but had to be content with the insurance payout of £1000 for it, which, with another £1000 for several electronic items then favoured by thieves, was a good deal more useful to us at that time than the objects themselves. This event caused me to think about realising some cash from other heirlooms, and prompted me to get a valuation of my grandfather's half-hunter watch and chain and three other gold watches. Being told that they were worth £2000, I took them to a dealer, whose own estimate was only £290. Later, a gold bullion dealer in Cowbridge Road bought two old silver watches for £20 and offered to sell the gold items on my half, for an estimated total of £525, to which I agreed. I also sold ten demijohns at an auction, not having made any wine recently, and sought another income opportunity by meeting the Principal of the Welsh College of Music and Drama, Edmund Fivet, with a view to teaching there. Barry Ferguson, organist of Rochester Cathedral since 1977, had recently retired at the age of 57 and was living in Shaftesbury, so Marian and I went over and had tea with him and his wife to discuss the pros and cons of early retirement.

By now Laura was playing her violin in the South Glamorgan Youth Orchestra, but she, along with some forty-five other members, decided to boycott their May concert in St David's Hall, having become thoroughly bored with the weekly rehearsals, begun in January, for

Mahler's second symphony. It is, of course, a wonderful work, and I have mentioned in an earlier chapter the first time I heard it in the same hall, but I considered the choice to be an ambitious ego-trip for their conductor rather than a suitable work for the young players under his baton. Undaunted by the walk-out, he invited back a number of former members, now at universities, offending the regulars even more, to make an orchestra of 144 players – but I was the only member of the family to go and hear it. We did however hear the orchestra's summer concert, when they were crammed shoulder-to-shoulder in the cathedral – a far from ideal venue for them. One Sunday in July combined a half-hour organ recital by me to precede the Festival Eucharist at Madley Church near Byford, and a dinner at Dyffryn House with our Kleeneze upline and downline couples, preceding a performance of *Twelfth Night* in the gardens. Never one to appreciate Shakespeare as I should, finding his extravagant vocabulary difficult to understand, I think I enjoyed the dinner more than the play, but the others evidently thought it was great.

The autumn choir term began ominously with another discussion with the Dean about what to do with Andrew Lewis, whose behaviour had been the subject of several meetings the previous terms (with and without his aggressive father). Another unfortunate event, as it turned out, was the promotion to full chorister status of little Rhys Harris, whose mother was a known trouble-maker. The ideal age for a boy to become a probationer is eight; experience showed that to start at a younger age was not beneficial, but simply meant remaining a probationer twice as long. Such was the case with Rhys.

Other September meetings included one at the deanery, when all the regular organists (my two assistants, with the parish organist Morley Lewis and his assistant Robert Court) tried to persuade the Dean of the necessity to have a new cathedral organ; a dinner at the Summer Palace, a fine Chinese restaurant opposite the ruined mediaeval bishop's palace, for a visiting vocal quartet from Russia, together with Clive and Hilary Westwood and John and Beryl Baldwin; and a conference at the City Temple in London, arranged by the RCO on the subject of organ-building, led by a panel of two dozen well-known organists and builders. A very unusual event occurred in October, when the Welsh language television channel filmed a spectacular Christmas Show in a 'big top' marquee situated in Margam Park between Cardiff and Swansea. The show featured the inevitable male voice choir and various solo singers, with a band led by an enthusiastic conductor who also acted as compere. There were jugglers, monocyclists, and some scantily-clad young lady acrobats. The organisers decided to include the cathedral choristers, so they were duly taught a couple of Welsh carols and appeared solemnly in their ruffs and red cassocks, standing stock still in their usual way; Oliver Lallemant sang a solo well-known at the time, *Walking in the air* from Howard Blake's musical story *The Snowman*. It was all great fun, and it was noticed that while awaiting their turn, one of the boys, a lively lad not yet eleven, was sitting with the pretty girls and chatting them up; he, Neil Hillman, will also feature prominently as this story unfolds.

When the autumn term began, I decided that my safest course regarding the now notorious Mrs Harris was to avoid any criticism of Rhys, for fear of instant repercussions. Ignoring my solicitor's advice, I had been persuaded by the headmaster to promote the boy, who had now served two years as a probationer, to chorister status, partly on the grounds that the school could not afford to lose pupils. Despite my decision not to speak to the boy, his mother telephoned Mr Gray in October to complain that I was still 'drawing attention to his facial twitch', implying that he was being picked on, and that some of the boys were calling him 'rabbit face'. Knowing nothing of this, or of her subsequent letter in which she threatened to transfer Rhys to Wells Cathedral School, I decided after half term to take steps to improve his performance. He responded so well that when I congratulated him, the other boys applauded him. Four days later I was summoned before the Dean and one of the canons and told that Mrs Harris had again complained of verbal abuse, and that the Headmaster had actually invited her and other parents to put complaints to him in writing, alleging that some of the school governors had requested this course of action. He refused to let me see any of the resulting letters, so I telephoned two of the governors, my friend Elisabeth Elias and yet another lawyer, John Griffith-Williams, who both denied all knowledge of such a request and advised me to phone the recently-appointed *Custos,* who happened to be the widow of Christopher Cory, the founder-director of the old Llandaff Festival. Accordingly I arranged an appointment to see her in her home, Penllyn Castle. Next day I angrily phoned Mr Gray to ask why he had passed the parents' letters to the Dean instead of to me, whereupon Mrs Cory, perhaps fearing my wrath, or simply confused at the direction matters were taking, cancelled the appointment to see me.

All these shenanigans were duly reported to Peter Jacobs, who had arranged for us to make another commercial recording with Priory Records in that month of November. This time it was a collection of settings of the evening canticles *Magnificat* and *Nunc Dimittis*[*], with the usual three evenings set aside for rehearse/record sessions. Neil Collier brought with him his new producer, who turned out to be Caroline Paschalides, a girl who once chaperoned my former pupil

[*] See appendix 1

Helen Burrows when I invited her out to dinner. Being new to the job, she was excessively particular in unsuitable ways, commenting on our style and even pronunciation – things which were immutable in the context of three three-hour sessions. The second and third evenings went very smoothly, though as a result of spending too much time over *Blair in B minor* we had to omit a little-known setting which Alan Gibbs had dedicated to us. Two days later we celebrated the tercentenary of Purcell's death by singing at Evensong his verse anthem *Rejoice in the Lord alway*, accompanied by a string orchestra of sixteen players picked by Andrew Wilson-Dixon from the Welsh College of Music and Drama, and Laura came home from Taunton for the weekend to hear it. After driving her back, I wrote to the Bishop offering to take the choir to sing at parish churches, as we used to do in my earlier years, but he failed to respond.

The following evening the Dean asked me to call on him after the full practice the following day. I thought that after so much good work with the choir, I was to be congratulated over a glass of wine. How far from the truth I was! Our meeting turned out to be very different from what I had envisaged, and had far-reaching implications.

Shown into the Dean's study, I found not just John Rogers but also one of the canons and, seated at the desk, the deputy chapter clerk, my friend David Lambert. Then, to my astonishment and dismay, the Dean addressed me formally, explaining that because several parents had written formal complaints, I was to be suspended from duty while an internal inquiry was carried out. My initial reaction was to complain bitterly. I said I would go straight to the Black Lion, where the choirmen could always be found after their late practice on Tuesdays, and show them the official letter that was handed to me, adding that the Dean might find he had no choir the following Sunday. I was told that while suspended I should have no contact with the boys' parents or the junior clergy, and that my case would be investigated by a County Court Judge, Philip Price, QC, who was also the Chancellor of the diocese of Monmouth. This seemed a very heavy-handed action, and I could not help thinking how differently the matter would have been handled in John Knapp's time as headmaster: he would have come round to show me the parents' letters and we would have sorted everything out amicably without resort to the law. It may be thought that the other Lindsay, Chapter Clerk, might have advised the Dean to take legal action, including the advice of a QC, to get his own back after his defeat over the telephone issue, but my recent enquiries have indicated that this was not so, and that the blame must be attached firmly to Lindsay Gray.

Immediately I began receiving messages of support: Mr Lallemant wrote a letter to Peter Jacobs, and the parents of another boy wrote in similar vein to the Chapter and the Governors. Michael Hoeg actually took Marian and me to dinner at the aforementioned Summer Palace. The men decided not to go on strike, as they felt the cathedral music needed all the support it could get, in the face of certain detractors and reluctant canons. Yet another lawyer came to my aid – the father of another chorister – and the loyal Michael Davidson, for many years in the choir, went to see the Dean. This, as it happened, was the beginning of another long-running saga; but it was not until the 14th December that Judge Price found time to come to the deanery to explain what form my investigation would take. It was clear that he had only a few letters to deal with, and intended to interview separately each of the six parents who had written them. For my part, I offered to set out concisely the circumstances surrounding each of the six boys, and to collect opinions from various people who I knew would write in my favour. At this point the judge lifted the ban on making contact with anybody – and not before time, I thought. Several of the choirmen called to show me the letters they were submitting, and I even had a surprise conversation with David Gwesyn Smith, the young baritone who had turned professional, calling from Amsterdam. Very soon I had recruited twenty character witnesses who agreed to write to the judge and put the whole business in perspective, having known me for many years.

All this activity left no time to send any Christmas cards at all, but the school matron invited me to join the choristers at the pantomime in the New Theatre, whereupon Laura and I returned from putting up decorations in Rozel Cottage in time to see *Dick Whittington* and be made to feel welcome; the boys had all signed a card expressing their good wishes. Dean John Rogers had predicted that my 'investigation' would all be done and dusted by now, but he could not have been more wrong: the judge would be very thorough, but worked on it only on Saturdays, and had as yet barely begun.

1996

As in 1994, my New Year began with a flurry of activity as a Kleeneze agent, delivering nearly a hundred catalogues, generating orders worth £157. Throughout January, being still suspended from duty, I concentrated on a recruitment drive, putting up advertisements in newsagents and sending one to the *South Wales Evening Echo* which resulted in nearly fifty phone calls from interested readers. A few of them came to see me at home, but mostly I visited their houses, conducting thirty interviews throughout Cardiff and neighbouring towns in twenty days, before submitting a second advert which generated another dozen enquiries. The purpose of all this activity was to encourage potential agents with my own enthusiasm and build up a group of, say, half a dozen keen people who would not only profit individually but entitle me (and therefore my uplines as well) to increasingly large bonuses. The snag was that very few of those who were initially interested pursued the business for any length of time.

After a few weeks my best colleague, Diane Lusardi from Bridgend, found a new way of earning money by visiting people's houses: market research. She joined a company with the ungainly name of Specialist Field Resources, and I decided to follow suit. A three-day training course in February set me on my way, with the occasional two-day survey in which I was expected to find about a dozen people to interview within twelve hours. In March I interviewed customers in a post office, was supplied with a large laptop computer – still something of a novelty, at least to me – and in April was sent to Gloucester to interview three dozen customers in a shopping centre. I was now firmly established as a professional interviewer, but still continued my Kleeneze work as well.

Despite my suspension, my cathedral salary was still being paid as if I were on a sabbatical term, and indeed it rose by the customary annual increment, although I had no work to do except for choosing the music to be sung. I ventured to apply for a post in the junior department of the Welsh College of Music and Drama, but was not appointed. As a further venture I embarked on a correspondence course in proof-reading, and wrote to forty-five publishers with a view to acquiring some unpaid work experience, only to find that they were all quite happy with their in-house proof-readers. I began to think that the company providing tuition existed more for its own benefit than mine, and in due course I approached several music publishers, thinking that my specialist knowledge would be in more demand. This resulted in only two assignments from people who already knew of me: Terence Gilmore-James, who asked me to check a set of organ pieces by one of his in-laws, Mansel Thomas; and someone else who sent me a setting of the evening canticles written by Bryan Kelly for the choir of Peterborough Cathedral, which I checked in return for a set of copies. I do not recall whether they sang it first, or whether our own performance in November was the premiere, but no further work of this kind was forthcoming, and I earned not a penny in this way. Juggling finances in one way and another, I considered taking £4000 out of an endowment policy and either converting the loft of Rozel Cottage or buying a stable block in the farmyard which it faced.

I was not the only man to be under suspicion at this time. James Adams, the head verger, being accused, like the bishop earlier in my career, of an activity known as 'cottaging', was fined only £100 but lost his job, soon taking up a similar appointment at Newcastle Cathedral. My old friend Michael Nicholas, who was making so many innovative developments as the first chief executive of the Royal College of Organists, came under criticism from the president, who at the time was the international recitalist Gillian Weir. I was present at a four-hour meeting of the council to discuss the matter in his absence, and was minded to speak up in his defence: we had been close friends since 1962 and it was because of his well-known efficiency that I had chosen him to be best man at my wedding. Most of the thirty-four members present had something to say, and opinions were well varied, but it soon became clear that there was a strength of opinion against him, and I began to wonder if my contribution on the basis of friendship might not carry enough weight to be helpful. I would have reminded members that it was Michael who drew up the plans for the college's revised constitution and had invented the title of chief executive; formerly the college was run by a president chosen by his predecessor, and a secretary and treasurer, none of whom was resident at the college, the office work being led by the Clerk. Although the post had been advertised, no candidate was deemed suitable, and Michael, who had not applied, was actually invited by Dr Philip Ledger to consider the post. His acceptance had meant leaving his very desirable post at Norwich Cathedral and renting a small flat in Bow. Deciding that he might like to have details of what was said, and by whom, I wrote down the salient points and posted them to him. It was resolved by twenty votes to fourteen that his services should be retained, subject to regular appraisals of a kind that were becoming normal practice in business circles.

The official investigation into my own conduct began in January, when Judge Philip Price summoned to his presence the parents who had written letters of complaint. Two more had jumped on the bandwagon, so to speak. One case was hardly worth considering, concerning a young chorister who had been taken away from the school at the age of eleven when his parents were unable to amass the necessary funds to keep him there. It emerged later that solicitors had advised the school governors to collect some evidence from the parents to see if they were justified in withdrawing their boy without notice or fees in lieu of same, in the course of which they alleged that I was partly to blame. Neither I nor anyone else had seen this correspondence. I noticed that the boy and his mother did not share the same surname, and it was also later revealed that there had been an acrimonious divorce causing problems which another parent, assuring the judge that the boy had not been victimised by me, thought needed a very detailed investigation; he was the only boy to have left the choir prematurely since 1983. The other involved Neil Hillman, the boy who had recently kept the dancing girls amused at the Christmas TV show. He was a known trickster, and one morning when I refused his request, minutes before the practice ended, to go to the toilet, he claimed later to have wet his pants, though I never discovered if there was any evidence of this. His mother had asked permission a few months earlier for the boy to have a family holiday in the first two weeks of term because her personal problems and financial situation had made an earlier holiday impossible. She lived alone, no doubt owing to the problems and stress that she claimed to have experienced 'during these past two years and more so the last few months'. Her complaint was enshrined in a single undated letter to the headmaster, which I did not see until the time of the investigation. Like the others, it alleged that my manner towards her son amounted to mental abuse, causing stress, tummy aches and the like, as a result of which she intended to take the boy away from both choir and school in July, several months before his twelfth birthday. I was allowed to listen to the interviews, which took place just around the corner from St Mary's in the office of the diocesan board of finance; Marian came with me on three of these occasions, but Mrs Harris persuaded the judge, against his will, to exclude her from her interview.

Nearly eight weeks had passed between the date of my suspension and the first of these interviews, which was with the estranged parents of Andrew Lewis. It emerged that the father had remarried only fifteen months earlier, following a five-year relationship, and the boy's allegiance was thereby split three ways as far as accommodation was concerned. The honour of becoming a Dean's Scholar was clearly a matter of great importance to Andrew, who was devastated when, despite the manoeuvrings of him and his father, another boy was appointed; he felt like giving up altogether, and it was suggested that his bad behaviour was an attempt to get himself expelled, not only from the choir but also from the school, where he had become unpopular. The judge quoted from seventeen letters written in by the parents of other choristers, and other adults who had witnessed Andrew's behaviour, amounting to a barrage of condemnation against him. Some of their comments about me were also given, commending for instance my 'quiet, lenient manner'. One couple were 'shattered and confused' that I was suspended 'for such childish and petty allegations', saying, 'He's not nasty; he just tells people what to do'. Choristers, it was said, had come to terms with my approach and were missing me. Michael Hoeg's comments in his practices were no less rude than mine, said one father. It was an extremely thorough interview which certainly gave Andrew's parents more than they bargained for, and I still have my five pages of notes to look back on with interest.

The following Saturday saw another long interview, this time with Mrs Hillman. For the guidance of the judge I had typed out a summary of each case as I saw it, for otherwise he would have had no clear picture of what all the fuss was about. With these notes as a starting point, he then had a deluge of fifty letters to read, including about twenty that I had invited specific people to write – present and former lay clerks and choral scholars, the parents (three of whom were lawyers) of choristers past and present, Michael Nicholas as RCO chief executive, Roy Massey as organist of Hereford Cathedral, Clive Westwood for obvious reasons, the cathedral's own succentor, chaplain and librarian, and my assistant Michael Hoeg; several past choristers wrote of their own volition in my support. Mrs Hillman made it clear from the start that she had not wanted her complaint to be taken out of proportion and threaten my position, and admitted that after some initial stress there had been no problem for the last six months. She had only intended to have a private talk to the headmaster, but he, having no jurisdiction over me (as I had reminded him earlier) asked her to put her complaints in writing to the Dean: it was, in her own words, drawn out of her by false pretences. It had been said that I did not treat every boy in the same way, but when asked to comment on this, she said that I only reproved a boy whom I actually saw doing something wrong, since the pressures of time in choir practices did not allow for further enquiry or the checking of allegations. She had hit the nail on the head here, and of course it was my responsibility to ensure that the service music was adequately prepared: there simply wasn't time to act like a school master, who has to combine the responsibilities of policeman, detective and jury while teaching and trying to maintain discipline. She had written only one letter, but still had to spend an hour and three quarters in front of the judge, and again I was taking copious notes which could provide material for a small book. I had spoken to her a number of times about her son, and was pleased to hear her say that she always found it perfectly easy to speak to me: 'You just have to make the effort to speak to a professional man and be determined' she said, adding that she and the other three plaintiffs should be shown what all the other parents had written about me, to put their complaints into perspective.

Lastly it was my turn to be interviewed, and with Marian beside me I took full advantage of the opportunity to explain at length my own problems in dealing not so much with parents, as with the authorities, including my constant struggle to improve my salary and pension prospects; altogether the interview lasted almost four hours. As if this were not enough, we were called before the judge again a fortnight later. For an investigation which the Dean had hoped would be completed before Christmas, it seemed intolerable that I had now been under suspension for nearly twelve weeks. I contacted Hambros, the legal advisers, who told me that suspension normally applied only in the case of a serious offence, that such a long period was unreasonable, and that I should tell my employers accordingly. I communicated this view to the Dean, telling him that the very fact of suspension was regarded by many as a stigma, and that it had already damaged my professional and personal reputation. Meanwhile he received a letter from the president of the Cathedral Organists' Association confirming my fears, and expressing the opinion that the time taken to resolve the matter was, after three months, becoming excessive. Dean Rogers told me that he expected to receive Philip Price's report within a week and that all procedures would be completed by the 10th March at the latest. When that date arrived, with still no sign of a report, I wrote to the Incorporated Society of Musicians, whose administrator wondered if relatively minor grievances were being used by the Dean and others (I thought of Lindsay Gray) for some wider purpose. He explained that the proper procedure was that any such grievances should have been put to me at a disciplinary meeting (which I suppose they were, though it was not designated as such) at which I should have been given an opportunity to respond (which I had, unbidden). If the employer felt that it was appropriate to give an oral or written warning, I must be given an opportunity to show improvement, and also had a right to appeal. Of course, there had been no warning, for what should I be warned about?

Easter came and went, and a fortnight later David Lambert anticipated that the judge's report, now running to twelve chapters, would be finished in time for a meeting of the Chapter on the 27th April (a full seven weeks later than the date anticipated by the

Dean). When at long last they had made their deliberations, I was invited to call at the deanery on the 6th May at midday. It was the May Bank Holiday, so I refused; they had kept me off duty for six months, and I was not going to spend a public holiday finding out if their actions were justified; besides, I wanted to know in advance what form the meeting would take. The meeting was duly postponed to the following day, by which time I had been in touch with an old friend of Marian's, then precentor of Hereford, who told me that the Dean of Hereford considered twenty-four hours' notice for a meeting, after so many months of waiting, quite wrong, and that I should take with me a professional colleague and not agree to anything without time for consideration. When I did meet Dean Rogers and David Lambert, who, it may be remembered, was still the deputy Chapter Clerk, I was told that the report had been accepted and that I was free to return to work. I chose a Tuesday Evensong, and was proud enough to process in with the choir instead of playing them in. Mrs Hillman, evidently full of remorse that her one letter should have contributed to her son's choir being without its choirmaster for half a year, was there to greet me after the service – a nice gesture, I thought. My reinstatement was not, however, as simple as that, owing to the conditions set out in the official letter of reinstatement handed to me by the Dean.

The Chapter, it said, had decided that I should be issued with a first written warning – but any indication of what I was being warned not to do was sketchy, to say the least. There was general criticism, wrote the Dean, of my approach to managing the choir, focusing almost exclusively on the collective good of the choir as a whole to the detriment, on occasion, of choristers as individuals who needed praise and encouragement as well as criticism and demands. Where had I heard this before? Well, my treatment of individual children had been the source of criticism received from the Associated Board, and I can only conclude that there was some justification for these complaints – I had evidently become, in the last few years, a rather unpleasant character, in the eyes of some people at least. The Dean's letter went on:

> Given the types of criticism made, the first written warning will be regarded as permanent, and you should be aware that in the event of further complaints against you which are found to be justified, you risk further disciplinary action being taken against you. Whether such further disciplinary action took the form of a final written warning or dismissal, would depend upon all the circumstances of the case at the time.

Tony Jeremy had already advised me not to co-operate until it was made clear to all concerned that I had been completely exonerated. He thought I had a possible case to sue for breach of contract, for denying me opportunities to enhance my reputation, with consequential loss of earnings. The ISM's legal helpline advised that it would be in order to ask for a reassuring statement to be issued to parents, failing which I could consider resigning and claiming constructive dismissal at an industrial tribunal – admittedly not an ideal solution, even if I were to succeed. One of my many legal advisers threw doubt on the legitimacy of the procedure in the first place, when I was not told in advance that the meeting at the deanery was a disciplinary one, nor was I invited to take a colleague with me. Moreover, a decision was reached without my being given a proper opportunity to defend myself, although of course I did put my point of view at great length to the judge, and the permanency of the so-called warning was considered unfair. I replied to the letter of reinstatement, requesting notification to parents that at least I now had the full support of the Dean and Chapter, and also that I should receive a full copy of the judgement to enable to me to decide whether to appeal against the written warning. I was also unhappy with a proposed press release, for what right had the general public to know about an internal inquiry? In particular I asked that the proposed denial of any sexual accusations should be withdrawn, being entirely unnecessary in the circumstances. The news that I had been invited to return to my post was sent to all the participants in the investigation along with the following paragraph:

> The Dean and Chapter are pleased that the lengthy investigation has now been concluded, and is currently considering implementing various recommendations contained within the report. The Dean and Chapter do not believe it is necessary or appropriate to comment in detail on the allegations which were investigated, or the view of the investigator on the various issues which were looked into, or the basis on which Dr Smith returns to work, which will be on 14 May. The Dean and Chapter are confident that all parties can now put this matter behind them and focus on the future.

On second thoughts, and on the advice of Gerard Elias, I had decided to return to work after only one week, for the well-being of the choir, provided I was allowed to see the report and decide what further action to take. At first it was decreed that I should read it in the cold mediaeval Chapter House, but the Dean offered me instead the relative comfort of his sitting room. I was allowed to make notes about the report, but not to copy any part of it *verbatim*. Moreover, because of its confidential nature David Lambert's young female assistant was given the unenviable task of remaining in the room while I made my notes – unenviable, because I was determined to make the most of the opportunity, and took three hours and thirty-five minutes to complete my task, but I did not think to notice whether she was crossing her legs.

The 'Report re allegations of emotional ill-treatment of some choristers' made very interesting reading, and even my notes on it filled fourteen pages. It began by mentioning the receipt of more than fifty letters and interviews with a dozen people, in the attempt to examine other sources of stress, including relationships between cathedral and school and me. In the course of reading 350 pages of documentation the judge had clearly taken a much broader view than that put forward by the parents of just four individuals, and this worked very much in my favour, with widespread criticism of the lack of communication which I had lamented for so many years. True, each of the four cases was dealt with in detail, exposing some of my own shortcomings, but there was heavy criticism of the two main protagonists, Mrs Harris and Dr Lewis. Of Mrs Harris the judge said there was *plain and compelling judgement against her by parents and staff; her complaints, shared with other parents, undermined the collective effort; she criticised Michael Hoeg, and declared of the Succentor that he had 'no right to be a man of God'.* New choirmen had to be warned not to correct her son, for fear of confrontation. Summing up her case, he wrote *I find nothing in the complaints made in respect of this boy which could possibly justify the description of emotional ill-treatment.* This was good stuff indeed, and I went on to read his verdict on Dr Lewis, who had claimed months before that my behaviour constituted gross professional misconduct and was probably unlawful. While conceding that the combination of complaints merited investigation, the judge wrote *I reject entirely any suggestion that the facts reveal emotional abuse within the Children Act 1989*, and added that Andrew's music scholarship awarded for entry to King's College, Taunton *reflects well not only on him, but on the training he has received, and suggests that he has retained a significant level of self-esteem and confidence.* Not one witness had denied that my choice of Dean's Scholars was proper and professional, and the judge entirely rejected the assertion made by the Lewises' psychiatric friend Michael Lewis, that as an alternative to an internal inquiry the local authority could exercise powers under Section 47. *As a judge nominated by the Lord Chancellor to conduct care cases*, he resoundingly concluded, *I have no hesitation in saying that the material available to me, let alone that available to Michael Lewis, simply does not begin to approach the necessary degree of gravity. I find no breach of duty under the Children Act 1989.*

Various witnesses had deplored my suspension and were critical of both the Dean and the Headmaster, but the judge evidently thought that the investigation was justified as there was medical evidence of stress, and a danger that the school (not to mention the choir) might lose four boys – but in fact two of them had already left. My position was made secure by his definitive statement that *it cannot be emphasised too strongly that nowhere in the mass of material... has there been the slightest suggestion that Dr Smith physically ill-treated any boy at any time, nor indeed that any physical contact had taken place whatever – no chastisement, throwing things or anything at all of that kind – and no suggestion whatever of any sexually inappropriate word or deed. He deals with the choristers collectively and the Song Room door is always open.* He paid tribute to Roy Massey's 'valuable description of the task of a choirmaster today in the face of a child-centred educational philosophy' and wrote that many experienced witnesses admitted that the huge commitment and skill required to cope with an exceptionally large repertory could involve 'much trial and a good many tears'. Although I was said to be on occasion less than diplomatic and not always sympathetic, the parents obviously valued my achievements and ability, and understood that strict discipline, hard work and commitment were required, while regretting that not enough praise and encouragement were given, and deploring the lack of communication and structure relating to choir matters. Every parent who wrote in agreed on the need for a high level of discipline and supported, in some cases strongly, my methods, but they also mentioned poor communication between them and me and the cathedral generally.

All the ten men in the choir had written to the judge, none of whom having witnessed any psychological abuse. I was considered sometimes unsympathetic and insensitive to the younger and less able boys, but my approach was similar to that of other choirmasters in their experience, dealing with a very heavy workload. One who thought I was 'not an approachable man' attributed this not only to my personality but to a lack of spare time caused by poor remuneration, while another rated me as 'a serious musician trying to do his level best with somewhat limited support'. Former choir members, looking back, had said that I rewarded good behaviour and singing, and dealt with bad behaviour firmly but not harshly. I was remembered fondly, wrote the judge, and was regarded as somewhat eccentric, with a curious sense of humour, if occasionally a bit thoughtless: the boys' characters had benefited from the 'priceless gift' of being in the cathedral choir.

Turning to wider issues, Judge Price identified my task as the need to balance collective unity with the welfare of individuals, and conceded that with such poor communication I was never told about choristers' work commitments or other musical activities. I was in effect working in isolation, and the Dean and Chapter, who had a responsibility for the boys' welfare, discharged it almost entirely through me. He noted that I was never invited to cathedral staff meetings as a matter of course, nor was I now, since John Knapp resigned, invited to lunches, concerts and social functions at the school. This situation should be remedied immediately. Because of the atmosphere more recently generated by the few, Marian and I no longer had parties at home for choir parents. The judge registered that the various disputes and difficulties I had described to him, relating to pay, pension arrangements, lack of heating, repair and proper maintenance of my house, culminating in the long-running telephone bill dispute, had marred several relationships that would have been valuable both to me and the cathedral. He realised that I had become disillusioned and dispirited because of my isolation within the communities of both cathedral and parish, and could understand why I should feel that a long period of suspension was poor recompense for my work over so many years. The judge acknowledged that I had to spend a great deal of time to trying to earn more money away from the cathedral and in fields unrelated to music, observing how sad it was that it needed an Inquiry to demonstrate that there were many who had respect and affection for me and admired my achievements.

A valuable feature of this lengthy report was the list of suggestions, directly aimed at the authorities, for ways of improving communications all round. The judge was dismayed at the mass of evidence about the place of the choir in the life of the cathedral, being seriously under-valued and having poor relations with the parish for many years. The professed aim of the worship of God was replaced by a dispiriting picture of personal conflicts and dissension. All suggestions I might make involving expenditure by the parish were likely to be refused 'because of their source rather than their merits', though he conceded that I should not bemoan the lack of accommodation for lay clerks when the parish could not balance the books. While it was thought that the choir did not maximise its potential for raising money for the cathedral, thereby reducing the burden on the parish, equally the cathedral failed to exploit the choir as one of its few potentially income-producing assets. It was very sad that the congregations failed to recognise our achievements, especially the recent recordings which had been well reviewed in national publications. Attention was drawn to the lack of support from Dean Davies over a period of sixteen years and many problems from that era, very sadly yet to be solved.

Summing up as if in court, His Honour Judge Philip Price QC enumerated twenty-seven points. They included the opinion that I had not behaved in an unprofessional way, that Rhys Harris had neither been demoted nor cruelly treated but that his mother was a persistent complainer, and that there had been no breach of the Children Act. I emerged as a good musician, if sometimes difficult to deal with, maintaining high standards of performance and the reputation of the choir, but ultimately disillusioned. For the future, there were recommendations for a properly constituted music committee, better communication all round, the official recognition by the Chapter and the school of the choir association, and the need to fit me into the life of the school. The concluding paragraphs expressed the judge's dismay at the history of personal conflict and unresolved problems, and the declaration that issues must be addressed and problems resolved as a matter of priority.

All this was most gratifying, of course, but I was still concerned about two aspects of the outcome: first, that there were no plans to disseminate any of the above to any of the many people who had contributed to it; and second, that I had been given what was described as a permanent written warning, which in effect made possible further action against me or even dismissal in the event of further justifiable complaints. The fragility of my position was borne home forcefully just a few weeks later, when we had to sing a Eucharist at 7.30pm on a Tuesday in honour of St Barnabas, following a full practice which began at 6pm. There is more music in a Eucharist than at Evensong, and we also had to rehearse a tricky setting by Walton for the following Sunday, so we were unusually pressed for time, the choir ascending to the vestry with just five minutes to robe for the service. This clearly upset Dr John Baldwin, the cathedral's non-stipendiary chaplain, who was on duty as the celebrant, though the boys and men dressed quickly and the service began on time (always a strict requirement). Unfortunately Dr Baldwin, who much of the time was pleasant enough, and had written to the judge in my support, had what is known as a short fuse. At the end of the Eucharist, when I came down from the organ loft after my closing voluntary, he was in the nave, still in his vestments but with a face like thunder, and began to berate me furiously over the supposed lateness of the choir. I was appalled that a man in holy orders should behave in such a way immediately after a sacred service, and I stormed out of the building in a rare burst of anger. As it happened, we had invited him, with the Westwoods, to dinner the following Friday, and I told Marian that his savage outburst rendered such a social meeting untenable. Evidently he shared my thoughts, for the next day brought a letter from him addressed to Marian. Far from apologising, he stated that he had reported the incident in writing to the Dean and the Chapter Clerk, and for good measure to the archdeacon as well, saying 'It appeared last night that absolutely no regard was being paid by the music department to the needs of the cathedral's liturgy – and that is wholly unacceptable and hence the course of action that we have followed. With that explanation, I am hopeful that you will understand why I feel it unbefitting to be with you on Friday night'. It says a lot for Clive that he, obviously sympathetic to our plight, invited Marian and me (though not Hilary, who seemed to think more highly of John than I did) to a five-course meal at the Celtic Manor Hotel, one of the most expensive restaurants in the area. It occurred to me that this episode was just the sort of incident that, if taken seriously, especially by the already antagonistic Chapter Clerk, could lead to my dismissal. I resolved never to take communion from John Baldwin in future, and to this day I have never forgiven him for such appalling behaviour, bringing the priesthood into disrepute in such a way. I am sure he would not realise that this episode was a contributory factor, if only a minor one, to my gradual disillusionment with the church and ultimately all things religious.

In view of these considerations and a number of other factors I decided to appeal against the Chapter's decision, as was my stated right, to the Bishop of Llandaff, the Right Reverend Roy Davies, stating my grievances and requesting some amelioration of my position. True to form, the bishop did not even speak to me, let alone invite me to see him, but six weeks later he passed the matter on to yet another QC, this time the chancellor of the diocese of St David's, His Honour Judge Michael Evans. 'When I hear from him', wrote the Bishop on 19 July, 'I shall get in touch with you and the Dean'.

Mrs Harris, true to her word, had removed Rhys from the choir altogether. It was customary at the end of the summer term for the Dean to conduct a short (and, it must be said, perfunctory) valediction to those boys who were leaving, and present them with a framed photograph of the cathedral. Lindsay Gray took exception to my failure to include Rhys in this way, writing to me that whatever dealings I may have had with his parents, the boy himself was conscientious and well-behaved, worthy to receive a leaving present in front of his parents and friends. No boy should be 'punished', he declared, on account of past actions of his parents. Incidentally, in response to Mrs Harris's false allegation in 1995 that Rhys had been demoted, I had immediately stopped publishing a list showing the boys' order of precedence, and abolished the long-established distinction between junior and senior choristers, with their attendant RSCM medallions on blue and red ribbons, so that no such complaint could ever be made again. I stated in reply to Mr Gray's letter that a joint decision had been made by the choir association, the Dean and me, to uphold the established policy that presentations were made only to boys who fulfilled their contract and left at the age of thirteen (Rhys being only ten). If we had taken other factors into consideration, such as parental behaviour, then Andrew Lewis would have been excluded, which was not the case. As it happened, another eight boys aged thirteen left on the same day, and Mr Gray evidently feared that my 'vindictive' approach would lead to more losses, but I reminded him that eight new boys had been recruited since the day I was suspended (surely a tribute to my reputation, I thought), leaving only one vacancy in the coming academic year, and furthermore that I was answerable only to the Dean, and not to him, in terms of choir management.

It was also during July that the Cathedral Music Working Party held a meeting at Southwark Cathedral, chaired by the Dean of Truro, and attended by three other English deans and four cathedral organists, where it was suggested that consideration be given at a future meeting to the Children Act, in relation to the recent difficulties at Llandaff, where I, although subsequently exonerated, had been suspended for so long for allegations of verbal abuse. The minutes record that concern was expressed over the way in which the situation had been handled by my Dean and Chapter and by the headmaster, and mention was made of the importance of establishing in each cathedral a child abuse officer. In due course this is what happened generally, except for the adoption of the title child protection officer. I wonder why no one thought of appointing choirmaster protection officers – but we shall come to that aspect later.

It will be recalled that after suffering a cold house for twenty-two years, and no longer waging a campaign about the telephone bill, I decided to request that central heating be installed at St Mary's. Of his own initiative, Adrian had carried out a survey on the 19th February into the temperature in various parts of the house, embodying his research in a typed report for me to send in to David Lambert, who was deputising at that time for Lindsay Ford the Chapter Clerk. A representative from British Gas had said that the most comfortable and most commonly adopted temperature throughout a household was 21° celsius. Only the sitting room, where our own gas fire had been on all day, and a very old electric radiant heater for four hours, satisfied this norm by 9pm. The temperature in the hall, the music room, and the first floor landing, which had only night storage heaters, had reached only 15 or 16, and the same figure was reached in my first-floor study only by using a separate plug-in radiator operating non-stop on maximum heat for seven days. Some of the heat from the storage heaters went up the stairs to the second floor landing, which registered 11 degrees, but unless a wall heater were switched on, the bathroom registered, as did Adrian's tiny room on the second floor, only 9, leaving the remaining three bedrooms as cold as 8 or 9 degrees above freezing. Admittedly it was the middle of winter, but our family had endured such low temperatures for nearly twenty-two years. I had been loath to mention central heating until now, because I was more concerned with improving my earnings, but I felt the time had come to put in a request for the kind of heating which for decades had become standard. I enquired whether a landlord was legally bound to provide proper heating, only to be told that open fireplaces were considered sufficient in this regard. True enough, all the living rooms and three of the bedrooms had flues, but in most cases the fireplaces had been blocked up before we arrived, and even if they hadn't, who in the last decade of the twentieth century could have been expected to carry hods of coal up two or three flights of stairs every day from the cellar? I complained to David that our fuel bills for the winter quarter had amounted to £660, so that by the time I had paid my share of 75% only £200 was left of my net salary for February. Surely the installation of central heating, I argued, as in all the other staff houses, would not only save us a lot of money, but in the long term would benefit the cathedral in the same way by drastically reducing its own contribution. I pointed out that my initial request, made more than two years earlier, had been totally ignored, even though I knew that three cost quotations had been submitted to the relevant committee. At least five months passed before Lindsay Ford, now back in office, wrote with the news that the finance committee were prepared to meet the 'reasonable cost' of installing central heating at St Mary's, but strictly on condition that any incidental costs such as redecoration should be met by me. I was incensed that the Chapter should expect me to pay anything in connection with the work: over the years I had spent thousands of pounds maintaining and improving the interior of the house, and I had no intention of covering the cost of any damage done by their workmen. 'Unless the finance committee will reconsider this bizarre proposal', I wrote, 'it looks as if we shall have to suffer a few more cold winters using separate appliances which are so much more expensive to run, to our mutual disadvantage'.

I had also taken the opportunity, during the temporary absence from duty of the Chapter Clerk himself, to raise once again with his deputy the vexed question of my pension. The figures indicated that if I were to retire the following year at 60, as I was still contemplating, after twenty-three years' service, my service pension would be only £1,000. My calculations based on my original expectations showed that the figure should be £4700, but that in order to achieve this a sum of about £40,000 would have to paid into the fund. 'There are many that think', I wrote, 'that something drastic must be done by way of compensation for the enormity of the negative impact made on me and my family by three months' suspension at the peak of My career'. The letter I had received about the proposed installation of central heating also stated tersely that the Chapter had refused to increase their contribution to the pension fund begun for me in 1991. Earlier in the year, Mr Ford's secretary had gone so far as to deny the existence of the quite separate endowment policy dating from my appointment seventeen years earlier, but the policy evidently came to light later, giving Ford an opportunity to tell me that no increase would be made to the contributions paid into it.

Having written to me about these two crucial issues, the Chapter Clerk wrote a second letter to me at the Dean's behest (or so he said) asking why I had been 'absent from duty' on three Saturdays in May and June without the Dean's permission. 'I have to put on record', he wrote, 'that taking leave without the permission of the Dean is a serious matter and I would remind you that you should seek his permission at all times'. I was able to deny this allegation, because I had missed only one whole Saturday when attending a conference in Birmingham; and on another I took an hour-long practice and then represented the cathedral at a dinner in Hereford given for the organists of several other cathedrals from as far afield as Southwell Minster. On this occasion, and on the third occasion, I had engaged not just one deputy but two, to ensure the smooth running of the services. For good measure I pointed out that on another Saturday I had turned down the opportunity to join the choristers on a day's outing to Alton Towers, deciding that my duty was to provide for Evensong and arranging extra practice time for the men, who sang the service with me while both my assistants travelled with the boys. What a pity my accusers never bothered to check the facts! I told him that it had never been the practice to ask permission for absence except for examining tours of more than two days' duration, and was mildly surprised when he wrote a single sentence in reply to say that the Dean did require that his approval be sought for any absence from duty.

My reinstatement as organist and master of the choristers was by and large, I thought, a vindication of my character and method of working, but there was more trouble to come very soon afterwards from a different quarter. The constant difficulties I had to face in my professional life evidently affected my judgement and manner as an examiner for the Associated Board, as described by two letters forwarded to me from discontented teachers. Only a month after resuming my cathedral duties I found myself examining string players in the Grand Pavilion at Porthcawl. Once again it was said that the younger candidates taking their first exams came out of the room feeling they had not been encouraged, and were upset by my apparent indifference; I was thought to be 'over critical and totally discouraging', one teacher saying that in future she would make a point of requesting another examiner who could respond more sympathetically to eager young pupils. It seemed to me that the more serious complaints from both teachers related to my actual marking standards; full and well-considered details were given of the exceptionally low marks I had awarded for much of the playing, much lower than they had ever seen in their many years' experience as peripatetic teachers working in the county of Mid Glamorgan. My own experience as an examiner dated back to 1969, but now I was the one whose confidence was being eroded. These candidates must have been exceptionally poor to have received such low marks, but I could not deny the reasonable comparisons made by seasoned teachers claiming that they had never complained before. I was admittedly reassured to some extent on the question of my manner, when the Board decided to address this aspect by inviting all examiners to one of a series of autumn seminars, to be headed by a chartered psychologist employed by a London firm of child consultants.

It is interesting to note that between the two adjacent examining days in question, I attended an evening meeting at Llandaff as a first step towards implementing the judge's recommendations: the absence of the Dean was covered by David Lambert and his legal assistant, and the choir association was represented by its new chairman, Jonathan Furness. Three main proposals were put forward:

    (a)   A choir handbook should be prepared, aiming to inform all interested parties about all aspects of choir life, e.g. pastoral care, uniform, timetables...

    (b)   A choir committee should meet on a monthly basis, to talk about things as they arise.

    (c)   A music committee would be formed to deal with recordings, (one a year was suggested), tours, concerts, purchase of music etc.

Six weeks after being asked, the new judge accepted the brief to hear my appeal, and after a further seven weeks I had still heard nothing from him. I reminded the Bishop that I wanted to report any further developments to the Cathedral Organists' Association at our November conference in Ely, but this was not to be, for a few days earlier I at last received an invitation to make my official appeal on 14 December, *nineteen weeks* after I had requested it. The Chapter was represented by a solicitor from the Cardiff firm Eversheds. I put forward my grievances about what I considered an inadequate outcome, and then waited yet another eleven weeks for the judge's conclusions, which carry the saga well into 1997 and will be summarised in the next chapter.

The first two of the innovative staff meetings took place in September and October, covering some useful ground, and a music committee was duly formed, its first meeting being on 8 October. I thought it significant that headmaster Lindsay Gray was not present for this, but the teacher in charge of boarding agreed to take the minutes, and the clergy were well represented by the Dean, a canon (the father of two of my former choristers), both priest-vicars, Jonathan Furness and the bass lay clerk Robert Adams. The purpose of this new committee was to promote the cathedral choir and to facilitate communications between all parties involved. We discussed ways of promoting the choir, such as singing a service every term at a parish in the diocese. In fact I had already approached the bishop about this, and had thanked him for advertising our offer to his clergy, but not one invitation was ever received from any parish. We also considered asking the BBC to offer us a broadcast Evensong, though I explained that we had been passed over because of the former Dean's reluctance to countenance ways of extending the service to last an hour. There was agreement that the Wales Tourist Board should be made aware of our choral services by the issue of a suitable leaflet, and to my suggestion that the cathedral shop should be open not just in the daytime, when we had few visitors, but more usefully during evening concerts, promoting our CD recordings and enabling members of the audience to purchase them. The most welcome news was that St Michael's Theological College had made available the use of a study bedroom and two flats for lay clerks (though on further enquiry I found the rent would have been prohibitive). I was able to announce that the magazine *The Organ* wanted to publish an article on the choir, that the BBC had offered small parts to four choristers for a broadcast of Britten's cantata *Saint Nicolas*, and that Welsh National Opera had asked for a chorister to perform in an Italian opera on tour during 1997-98.

Something unusual happened in September. In the last chapter I wrote that I had taken my grandfather's half-hunter watch and Albert chain to a gold bullion shop to be sold, along with other items. I received some money for the sale of one of the watches, only to learn that a thief had hurled a brick through the shop window and stolen the gold chain, so I received £206 including the insurance claim.

Because of the great exodus of boys in July, we were down to fewer than ten choristers, but they were all doing well and at some services we managed surprisingly well with only half a dozen really efficient boys plus a few probationers, even on Christmas Eve. I was not discouraged, because of the substantial number of boys in training, for I had accepted no fewer than nine new boys since my return to duty, out of an unusually large field of sixteen applicants – not a bad tribute to my recovering reputation, I thought. In October I invited one Andrew Mitchell, a bookseller, to buy some of my unwanted items: he did not buy any, but it transpired that he was related to

Marian's family, and his family tree revealed that he was Adrian's third cousin! On the same day I went to Waterstone's bookshop in Cardiff and introduced myself to Charmian Cawood, the elder daughter of my girlfriend in the sixties, Mary Wilcock, whose ex-husband was a violin teacher then living in Penarth. Earlier in the year, at an organists' conference in Wells, I had come across Andrew Nethsingha, Organist of Truro Cathedral, who divulged to me and Anthony Crossland (his former colleague in Wells) that he had just ended a relationship with Mary's younger daughter Harriet. What a string of coincidences!

The week before Christmas included not only our customary party at home, with Laura's help, for fourteen boys, but also a tea party for some of the men and a dinner-dance organised by the choir association in the great hall of Caerphilly Castle, an imaginative concept though not well organised, with a decidedly basic meal and dancing to a rock band, which seemed inappropriate. The choir sang carols before dinner, and afterwards Mrs Hillman, whose unfortunate letter a year ago had inadvertently caused so much trouble, made a point of asking me to dance, a gesture which was much appreciated. We somehow managed to do justice to the service of nine lessons and carols with only six choristers, two probationers, and two former Dean's Scholars who had volunteered to come back and help out, as they did again on Christmas Day with a complement of seven men for Schubert's *Mass in G.*

1997

Before resuming my main work as a Kleeneze agent and market research interviewer, I gave a rare organ recital, having been invited by an old friend from my Salisbury days, then Vicar of Stoke Gabriel in Devon, to share an evening with a tenor from Exeter Cathedral, alternating arias with organ pieces. The resulting programme was much too long, but Marian and I enjoyed pleasant company, staying overnight. I was persuaded to play for the Sunday morning Communion service, which was followed by a traditional lunch party in the Vicarage.

For one of the first market research projects of the year I was required to travel to London and stay there overnight. Apparently there was a shortage of interviewers for a survey about the 'quality' national newspapers, and some people had been sent from Scotland for the same reason. On collecting the survey material, I was surprised to find that I then had to travel right across London and interview in Redbridge Lane, Ilford, only half a mile from my old home. I encountered very few 'broadsheet' readers, and only one of them was prepared to answer questions, so I decided to make a detour and call at my old address, but unluckily no one was in. At a meeting of interviewers I was interested to find that many of my colleagues were working for more than one agency and could pick and choose their preferred type of survey. I signed up with a local company called Beaufort Research, and for the next couple of years interspersed their offers with those from Specialist Field Resources, including some telephone work from an office in Cardiff; this was paid by the hour, irrespective of the number of successful calls made, but the rejections far outweighed the results and I soon lost interest.

In May I joined another organisation called Research Services Limited and stayed with them for the next six years, by which time they were known as IpsosRSL. Yet another venture began in February, when I became an interviewer for a high-class Introduction Agency (commonly known as dating) called Sirius. Men and women seeking partners would pay hundreds of pounds to join, and it was my job to visit new applicants in their homes, make conversation for an hour and write a paragraph describing them for the benefit of potential partners. In some cases I had to travel considerable distances – one day as far as Langton Matravers in Dorset. These assignments came rather spasmodically and were not well paid, but I met some interesting people who were often in high-powered jobs which allowed little time for normal socialising; their holiday activities often seemed to feature exotic things like swimming with dolphins in the Indian Ocean and touring Antarctica on a sledge drawn by huskies. One of them admitted to being in charge of a section of the Prince's Trust, with regular access to Prince Charles. In another case, when calling on a gentleman in Cardiff, I was surprised to spot on his mantelpiece a photo of one of my choristers, and found that the boy was this man's son, but he declined my offer to leave and send along another interviewer, so I carried on asking questions. It was not part of my remit to discover how many of my respondents found the love of their life, but at one point I did telephone a handful of people to ask how they had fared, and I recall one young lady librarian telling me that the nicest person she had met was actually me!

At the end of February I was at last vouchsafed a twenty-page report by Judge Michael Evans QC, Chancellor of the Diocese of St David's, on my appeal against certain aspects of the outcome of the long investigation of 1995-96. My objections were basically two-fold. First, that I was given a 'first written warning' which should be 'regarded as permanent'. I pointed out that at the time of my sudden suspension from duty on 21 November 1995, there had been no previous disciplinary meeting nor any kind of verbal warning whatsoever. Second, I felt that the many people who had taken the trouble to write in support of me, not to mention my colleagues at other cathedrals who knew of my plight, had a right to know rather more about the outcome of the inquiry. The fact that the complaints made about me by three of the four parents had been dismissed, was not mentioned in the public statement issued by the Chapter upon my reinstatement, nor were the many criticisms directed by the judge to the Dean and Chapter. Chief among these was that they had taken no action to implement the provisions of the Children Act 1989 which came into force in 1991.

In his reply to my appeal, the judge specifically mentioned the John Baldwin incident recounted in my last chapter, writing

> Dr Smith quoted the anecdote about the action of a junior member of the Cathedral staff in support of his feelings. In my judgement that story raises an issue of management, but not the management of the choir.

Concerning my suspension, Judge Evans wrote, 'I cannot say that suspension was a course outside the band of reasonableness' and, in effect, that its length could not have been predicted. Little had they known that the inquiry would generate some 350 pages of documentation, very largely in my favour! The appeal judge acknowledged that steps had already been taken to implement Judge Price's recommendations regarding administration and management, but added

> The question for me is whether these measures should have been in the reasonable contemplation of anyone who was concerned with the good of the choir and the welfare of the young *before the complaints were made*. I feel bound to say that most of what Judge Price recommended should have been obvious to anyone concerned with the welfare of young children. The Dean and Chapter should not consider themselves entirely blameless in this matter. Dr Smith told me that one of the problems had been that there was no one on the staff of the Cathedral, from the erstwhile Dean downwards, who had had any real interest in the music produced by the Choir for the services.

Conceding my own faults in handling certain situations, the judge offered some justification in that

> Part of the explanation lies in his own formative years when he learnt his undoubted skills. They were in a different age and climate. Things which could be said and done twenty or thirty years ago are not acceptable now. The limits of behaviour which many took for granted in earlier days, are now not acceptable.

He also recognised that Neil Hillman, the only boy whose case had been upheld, had gladly accepted an offer to sing tenor in the choir when his voice broke, even though he might easily have taken the chance to opt out, while still retaining his chorister scholarship. He concluded that giving me a 'first written warning' was 'within the ordinary range of reasonable behaviour for an employer in the circumstances', and that

> although the Dean and Chapter and the Cathedral School ought to have considered the wellbeing of the junior members of the Choir more closely, the onus of constructing proper relations between the Choir and the School, and the Choir and the Chapter, must primarily be upon the Master of the Choristers... it is natural that the Chapter and School should turn to the Master for guidance and not the other way round.

Judge Evans gave little attention to my complaint that the public statement issued by the Chapter did not admit that the complaints of three of the parents out of four had been discounted: he merely stated that I had approved the statement, subject to the omission of its assurance that there had been no allegations of sexual or physical abuse. He rightly assumed that such a negative reference might, in my view, have encouraged a 'no smoke without fire' response. It was for the cathedral authorities to decide, he concluded, what use might be made of the material provided, adding the suggestion that an open discussion of the management problems would be of considerable help.

Thus came to an end the second of the two major confrontations of my time at Llandaff. I think this one was less controversial than the saga of the telephone bill, and that I was appreciated all the more by its outcome. It did little to assuage the opposition of the Chapter Clerk, to whom I appealed a few months later for funds to advertise for new lay clerks. He still insisted that to advertise in national music magazines was unnecessary in such a place as Cardiff, which he imagined was well able to supply its own suitable singers. I tried again to explain the true situation, by writing:

> I can only say that such advertising has over the years produced a cross section of applicants, both from the locality and further afield. Recent lay clerks and choral scholars have come from Petersfield, Wrexham, Lichfield, Manchester and Edinburgh. Singers in the Cardiff area may well like to join us, but unless vacancies are advertised in the journals that are recognised in this field, how will they know that they exist? The problem recently has been not the appointment as such, as the ability to keep men for more than a year, when they realise that other cathedrals offer better pay and conditions. Three out of our last four leavers moved on to Hereford, Wells and Chichester, where they are paid between twice and four times as much and also occupy accommodation provided by the Cathedral.

A few chapters back I predicted that the name of Russell Warren would appear again. He was a popular teacher of several subjects at the cathedral school, including divinity and science, and also played the flute. In the latter capacity he ran a wind ensemble for the children and taught the flute to our younger daughter Laura, who achieved a Distinction in the Grade 4 examination before deciding to specialise in violin and piano. Russell was one of those who soon took a dislike to headmaster Lindsay Gray and his supposed machinations. In 1996 he had sent a very long list of complaints to the school governors on being issued with a redundancy notice, followed by a further long letter six weeks later, but to no avail. He had already attempted suicide by taking an overdose. I mention this because he also considered that underhand measures were being implemented regarding my own situation. Shortly after my reinstatement in 1996 he was told by one of the teaching staff that Mrs Dinsmore, the lady in charge of choristers' boarding, had complained to Lindsay and to Michael Hoeg that the boys' behaviour had markedly declined, and that he suspected that a 'second strike' against me was planned. In view of his own mental state, one cannot be sure that this was so, but in March 1997 he again wrote to me, expressing concern that the headmaster had appointed a new head of science who had shown interest in cathedral matters and was already being described as a 'liaison' between school and cathedral. Russell's informant was said to be strongly of the opinion that this move was another attempt by Mr Gray to push me 'further towards the side-lines'. As it turned out, this man, Huan Kenworthy, joined the music committee in the autumn and seemed to be quite benevolent towards me, but the views passed on by Russell were symptomatic of the impression of 'divide and rule' tactics attributed to Lindsay Gray at that time. The music committee met in February and May, covering a wide-ranging agenda, and I felt it was useful to share my concerns and plans with a group of interested people for a change, but it did not go unnoticed that the headmaster did not attend; I presume he preferred to quiz the minutes secretary afterwards (who was none other than the aforementioned Mrs Dinsmore).

During the first week of March I drove to Wells in time for lunch at the cathedral school, on the occasion of the annual 7-a-side football match for cathedral choristers from the south west. I missed the football, driving on to Taunton instead, where I picked up Laura from King's College and took her back to Wells in time for Evensong sung by the teams from twelve cathedrals – impressive in sight and sound. Returning to Taunton, we witnessed a school show involving jazz, song and sketch. After an overnight stay, I was back in Llandaff next day to spend six hours playing the organ accompaniment to a Welsh choir's rendition of Stainer's *Crucifixion* which was being filmed by a local television company. Unbelievably the next day included another six hours' filming, after which I went to London for the RCO council meeting, when the President Martin Neary explained the outcome of the inquiry into the efficiency of Michael Nicholas as chief executive, which was that, one way or another, he would relinquish the post in return for a year's salary. The secretary, my old university friend David Pettitt, told me privately that Michael's allegedly offhand manner had upset his office staff at the RCO's headquarters at St Andrew's, Holborn, and that there was no doubt he had to go. Martin Neary's predecessor as president, Gillian Weir, had criticised Michael's organisational ability, which I also found hard to understand. It was odd that two men who had been at Oxford with me, and who had each shared European holidays with me, should be on opposing sides in this unfortunate affair. I felt particularly sorry for Michael, who had left a prestigious post at Norwich Cathedral, with a house in the close, to take this newly-created position, living in a one-bedroomed flat in east London

Meanwhile my own work as a musician was also coming under scrutiny again, following the complaints that had been made about me as an examiner to the Associated Board of the Royal Schools of Music. It was among all this activity in the Spring term that I also met the board's newly-appointed chief examiner, Clara Taylor, in London to discuss my shortcomings. It was arranged that I should examine in London on three consecutive days under the scrutiny and supervision of three moderators, who would assess my marking standards and general demeanour. I had a fairly intense session with one Sally Wainwright in Windsor, followed by a more relaxed day with Nigel Carver in Wimbledon. That evening, Rachel took me to see *Oliver* at the London Palladium, perhaps to keep my spirits up before my final session with Clara Taylor. Reassuringly, Clara pronounced me fully fit again as an examiner, ready for further work in the ensuing summer, and indeed my work in mid Wales, Dorset, Somerset, Sussex and Kent over a period of four weeks in June and July apparently attracted not a single complaint. What happened later in the year was to alter the picture considerably, however.

Easter Day featured another unseemly and bad-tempered outburst by Father John Baldwin. The Book of Common Prayer in use in Wales provided two alternative endings for the Eucharist, and it fell to Dr Baldwin to use one of them – either the Blessing or the Dismissal ('Let us proceed in peace', the congregation responding 'In the name of the Lord, Amen') – to be followed at once by organ music while the so-called sacred ministers and the choir processed out of the cathedral. Easter Day, the most important Sunday in the Church's year, merited loud, triumphant music, which I duly provided after Fr Baldwin had pronounced the blessing (though I would have expected the bishop, if present, to do this). Unfortunately he tried to add the dismissal, which of course was completely drowned out by my joyful chords. Predictably this mishap brought out the worst in him, and there was another confrontation when I finished my voluntary. He refused to admit that the two endings were alternatives, even when I said that in all my twenty-three years as organist (or ever since the book was published) no one had ever flouted the rubric. He was furious, but I realised afterwards that he, with his work at the church's administrative offices in Cardiff, had prior knowledge of the forthcoming edition of the prayer book which apparently did allow the two texts to be juxtaposed, and had simply confused the issue. His attitude only reinforced my reluctance to pay homage henceforth to the Church as represented by such a priest.

The summer term was remarkable for a number of musical ventures with the Cathedral choir, carefully interwoven among my busy examining schedule. The HTV company made a half hour documentary programme about us, filming part of an Evensong and including interviews with the headmaster and me. The latter was filmed in my study at St Mary's, just a month before my sixtieth birthday and as luck would have it, on the very same day that a plumber was installing the central heating for which we had waited twenty-four years, so that the TV crew had to step over gaps in the floorboards to get into the study.

The Choir Association gave me a surprise party in the parish hall during the week of my birthday, attended by many of the choristers' parents, and the chairman Peter Jacobs made a nice speech. The actual birthday (7th June) was also the thirtieth anniversary of my engagement to Marian, exactly half a lifetime before, and we celebrated the occasion together, not with a party, but by crossing the Channel by ferry from Ramsgate to Ostend and spending a long weekend in Bruges, including a meal with my cousin Colin and his wife, who happened to be passing through at the time. I received a considerable amount of money at this time, from a lump sum in respect of a pension accrued from my school-teaching days, plus a couple of maturing endowment insurance policies; as I liked to say, my ship had come home at last.

The day before setting off to examine in Llandrindod Wells, I directed, for the ninth and last time, a live broadcast of Choral Evensong for the BBC, and from mid Wales three days later I drove to a village church in Oxfordshire for the wedding of an aristocratic bride named Larissa Heber-Percy and her bridegroom Justin Hardy. The full resources of the cathedral music, plus two trumpeters, had been engaged to provide a sumptuous programme of music which included no fewer than eighteen items: it was all organised by a man called Orlando Murrin, and a coach was laid on to take us all to the church. At the reception afterwards I was introduced to a lady who turned out to be the mother of the Marquess of Blandford, but I never discovered the identities of any of the other guests, no doubt of similar distinction. The modest little church was bedecked with flowers in every conceivable cranny, and we received over a thousand pounds in fees for our much-appreciated efforts.

Around that time, more appreciation was shown in national reviews of our most recent recording with Priory Records, albeit made in 1995, in the series of *Magnificat and Nunc Dimittis* settings.* The house journal of the RSCM, *Church Music Quarterly,* said

> It is a pity that we do not hear more from the fine choir of Llandaff Cathedral. Their two new recordings are quite splendid, and director Michael Smith draws some beautiful sounds from his singers, who are alert and sensitive.

An article in *Church Times* had Roderic Dunnett writing in similar terms:

> I have a personal *penchant* for Llandaff. There is a warmth and commitment to their (paradoxically) English-cathedral open sound. They find amplitude in Christopher Knott and Gerald Near (with Howellsy tenor solo), guts in Purcell, shapeliness in Farrant, style and spirit in two fine trebles' services from Stanley Vann and Richard Shephard.

while Dr Brian Hick, proprietor of *The Organ* magazine, wrote:

> One of the real benefits of this series is that it not only records cathedral choirs who might not otherwise be heard, but allows us to hear settings which might otherwise go unnoticed. This new recording is no exception. The singing, particularly the boys' voices, is exceptionally refined and sweet, with no sense of the hard edges or strain which have marred other choirs I have been listening to recently.
>
> There are familiar works by Purcell and Howells, but I particularly enjoyed Christopher Knott's *Third Service* which, though stylistically close to Howells, has a voice of its own and a gentle, captivating reflectiveness. Richard Shephard's *Llandaff Service* was written in 1986 to commemorate the memory of Paul Dallimore, a Llandaff chorister... It is a moving and very sensitive setting and sung with utter conviction. The CD also includes settings by Gerald Near, Hugh Blair, Alan Gray and Stanley Vann.

Brian Hick had already shown interest in Llandaff by coming to inspect the cathedral organ, a visit resulting in a long and far from complimentary article in his magazine, with a cover photograph of the pulpitum arch bearing the 'positive' organ in its notorious concrete

---

* See details in Appendix 1

cylinder. I had the opportunity to distribute copies of this issue to each of the canons, when at one of their quarterly meetings I was allowed to spend half an hour putting the case for a new instrument, but although I had also presented a stack of copies to the cathedral shop, the Dean had already banned them from sale. The article said virtually everything that needed to be said on the subject, but with my own retirement in mind I had little to hope for in this respect.

Sunday 22nd June was the centenary of Queen Victoria's Diamond Jubilee service on the steps of St Paul's Cathedral, when the choirs and bands had been under the direction of my ancestor Sir George Martin. I duly marked the occasion by performing at the end of Evensong the *Te Deum* which he had composed for the occasion (and which I had introduced to Llandaff in 1977 in honour of Queen Elizabeth II's Silver Jubilee), The anthem that afternoon was by Sir John Stainer, Martin's teacher and predecessor. On the same evening I provided organ accompaniment for several hymns in a four-hour recording session for *Songs of Praise* on BBC television.

Ten years earlier I had been greatly impressed by the international congress of the Incorporated Association of Organists, held in Cambridge. History was about to repeat itself in more ways than one. I did not attend such gatherings annually, but this year it was the unusual place which attracted me, namely the city of Haarlem in the Netherlands, known above all for the spectacular baroque organ which dominates the west end of the church of St Bavo. The week was planned on a much more modest scale than the Cambridge event, but included a master class and a recital at St Bavo's and some very interesting visits to organs in various kinds of buildings. There was a coach trip to the Royal Concertgebouw Hall in Amsterdam, followed by a boat trip on the canals, and I was very soon keeping company with one of the few other single travellers, a lady in her early forties called Gail, who was a school music teacher and church organist from Glasgow. On another coach trip to Utrecht I decided to sit with someone else, for fear of monopolising her unduly, but while dining that evening back in Haarlem we enjoyed each other's company so much that she agreed to boycott the scheduled harpsichord recital and spend the rest of the evening with me at a local cinema where Rowan Atkinson's comic film *Bean* was being shown. In retrospect I somewhat regretted that we both missed a coach trip the following day to hear the famous 18th century Schnitke organ at the St Laurentskerke in Alkmaar.

It was on the last day of August that I turned on the television for the morning news bulletin and heard the shocking and almost unbelievable announcement that Diana, Princess of Wales, had died following a car crash in Paris. There is no doubt that this item of national news had the greatest impact on me of any in my lifetime (for I was only two when Britain declared war on Germany in 1939, and when the attack on the World Trade Centre took place in New York in 2001 we were campervanning in Canada without access to the breaking news). One of the oddest musical assignments came my way six days later, when Diana's funeral service in Westminster Abbey was relayed live to a giant television screen in Llandaff Cathedral by way of a national homage for the people of Wales. I telephoned Martin Neary, the Abbey organist at the time, for details of the hymns, as my brief was to synchronise my playing with the singing at the funeral itself – which I did with the aid of headphones. People had begun laying flowers around the large stone preaching cross between our house and the Cathedral, and as the days went by an enormous pile of floral tributes was created, supplemented by more flowers on the grass around the nearby ruins of the old belfry. History, of course, records similar tributes throughout Britain, marking the unprecedented outpouring of emotion to which this sad accident gave vent.

Cathedral matters were now dealt with not by correspondence with the Chapter Clerk (there had been none since May) but by the occasional meetings as proposed by Judge Price. The so-called staff meetings in the headmaster's study were not always particularly good-natured, for Michael Hoeg felt obliged to support his boss, while my own backing was provided by Matthew Tomlinson, a very supportive priest vicar. There were sometimes differences of opinion about the promotion of choristers, especially when I appointed two Dean's Scholars who were a form below another boy who was a prefect, and slight friction concerning Lindsay Gray's girls' choir, which after Whitsun was allowed to sing the occasional Evensong on a Wednesday – a precedent which was the thin end of the wedge, as it turned out. Lindsay managed to talk the Dean into allowing the girls to sing Monday Evensongs regularly from September. This had been the prerogative of the choristers for many years; I do not remember being consulted, and the break with tradition took the boys' parents by surprise. The headmaster tried to make a case for easing the burden on the choristers, but it wasn't as simple as that. The repertoire available for boys' voices is quite considerable, but reducing the opportunities to sing it, from twice a week to only once a week, meant that the interval between trebles-only settings and anthems was doubled. Not only did this reduce their ability to remember the music, but it also meant halving their repertoire of psalms, with similar consequences. The only advantage to the boys was that more time could be spent at their Monday morning practices on music for the rest of the week; for it must be borne in mind that except in the case of new music which was unknown to everyone, rehearsals for the seven weekly services were not begun until the Monday of each week. It was made clear that the girls' choir was not part of the Foundation, and indeed until July 1999 they were designated a 'visiting choir' on the printed monthly service schemes, but meanwhile Lindsay subtly began calling them 'the Cathedral School Girl Choristers' and by the end of the decade this title no longer appeared as a mere footnote but was incorporated into the relevant dates.

The April staff meeting was held at the deanery, and with only Matthew and the Dean present, I was able to introduce a list of twenty items for discussion. I announced that I had compiled, for the guidance of probationers' parents, a note of the skills required of a boy in order to be promoted. We were down to only eleven choristers, and with four more due to leave in July we really needed to increase the number to fourteen for September. (In fact one boy was taken away in April because his parents were dissatisfied with the school). I felt it necessary to point out that promotion was not an automatic procedure, for, unlike a school choir which could accept children of a fairly wide range of ability, a cathedral choir had to consist entirely of efficient boys and men, with no passengers. I explained that the majority of boys in the past had learned enough in their first year to be reasonably independent in musical terms, and that in the past ten years five out of every six probationers had made the grade and become successful choristers. It may interest the reader to know what my criteria for promotion were:

1. The ability to sing any psalm in our normal repertory with the correct pointing and without stumbling over any words. Each phrase, ending with a colon, full stop or asterisk, must be sung with one breath.
2. The ability to sing at sight a melodic line consisting of upward and downward intervals of a second and a third, and repeated notes, with a simple rhythm comprising minims, crotchets, quavers, dotted minims and dotted crotchets, and (at least by the second attempt) to fit in the words correctly.
3. A pleasant vocal tone which will blend with the other treble voices.
4. A reasonably confident and enthusiastic manner.

I went on to say that the exodus of no fewer than ten choristers in 1996, twice the normal average, had created an unprecedented situation, especially as none of the present probationers had served for as long as three terms. At subsequent meetings I stirred up some controversy by suggesting that if the school proved unable to attract suitably able boys for the choir (perhaps because of the demise of boarding) it might forfeit the right to occupy premises owned by the cathedral, which historically were provided at a 'peppercorn' rent in return for the provision of choristers. Dean Rogers felt bound to reassure the headmaster that, should the choir discontinue, the cathedral would not evict the school! I privately noted that the average number of candidates attending voice trials in any one year had plummeted from seventeen before Lindsay Gray's appointment to only nine since he arrived, with only four internal applicants in the current year.

For comparison, I asked Dr Edward Higginbottom, Organist of New College, Oxford, how he dealt with his probationers. He described their timetable, and in sight-reading he expected an ability to recognise most of the intervals in the chromatic octave, and to be able to sing not only seconds and thirds but also rising fourths and sixths, so I reckoned that my criteria were not excessive in that respect. Luckily I was able to select four promising new boys by September, but by November only one boy had served as a chorister for more than a year and a half, so it was a close call. It seems that all cathedral organists experience this kind of thing at least once in their tenure of office, but somehow our choirs continue to survive and flourish.

No one attended the music committee meeting scheduled for July – probably because word got round that I would be away examining – but in September Lindsay duly introduced Huan Kenworthy, as predicted by Russell Warren, and a useful range of topics was discussed, notably ways of advertising for and attracting boys and men to the choir. The participants were representative of the school, the boys' parents, the lay clerks, the junior clergy and the Chapter, and my only regret was that such meetings had never been held during the twenty-four years since my appointment. The committee was limited by being only advisory, but a useful little booklet was produced to explain to choristers' parents the routine workings of the school and cathedral and the functions of the various people with whom the boys would come into contact, and we did manage to secure an engagement to sing a Festal Evensong at a parish church in the diocese, to celebrate the centenary of St Theodore in the industrial coastal town of Port Talbot.

A week's examining in Banbury allowed me to meet Laura, now in her first term reading Music at Oxford, to dine with friends in Chipping Norton, and at High Table in Christ Church, and see Laura playing the violin at a concert in Merton College Chapel. It was after our great Advent Procession service that I drove to Bristol for the evening flight to Glasgow to spend a few days with Gail. The elaborate service music had gone exceptionally well, with only ten choristers and eight men, and as the plane rose into the night sky and I sipped my gin and tonic, I felt very lucky and much at ease with the world. I was then considerably taken back to find that Gail was not at the airport to meet me: it turned out that she was offended that I had not contacted her often enough since I had made my arrangements. There was worse to follow, for my hotel was not far from her flat, and in consequence a long way from the examination venue, and next morning I had to wait half an hour for a taxi, arriving late; this did not augur well for my declining reputation as an examiner. Each evening I met Gail for meals, and one of these was followed by concert by the Royal Scottish National Orchestra playing the only performance I have heard of Mahler's Seventh Symphony. Her propensity for avoiding being seen with me was in evidence when I bumped into an old college friend in the foyer: she quickly disappeared, and also declined to accompany me to Edinburgh when I went to inspect (for future reference) the new organ at St Giles's Cathedral. After my last day's examining she saw me off at the airport, and we never met again.

December brought the usual plethora of carol services by various schools and organisations. I had the right to receive a fee for most of them, even if they provided another organist, and this time I collected £850 for not playing at ten services. The next day the *South Wales Evening Echo* published a very nice article about my approach to the festive season, along with a large photograph of me at the organ.

Rachel came home for Christmas, having been employed for some months as an editor of classical CD recordings for the well-known company Chandos, based in Colchester. A banquet at Caerphilly Castle was arranged by the Choir Association in collaboration with the Friends of the Cathedral School, thus allowing parents of other boys to hear what the choristers could do. The full choir sang ten carol settings before the meal and I danced with several of the boys' young mothers afterwards. The family missed the Christmas Eve service of nine lessons and carols by setting out the previous day for Byford, so I was alone at St Mary's when I awoke on Christmas Day and directed Stanford's Communion Service in G at the morning Eucharist, but the whole family was at the cottage when I arrived for a late lunch with them.

1998

February brought an unexpected and wholly unwelcome blow in the form of a letter from the director of examinations at the Associated Board. In the summer of 1997 I had examined 370 candidates without receiving a single complaint. It was a different story with my Glasgow visit, however. My late start on the first morning was not mentioned, but at least three formal complaints had been received, and they were sufficiently serious to result in several re-sits and the issue of free-entry vouchers for some candidates and letters of reassurance and apology to others. I was alleged to have been 'frosty in the extreme', to have made unnecessary, derogatory and unprofessional remarks to candidates, and even to have 'directed rude and abrupt orders' to an accompanist. It was said that I had made no attempt to put candidates at their ease but had in one case made a little girl feel 'uncomfortable and stupid'. It was not only in Glasgow that I fell so far short of the Board's expectations, for several more serious complaints, making an overall total of eight in twelve days' examining, had come from the teachers of candidates I had examined in Banbury in November. One correspondent wrote: 'All this child, and many others, got was a dry and scaring experience, the remarks from which read like a car instruction manual'. My attitude to candidates from Bloxham School was reported as 'supercilious and condescending'. These indictments could hardly have been more damning, and they left me dumbfounded. I was deeply disappointed to read Philip Mundey's conclusion, enshrined in terms that were typically kind and understanding, but nonetheless devastating:

> These complaints emanate from diverse sources and I realise how upsetting they are to read, but this feedback, married to previous concerns about the all-important question of personal approach to examining, has left us with no option, unfortunately, but to withdraw your name from the panel of examiners. Your work for the Board over the years has been much appreciated, and we are very sorry that we can see no way of continuing it. However, please do allow us to wish you every success in all your other professional activities.

This was a sad irony, as Philip admitted at the start of his letter, for he had just received my request for more examining overseas. Indeed, such had been my performance in the summer exams that Richard Morris himself, as chief executive, had asked me at an autumn seminar in Bristol if I would like to be offered an international tour again.   I considered each of the complaints in turn, and wrote a detailed letter in an attempt to refute some of the allegations and justify others. For example, a correspondent from Northamptonshire asked about my written reports 'What about a tiny bit of praise; where's the reference to the music?' Fortunately we examiners kept carbon copies of our reports, for just such an eventuality, and I was able to send in copies of all those I had written at the Banbury centre. *Every one* of them referred in detail to the music played and included words of praise and encouragement, nearly always placed at the beginning of each remark, as required by the Board. Even a total as low as 90 out of 150 elicited positive comments like 'the notes were right', 'this worked rather better', 'most of the notes were found'. Philip Mundey did not deny my claims, and accepted that my mark forms were by and large very acceptable, but there was no denying the impression that so many had of my failure to 'handle that fragile relationship in the examination room'. I had pointed out my unblemished record in the summer, and had given an assurance that this would be restored henceforth, but Philip explained

> It is because we cannot now be confident that you will consistently apply the improved manner of which you speak, and that your manner has previously been called into question, which has led us to take the decision not to offer you further work, and I am afraid that we can see no grounds for reversing that decision. Again, let me say that we are genuinely sorry that things have not worked out, despite the efforts we have all made to achieve a satisfactory outcome.

After twenty-nine years as an examiner I had fully anticipated many more years' work, for there was no longer a stated retirement age, and I knew several other examiners who were years older than myself. Having spent months in the Far East, southern Africa and New Zealand between 1979 and 1990, I was looking forward to further assignments in some of the ninety or more countries in the Board's worldwide net. My only consolation was to be accepted as a member of the panel of Theory markers. This entailed marking 500 or more papers a term from all over the world 'in the comfort of my own home', and without having to meet a single candidate in the flesh. The work was well paid, and at least it entitled me to attend the grand annual meeting and luncheon at the London Hilton.

Eight boys attended the January voice trial, from which Lindsay Gray was excluded by the Dean on the grounds that although he had a right to test their academic potential, an assessment of their musical ability was a matter for my own judgement.. In addition to the setting up of regular meetings as a result of the 1996 inquiry, it had become the custom, in accordance with the 1989 Children Act and the 1993 Home Office code of practice entitled *Safe from Harm,* that my choir practices with the choristers should be attended by another responsible adult, as much for my protection as theirs. Not until nearly a year and a half after my reinstatement did the Welsh bishops set out their interpretation of the law in a document styled *The Care and Protection of Children*, and it was only in in October 1998 that the cathedral issued its own child protection policy. The Llandaff diocesan authorities were even tardier, and by the time their own code of practice was published (*ten years* after the 1989 Act was passed) I had already handed in my notice.

The headmaster made a further attempt to give the impression that his choir girls were on a par with the cathedral choristers by advertising a voice trial for new recruits a week after the customary January Trial for new boys, and in the same advert in the *South Wales Evening Echo* under a school heading. Cathedrals which had inaugurated girls' choirs, had done so at the instigation of their Chapters after much discussion and preparation, not least in matters of finance. In all my years at Llandaff, no one had ever suggested to me that we needed a girls' choir – even choristers' parents who had daughters – and there was still a body of support for the idea that the centuries-old tradition of all-male choirs should be rigorously protected. An article in *The Times* drew attention to a report issued by the Friends of Cathedral Music, saying

> Boys are increasingly unwilling to join choirs where girls are admitted because they do not want to be seen doing 'girlish things'... Boys who are prepared to dress up in white surplices and triple ruffs if they sing with men, begin to think twice if girls appear alongside them – yet it has become politically unacceptable to have all-male choirs: "It's all right to destroy centuries of tradition for the sake of political correctness".

Those cathedrals that have instituted girls, beginning with Salisbury in 1991, have in fact kept them separate from the boys, although more often than not they do sing with the men. One of the problems is seen as the sheer cost of financing, robing, and in some cases housing, two separate choirs, which can run into thousands of

375

pounds. Lindsay's advert, rather craftily in my opinion, stated that successful boys would 'gain 66% of school fees per annum' while 'awards up to £1000 per annum' would be made to successful girls. A dozen boys were auditioned, of whom half were already cathedral school pupils, and I accepted three of them.

At my early morning practices before school, the Dean took responsibility for the required supervision duties, taking turns with the two priest vicars. On arrival in the song room on the last Friday of January, however, I was surprised to find an unknown lady sitting in the corner. She turned out to be a Mrs Lovell, wife of the school's deputy head. She remained there for the whole of the practice, having expressed surprise that no one had told me that she was coming, and afterwards explained that the governors had requested that my practices should be observed by a representative of the school. When I phoned to speak to the headmaster, his secretary said that he was too busy to speak to me. Evidently Mrs Lovell was unaware that the cathedral staff had long ago assumed this responsibility. I had been taking choir practices for forty years, and although I would have acceded to any reasonable request to watch any one of them, I objected strongly to being inspected at someone else's request and without my permission. I was determined to put Lindsay Gray firmly in his place, and started by telephoning the precentor, and the *Custos*. For good measure I also consulted the legal department of the Incorporated Society of Musicians and wrote a formal complaint to the Dean, who, as one of the governors, knew nothing of such a decision; many years later he divulged that when the board of governors actually did try to interfere, he threatened to resign his membership. The following morning, a Saturday, Mrs Lovell again appeared, and was immediately evicted from the premises by Matthew Tomlinson, the priest vicar on duty, who summoned the Dean for support. I immediately wrote to the clerk of the school council, at the request of the precentor, to establish whether the decision to send an employee of the school to be present at each of my boys' practices on cathedral premises was made by a full meeting of the council, and if so, when. If not, I added, on whose authority was the edict made? Next morning I telephoned another governor whom I knew slightly, who also denied knowledge of the headmaster's plot. I received no reply from the clerk, but I did hear that the Dean called a meeting soon afterwards with the precentor and two of the governors to discuss 'difficulties' with the headmaster – who then cancelled the staff meeting scheduled for the following morning. At a party held in the School for choristers' parents I met the newly-appointed matron, whose very popular predecessor had been sacked.

If my own work was to come under scrutiny, supposedly in the interests of the boys (though I suspected a different agenda), I was careful to preempt any possibility of dangers elsewhere. I responded to a request from someone I knew who asked what measures were in place to look after any boy who might become ill during a service, by asking for a rota of parents to be available for such an eventuality, and drew attention to a potentially dangerous leaning tombstone adjacent to the boys' route to the song room. These requests were in recognition of advice from the Cathedral Organists' Association that all safety procedures be put in writing, in case subsequent enquiries were made.

I also investigated the truth of Lindsay Gray's claim that one purpose for having a girls' choir to sing on Mondays was to reduce the burden on the boys, as other cathedrals had done. I found that a survey little more than a year earlier had shown that there were 'official' girls' choirs at sixteen cathedrals, and that in nine of these the introduction of girls had actually increased the number of sung services. In only three cases had the number of boys' services been decreased, and these were cathedrals where they had previously sung eight services a week, as compared with our seven. The headmaster, who had agreed in March to advertise the May voice trial in four appropriate publications as agreed by the music committee, had failed to do so, and I sensed some reluctance to finance such adverts because the school had recently had to advertise for several new teachers. It would seem strange, I told the Dean, if they were unable to spend a few hundred pounds advertising for boys, while providing thousands of pounds worth of scholarships for girl choristers. I noted also that I had not been sent any report forms for the choristers, as agreed; failing to write their reports could again lay me open to censure, I thought. Furthermore, the school calendar, which had not been sent to the Dean and me for checking (as previously agreed) contained many errors concerning the choristers. I wrote to the Dean:

> The concert scheduled for 1 May (two days after term begins!) coincides with Eucharist sung by the Choristers, half of whom are in the school's Chamber Choir; and if parents take any notice of the dates for half term we shall have only half the Choristers on Whit Sunday (the day-choristers returning the following morning) and none at all on All Saints' Day, which falls on a Sunday. Also, the times given in the Music Calendar for weekday morning practices are *all* incorrect, as is the spelling of the names Barnabas and Shephard. Surely such a proliferation of mistakes does no credit to the Cathedral School.

On one occasion I was rebuked by Lindsay for mis-spelling

one word in some information I had provided: it seems that he, a Cambridge graduate, did not know that *till* is a perfectly legitimate alternative to *until*.

The headmaster sometimes put in a plea for the promotion of boys from probationer to chorister status. Sometimes I was able to agree, but not always. A case in point was a boy called Charles, whom I had admitted when he was not yet seven. This was a mistake, for in such rare cases I always found that after a whole year as a probationer, the boy was no more ready to be promoted than a boy of eight who had just joined. Charles seemed to be in a dream half the time, and made little progress. Mr Gray put forward considerations regarding the boy's home circumstances, including the death of his father in a fire, and expressed regret that I was proposing to promote two boys who had joined us more recently. For some reason now forgotten I was contacted by no less a musician than Sir David Lumsden on the boy's behalf, but I stuck to my guns and made the boy wait until he was ready for promotion in September. In the past twenty-two years, I explained, only three boys had become choristers before the age of nine and a quarter; moreover, Charles, still several weeks short of his ninth birthday and the youngest of the probationers, was by no means the keenest or most efficient.

There were developments of a more constructive nature concerning the cathedral organ. Dean Rogers had asked me before my suspension in 1995 for a report on the organ and my recommendations for a replacement, and upon my reinstatement I had given him the names of two experts in the field who might provide an impartial opinion. The magazine article published in the summer of 1997 must have made an impact, for at last it was agreed to appoint an official adviser, and my old friend Dr Roy Massey agreed to look into the possibilities and write a report, for a fee of £2000. Meanwhile I had approached each of the organ builders we both had in mind, asking them where I might play representative examples of organs they had built in the past ten years. I made a plan and set off for London, where I played at St Barnabas's in Dulwich, St Peter's Eaton Square, St Michael's Chester Square and St Martin's-in-the-Fields. After dining with Adrian at my Club near Marble Arch and staying overnight, I visited Bromley Parish Church before getting a train to Nottinghamshire and visiting Southwell Minster before returning home. Next day I was in Bath Abbey, where the organist Peter King gave me a 40-minute recital on a fine organ built by William Hill in the nineteenth century and quite recently rebuilt and added to by the German firm Klais. This was not the only instrument to have been the work of several builders over time, and there were comparatively few opportunities to see a completely new instrument – the most notable being at Dulwich by

Kenneth Tickell and at St Peter's, Eaton Square by the Irish builder Kenneth Jones, who had also rebuilt the fine five-manual organ in Tewkesbury Abbey, where my tour ended with a choral Evensong. I calculated that my travels, with the attendant loss of earnings through time spent organising and carrying out my plan, cost me £350, but as the Chapter were already paying Roy, I received nothing by way of reimbursement. Later I had an opportunity to try out the two organs installed in 1995 by Mander at Chelmsford Cathedral, and was invited by Roy to play several organs in Birmingham, where I realised that he had a strong inclination towards Nicholson's of Malvern. Marian and I went to Malvern one day and were shown round the organ works, after Roy and I had met the managing director and a colleague at the New Inn, St Owen's Cross, where we had pored over their specification and design drawings while waiting for dinner to be served. Five builders were invited to tender, and it is interesting to note that by the time Nicholsons were actually awarded the contract *ten years* later, Andrew Moyse was still in charge, but there was a new organist, a new dean and a new adviser, so slowly do the wheels grind at Llandaff. When our parish organist Morley Lewis heard about the plans we were making, he told the Dean that we should be approaching at least two notable builders from Europe, and managed to get permission to make a unilateral approach to Klais in Berlin and the famous Danish firm of Marcussen, an example of whose work I went specially to Manchester to hear, at the new Bridgewater Hall. Neither Roy nor I was inclined to invite builders from abroad, believing that an organ used mainly to accompany music written for Anglican worship would more fittingly come from the British Isles; and I did not even meet the man from Marcussen who came during the summer vacation. Morley was also responsible for bolstering the organ committee by adding several members of the PCC whose knowledge of organs was negligible, and after a few meetings the whole scheme fizzled out because no one knew what to do next, especially with regard to raising money. The whole exercise had proved to be futile, encouraging me again to consider retirement.

Following my return to work in 1996 there were several instances of organists known to me (in addition to Michael Nicholas) being accused of wrong-doing, and I now realised that my case was insignificant in comparison with both the indictment and the outcome in every case. One of these involved the Secretary of the Glamorgan committee of the RSCM, which I chaired; he was Christopher Norton, a parish church organist in Neath and a successful primary school teacher. He was accused by two small girls of mildly sexual behaviour during lessons, and was banned not only from the school but from living in the vicinity. Adrian and I went along one afternoon to hear part of his trial in Swansea Crown Court, and what we heard sounded sufficiently damning to convict him, but in the course of four weeks it was revealed that the girls had been set up by a gang in their class who had threatened dire consequences if they did not invent the story against their teacher. He was acquitted on all nine charges, but was still subject to parental threats and was unable to resume teaching at that or, as it transpired, any other school. The Organist of St Asaph Cathedral, one Huw Davies, was also falsely accused and required to move away from home pending trial. He was virtually forced to resign, and although found innocent he never returned to cathedral music. Most public of all was the accusation against Martin Neary (he who had overseen the dismissal of Michael Nicholas) who as Organist of Westminster Abbey upset his second Dean by the manner in which he dealt with the finances of choir recordings and tours. His battle with the Abbey authorities made headline news and was the subject of at least one national newspaper's colour supplement. A fund was even set up to help pay for his appeal (I contributed my widow's mite) which was conducted by a judge rejoicing in the name of Lord Jauncey of Tullichettle who upheld the Dean's decision that Martin should go. Whatever I and others may have thought of Martin's limitations as a musician, I had always regarded him as a man of integrity, and wondered if, as one of Her Majesty's Judges, Lord Jauncey was obliged to support the Dean who also enjoyed a royal appointment in a 'royal peculiar'.

On the family front, Rachel bought a lovely little house facing across a large triangular green in the really delightful town of Brightlingsea on the Essex Coast, ten miles from her work in Colchester, and Laura, now well established in Oxford, was elected President of Oriel College Music Society. She was less than happy with her personal tutor, who had replaced the man she had expected to supervise her work, who had taken up a post in America. I phoned one of the lecturers whom I had known as a fellow student to ask what could be done, but it only later when Laura plucked up courage to speak to the Provost of Oriel that some better arrangement was made. In late February we heard Oriel College Chapel Choir sing a service in Brecon Cathedral, and I attended a memorable concert in the grand Victorian chapel of Keble College, Oxford, in which Oriel was one of the eight college choirs participating. Each choir sang one anthem, and at either side of the interval they joined forces to sing the two great anthems *Hear my words, ye people* and *I was glad when they said unto me* by Hubert Parry, a former Oxford Professor of Music, to celebrate the sesquicentenary of his birth. Even more memorable were the two performances of Tallis's 40-part motet *Spem in alium nunquam habui* which began and ended the concert. It was pleasing to note that one of the organists taking part was Benjamin, organ scholar of Lincoln College and the son of my old friend Michael Nicholas, and that the Tallis anthem was conducted by the niece of my more recent friend Gerard Elias. The Oriel Choir included of course Laura, and also Alice Stainer, who was to remain a friend of our family long afterwards. Laura's non-musical activities included rowing in her college's First Ladies' Eight, which involved a very arduous daily routine of training both on and off the river and participation in the Torpids races in March and the Summer Eights in May.

The scope of my own work as a researcher was extended beyond the regular interwiewing of respondents in their own houses to the radio listening survey known as RAJAR, which involved distributing diary booklets to a number of people in strict accordance with a quota to ensure a random cross-section of the public, persuading them to keep a record of every radio station they heard during the week, and then collecting them. Pay depended on the number of books completed and returned, but it worked well and it was one of my favourite surveys for years to come.

My friend Joanne, who at some time after 1993 had actually moved into a flat on the Cathedral Green without my realising it (even though she attended the local RSCM committee meetings at my house), left Llandaff in March to become an assistant verger at York Minster. She maintained her enthusiasm for cathedral music by engaging singers from time to time to form a 'visiting' choir, and in August a choir of thirty-eight singers sang a weekend's services in Llandaff. Another musical enthusiast was James Webb, a young lay clerk who composed some good church music, and was commissioned to write an anthem for the centenary of the Children's Society, commemorated at two services on the same day in October; even I was inspired to write music for a youth brass band participating in the service, to enhance the hymn *Thine be the glory* to Handel's tune *Maccabaeus*, incorporating what I thought was a thrilling upward modulation and a descant for the last verse.

November saw a change in our fortunes, when we collected £75,000 in proceeds from the sale of our flat in The Old House, Cathedral Green, enabling us to pay off the last £18,000 of our mortgage on Rozel Cottage and over £7,000 of credit card debts. In the same week I celebrated by dining at High Table at Christ Church, where I met Peter Jay, whom I had known as an undergraduate and who had become Britain's ambassador to Washington. I found myself sitting next to his guest, John Simpson, widely known as the BBC's chief foreign correspondent and a familiar figure from television reports. For once I felt rather inadequate with my limited knowledge of foreign affairs, but I find it is always possible to make conversation, even if one's experiences of life do not have much in common.

Choristers leaving the cathedral after evensong in the summer term, 1992 followed by Michael Hoeg and watched by singing-man Alastair Clarke and Marian.
Ten years later the probationer in the centre, Oliver Lallemant, became Organ Scholar of Trinity College, Cambridge

Old Barn Cottage, Bowerchalke, Wiltshire,
Bought in June 1999 for our retirement.

1999

It was perhaps fitting that the last year of the millennium should see the departure of several key figures in the life of Llandaff Cathedral. First to retire was the Bishop, Roy Davies, who of course had had no impact on my life at all: even when we had invited him to dinner a few years earlier, he had not reciprocated with even so much as a drink, and when I had appealed to him following the great inquiry he had engaged a judge to do the work without even speaking to me. Our only contact since his enthronement had been when I engaged him to speak the narrator's part in Howard Blake's choral work about the life of St Benedict, entitled *Benedictus*. His final Evensong in January was somewhat marred by the unannounced decision to film the service, without my permission. Fortunately I spotted a camera forty minutes earlier and was able to obtain an assurance from the Dean that the appropriate fees would be paid to the singers and organists: I cited the requirements of the Incorporated Society of Musicians and he had no option. That very day, the treble voice of the last Dean's Scholar to see me out, Sam Furness (Jonathan's eldest son) showed signs of breaking, an event which contributed to unforeseen and sinister consequences, as we shall see. Clive Westwood, who has figured here and there in these memoirs, had attended only one meeting of the music committee before he too bowed out in favour of David Jones, a banker and amateur organist who had given me sound financial advice and was to be instrumental in securing my immediate future. The choir completed three visits to the Three Choirs Cathedrals by singing Evensong at Gloucester in May, after which Robert Adams, a very loyal, genial and efficient lay clerk, retired after thirteen years' service.

In the course of conversation David put forward the view that, having made a £30,000 profit on selling our flat next door, we should put Rozel Cottage on the market. We had not stayed there for several months, but for years I had envisaged retiring there, until various considerations turned our thoughts to a return to Wiltshire, where we had lived in the early years of our marriage and where Marian's mother was about to enter her nineties in a residential home. We spent only one day looking at houses and cottages, and a few days later paid £125,000 for Old Barn Cottage in Bowerchalke, with only two bedrooms but a lovely big garden looking out over fields and hills. Our first plan was to let it to holidaymakers through an agency, as we had done for so many years in Herefordshire, but later, having spent much of our summer holiday there, we decided that the time had come to leave Llandaff at the earliest opportunity, and live in Bowerchalke permanently.

I had become rather disappointed with the general quality of applicants for our dayboy places, and in fact appointed only three out of a dozen applicants at the January voice trials, half of whom were already pupils at the school. In an attempt to improve things I arranged for a lady singing teacher at the school to give newcomers some vocal tuition. There were exceptions, one of whom on this occasion was a boy called James Eager, the son of a professional trombonist, who after my retirement was nominated BBC2 Choirboy of the Year. On succeeding Jonathan Furness as Choir Association chairman in the autumn, Mr Eager volunteered to set up a Saturday morning theory class specifically for choristers. Jonathan had persisted in vain with his attempts to persuade me to let the choir make an annual recording, but I was reluctant to embark on any project unless it involved the men professionally, preferably with national distribution, especially as the cathedral shop was operated in such a lamentable way that the women behind the counter scarcely knew of the existence of any of our CDs – and indeed Priory Records had given up on Llandaff sales for this very reason. I could understand why parents wanted a memento of their boys' contribution to the choir, but our previous recordings had already covered many of my favourite items, and my enthusiasm for extra-mural schemes of this sort had long begun to fade. I continued to seek out suitable lay clerks for the Choir, finding amongst others two men, an alto and a bass, from the choir of the Roman Catholic cathedral: they were good value, but unable to sing for us on Sunday mornings owing to their prior commitments. Another reliable singer of some years' standing, Dr Alastair Clarke, had his own loyalty to a Baptist chapel where he played the organ at their Sunday morning service. This meant that the number of men seen and heard by the majority of listeners (I should say *worshippers*) was always less than the full complement of up to ten men who could be heard on a Tuesday evening, which I thought was a pity. After I left, I believe the alto and bass were banned by the organist of the Metropolitan Cathedral from singing in Llandaff at all: he was also headmaster of the school where they taught, and so presumably had a hold over them. It took me some time to persuade Ken Hall, the administrator responsible for the day-to-day expenditure, that his allowing our singing-men's pay to remain below the recently introduced national minimum wage was unlawful, but when I told him that a tax inspector was on his way, he soon made the necessary adjustments. I also persisted in observing the health and safety requirements that were coming into force at this time.

The woman appointed to oversee these matters had failed to provide either a first aid kit or a telephone in or near the song room. Being under scrutiny myself, it seemed advisable that I should check the responsibilities of others, but the nearest first aid kit remained locked up in the bishop's vestry (for which I had no key) and the telephone, already stolen twice, was never replaced in my time.

I tried to encourage the cathedral shop to promote our recordings, but my persuasive letter was passed around until it reached the PCC, so nothing was done. I did manage to persuade someone to produce some attractive leaflets advertising the cathedral (an idea which had been anathema to the previous Dean), and I may have had some influence on a scheme to floodlight the building (Dean Davies having been responsible for the actual removal of the existing floodlights). At intervals since the summer of 1996 I had put my oar in with a local county councillor in an attempt to improve in various ways the look of the Cathedral Green (designated in 1968 as a conservation area), referring to the poor condition of the ruined mediaeval bishops' palace, the unsatisfactory mixture of lamp posts of different styles, and the question of regaining the floodlighting. At least one of these requests reached the director of planning, while another reached the director of property services via the unusual route of the director of sports and leisure, such are the mysterious workings of local government. I also raised the possibility of road signs to direct Cardiff visitors to the cathedral and its treasures. If Hereford Cathedral could incorporate the *Mappa Mundi* into its road signs, I suggested, what about Llandaff promoting its Epstein statue, its Rossetti triptych, or its John Piper windows? Eventually my persistence began to bear fruit, with the proposed formation of a small working group of councillors, council officers and representatives of the cathedral, but with the proviso 'However, the matters you indicate in your letter have not proved susceptible to quick approaches, even though we all feel them to be issues of importance'. Par for the course, I thought. By April 1999 I was still pursuing my ideas with Councillor Greg Owens and, congratulating him on his apparent success with regard to floodlighting plans, I wrote:

> I am prompted to ask why there are still no proper road signs indicating where the Cathedral actually is. Only recently the Organist of Hereford Cathedral (which, as you know, is well signposted) got lost when visiting the Dean to advise on a new organ. Last week I was driving through Glasgow on the motorway, and saw *three* successive signs directing motorists to the Cathedral, a building of much less historic importance than ours: first a large brown sign, then a blue one, and finally

a white one. Someone here told me recently that he had seen a brown sign leading to a rabbit farm! In Cardiff it is easy to find the leisure centres, but go to Fairwater (a district adjoining Llandaff) and the only 'attraction' nearby is apparently the ski slope!

On the question of floodlighting the cathedral, Councillor Owens acknowledged that it was our mutual correspondence which had prompted him to draw together the necessary groups of people, adding, 'I am grateful to you for providing the impetus for this initiative to be revived'. I discovered that the cost of reinstalling floodlighting would be £29,000 and that contributions would be forthcoming from the Electricity Board, the Council and the Friends of the Cathedral. Not until at least a year after I left did the scheme come to fruition, aided by a £40,000 grant from the Friends of the Cathedral, and now that the feature is up and running, no one would guess that it was instigated by me. My plea for road signs did not bear fruit in my time; I had been told years earlier that such signs to places of worship and tourist attractions had to be financed by the proprietors, and my assertion that such funding might be handsomely repaid by income from the resulting increase in numbers of visitors fell on deaf ears, both then and on this occasion. Once again the Chapter (under a new dean) waited until I was well out of the way before sanctioning the spending of £6,000 (also provided by the Friends) on 'brown' road signs at key locations to advertise the cathedral.

Plans for building a new organ had foundered, partly owing to the choice of parishioners admitted onto the organ committee, one of whose main claim to distinction was his status as secretary of the International Football Association Board. Although no fewer than seven builders had submitted specifications, the project was found dead in the water, not to be revived until after I retired, when the Friends received a letter from their treasurer, Sir Donald Walters in November 2000, mentioning the developments noted above and saying:

> On 1 September our new Organist and Choirmaster, Richard Moorhouse, joined us from St Paul's Cathedral. There are exciting plans for the development of music at Llandaff, and as demonstration of our support the Council of the Friends has increased our donation for music from £8,000 last year to £15,000 this year. With Richard in post, steps will now be taken by the Dean and Chapter to ensure that the Cathedral will have an organ that will serve the needs of the cathedral in a proper manner.

What, I wonder, were these 'exciting plans for the development of music'? Perhaps one day I will learn how it developed. And how was it suddenly possible to almost double the Friends' contribution to the music, when for years it had been restricted and virtually unchanged? Why did they have to wait for a change of regime before recognising the need for a new organ? Had I not first put forward such a proposal twenty-three years earlier, and had the 1997 plans of seven organ builders been forgotten? Perhaps the Friends had never been told about them; was that my fault? I can only assume that I was considered a thorn in the flesh, and that no one was really prepared to adopt any of my ideas.

The boarding of some fifty pupils in a big house known as The Lodge had by now been gradually phased out, leaving only two girls and just one chorister, an eleven year old boy called Thomas French, whose home was part of a castle in Scotland. I have already mentioned my reservations about the quality and quantity of food supplied to the boys, especially at weekends, and I believe several local boys had taken advantage of the opportunity to live at home at least partly for this reason. It evidently seemed to Tom's parents that supervision had become very lax following the sacking of matron Heather Jenkins. They knew that Lindsay Gray had moved from the house provided for him on school premises to a village some miles away, where he became the parish church organist, and were under the wrong impression that Michael Hoeg had moved out permanently into his own flat and that housemistress Joanne Dinsmore was soon to follow suit. Their grievances were embodied in a very long letter to the headmaster in the Easter holidays, giving detailed descriptions of conditions in the boarding house as found when they came to see their son on Good Friday. They were so disturbed by the change in the boy's health and attitude that they consulted their GP, who referred him to a consultant paediatrician, who expressed concern about Tom's depression and weight loss, which the boy attributed to being underfed. Mr French's three-page letter, listing nine specific complaints which made very disturbing reading, was copied to the Dean and a social services inspector who later told me that conditions at the Lodge had changed dramatically since John Knapp's time, with a poor choice of food at tea-time replacing the cooked meal formerly served before Evensong. I forwarded a copy to the School *Custos*, and reminded them both that when similar accusations were made a few years earlier about my own responsibilities, an official inquiry was held, and I expressed the hope that these allegations would be taken equally seriously. In fairness it must be said that they were all firmly rejected by Lindsay Gray, whose lengthy reply, defending his move to Peterston-super-Ely and stressing the 'very high standard' of the catering, concluded by saying:

> The boarding staff are astonished at the tone and substance
> of your letter. Both Joanne and Julie, in particular, felt very
> upset because I know they have spent an enormous amount of
> time with Tom and he has received some wonderful treatment
> over the last few terms, particularly in the last months when
> there have been so few boarders.

Joanne Dinsmore, the housemistress, submitted a very long and detailed account of the boarding conditions as she saw them. It read very convincingly indeed, and she must have felt just as aggrieved as I had a few years earlier. As for Mr Golley, the school *Custos,* he refrained from commenting on these issues and my concerns about the effects of losing the boarding facility, restricting his reply to suggesting that Gloucester and Norwich Cathedrals and New College Oxford had adapted successfully to non-boarding and without depletion of numbers. He overlooked my request that boarding should still be available as a temporary expedient, to allow for parents to go away for the occasional short break or on business, and declined to provide details of the new conditions relating to the care of choristers in the light of their changed status. I pointed out in my reply that our reduced catchment area was matched by the recent decline in musical talent, and that more than half of recent applicants were already pupils at the school. I was skating on rather thin ice here, and the *Custos* had little difficulty in refuting my arguments.

In most ways the first few months of the year progressed quite smoothly. In addition to my regular duties in the cathedral I continued to mark some 500 music theory papers each term from all over the world. These months, as it transpired, represented calm before the storm, for no sooner had I responded to the 'French connection' than big trouble started for me again.

To make sense of this part of my story I need to go back to May 1994, when the candidates at an extra voice trial included an 8-year-old boy called James Sykes Hagen from a village called Tonyrefail. His performance was not promising, but as he became a pupil at the school anyway, I agreed to hear him again nine months later, by which time his home was apparently in Pontyclun. He was one of three boys who joined us as a probationer in September 1995, one of whom, Gwilym Evans, became Dean's Scholar after only two years, made a personal CD and appeared on stage singing a duet with the renowned child star Charlotte Church (formerly a pupil at the school) before winning a scholarship to Eton. By the end of his first term James had had enough, and left. Maybe he was too homesick, as he had predicted at his first audition. The following September he plucked up courage to start again, and by the time he became a full chorister in June 1997 (with special pleading in his favour by Lindsay Gray, backed up by Michael Hoeg) he was already eleven and a half. His voice lasted only eighteen months before breaking, so that when the choir returned for the spring term 1999 there were two boys unable to sing treble, the other being Sam Furness, who had also joined us in September 1995 but had now been a Dean's Scholar for a term. Sam was a very competent musician, and he took no persuading to move to the back row and try singing tenor (in later life he became a choral scholar at St John's, Cambridge). For the sake of fairness and to avoid a charge of favouritism, I reluctantly extended the same privilege to James, who was less experienced and much less competent. By the end of term the lay clerks were complaining, and it was clear that the experiment had failed. This is where I made a mistake. I should have taken the bull by the horns and contacted his parents after Easter to explain why I was retaining the other boy and not him. It was only when he arrived with the other boys at the beginning of the summer term that I told him that with a full complement of tenors we would have to 'pension him off'. When he reappeared on the Sunday morning I sent him away, not surprisingly incurring severe criticism from his mother, who was called, rather confusingly, Dr Meriel Sykes Hagen Newton. She wrote to the Dean in no uncertain terms, typing her letter in big bold print, about the 'dreadful and sarcastic' way I had treated her son, asking whether I was entitled to make unilateral decisions and to 'humiliate a child in front of his peers'. Was I, she asked, a trained teacher who has been taught how to deal with children and adults alike? She considered my manner unchristian, adding that James wanted to become a priest when he grew up. She had the grace to admit that she had never had cause to complain about me before, that James had never said anything bad about me, and that he truly admired and respected me. But she thought it unfair that another boy was continuing to sing tenor, and requested her son's reinstatement with the men, failing which I should be suspended owing to my 'awful unprofessional conduct' pending another investigation and judgement upon me.

After discussing the matter with the Dean I wrote a short conciliatory letter to Mrs Sykes Hagen, apologising and explaining that my decision to let James stay in the choir for a while was out of consideration for his feelings, rather than for the good of the choir as a whole (for had I not been criticised in the past for doing just the opposite?). I told her that the Dean considered this a misjudgement on my part, and had decreed that in order to avoid misunderstandings in the future, a treble would not return to the choir in another capacity unless I were convinced that his musical ability matched that of the men (as was manifestly the case with Sam Furness, though I refrained from saying so). A complicating factor was that James had been looking forward to singing at a special service at the end of May in the presence of the Queen and the Duke of Edinburgh, to mark the opening of the newly-created Welsh Assembly. His mother told the incredulous Dean that James had already written to the Queen, 'telling her all about himself, and the fact that at the end of term he would be the first boy to go from us to Gordonstoun School'. (I wondered how such a quiet, self-effacing boy would fare in that notoriously tough establishment.) A few days before the royal event the Choir Association received a long letter from the boy's father, a former solicitor who signed himself Robert H Newton. I never understood the true status of the parents, but later assumed that he was a the step-father: as I have observed earlier, most of the problems I encountered with boys emanated from unstable home circumstances, and I note also that their address had changed twice since his first attendance at a voice trial. The Dean, following the correct procedure, had referred the parents' complaint to the diocesan child welfare officer, who spent two hours discussing my behaviour with them. Mr Newton, possibly influenced by his apparently more belligerent partner, expressed dissatisfaction with various aspects of chorister life, asking:

1. Why are the parents not told the contents of Music Committee meetings?
2. The singing teacher: was the post advertised? Who appointed her? Does she have specialised training in vocal and choral music? Is she a professionally trained teacher? Was her appointment approved by the Dean and Dr Smith? Is she paid? If so, by whom?
3. Why do parents have no feedback from the Choirmaster? Why silence from the Cathedral Choir?
4. Why are the same boys chosen time after time to sing solos?
5. Is the Cathedral Choir open to inspection? If so, when was the last inspection? What was the outcome of the report?

He went on to complain strongly that Marian was allowed to teach the piano to any chorister, alleging that matters concerning the choir could easily be discussed in a way that was unfair to others who could not afford lessons, or who lived further away. He also complained at not having received the most recent choir photographs, and that no recording had been made during his son's four years in the choir (actually the boy had been a chorister for only four *terms*). As the Choir Association's chairman, Jonathan Furness replied in a well-balanced way to every point made, in a letter four pages long. After due discussion, and to placate the parents, it was decided to let James attend the royal occasion, not as a member of the choir, but dressed in school uniform. He joined in the procession and took his place rather sheepishly in a seat east of the choirstalls, amongst the canons. People watching the service on television probably thought he was the head boy. The service itself was deliberately ecumenical, to reflect the multi-cultured aspects of the Principality, so that the choir's participation was minimal, but the Dean received a grateful letter from Buckingham Palace, signed by Sir Robert Janvrin, the Queen's Private Secretary, thanking the Dean and saying:

> Her Majesty and His Royal Highness thought that the Service captured the nature of the very special day and much appreciated the whole occasion. They have asked if their thanks could be passed on to all those who played a part, however small, behind the scenes to ensure the service ran so smoothly, and in particular to the organist, musicians and choir for the marvellous music which is such a notable part of this service.

Equally gratifying was the receipt of over £2,500 in fees for the organists, lay clerks and choristers, largely on account of the filming of the service for national television. Less welcome was the letter awaiting me on return from the half term holiday from the aforementioned child welfare officer, a parish curate called Sally Davies, referring to James Sykes Hagen. I told her in reply that although neither of James's parents had written anything to me, as was required by the terms of our *Notes for Choristers and their Parents*, I had written them an apologetic and explanatory letter. I added that Mr Newton's letter to Jonathan had been copied to all the boys' parents, and moreover that James's retirement from the choir had been discussed at length by the music committee, chaired by the Dean, before the parents complained, when my ruling was upheld by the Dean on the recommendation of a canon who was the chairman of the child protection board itself. I offered my house for a meeting with Sally Davies, Jonathan Furness and the parish's child protection officer, but evidently this was deemed unnecessary in the light of my letter. Fr Matthew Tomlinson confided in me that Mrs Sykes Hagen had been 'astounded' when James (who had no such ambitions) was not made Dean's Scholar, and had also complained to the headmaster when he was not made a prefect. Moreover, Michael Hoeg would not have him in the school chamber choir at all.

In the summer of 1999, I was engaged with arrangements for the installation of the new bishop of Llandaff, the Right Revd Barry Morgan, then bishop of Bangor. Like his predecessor, he refused to

391

refer to his installation as an enthronement, but I managed to persuade him to include Bruckner's stately anthem *Ecce sacerdos magnus* (having already engaged its three trombonists) which at first he had thought unduly congratulatory. We included Rutter's lovely setting of the blessing *The Lord bless you and keep you,* a psalm by Mathias, and a mixture of Welsh and English hymns. In Parry's anthem *I was glad*, we again incorporated a revised text for the original royal greeting by substituting the words *Vivat episcopus, vivat episcopus Llandavensis.*

We spent the whole of a seven-week summer holiday at our new home in Bowerchalke, and it was on my return to Llandaff in September that I was notified of 'an anonymous referral' to the county council's child protection unit, and the fact that subsequent enquiries under the provisions of the Children Act had been completed. What I did not know was that an astonishing series of three or four meetings had taken place at the social services office, involving at least eight people, to discuss my future. Lindsay Gray attended most if not all of the meetings, putting his oar in by naming certain parents who had at any time expressed misgivings about my leadership. Sally Davies was involved, together with two or three social workers, and I was invited to meet Sally and the unit's manager at their Cardiff office. On arrival, I took the initiative by placing myself at the head of the table to give the impression that I was chairing the meeting. I was told that a few of the parents had expressed dissatisfaction with my dealings with the choristers. Suspecting that Lindsay Gray was behind this, I demanded to know their names, only to find that two of them had left the choir a year earlier and that the rest had been dealt with in the official inquiry of 1996. In one case, the father of a boy who was already nearly twelve when he became a chorister, was incensed when two younger but more experienced (and better) boys were appointed Dean's Scholars. I voiced strong criticism of the way that people had been discussing me for several months behind my back, and threatened to write to my MP to complain about the time that they had wasted. The manager admitted that because they were obliged to follow up every allegation received, my case was by no means unique, and that the resulting departure of staff from the department was a cause for concern. No wonder social workers have a bad name, I thought.

My last meeting as a member of the music committee was chaired, in the absence of the Dean, by the precentor, Canon Malcolm Ellis. Previous holders of this nominal position on the Chapter had had no contact with me, with the exception of Clive Jones many years before. By constitution precentors had no official duties, their normal work being carried out vicariously by the priest vicars (hence the title of these younger priests) but Malcolm Ellis, like Dean Rogers, did take take some interest, even inviting Marian and me to tea (an unheard-of privilege), but as a Chairman he was so vague and bumbling that I thought he must have some mental illness. There was much discussion about many aspects of running the choir, and in the absence (again) of the headmaster, there was scope for the new choir chairman (Mark Eager) and a new lay clerk representative to make their contribution. An extra voice trial in July had attracted four boys and produced my last chorister, an Indian boy called Ranjit Sambi (who, like three of his predecessors, later secured a scholarship to Eton). It became clear that no further progress had been made on the proposal that a choral foundation be set up along with the organ appeal, and in fact the organ committee had not met since at least April and was unlikely to meet until a new Dean had been appointed. I did not mention that I had decided to retire, but complained about some of the working conditions mentioned above, that our 'singing men' (those paid on an *ad hoc* basis) were still receiving less than the national minimum wage, and that the work of the Dean's secretary left much to be desired. This young lady's responsibilities included typing out the *Weekly Notes* to be distributed to members of the congregation on Sundays. Many of the dates and times conflicted with those given in *The Llandaff Monthly* and the single-sheet leaflet was always full of mistakes of all kinds. Some months earlier I had volunteered to check all the proofs, but it was a matter of chance whether my corrections were incorporated into the finished article. The notes issued on my last Sunday, giving details of the Christmas services, included at least thirty mistakes of all kinds.

Before the time of my suspension in 1995, Marian and I had discussed ways and means to retire when I became sixty in 1997. But on my reinstatement in 1996 and the exodus of far more boys than usual, I was quite keen to restore my image and show what more I could do for the cathedral. Early in 1999 we again thought about retirement, and while staying at Old Barn Cottage during the summer we realised that this was our new home. We had at first intended to let it to holidaymakers, as we had for so long with Rozel Cottage, and indeed had already appointed new agents, but on payment of a penalty we withdrew from the contract and directed our thoughts ahead. Suspecting that I had not heard the last of the Sykes-Hagen affair, I approached the Dean (who had already announced his forthcoming retirement in the autumn) saying that although I felt my time had come, I could not afford to retire unless he could arrange a generous financial package to tide me over some way towards my sixty-fifth birthday when I would receive the state pension. I made it clear that if necessary I would be prepared to fight my corner once more against all comers, but that I had become weary of having to defend myself. He had nothing to lose, of course, in supporting me, and asked me how much money I would like! I was reckoning in the region of twenty-five thousand pounds, I told him optimistically – and he said he would look into it. I drafted five sheets of ideas to present to the Chapter in support of my request for early retirement – though in fact my service agreement made no mention of a retiring age, so it was my choice anyway. At the age of 62 I noted with interest that my counterparts at five other cathedrals had recently retired when under 64, including my close friends Richard Seal at Salisbury and Michael Nicholas at Norwich. In the event, I condensed my five sheets into a couple of paragraphs in my letter of resignation, and for posterity I reproduce them here:

Dear Mr Dean,

You will be aware that in recent weeks I have become increasingly disenchanted with the conditions under which I find myself working. The abolition of boarding for choristers has not only restricted the catchment area, formerly nationwide, to the immediate locality, but has subtly changed the ethos of choir management. Recent legislation has affected teacher-pupil relationships for the worse and has made choirmasters far more vulnerable to criticism, inhibiting the 'personality' aspect which is a vital ingredient in creating the individual style that each cathedral organist produces from his choir.

For twenty years I worked amicably and successfully with three headmasters, and enjoyed making music with a long succession of boys and men. I find my relationship with the present Head to be increasingly stressful, and we often adopt conflicting attitudes to what should be an experience joyfully shared between two professionals. For several years I have felt hounded and victimised, and I no longer have the will or energy to be constantly defending myself and refuting allegations supposedly made against me. I feel that such problems call for a younger man more in tune with current trends and the stringent demands of modern teaching philosophies. Although on the surface it may seem that cordial relations are maintained, there is in fact an undercurrent of insidious behaviour on the Headmaster's part which has long been recognised by those who know me well, and which seems calculated to undermine my authority (such as it is) and endanger my professional reputation. I have done my best to deal with this harrassment ever since 1994, but the strain has begun to tell, not only on me but on my wife, and I see no indication that the situation will improve; in fact I suspect that the reverse is the case, with consequent sapping of ones enjoyment and enthusiasm.

I went on to put my case for a golden handshake, summarising the history of my earnings and pension provision for one final time thus:

> It was recognised in 1988 that my initial salary in 1974 was equal to thirteen fifteenths of an incumbent's stipend, and that in the intervening years this proportion had been seriously eroded. Therefore a decision was made that the calculation be restored, and thus it has continued. There were, however, nine years (1980-88) when my salary dropped to a much lower proportion, causing a shortfall of £15,118 which was never made up.
>
> If the annual premium paid toward my pension, set in 1985 at £384, had been raised year by year to keep it at 10% of salary, a further £7,892 would have been contributed to the fund, producing a much healthier pension than the £1,630 per annum currently predicted at the age of 65.
>
> In these ways the Chapter has, in effect, made a saving of £23,000 in the course of the last eighteen years, which with the accrued interest might legitimately have been regarded as part of my remuneration. I put this to you in the hope that at least some of this 'lost' money may now be made available, bearing in mind that an increased pension contribution would have generated a great deal more over the years.

I was very fortunate to have the support of David Jones, my financial adviser (who was one of the cathedral stewards) and also a certain amount of sympathy from Ken Hall, the administrator, both of whom had influence with the Dean – who also had my interests at heart. David was in a good position to negotiate between us, and to my considerable surprise I was offered a whole year's salary plus a further three months' earnings in lieu of notice, amounting to a staggering tax-free sum of £16,343 which more than equalled the shortfall of £15,000 which I had lamented years before, so perhaps justice was done in the end. I was told that the Chapter would also continue to pay my pension premiums until my sixty-fifth birthday, but in the event these were paid to me in cash, adding another thousand pounds or so to my haul. It was on 30 September that we discussed these retirement measures, so I was rather taken aback to receive, the very next day, a rare letter from the Chapter Clerk Lindsay Ford (who, be it noted, had kept a low profile for several years) in these terms:

The Dean has received the observations of the Child Protection Unit which undertook the recent investigation into the complaints which they discussed with you at your recent meeting. I regret to have to inform you that they have recommended "that Llandaff Cathedral commence a formal Disciplinary Investigation in respect of Sykes Hagen's allegations". They recommend that the Investigation incorporates the matters raised by Thirkettle and Morgan to "illustrate a pattern". The Dean will be seeking advice upon the conduct of the Investigation, and I will be in touch with you about that as soon as I am able.

With the usual breakdown of communications he evidently knew nothing of my offer nine days earlier to retire, and had to add sheepishly in his own hand 'I have since spoken to the Dean and understand you have had a recent meeting which would supersede the above'. When accepting the financial terms of my proposed retirement, I told the Dean that I would have to consider whether it would be in my best interest to postpone my retirement, in order to defend myself one more time against a manifestly unreasonable complaint and to re-establish my integrity before leaving. David Jones confided to me that 'the knives were out' and that the Chapter Clerk had gloated evilly 'We'll fight him in the courts'. My feeling is that they all secretly feared taking me on again, because I had always beaten them in the past, and was all the more likely to do so again. The letter from the CPU unwittingly strengthened my hand and virtually ensured my generous settlement. Even then the Dean managed to get it wrong, by writing to offer me only a year's gross salary and declaring that my employment would end on 31 October. When I protested, he amended the offer to extend my employment until 31 December, allowing me to remain in St Mary's for a further ten days, and adding the agreed three months' salary. I made sure they incorporated the 3% increment to which I would be entitled in the new year. Having seen to my future, Dean Rogers himself retired on 21 November, when a unique Evensong was sung by all four choirs, the cathedral choir being joined by the girl choristers, the parish choir and the parish singers in singing Noble's setting of the canticles in B minor and Charles Wood's anthem *O thou the central orb* which I had first known as a choirboy in about 1945. Between his retirement and mine came the choir association's Christmas banquet, again planned for Caerphilly Castle but because of icy conditions held rather disappointingly in the school sports hall. The occasion was somewhat marred by an incident involving the father of one of the boys who accused the lay clerks, seated with Marian and me at high table, of being cheapskates for asking for more wine on the house. They had made their contribution by singing a selection of carol arrangements before the dinner, and were the guests of the Association. Aware of that body's sometimes slightly grudging attitude to the men, Spencer Basford stood up and threatened this man, pushing him to the ground. Several of us gathered round to prevent a fight, diffusing the unpleasantness, and dancing with some of my favourite ladies after the meal went some way to ameliorate the situation, but I could not help thinking that such animosity might have been avoided at my very last social occasion there.

At my own last Sunday service on the previous afternoon, featuring Sir George Dyson's theatrical canticles in D and Sir Hubert Parry's great setting for 8-part choir of Milton's text *Blest pair of sirens*, a very well-worded and gratifying farewell speech was made by the new bishop, who presented me with a relatively modest cheque supposedly representing a gift from the congregation (which numbered no more on that occasion than on any average Sunday). As the Choir processed out I had great pleasure in playing the whole of that song made famous by Frank Sinatra, savouring its full text on the copy in front of me and building to a climax as the choir left the nave to the refrain *I did it **my way**.* My very last service was the Eucharist on Christmas Day, at which Mozart's Mass in D was accompanied by a string quartet which included Laura (violin) and Rachel ('cello), the anthem effectively welcoming my forthcoming new life with Percy Fletcher's setting of Tennyson's words *Ring out, wild bells, to the wild sky.* This time we did not engage handbell ringers, but in welcoming the New Year and returning to England there seemed to be hope in the words

> Ring out a slowly dying cause,
>   And ancient forms of party strife;
>   Ring in the nobler modes of life,
> Wth sweeter manners, purer laws.

> Ring in the valiant man and free,
>   The larger heart, the kindlier hand;
>   Ring out the darkness of the land
> Ring in the Christ that is to be.

Under the editorship of Dean Rogers, *The Llandaff Monthly* had become much less formal and more personal. A new priest vicar, aptly named Father Parrish, introduced a series of profiles, compiled from interviews, of prominent members of the parish. I knew all of them by name, but almost nothing else about them owing to my minimal involvement with those who never came to our choral services. The April issue actually included an article about me and Marian and our family, covering two and a half pages on our lives together, and in December the other prest vicar Matthew Tomlinson (who shortly afterwards also left to become Vicar of St Augustine's, Edgbaston – another good man gone!) generously wrote:

> The end of 1999 marks the end of an era for Llandaff Cathedral. It is with great sadness that we must say goodbye to Dr Michael Smith after 25 years as Cathedral Organist. It is inevitable that Michael, who has seen four different bishops of Llandaff and worked under three Deans, should have left his inimitable mark on Llandaff, not only with his magnificent musicianship and his attention to detail, but also his keen wit and great sense of humour. His vast experience, and his gift of choosing just the right music for each service, is extraordinary and seems effortless. Humour has rarely been absent from Choir practices under Michael's direction, but nor too has a great sense of fairness and an emphasis on teamwork which has produced over the years a very distinctive Llandaff sound. We wish Michael and Marian every happiness in the next stage of their lives in rural Wiltshire.

The last issue I saw of that magazine included an even more fulsome tribute by my trusty second assistant, David Geoffrey Thomas. I had reason to be grateful for his unstinting loyalty and helpfulness, and presented to him, at a little ceremony in his flat attended by the lay clerks, a limited-edition print of a coloured drawing of the original Royal College of Organists' building in South Kensington, by its consultant architect. His own tribute read thus:

> On Christmas morning 1999, Michael conducted and played his final service in Llandaff Cathedral. Throughout the years that I have known Michael he has been an inspiration to me. After Sunday Evensong I have witnessed him play phenomenally difficult pieces – 'sailing' through them without batting an eyelid. I remember on one occasion a piece he played by Reger. Organ music by Reger is very difficult: the pages are black with notes. He ploughed through this, page after page with the greatest ease, and when he came to the end he turned to me and said 'Did you spot the deliberate mistake?' Whereupon he turned back about half a dozen pages and, amid the blackness of notes, pointed to one in the middle and said, 'There, I played a wrong note!'
>
> His playing was truly remarkable. It is ironic that when the organist plays the voluntary at the end of the service the

congregation stand up, start talking to one another and walk out, thus missing what is essentially a part of the service. In France, things are very different: at the end of the service the organist plays for half an hour and nobody moves – the whole congregation sit and listen, and when the organist has finished they applaud! Food for thought.

The daily sung services here seem to be something of a secret – the preserve of a small clique of people who turn up. There are six cathedrals in Wales, but ours is the only one capable of maintaining a sung service every day (except Wednesday). This is a tradition unique to the British Isles and here, in Llandaff, unique in Wales. Over the years Michael has taken great care to choose music from the wealth of the sacred repertoire and lead a professional choir to sing it - all on a daily basis. It is sad, in a way, that only a few come to hear this. It is a God-given resource – cherished by a few, missed by the many. Michael once told me that at one of the Cathedral Organists' conferences, all the delegates were asked to take along their monthly music schemes. Ours was the best of all the cathedrals, and we are grateful to him and Qualitex Printing for this. When choosing the music, Michael has always read the Lessons before making his choice. Consequently, the anthems have always reflected the readings and/or psalms – a perfect match.

I have always cherished being in the loft with him. Not only has his playing been inspirational, but his sense of humour and sharp wit has also been something to relish. This, however, is best left unwritten, as the spoken word is always more effective and thus shall remain the preserve of his immediate colleagues – Michael Hoeg and myself!

We who love the Anglican musical tradition are grateful to you, Michael, for the years of sterling service you have given us here in Llandaff – keeping the unique tradition of some of the best sacred music in the world alive in this part of Wales. I, for one, shall miss you greatly. Thank you for being here, and very best wishes to you for a very happy retirement.

On the last day of my career, of the decade, of the century and of the millennium, I wrote a letter to the bishop, describing in some detail the machinations of the headmaster, suggesting that he might pass on the information to the new dean, as yet to be appointed. Typically there was no acknowledgment, let alone a response, so when I was safely settled in our cottage at Bowerchalke I sent him my new address. It was not until March that he wrote back, admitting that he had only just come across my letter, buried under a pile of post-Christmas mail. After taking so much trouble to set the record straight, I thought this example of inefficiency was quite disgraceful. He said he had read my letter very carefully, and that he would need to read it again and consider the implications. Not so long afterwards he became Archbishop of Wales, upon the appointment of his predecessor Rowan Williams as Archbishop of Canterbury. His brief response to me was the last letter relating to my time at Llandaff – or so I thought.

The final insult came more than two years after my decision to retire, in the form of a letter from the Department of Education and Skills, which I read with sadness not unmixed with a sense of injustice, after all those years of hard work and achievement. It was like a final twist of the knife:

> The Secretary of State has been made aware of your resignation from your post as Cathedral Choir Master at Llandaff Cathedral. The Department of Health informed us of allegations, referred to them by Cardiff County Council Social Services, that your behaviour towards choir boys was unacceptable and that parents had complained that their children had been unfairly and cruelly treated by you.
>
> The Secretary of State has decided on the basis of the information put before her that she will not, on this occasion, take any action under regulation 5 of the Education (Restriction of Employment) Regulations 2000 (SI 2000/2419), which empowers her to bar or restrict the employment of people in relevant employment on medical grounds, on the grounds of misconduct (whether or not he/she is convicted of a criminal offence), or on the grounds that the person concerned is not a fit and proper person to be employed as a teacher or worker with children and young persons.
>
> I am however to express the Secretary of State's concern that you have placed yourself in a position where such allegations could be made against you. You are advised that in future you should take great care to avoid placing yourself in a similar position where further allegations could be made.

How different from the verdict of my closest colleagues! The letter was signed by someone representing the teachers' misconduct team (yes, *misconduct*!) on behalf of Estelle Morris, who herself resigned a little later as Secretary of State, admitting that she was not up to the job. No wonder then, that she took so long to look at my case! At least I *was* up to the job, and had stuck at it for more than a quarter of a century. Not long afterwards, our Chapter Clerk resigned for personal reasons and was not invited to preach again. I, however, having successfully survived four bishops, three deans and four headmasters, was now free to retire, with my lovely wife, our younger daughter, a golden handshake and feelings of achievement and contentment, to our thatched cottage in the Wiltshire countryside.

EPILOGUE

Our retirement together to a small thatched cottage in the Wiltshire village of Bowerchalke, predicted to last indefinitely, was tragically cut short by Marian's death from inoperable brain cancer in October 2003, a few days after her sixtieth birthday. She had been in demand in the Chalke Valley as a professional piano teacher and a qualified gardener, creating horticultural designs for others as well as ourselves. The choir and organists of Salisbury Cathedral provided the music at Marian's memorial service, which was conducted by Canon Jeremy Davies at All Saints' Church, Broad Chalke. Llandaff Cathedral and Parish were represented by Dean Rogers and two churchwardens.

The name Mary Wilcock appears more than once in the foregoing memoirs, and in due course we met again for the first time in forty years, bought a house together in Hereford with extensive views over the Wye valley, and were married in September 2006.

Lindsay Gray was appointed in 2008 in the prestigious and international post of Director of the Royal School of Church Music, but unlike his five predecessors whose tenure averaged sixteen years, decided to seek pastures new after little more than four.

I have paid little heed to the fortunes of Llandaff Cathedral since then, but as I prepare these memoirs for publication in 2013 it has come to my notice that in some ways matters have deteriorated even further. Following the ministry of Dean John Lewis, who had succeeded John Rogers, it seems that the Bishop filled the resulting interregnum by taking on more responsibilities himself. As the dean of Llandaff is also vicar of the parish, and the present bishop is also the Archbishop of Wales, it was jokingly suggested that his title should read *The Reverend, Very Reverend, Right Reverend and Most Reverend Dr Barry Morgan*. Eventually he solved this anomaly in a most unexpected way, breaking with centuries of tradition by boldly appointing a woman as Dean; but after only a few weeks her resignation, not fully explained, was announced in the national Press.

Some ten years after my retirement a group of people, valiantly led by my successor Richard Moorhouse, managed to raise more than a million pounds for the new organ for which I had fruitlessly campaigned in 1977 and 1997. My trusty assistant Michael Hoeg played the new instrument at Easter 2010, but by the end of the summer term had retired after nearly thirty years in office and moved to Cornwall. A shortfall in the fundraising caused a delay of three years before the instrument was completed in all its considerable glory – for it has been compared favourably with some of the best organs in Europe – and I was delighted to find the nave packed to the doors when I made a rare return visit this month to hear a recital given by Robert Quinney to celebrate this very notable achievement.

How ironic it is that earlier *in the same week* the Chapter (still Dean-less) had announced that to help pay off their current deficit of £81,000 they intended to make the assistant organist and all the lay clerks redundant. In what other cathedral would the authorities, having sanctioned the spending of a fortune on the finest British organ to be built in decades, implement the imminent loss of the man who was appointed to play it, and the choir it was designed to accompany? Is the musical tradition of Llandaff Cathedral now destined to fall into oblivion? I often regretted going to Llandaff, but the tribulations I encountered and at least partly overcame in the latter part of the twentieth century seem to fade into insignificance in the light of these revelations. However, it must be admitted that my experience of the inner workings of a Welsh cathedral left me disillusioned, and was partly responsible for my gradual alienation from the Church and indeed religion in general.

23 November 2013

APPENDIX 1

CD recordings made by the cathedral choir in 1994 and 1995 may be obtained from www.prioryrecords.co.uk :
PRCD510 Great Cathedral Anthems, Volume 6
PRCD551 Magnificat & Nunc Dimittis, Volume 8

APPENDIX 2

LLANDAFF CATHEDRAL CHORAL SOCIETY

Concert programmes 1974-91

1974	Bach	Christmas Oratorio, parts 1-3
1975	Brahms	German Requiem (in English)
	Bernstein	Chichester Psalms (in Hebrew)
	Mozart	Solemn Vespers, K.339
	Honegger	King David
	Handel	Messiah
1976	Duruflé	Requiem
	Vaughan Williams	Dona nobis pacem
	Bach	St John Passion
	Handel	Messiah part 1 + Hallelujah
	Bach	Magnificat
1977	Brahms	Liebeslieder Waltzer (soloists)
	Rossini	Petite Messe Solennelle
	Blow	God spake sometime in visions
	Purcell	My heart is inditing
	Handel	Zadok the Priest
	Martin	Te Deum
	Parry	I was glad when they said unto me
	Stanford	Coronation Gloria
	Walton	Te Deum
	arr.Jacob	God save the Queen
	Mendelssohn	Elijah

1978	Handel	Sixth Chandos Anthem
	Vaughan Williams	Five Mystical Songs
	Britten	Rejoice in the Lamb
	Kodály	Missa Brevis
	Schubert	Mass in G
	Mathias	This Worldes Joie
	Bach	Cantatas 57 & 140
	Britten	Saint Nicolas
1979	Dvořák	Stabat Mater
	Elgar	The Dream of Gerontius
	Handel	Messiah
1980	Bach, C.P.E.	Magnificat
	Haydn	Theresienmesse
	Fanshawe	African Sanctus
	Bach	Mass in B minor
1981	Gabrieli	In Ecclesiis
	Bach	Cantata 118
	Bruckner	8 Latin motets
	Vaughan Williams	O clap your hands
	Faurè	Requiem
1982	Beethoven	Missa Solemnis
	Liszt	Psalm 13
	Kodály	Psalmus Hungaricus
	Bernstein	Chichester Psalms
	Stravinsky	Symphony of Psalms
	Mozart	Mass in C minor
	Handel	Dixit Dominus
1983	Bach	St Matthew Passion
	Elfyn Jones	Give me the wings of faith
	Rossini	Petite Messe Solennelle

	Handel	Messiah
	(various)	Carols
1984	Mozart	Requiem
	Vivaldi	Gloria
	Elgar	The Kingdom
	Bach	Magnificat
	Britten	Saint Nicolas
1985	Walton	Belshazzar's Feast*
	Poulenc	Gloria
	Patterson	Mass of the Sea
	Mendelssohn	Elijah
1986	Britten	War Requiem*
	Elgar	The Music Makers
	Holst	Hymn of Jesus
	Brahms	German Requiem (in German)
	Vaughan Williams	Five Mystical Songs
1987	Orff	Carmina Burana*
	Lambert	The Rio Grande
	Blake	Benedictus
	Parry	Ode on the Nativity
	Vaughan Williams	Fantasia on Christmas Carols
	Finzi	In Terra Pax
	Hoddinott	Bells of Paradise
1988	Berlioz	Grande Messe des Morts*
	Bach	Mass in B minor
1989	Stainer	The Crucifixion
	Vaughan Williams	The Old Hundredth
	Purcell	Funeral Music for Queen Mary

	Bach	Cantata 118
	Nevens	Te Deum
	Vaughan Williams	O clap your hands
	Rutter	Gloria
	Bruckner	Locus iste a Deo factus est
		Ecce sacerdos magnus
	Parry	I was glad when they said unto me
	Bruckner	Mass in E minor
	Faurė	Requiem
1990	Dvořák	Mass in D
	Rutter	Requiem
	Brahms	German Requiem (in English)
	Poulenc	Gloria
1991	Vaughan Williams	Dona nobis pacem
	Duruflė	Requiem
	Bernstein	Chichester psalms

*with other choirs, in St David's Hall

Note: Until 1988 five out of six concerts were with a professional orchestra, almost always comprising members of the BBC Welsh Symphony Orchestra.

APPENDIX 3

The lay clerks, choral scholars and singing men, 1974-99

Robert Adams
Gary Beauchamp
Brian Burrows
Paul Daly
Maldwyn Davies
Geoffrey Davison
Philip Drew
Gervais Frykman
Jonathan Hibberd
David Cynan Jones
Charles Lewis
Ivor Meredith
Matthew Mudge
Julian Paisey
Alex Pridgeon
Gary Savage
Peter Smith
Francis Taylor
Peter West
Roland Woods

Spencer Basford
William Bokerman
Stephen Challenger
Michael Davidson
Mark Davies
Terence Dickens
Neil Evans
Timothy German
Marcus Hopkin
Alun Jones
Ralph Lock
Charles Moore
Nicholas Murdoch
Timothy Parish
Ian Roberts
David Smith
Michael Steer
David Truslove
Alan Williams
Colin Wyver

Timothy Bateman
Timothy Brookes
Alastair Clarke
Jeremy Davies
Martin Davies
Andrew Dobbins
Peter Foster
Stephen Hamnett
Brian Inglis
Christopher Larley
Christopher Mayled
Deiniol Morgan
Simon O'Connor
David Pounder
Kenneth Robinson
David Gwesyn Smith
Timothy Symonds
James Webb
Edward Williamson

Assistant Organists Anthony Burns-Cox
Michael Hoeg

Honorary Deputy Organists Morley Lewis
David Geoffrey Thomas

Choir Librarian Ralph Stephens

The 139 Choristers of Llandaff Cathedral, 1974-99

David Holme
Rhys Neale
Mark Luther
Howard Jones
Andrew Yeo
Anthony Perkins
Francis Burling
Edward Boreham
Philip Jones
Simon Lewis
Stuart Joyce

Peter Lake
Andrew Hinton
Timothy Johns
Stephen Johns
Paul Fox
Stephen Sharples
Christopher Drew
David Hubbard
David Pinnell
Dylan Kelly
Timothy Jones

Neil Wootten
Tony Jenkins
Andrew Lake
Philip Sharples
Richard Muir
Peter Jones
David Shepherd
Peter Snelling
Mark Dyer
Peter Fox
Giles Meredith

Redmond English
Damian Kelly
Robin Davies
Richard Johnson
Justin Hinchliffe
Geraint John
Gavin Rowarth
Philip Herbert
Robert Williams
Ceri Evans
Dan Edwards
Paul Dallimore Carter-Armson
Roger Saunders
Christopher Parsons
Edward Adams
Steven Moss
Benjamin Halsey
Edward Knapp
William Davies-Jenkins
Thomas Hibberd
Huw Lewis
Richard Norman
Jack Emery
Nicholas Mills
Timothy Belcher
James Bull
Robert Milton
Gwilym Evans
Thomas Morgan
Charles Oram
Jack Furness
Rhys Jenkins
Benjamin Gwinnutt
Rhys Mansel
Ranjit Saimbi

Jeremy Mannings
Guy Ledger
Timothy Lewis
Peter Hedderly
Ceri Morris
David Howard-Jones
Mark Rowarth
Stephen Hurn
Robert Hooke
David Cantrell
Rhodri Crookes
Roland Mumford
Timothy Humphreys
David Butler
William Davey
Benedict Davies-Jenkins
Edward Jones
Jonathan Robson
Miles Lallemant
Edward Crockett
Edward Austin
Andrew Lewis
Tristan Aldridge
Sebastian Clarke
Matthew Ashment
Neil Hillman
Joseph Adams
Gwilym Mumford
Samuel Furness
Samuel Palmer
Thomas French
Patrick Scaglioni
Nathan Eager
Rhys Owen
Ian Winter-Jones

David Snelling
Nigel Ledger
Timothy Batty
Alexander Wotke
Justin Lewis
David Elias
Jonathan Greatorex
Robert Elias
Julien Sweeting
Bobby Sastry
Timothy Fundell
James Elias Andrew
Matthew Craze
Andrew Richley
Richard Jeremy
Darren Roberts
Gareth Campbell
Charles Jeremy
Robert Samuelson
John Crockett
Christopher Spurgeon
Oliver Lallemant
Grant Baldwin
Robin Jacobs
Laurence Peckham
Rhys Harris
James Gallavin
James Sykes-Hagen
Giles Thirkettle
James Hooper
Thomas Bentley
David Mahoney
Joel Ferrand
Robert Furness
James Eager

The 16 Priest Vicars

Clive Jones
Richard Evans
Derek Belcher
David Adlington
John Redvers-Harris
Robert Parrish

Paul Lyons
John Jenkins
Graham Holcombe
Steven Kirk
Nicholas Court

Raymond Bayley
Terence Doherty
John Ward
Nigel Hartley
Matthew Tomlinson